THE AGRARIAN VISION

Culture of the Land: A Series in the New Agrarianism

This series is devoted to the exploration and articulation of a new agrarianism that considers the health of habitats and human communities together. It demonstrates how agrarian insights and responsibilities can be worked out in diverse fields of learning and living: history, science, art, politics, economics, literature, philosophy, religion, urban planning, education, and public policy. Agrarianism is a comprehensive worldview that appreciates the intimate and practical connections that exist between humans and the earth. It stands as our most promising alternative to the unsustainable and destructive ways of current global, industrial, and consumer culture.

The Agrarian Vision

Sustainability and Environmental Ethics

Paul B. Thompson

THE UNIVERSITY PRESS OF KENTUCKY

Scholarly publisher for the Commonwealth,
serving Bellarmine University, Berea College, Centre
College of Kentucky, Eastern Kentucky University,
The Filson Historical Society, Georgetown College,
Kentucky Historical Society, Kentucky State University,
Morehead State University, Murray State University,
Northern Kentucky University, Transylvania University,
University of Kentucky, University of Louisville,
and Western Kentucky University.
All rights reserved.

Editorial and Sales Offices: The University Press of Kentucky
663 South Limestone Street, Lexington, Kentucky 40508-4008
www.kentuckypress.com

14 13 12 11 10   5 4 3 2 1

Library of Congress Cataloging-in-Publication Data

Thompson, Paul B., 1951–
  The agrarian vision : sustainability and environmental ethics / Paul
B. Thompson.
      p.   cm. — (Culture of the land: a series in the new agrarianism)
  Includes bibliographical references and index.
  ISBN 978-0-8131-2587-9 (hardcover : alk. paper)
  1. Sustainable agriculture—United States.   2. Environmental
ethics—United States.   3. Agriculture and state—United States.
I. Title. II. Series: Culture of the land.
  S441.T48 2010
  630—dc22
                              2010007781

This book is printed on acid-free recycled paper meeting
the requirements of the American National Standard
for Permanence in Paper for Printed Library Materials.

Manufactured in the United States of America.

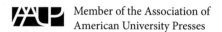   Member of the Association of
American University Presses

For Diane Thompson, local food advocate

Contents

Acknowledgments

This book is a follow-up to my book *The Spirit of the Soil: Agriculture and Environmental Ethics*. In response to an invitation from Norman Wirzba and Stephen Wrinn, I assembled a collection of mostly previously published essays and received extremely helpful comments from University Press of Kentucky reviewers. The result bears little resemblance to that original collection. Several proposed chapters were dropped altogether, and two totally new ones were written. Most of the other chapters have been so thoroughly revised and amended as to constitute new works. But assembling and revising those essays took me back to some that had been written more than twenty years ago. I fear that many of the individuals who helped me with those articles have now faded from memory. But I can name several colleagues who have been frequent interlocutors and have helped shape my thinking on sustainability and agrarian ideas for many years. Foremost are Richard Haynes and Jeffrey Burkhardt, fellow conspirators since the beginning of the quest to invent something called agricultural ethics. At about the same time, I met five people from the rural social sciences who became great friends and had a tremendous and continuing influence on my thought. Three of them, Bill Browne, Fred Buttel, and Glenn L. Johnson, have passed on in recent years. Thankfully, I continue to enjoy my interactions with Larry Busch and Kate Clancy. More recent colleagues who have been informal critics of my work include Gary Comstock, Laura Westra, Clark Wolf, Rob Streiffer, Jennifer Welchman, Bryan Norton, Ben Mepham, Michiel Korthals, Peter Sandøe, and Ben Minteer. Colleagues who have subjected my work to useful criticism in print include Fred Buttel and Larry Busch, as well as Kathryn George, Mora Campbell, Eric Freyfogle, and Carolyn Raffensperger.

This project really got under way in connection with a National Science Foundation grant awarded in 1992 when I was on the faculty at Texas A&M University. I worked closely with a group of colleagues there in the early stages, and each of them is responsible for some part of my current thinking on sustainability. They are, in alphabetical order, Harry Cralle, Wesley Dean, Bruce Dickson, Susan Gilbertz, Adolf Gunderson, Thomas Hilde, Jimmy Killingsworth, Alex MacIntosh, Tarla Rae Peterson, Gary Varner, and Don Vietor. Additional financial support was provided by the W. K. Kellogg Foundation through its gift of funds to endow the W. K. Kellogg Chair in Agricultural, Food, and Community Ethics at Michigan State University. In addition to anonymous reviewers, the manuscript was read (at various stages in its development) by MSU colleagues Sandra Batie and David Wright. All these reviewers made exceedingly helpful suggestions, though I must admit I could not incorporate everyone in the final text. Invaluable technical assistance was provided by Ellen Link, Linda Lotz, and Julie Eckinger. I, of course, maintain responsibility for any remaining flaws.

Although all the previously published materials in this book were extensively revised, I would like to thank the original publishers for permission to reprint portions of the following essays:

Chapter 2: "The Reshaping of Conventional Farming: A North American Perspective," *Journal of Agricultural and Environmental Ethics* 14 (2001): 217–29.

Chapter 3: "Agrarian Values: Their Future Place in U.S. Agriculture," in *Visions of American Agriculture*, ed. W. Lockeretz (Ames: Iowa State University Press, 1997), 17–30.

Chapter 4: "Agriculture and Working-Class Political Culture: A Lesson from *The Grapes of Wrath*," *Agriculture and Human Values* 24 (2007): 165–77.

Chapter 5: "Farming as Focal Practice," in *Technology and the Good Life?* ed. E. Higgs, A. Light, and D. Strong (Chicago: University of Chicago Press, 1999), 166–81.

Chapter 7: "The Philosophical Rationale for U.S. Agricultural Policy," in *U.S. Agriculture in a Global Setting: An Agenda for the Future*, ed. M. A. Tutwiler (Washington, DC: Resources for the Future, 1988), 34–44.

Chapter 8: "The Social Goals of Agriculture," *Agriculture and Human Values* 3, no. 4 (1986): 32–42.

Chapter 10: "Sustainability as a Norm," *Techné: Technology in Culture and Concept* 2, no. 2 (1997): 75–94.

Chapter 11: "Agricultural Sustainability: What It Is and What It Is Not," *International Journal of Agricultural Sustainability* 5 (2007): 5–16.

Introduction

Sustainability and Agrarian Ideals

How can we make our society and our lives more sustainable? What would it mean for us to try? When Thomas Jefferson assumed office as the third president of the United States, he faced a sustainability crisis of his own. The new republic was straining to recover from debts incurred while opposing the British in the Revolutionary War. Although historians of the United States seldom mention the fact, many colonials chose to relocate their businesses after the Revolution, seeking a more stable economic and political environment. The United States' chief international ally was France, which had endured a decade of revolution itself. Jefferson not only had to find some way to rebuild the economy of the new nation; he also had to do it in an manner that would fend off predatory European states still looking to recolonize the North American continent, should the government of the United States falter. What is more, events in France had demonstrated how experiments in democracy could abuse power as well as how they could fail. Could the American experiment in democracy survive? Was it sustainable?

Jefferson would not have used the word *sustainability* to describe his challenge. His sustainability crisis was primarily political, whereas ours is environmental. Jefferson's response may serve as a model for us nonetheless. The urge to live sustainably is fast becoming a theme for contemporary politics and environmentalism, and it is easy to forget how recently *sustainability* entered our vocabulary and our mind-set. *Our Common Future* (also known as the Brundtland Report) brought the phrase *sustainable development* into widespread circulation in 1987. The report was the product of the World Commission on Environment and Development (WCED), an international working group that hoped to define a new consensus to guide thinking on global environmental issues in general and on economic growth in developing countries in particular. It sparked an intense conversation among economists, ecologists, and other development specialists about the need to conceptualize global development processes in a way that was attractive to both industrialized and industrializing nations.

Today, *sustainability* has become a byword for many people who never heard of the Brundtland Report. They are concerned about both local and global environmental issues. They have begun spin-off conversations about sustainable cities, sustainable growth, sustainable energy policies, and even sustainable architecture in the first decade of the twenty-first century. Responses to climate change may be the leading focus in the coming round of policies intended to achieve sustainability. Reports from the Intergovernmental Panel on Climate Change have shown that the trajectory of global growth in energy use simply cannot continue. The efforts of former vice president Al Gore have brought both the processes and the likely impacts of climate change to the attention of a broad public. People have recognized that our world is at risk from rising sea levels, the flooding of coastal areas, probable declines in farm production, and shifts in ocean currents that could make the planet virtually uninhabitable. Awareness of these challenges is growing.

This book emphasizes the philosophical and conceptual side of those challenges. The *un*sustainability of the patterns inherited from the twentieth century is taken for granted, and I do not try to prove it. My primary audience is people who have learned the first lesson of environmentalism and are ready to move ahead. Most of them will agree that our current ways of understanding the moral basis of sustainability are inadequate. Current modes of ethics conceal the complex way that norms of human action both shape and are shaped by the natural world. In doing so, they force conversations on sustainability into an awkward vocabulary incapable of expressing the sense in which sustainability is a moral ideal.

Moral ideals illuminate human aims and aspirations while remaining open-ended or even vague in their details. They orient our thinking even while requiring considerable specification before they can be acted upon. Far from being utopian or fanciful, moral ideals connect us to the hopes, aspirations, and wisdom of ages past, even while leaving room for discovery, innovation, testing, and revision in the future. Jefferson drew on nearly forgotten ideals related to farms and farming in resolving his own sustainability crisis. My claim is that those lost ideals provide an apt starting point for fashioning our own concept of sustainability.

The way past societies dealt with questions we now associate with sustainability was tied closely to debates over agriculture. Some of the reasons for this link can be stated succinctly. A society that cannot be fed cannot endure. Past societies had a keener sense that matters ranging from global trade to military security depended on a viable agriculture. They knew where their food came from and where at least some of their vulnerability to hunger lay, as well. More subtly, virtually everyone who lived prior to the twentieth century was much closer to the land than the average well-educated suburbanite of the twenty-first century, which meant that they had at least an implicit knowledge of farms and farming practices. They thus had some grasp of their dependence on secure processes of ecological and social reproduction. A good, firm picture of what it takes to keep a farm going provided them with an enormously useful set of metaphors for understanding what it takes to keep society going. The challenge for sustainability is to make that picture meaningful for people who live in cities and have little personal contact with farming.

For Americans, Thomas Jefferson (1743–1826), third president of the United States and author of the Declaration of Independence, is the emblematic progenitor of agrarian ideals. It is not quite true that Jefferson invented these ideals, but he, along with the other founders of the American republic, lived through a period in which the future of the American polity and its way of life were far from assured. They had a visceral understanding of sustainability (even if they had never heard the word) that was forged in conflict, personal risk, and the very real possibility of failure. That Jefferson saw farmers as "the most valuable citizens" during the Revolution and the early years of statehood is well known, though few have paused to think why. In this book, I organize many themes around Jefferson as an emblematic figure because his shrewd wisdom in praising farmers is indeed a model that present-day advocates of sustainability would be well advised to understand and emulate, but this is not a book about Jefferson or his time. It is our own time that is the focus of sustainability here.

To understand and move toward sustainability, a society needs to have some conception of how its institutions and practices intersect and connect with the natural cycles of production and reproduction. It needs to understand how its own sense of community identity is either reinforced or disrupted by those cycles and how, in turn, those cycles are reinforced or disrupted by human practice. Although ecology and environmental science are beginning to discover and explain some of the linkages between human and natural systems, we are still far from being able to articulate how these linkages can be translated into a moral vocabulary dominated by ideas of decision making, impact analysis, and trade-offs among intrinsic or instrumental values. It is ironic that Jefferson's nearly forgotten words of the moral and political significance of farming illustrated such linkages in ways that were transparent and easily understood by all. These agrarian ideals guided human practice in ages past and proved to be effective in shaping human conduct.

Any contemporary usage of agrarian ideals must be revised and reinterpreted in numerous ways. First and foremost, these ideals need to be made relevant to urbanites, something that can be done by focusing on food rather than farming. They need to be updated in light of contemporary environmental science. Agrarian ideals also need modification with respect to some of the less savory ways in which agrarian thinking has rationalized racist, paternalist, and colonial ideologies. What I recommend in this book is a fresh look at the moral significance of food and farming, but one that is informed by the way agrarian ideals of past times were taken up by societies in action-guiding ways. I begin with the philosophy of agriculture and explore its ties to venerable traditions in ethics and political philosophy. I show how agrarian ideals supplement and complete conversations in environmental policy that have become too narrow to engage the moral imagination of nonspecialists. I elaborate on agrarian ideals that emphasize concepts of virtue and moral character. I review debates on sustainability and show how discussions of sustainability grounded in systems ecology might be deepened and given normative bite through an adaptation of agrarian ideals. I do *not* argue that we should go back to Jeffersonian conceptualizations of agriculture and its moral significance, much less that we should return to Jefferson's way of farming. A philosophy of sustainability needs a healthy dialectic—a robust exchange of views—that is informed both by moral and political philosophies that emerged in the Enlightenment and matured in the twentieth century and by environmental ideals that were once expressed in connection with farming and that date back to the ancient Greeks.

This book is preparation for that exchange, that dialectic. It aims to open up the dialogue on sustainability, but not to complete it.

Agrarianism

The very idea of agrarianism is not well understood by many scholars, activists, or environmentally enlightened citizens today. One can argue that the term is primarily associated with land reform movements aimed at breaking up large parcels assembled under colonial domination. Indeed, the online version of *Merriam-Webster's Dictionary* defines agrarianism as "a social or political movement designed to bring about land reforms or to improve the economic status of the farmer." Yet agrarianism is sufficiently well known in other quarters to have prompted a Wikipedia entry that offers the following summary:

Cultivation of the soil provides direct contact with nature; through the contact with nature the agrarian is blessed with a closer relationship to God. Farming has within it a positive spiritual good; the farmer acquires the virtues of "honor, manliness, self reliance, courage, moral integrity and hospitality" and follows the example of God when creating order out of chaos.

The farmer "has a sense of identity, a sense of historical and religious tradition, a feeling of belonging to a concrete family, place and region, which are psychologically and culturally beneficial." The harmony of this life checks the encroachments of a fragmented, alienated modern society which has grown to inhuman scale.

In contrast, farming offers total independence and self-sufficiency. It has a solid, stable position in the world order. But urban life, capitalism and technology destroy our independence and dignity while fostering vice and weakness within us. The agricultural community can provide checks and balances against the imbalances of modern society by its fellowship of labor and cooperation with other agrarians, while obeying the rhythms of nature. The agrarian community is the model society.[1]

As a philosophical tradition, agrarian thought emphasizes the idea that farming practices have the power to shape the moral character of the individuals who engage in them, and that a society's farming culture—its means of subsistence—reverberates through all its institutions. Agrarian ideals are moral and aesthetic ideals. They describe a way of life as it ought to be lived. They articulate aspirations for both individuals and family groups. They apply equally to regions and towns and can be expanded to express ideals for entire civilizations. They celebrate an agriculture shockingly unlike the agriculture that industrialized countries have today.

Writing in the first decade of the third millennium, one cannot help but notice that people who have lived their lives in industrialized nations are unlikely to have experienced genuine hunger, much less to have spent much of their working lives growing food. Most devote much less than half their disposable income to food; in many cases, the percentage is less than a tenth. The agricultural production system that has made this possible is a relatively recent creation, and it depends heavily on coal and oil not only for the fuels that power machinery and transport but also for the manufacture of key farm inputs such as fertilizers and pesticides. What happens now that the supply of fossil energy is beginning to contract? Does this whole system collapse in a heap? Do other factors such as pollution, competition for water, or climate change add even greater pressure to a system already near the breaking point? And what are we to say about the two-thirds of the world's population who do not share in the largesse of industrial agriculture? Would greater economic development bring them in? And if it did, wouldn't that only place an even greater strain on the system? In short, is a food system of the sort we have now *sustainable*?

These are exceedingly important questions. Just as the analysis in this book is intended to help us think more pointedly about the sustainability of our society in the face of challenges brought on by climate change or loss of wildlife habitat, it is also intended to help us think more critically about the sustainability of agriculture itself. Yet the book *does not* attempt to answer these questions, nor does it assemble the facts and figures about present-day agriculture that would be needed to do so. One might also expect a book on food and farming to recommend changes in farm policy or changes in one's personal food habits. Indeed, good, honest, practical advice based on my general premise *would* urge people to pay more attention to what they eat: Learn where your food comes from. Frequent your local farmers' market or join a community-supported agriculture organization, because these are excellent ways to become acquainted with farmers, thereby gaining some appreciation of the challenges they face. Such initial moves might lead one gradually and inevitably to a more sophisticated understanding of the way our food system connects with the more obvious sustainability issues associated with globalization or climate change. I am all in favor of such practical advice, and I hope my readers will consider it seriously. But this book aims to supplement and amplify that practical advice with a philosophical analysis of why thinking in terms of agrarian ideals might contribute to sustainability.

One of the most widely known twentieth-century sources on agrarianism is M. Thomas Inge's *Agrarianism in American Literature*, a compendium of agrarian imagery and stories. In his introduction, Inge summarizes agrarian themes by noting five key tropes:

1. *Religion*. Farming reminds humanity of its finitude and dependence on God.
2. *Romance*. Technology corrupts; nature redeems.
3. *Moral Ontology*. Farming produces a sense of harmony and integration, while modern society is alienating and fragmenting.
4. *Politics*. Rural autochthony provides the backbone for democracy.
5. *Society*. Rural interdependencies and reciprocities provide a model for healthy community.

Literary works that sound these themes qualify as agrarian, especially when they contrast these themes to notions associated with industrial production or city life. In the 1930s the so-called Vanderbilt Agrarians—a group of English professors and literary types associated with Vanderbilt University in Nashville—tended to write as if the contrast could be drawn in terms of the urbanized and industrial North versus the still rural and agrarian South.

I want to avoid a treatment that demonizes the city in this way, for most of us do and in fact must live in cities if we are to live sustainably. Nevertheless I must admit that literature centered on rural life is an apt mode for developing an agrarian view. Allowing a story to play out at length, allowing the reader to develop insight into the mentality of a story's characters, and then allowing contrasting mentalities and attitudes to express themselves in fleshed-out and detailed situations can provide knowledge by acquaintance that would be difficult to articulate in terms of succinct principles or rules of conduct. Moral advice can be given in the vein of emulating what one thinks a particularly admirable person (real or fictional) would do in a given situation. I thus do not deny that there is resonance between the literary depictions offered by Inge and the agrarian ideals I put forward as a new way to think about sustainability. Nevertheless I do not, with one prominent exception, rely heavily on literary works to develop my conception of agrarian ideals. I focus instead on farming itself and reprise some contrasting ways that people have understood agriculture to have moral and cultural significance throughout the ages. I do not attempt to summarize agrarian virtues, but neither do I engage in extended character studies or attempt to create models for all of us to emulate. The focus is on how a nearly forgotten way of understanding agriculture's broad and deep cultural significance can be a keystone for thinking about sustainability.

Between Agrarianism and the Ideal of Sustainability

If one takes a broad view, debates over sustainability go back centuries, though one would be hard-pressed to find this particular word being used much before the last half of the twentieth century. Within such diverse areas as military matters and sea power, on the one hand, and religiosity and the virtues of humility, on the other, human beings have pondered the principles and practices that support permanence or resilience in farming methods and farming peoples. The reasons why range from the obvious (armies need food) to the obscure (farming people are alleged to be naturally pious). Yet this wealth of ideas and speculation is all but untapped for our contemporary understanding of sustainability. How might we learn to think about sustainability from this lore of permanence and resilience in agriculture?

The contrast between industrial and agrarian philosophy will be thematically developed and expanded throughout the chapters of this book. I am primarily interested in the debates occurring within my own time—even within my own community. I have many friends and neighbors who have been motivated by the likes of Michael Pollan or Vandana Shiva. Some of them have undertaken pretty radical changes in their relationship to food. Indeed, I am married to someone who fairly recently began to refer to herself as a "local food activist." If these are taken to be symptoms of an agrarian mentality, then agrarian philosophy would appear to be on the rise. Yet the majority of my students and my neighbors seem to be fairly satisfied with the industrial food system, and even those who opt for organic or local food may have personal health primarily in mind. Although sustainability is becoming a broadly shared ideal, many environmentally committed Americans do not perceive any strong connection between sustainability and agriculture. One goal of this book is to change that perception.

My focus is implicitly on the United States, though much of what can be said about the United States applies to the rest of the industrialized world as well. The limitation in my scope is partly a matter of convenience in that, as an American, American history, culture, and agricultural policy are subjects with which I am concerned and familiar. But it is also true that agricultural practices tend to evolve in relationship to local geography and politics. A philosophy of agriculture—and, by extension, sustainability—is thus appropriately attentive to dimensions of place or locale, on the one hand, and local or regional history, on the other. Hence the qualities and endowments of particular places are themes that recur in the ideals of permanence and resilience that have been expressed in the past. These themes stress the need to maintain attitudes and practices that answer to these endowments in ways that are at least thought to be peculiar to them. As we shall see, belief in and attentiveness to characteristics that make a given place "special" are hallmarks of agrarian philosophy.

The United States is much too large a geographic unit to have determined a particular approach to farming and ranching based exclusively on soil and climate, but the legal environment for land tenure and the policy environment for agriculture are established mostly at the federal level in the United States. What is more, the intellectual and political history of the United States is, in fact, deeply informed by ideals of permanence, settlement, and prosperity that hark back to its origins. The influence of federal policy began with the Louisiana Purchase in 1803 and took a formative shape with the Homestead Act of 1862. This law encouraged western settlement by offering land title to anyone who would occupy and improve a plot of land (originally 160 acres) over a five-year period. The developmental and egalitarian goals of this federal policy were deeply interwoven with a set of values that linked responsible citizenship and economic prosperity (if not sustainability) to farming. The formative influence of federal policy in the United States was buttressed by laws that created the Department of Agriculture (also in 1862) and expanded the support of agricultural research in 1889. The political dominance of federal policy became solidified when the first of a series of "farm bills" was passed in 1933. Since then, if not before, agriculture in America has been a national affair.

Thus, when I write *we* or *our,* I tend to mean all Americans. This is a fuzzy *we,* in that many of the agrarian cultural themes that shaped the United States also shaped other nations where European farming practices displaced indigenous cultures and came to dominate the landscape— places like Canada, Australia, and temperate regions of Latin America. It is a bit less inclusive of Europe itself. In subtropical European climates, the latifundia of ancient Rome tended to compete with vestigial agricultural practices dating from before European invasion. In these biological and cultural environments, the shape of agrarian argument and the resulting history of political development that I describe in this book undoubtedly look somewhat unfamiliar. So I make no pretense to speak for everyone. Nevertheless, non-Americans are welcome to identify with my first-person plural perspective and adapt it as need be. Hopefully a few will choose to do so. The overall goal is to develop a vision of sustainability that has been enriched by a better appreciation of agrarian ideals. And this is not a topic that should be confined to an American perspective.

Later in the book I shift away from agrarian heritage and undertake an examination of sustainability as the idea has developed over the last three decades. The signal event here was the publication of *Our Common Future,* mentioned earlier. The WCED, chaired by Gro Brundtland, offered the idea of *sustainable development* as the guiding light for economic growth in countries where industrialization had failed to lift the majority of the population from conditions of extreme poverty. *Our Common Future* called for development that "meets the needs of the present without compromising the ability of future generations to meet their own needs," and this phrase continues to be associated with definitions of sustainability today. But the report was intended to be more than a slogan. It was intended to provide a basis for global agreements on trade and environment, on the one hand, and for industrial and technological expansion projects conducted under the aegis of national development agencies or multinational organizations such as the United Nations or the World Bank, on the other.

As such, it became important to specify the WCED's definition more precisely. Many of the first efforts to do this were undertaken by the professionals who were already involved in the negotiation of international agreements and the management of development agencies before the Brundtland Report was issued. Many of these professionals were economists, and the tools they deployed to specify sustainable development were derived from the tools they had been using in development theory all along. At the same time, the WCED aimed to bring *environment* into development planning, and professionals devoted to the management of natural resources (such as fisheries or natural habitats) had their own ideas about what sustainability involved. This situation set the stage for at least a decade of wheel spinning and miscommunication, even as it created an opportunity for some rather abstruse theoretical constructs to become entrenched in the day-to-day execution of plans oriented toward sustainability.

My contention in this book is that farms, farming communities, and the agricultures that support entire civilizations are excellent models for the complex kinds of ecosocial hybrid systems that need to be sustained if our society is to achieve sustainability at all. Of course, our own agriculture *is* one of the complex ecosocial hybrid systems we need to sustain, and as already noted, one can question whether our current hybrid is all that sound. But my focus, again, is on the way agrarian philosophies—philosophies developed to probe and promote the appropriate relationship between agriculture and larger society in the past—model the kind of *thinking* we need in order to ask and answer questions about a sustainable society. An adequate environmental philosophy certainly needs to adapt and expand on the model suggested by agrarian ideals, so this book is only a start, at best.

Ethics and Environmental Philosophy

Beyond my primary audience of motivated environmentalists, my secondary audience is environmental philosophers in particular. The word *ethics* brings up vastly different associations for different people. Here, it is an attempt to identify and express the principles that undergird and provide guidance for human action. Human action, in turn, is understood broadly to encompass both actions undertaken by individuals and policies or collective actions undertaken through organized forms of agency. My concern with ethics is not wholly general, however, but is focused on questions that arise in connection with the project of sustainability. This places the inquiry within the domain of environmental philosophy. Environmental philosophy articulates and defends basic principles for understanding and addressing environmental issues. An environmental philosophy is an explicit statement of norms, values, and working principles intended to guide our thinking and practice with respect to the preservation, utilization, and appreciation of nature and for the conservation of natural resources, as well as the addressing of specific environmental problems such as pollution, biodiversity loss, and climate change. It can be thought of as the philosophy behind environmentalism.

In relation to ethics, environmental philosophy is also an activity intended to sharpen and improve human conduct. Speaking very broadly, anyone involved in activities intended to protect or remediate the environment has an underlying philosophy. They believe that their actions on behalf of the environment are worth doing, and they also have beliefs about both causes of and remedies for environmental harms. They are keenly aware of some such beliefs but may not be particularly cognizant of others. Indeed, people rely on a number of implicit beliefs or assumptions in everything they do. One example of the hidden complexity of this background is the child who asks a series of "Why?" questions. "Why do I have to eat my oatmeal?"—To be strong at school. "Why do I have to go to school?"—To get a job when you are older. "Why do I have to get a job?"—To make a living. "Why do I have to make a living?" Eventually the frustrated parent answers, "Just because." It is not that one has truly run out of reasons but that one's knowledge at these deeper levels has become tacit and is not easy to articulate or express.

There is always a fair amount of vagueness and ambiguity in tacit knowledge, and this accounts for the fact that it is not unusual for two or more adults to start out working together on some project only to discover later that they had very different (but unstated) assumptions about why the project was important or what it would take to complete it. Thus, a more specific way to understand environmental philosophy is that it attempts to lay out implicit assumptions behind the protection or preservation of the environment and to subject those activities to the kind of critical examination necessary to anticipate failures due to such misunderstandings. Anyone might participate in this kind of "laying out." But a relatively small group of people has dedicated the time and energy to reflect on their own tacit knowledge, carefully express these assumptions (usually in written form), read the efforts of others, and, finally, engage in critical dialogue aimed at mutual understanding and the most robust configuration of a platform for environmental action. These people are environmental philosophers, whatever training they might have.

The Argument of This Book

Succinctly stated, the first five chapters consider an implicit debate in the philosophy of agriculture that has raged for the last 100 years (if not the last 3,000 years): what principles should guide the way human beings farm or raise livestock? The debate is implicit because many of the participants had little sense that they were debating, nor did they have any idea that there was such a thing as the philosophy of agriculture. Chapter 6 on food and community is the pivot point. I then turn to public policy and sustainability in chapters 7 through 12. There I examine competing views on what kind of goal or value sustainability is and review how sustainability has been portrayed during the last few decades. Finally, in the conclusion I offer a discussion of how agrarian thought—historically associated with the philosophy of agriculture—might inform our thinking on sustainability and the good life.

Chapter 1 provides an initial statement of the argument for bringing agriculture to the forefront when we discuss the ethics of humanity's relation to the environment. It introduces how we tend to think of environmental issues in ethical terms. *Ethics* here simply means thinking in terms of "oughts"—goals, duties, norms, or visions of what people should do and where society should be heading. For the most part, ethical thinking on the environment has tended to ignore agriculture in recent years, despite the fact that agriculture is a keystone for human-environment interactions. The chapter continues with a whirlwind tour of agricultural ethics and introduces the broad framing of industrial and agrarian philosophies of agriculture.

Chapter 2 continues the theme of industrial versus agrarian philosophies of agriculture and offers a brief history of how these developed in American history. Jeffersonian agrarianism is given a more fulsome treatment, and I examine how it differed from the ideas of the New England transcendentalists, who first fashioned a uniquely American philosophy of nature. Agrarianism is treated succinctly in terms of three key substantive principles: farmers make the best citizens, all politics are local, and self-realization is a community thing. Though too simple, this treatment allows a consolidation of the agrarian philosophy as it relates both to sustainability in general and to agriculture in particular. I also argue that many people who thought they were opposing industrial practices in agriculture have actually reinforced the industrial philosophy of agriculture. This is not *wholly* bad, for the political and moral tradition of liberal political philosophy has been responsible for important social reforms. Yet the agrarian ideal articulates political values increasingly absent from our public conversations, to our detriment.

Chapter 3 explores the industrial-agrarian contrast by examining philosophical rationales for alternative visions of the future of American agriculture. The political ideal of secure property rights reflects one strand of thinking, and the goal of efficiency reflects another. Together, these ideas lend support to an industrial philosophy of agriculture. The philosophy that supports an agrarian alternative to the industrial vision is less easily developed with a linear logic model. It is composed of a number of virtues reinforcing and constraining one another in an ecological manner. Some virtues refer to individuals, whereas others are more collective or community based. In this chapter I focus on two virtues—stewardship and self-reliance—that begin to articulate the basis for an agrarian vision. The chapter concludes with the suggestion that some parts of the United States may be more conducive to one vision, while other parts are more conducive to the other. As such, the tension between these visions can be partially mitigated to the extent we can think of policies (and, implicitly, philosophies) as having an inherent connection to place.

Chapter 4 is a more thorough examination of the links between sociopolitical philosophy and competing visions of agriculture. I offer a new reading of John Steinbeck's classic Dust Bowl novel *The Grapes of Wrath*. I use themes and characters from the 1939 novel to illustrate how libertarian, utilitarian, egalitarian political philosophies converge around an industrial mentality, whereas agrarian philosophical ideals situate moral character and group identity in relation to values that privilege links to the land and a sense of place.

Chapter 5 returns to present-day environmental philosophy and articulates a version of agrarian ideals in light of writings by Albert Borgmann and David Strong on focal practices. Focal practices are a counter to the pace and texture of modern life, in which meaningful encounters with nature and other people are all too rare. Borgmann's philosophical development of this idea is discussed, and his approach is followed into an examination of farming and "the culture of the table." I end the chapter by arguing that, in the end, place as revealed and understood through practices of good farming and good eating is quintessential to our understanding of what makes life worth sustaining.

Chapter 6 is the centerpiece of the book. It begins with a return to the themes of environmental philosophy introduced in chapter 1. Relying on the writings of Mark Sagoff, I illustrate how agrarian ideals provide a counterpoint to the ways contemporary thinking on the environment has drifted away from ideas and practices that bind land and people into a community. The chapter concludes with a discussion of how eating together can be a way to rebuild focal practices of solidarity among people and with their broader environment, pointing us toward a community of hope that is oriented toward the ideal of a truly sustainable society.

Chapter 7 moves the focus of the argument decisively toward policy and argues that agricultural practices have a symbolic significance that is underappreciated in U.S. farm policy. Our dominant language for debating farm policy has been profoundly shaped by a European philosophical tradition that frames political life as a social contract among self-interested individuals. Thus the bargain struck by competing interests has been a powerful model for understanding agricultural policy. Alternatives to this model attempt to specify values that override or transcend the self-interest of one or more parties to the bargain, and such alternatives draw heavily on agrarian ideals.

Chapter 8 brings the discussion closer to the concept of sustainability as such by examining agriculture's "social goals," which go far beyond the simple production of food. Social goals are not necessarily aspirations or values sought by a particular individual but desiderata that we associate with agriculture at a holistic, social level. Many of the classic agrarian ideals discussed in the first seven chapters are best understood as social rather than individual goals. There are two key lessons here for sustainability. First, it is at least logically possible for a society to achieve agrarian or sustainability goals without anyone actually dedicating themselves to these goals in their individual practice. Second, it is at least logically possible for a society in which virtually everyone is committed to these goals to fail at achieving them. These points should make us humble, and they are important to set the stage for thinking about the deep meaning of agrarianism and its relationship to sustainability.

Chapter 9 discusses the 1987 Brundtland Report and the way it shaped thinking on the idea of sustainable development. I review some technical ways of defining and implementing sustainability that were developed in the decade after the report, along with the considerable body of literature addressing agricultural sustainability that existed well before the report came out. The chapter concludes with a discussion of some ideas that reach back to the first half of the twentieth century, including a discussion of the philosophical roots of today's thinking on organic farming.

Chapter 10 shows that one approach to sustainability is based on economic models and can be understood in terms of resource sufficiency, whereas another set of approaches drawn from ecology understands sustainability in terms of functional integrity. I review debates between and among advocates of alternative approaches in which the key issues turned on "weak" versus "strong" sustainability. These approaches might well be merged at the mathematical level. But they differ in that they tend to shape the values or the ethical questions asked about sustainability in importantly different ways.

The ethical distinction between resource sufficiency and functional integrity is further articulated in chapter 11, and I give some examples of how different types of ethical questions tend to be asked. I compare sustainability with other "essentially contested ideals," such as causality or justice, and conclude that even though we are not likely to settle the debate over sustainability (as tends to be the case with ideals), it is nonetheless important to continue it. Here, I also acknowledge "nonsubstantive" uses of the term *sustainability* and argue that although these have a place in our discourse, it is important to keep more substantive claims before us.

Chapter 12 follows up on the recent trend to identify sustainability as a social movement (or a coalition of social movements) and examines how this helps—but can also hurt—our ability to think clearly and ethically about sustainability. It includes a discussion of how sustainability is implemented through the selection of "sustainability indicators" and provides an example of indicator selection for a livestock production facility. It concludes by revisiting the concept that overcoming social conflict can be understood as working toward sustainability.

The book ends with a return to Jefferson and a reprise of the way agrarian ideals might revitalize environmental ethics and contribute to a more productive and engaged public conversation on sustainability. The schema from Inge (cited earlier) is revisited, and I suggest how each element in his agrarian typology needs to be rethought and reconceptualized in order to pursue a sustainable future. A public motivated and guided by agrarian ideals will have better philosophical resources with which to articulate our relationship to the natural world and our dependence on the continuing viability and integrity of natural ecosystems. We will, in short, be better equipped to debate and work at sustainability.

CHAPTER 1

Sustainability and Environmental Philosophy

The word *environmentalism* is often used to indicate a loosely organized social movement that emerged in the closing decades of the nineteenth century, leading to the formation of national parks and wildlife preserves. The most active early period in the United States coincided with the terms of President Theodore Roosevelt (1858–1919), which saw a considerable emphasis on conservation and an expansion of the national park system. Environmentalism enjoyed a resurgence during the 1970s with the passage of key environmental legislation such as the Clean Water Act and the creation of the Environmental Protection Agency. It has reemerged in recent times in connection with the opposition to globalization and in response to climate change. The idea of sustainability has considerably broadened the concerns of the environmental movement and, at the same time, has helped bring environmentalism itself into the mainstream.

Sustainability and environmental action alike involve implicit, unstated assumptions about the principal aims and focus of the environmental social movement. As we shall see, environmental philosophers often emphasize wild nature, but many ecologists and geographers who tackle environmental problems start with the human impact on land and water more generally. This starting point quickly leads them to agriculture. The Food and Agriculture Organization of the United Nations reports that 5,872,738 hectares of the world's 13,048,300-hectare landmass are used for agriculture: when small garden plots and marginal lands used for occasional grazing are included, slightly more than half the land on planet Earth is used for plant and animal production. Another third consists of forests and woodlands. The remaining 4,002,828 hectares can be categorized as (1) deserts, tundra, and swamps not habitable by human beings; (2) wetlands and savanna set aside for recreation and wildlife preservation; (3) lands used for mining and manufacturing; and (4) urban areas. In the United States, about half the landmass is used for agriculture; in the United Kingdom, the figure is 40 percent. Excepting multiple-use forests, U.S. lands set aside specifically for conservation or recreation (including uninhabited deserts, swamps, and high mountain ranges) make up a mere 20 percent of the total.

From one perspective, then, agriculture is a key to humanity's impact on the environment. Sustainable land use cannot be thought of strictly as a matter of protecting island ecosystems from all human use, however important that continues to be. If we shift from land to water, we note that agriculture uses the largest share of fresh water. In fact, Lester Brown, founder of the Worldwatch Institute and coiner of the phrase *sustainable development,* has always believed that food production is the key to sustainability. He wrote, "There is a tendency in public discourse to talk about the water problem and the food problem as though they were independent. But with some 70 percent of all the water that is pumped from underground used for irrigation . . . the water problem and the food problem are in large measure the same."[1] Thus, even when our focus is narrowed to environmental sustainability (that is, before we even begin to ask about fairness, justice, or whether the human population will have enough to eat), we note that a very large portion of what we take to *be* the environment—nonurban land and water—is caught up in agriculture.

The agricultural focus can be expanded even further if we take a science or policy perspective. In many cases, the science underlying forestry and fish and wildlife management resides in institutions that originated as colleges of agriculture. This is because basic science disciplines traditionally eschewed applied problems, so agricultural colleges became the natural home for all manner of applied biology. In most nations, executive policy for the management of forests and fisheries resides in the same ministry as agriculture. For good or ill, the lead administrators of agencies devoted to policy making for biological systems often have farming backgrounds and perspectives. Agriculture is, in this broad sense, the human management of ecosystems, and all natural ecosystems are increasingly being viewed as in need of management, if only to shield their natural functions from impact by the ever-expanding human species. To this way of thinking, agriculture represents the ensemble of ways in which the human species both shapes and is shaped by the ecosystems that human beings inhabit. Although I do not presume to use the word *agriculture* quite *this* broadly, the way that some of our key intellectual and political institutions are tied to agriculture is worth keeping in mind.

Such considerations can lead one to the judgment that agriculture is critical for environmental quality and sustainability, but there has actually been very little discussion of agriculture within the subgroup of people who have developed environmental ethics as a philosophical subject. This component of environmental philosophy emphasizes the norms, principles, or "ought" statements implicit in environmentalism. It also encompasses the way more general ideas in ethics and political theory intertwine with our attempts to act appropriately with regard to the environment in both our personal and our larger social lives. To the extent that sustainability is an encompassing or guiding principle for addressing social problems, it is a central topic for environmental philosophy. To the extent that basic value orientations, framing assumptions about nature and society, or humanity's accumulated traditions for acting collectively and adjudicating disputes are important to sustainability, environmental philosophy is central to sustainability. Ideas and debates in environmental philosophy can come from anywhere, but their integration with broader traditions of thinking in the sciences and in ethics, politics, or the law can be more easily achieved when people trained and specializing in those areas take a prominent role. Thus, better integration of agriculture *and* philosophy into our thinking and action on sustainability is a critical task for the near term.

Environmental Philosophy and the Neglect of Agriculture

Environmental ethics is not limited to people who have academic degrees in philosophy. Aldo Leopold (1887–1948), generally hailed as one of the founders of present-day environmental philosophy, received his advanced training from Yale University's School of Forestry. Leopold's philosophy of "adaptive management" was originally developed to ensure a thriving population of game for hunters, but it has now been expanded into a general way of thinking about resource management and sustainability. Leopold himself was quite cognizant of agriculture. At one point he wrote, "There are two spiritual dangers in not owning a farm. One is the danger of supposing that breakfast comes from the grocery, and the other that heat comes from a furnace."[2] This aphorism aptly encapsulates some of the key themes one can draw from agrarian ideals, and I return to Leopold's thinking several times in this book. But although Leopold is in many respects the prototypical environmental philosopher, his willingness to take agriculture seriously is *not* typical.

In fact, most environmental philosophy has been shaped by the early history of international movements to establish national parks and to preserve wildlife populations. It was focused on that comparatively small portion of the landmass that was to be set aside and protected *from* agriculture, and it was preoccupied with developing good reasons to do just that. The debate between John Muir (1838–1914) and Gifford Pinchot (1865–1946) over the future of American wilderness set the stage for an environmental ethics that has largely ignored land and water used for farm production. Muir was a Scot who spent most of his later years in the United States, writing a number of influential books on the American West and eventually founding the Sierra Club. Disciples of Muir believe in the preservation of woodlands and other wild areas. They argue for the intrinsic value of ecosystems and have developed ethical approaches that are ecocentric, in that they view the natural world as having moral value and significance wholly apart from any use humans may have for it. They decry those who decide nature's fate by calculating the economic value of wild species or habitat, and they support political initiatives to remove natural areas from the threat of development by timber and mining companies or by public water projects.

Pinchot founded the School of Forestry at Yale and was a leader of the U.S. Forest Service, as well as governor of Pennsylvania. Disciples of Pinchot argue for the conservation and wise use of nature, but they see no problem in describing forests and protected areas as resources that must be set aside for future use. They think of environmental ethics in terms of duties to future generations of human beings. They are thus anthropocentric, considering the moral value we associate with the natural world to reside ultimately in the way human beings place value on it. For example, the subjective feeling of well-being a human being experiences simply by knowing that certain ecosystems exist provides the ultimate basis for setting aside parks and wilderness areas. This kind of well-being may indeed be subject to an economic treatment, and environmental economists have developed sophisticated techniques for estimating so-called existence value. In real life, Pinchot and Muir were frequently political allies. Thus, anthropocentric conservationists may support many of the same political goals as their ecocentric preservationist counterparts, but the anthropocentrist sees nothing inherently wrong with weighing nature's loss against humanity's gain.

Muir and Pinchot represent two ways of understanding environmental values, and their respective philosophies also arose in debates over the future of African wildlife and European woodlands. This type of debate continues to be crucial for the fate of endangered species, such as the giant panda, and for the more than one-third of the world's landmass that is now forested. It usefully illuminates issues related to the way urban encroachment, energy consumption, and thermal pollution threaten large land areas where human use has, until recently, had only a marginal and indirect effect on wildlife and ecosystem processes. Yet by organizing one's entire environmental philosophy around the dichotomy represented by the perspectives of Muir and Pinchot, environmental ethicists fall prey to two related dogmas. If unquestioned, this habit of mind limits our ability to ask the right questions about sustainability.

Two Dogmas of Environmental Philosophy

The dichotomy of ecocentric and anthropocentric thinking has been reinforced by two assumptions, two elements of tacit thinking that have become dogmas in philosophical discussions of the environment. First is the dogma of pristine nature, the presumption that the best environment is one completely devoid of human impact. In *Second Nature*, Michael Pollan recounts the story of Cathedral Pines, a natural preserve in Cornwall, Connecticut. It seems that in 1989 the pines fell prey to a particularly violent storm, and the once venerated park became an eyesore of rotting stumps and dense undergrowth. What to do? One contingent of townsfolk argued that fires and storms are natural events and that the unsightly state of Cathedral Pines was entirely consistent with the preservationist goals that guided its establishment. Hence, their solution was to do nothing; the pines would eventually come back on their own. Others stressed the pines' contribution to local history and culture and noted that the area would not return to its former state for 100 years. They urged a management scheme of reseeding and brush control. Was Cathedral Pines another episode in the contest between ecocentric preservationists and anthropocentric conservationists? The story continues. As Pollan points out, Cathedral Pines was actually a second-growth forest, replacing hardwoods that had been cleared by European settlers in bygone days. The pine trees there never would have become established without drastic human intervention. Even the hardwoods that had gone before had been managed by Native American residents of the region. The pristine nature prized by everyone, it seems, was nowhere to be found.

The type of environmental philosophy that created the dilemma of Cathedral Pines was the target of a blistering attack by historian William Cronon, who called it "getting back to the wrong nature." Cronon documented human impact on American environments prior to the arrival of European settlers. His work exposed how the belief in pristine nature served to rationalize European conquest of American lands and peoples alike. Europeans obviously knew that there were indigenous tribes, but because they saw the land as untamed wilderness, as pristine and unaffected by human beings, subjection of the people living on this land became part and parcel of the subjection or taming of the land itself. It was, in a philosophical sense, as if their interactions with plant and animal species were wholly natural, meaning "not human." For conquistadors and colonists who saw pristine nature as morally unimproved, this was an invitation to displace native peoples. But Cronon notes that simply inverting this judgment, so that we now see pristine nature as something to be preserved, leaves us in a very curious position with respect to the people who were an indispensable part of those ecosystems. Were Native Americans savages whose very wildness rendered them incapable of thoughtful ecosystem management? Did they deserve to be "preserved" along with the wild nature of which they were a part? The offensiveness of this suggestion refutes any serious attempt to use the dogma of pristine nature as an ethical principle for understanding sustainability.

The second dogma is more subtle. Much of the environmental policy in the United States has been guided by the preparation of environmental impact statements, and similar technical studies are used in most industrialized democracies. In these policy instruments, analysts use biology and economics to predict the effect a construction project, a management scheme, or a public policy will have. Economists assign value to these impacts using techniques that have become controversial among environmentalists and philosophers. But the assumption that the acceptability of the activity turns on the acceptability of the predicted outcome has not been so controversial. We (that is, society) are expected to choose between one studied activity and another (or alternatively, to choose neither), based on the projected impact of the action. This can be called the dogma of environmental impact.

best principle is pristine, best consciousness is less impact — these thoughts leave out agriculture

This kind of impact-based thinking is not to be sneezed at. Many credit Rachel Carson (1907–1964) with sparking the environmental movement by calling the public's attention to the environmental impact of the widespread and indiscriminate use of pesticides. Her book *Silent Spring* is important for environmental ethics because it established one model for arguments that use environmental science to influence human action. In this model, the best empirical science is used to establish the actual, likely, or potential consequences of an activity—anything from using pesticides to building a dam. These scientific studies are then summarized for the general public in books like *Silent Spring*. Although such books provoke outrage and can stimulate needed reform, they typically do not make any explicit statements about *why* the predicted consequences are ethically unacceptable. Authors like Carson allow readers to supply their own moral values, and in the case of declining songbirds, that was enough to provoke action. But the more subtle problem is that the dogma of environmental impact draws a sharp line between the prediction of an outcome, which is a task for science, and the formulation of values to be used when determining what kinds of outcomes are acceptable or desirable. For the most part, environmental philosophers have been willing to accept this division of labor, confining *their* debate to why impacts are significant, which sometimes takes the form of questioning the numbers generated by economists.

This tag-team approach, in which scientists predict and philosophers or economists value, fits nicely with the picture of ethics that held sway throughout the twentieth century. It is a picture that offered two main options for understanding how ethical norms influence human conduct. *Consequentialism* is the view that any sound argument about the ethical acceptability of an action or activity *must* turn on claims about the outcome of that activity. In classical utilitarian ethics (of the sort Peter Singer has applied to animals), there is the additional presumption that only outcomes that affect the welfare (health, wealth, and well-being) of creatures capable of subjectively experiencing satisfaction or dissatisfaction can have ethical significance. The alterative *deontological* approach stresses rights and duties. Here one might argue that some outcomes are totally unacceptable because they violate rights or fundamental freedoms. A land-use policy that involves allowing a former wetland to flood might be viewed as unacceptable because the outcome is inconsistent with the property rights of certain landowners, for example. In either case, our reflection on the ethics of environmental sustainability drills in on the values we associate with the outcome or impact of our actions. Consequentialists hold that ethics is exclusively about determining the acceptability of an action or policy by examining trade-offs among outcomes or consequences, whereas deontologists specify a set of outcomes that entail nonnegotiable duties.[3]

It is also possible to broaden one's environmental philosophy by adopting an ecocentric scheme of valuation. In the preceding examples, the value of environmental impacts was derived from human satisfaction or use. One might easily recognize that many animals experience feelings of satisfaction or suffering that can be traced to the quality of their habitat, so one can question anthropocentrism without questioning the dogma of environmental impact. What is more, one can be more broad-minded still by insisting that it is not a matter of trading off benefits and harms to people and wildlife. One might insist that we think of living things or even complex entities such as species or ecosystems as having a *right* to exist. Environmental philosophers who are this broad-minded do not think of themselves as consequentialists, but it is important to see that even so, it is environmental impact that violates these rights. Here too, the dogma of environmental impact remains unquestioned.

I do not dispute that consequences matter when it comes to ethics, but the exclusive focus on outcomes or impacts has some disturbing implications. The dogma of environmental impact makes it easy to think of values as being wholly independent from facts. In the anthropocentric or utilitarian tradition, they might reside in the subjective pleasure or displeasure that human beings associate with their personal well-being. An ecocentric approach has often proceeded by trying to establish that ecosystems or nonhumans have rights that are violated when certain types of outcomes materialize. But in either case, science predicts the outcome, and then some subjective act or cultural tradition is drawn on to assign a value to that outcome. Since ecosystem processes are presumed to be proper objects of scientific study, this means that ecosystems play no role in actually *creating* values. The value process is radically separated from anything we call "nature" and lies entirely in a sphere we might call "social" or "cultural."

The general philosophical problem here is that the nature-culture divide is actually very difficult to maintain. Science itself is a cultural activity, and it is shot through with value judgments (a point that is central to the discussion of sustainability that begins in chapter 8). More pointedly in the present context, combining the dogma of environmental impact with the dogma of pristine nature creates a disastrous environmental ethics for cultivated ecosystems (that is, for agriculture). Agriculture by its very nature and intention involves an impact on nature. However ethical imperatives for land use are expressed, the result of any call to limit the environmental impact from agriculture means the less agriculture, the better. However, if agriculture is to be minimized on a per-acre basis, it must be practiced as intensively as possible on those acres. This reasoning categorically supports industrialized agriculture over organic or low-input alternatives. It reaches its logical conclusion in an agriculture that consists of slime pits where genetically engineered microorganisms efficiently transform sunshine and nutrients into biomass, which is then piped into factories where more genetically engineered microorganisms transform the biomass into something that resembles edible food. If this is not your idea of what sustainable agriculture looks like, you, like me, want to look elsewhere for an environmental ethic of sustainability, at least insofar as sustainability has anything to do with agriculture.

The Philosophy of Agriculture: Ancient Greece

Many so-called environmental impacts are better conceptualized not as consequences, outcomes, or end points that are the *result* of human action but as components in dynamic feedback systems that regulate both ecosystem processes and a wide range of human interests. In this connection, it is useful to recall the difference between moral philosophies that emphasize case-by-case decision making and the pattern of moral thinking characteristic of classical Greek philosophy, where human actions are thought to reflect and be shaped by broad aspects of the social and natural milieu. Victor Davis Hanson, a contemporary scholar of the ancient Greeks, believes that philosophers such as Socrates (circa 469–399 BCE) and Plato (circa 429–347 BCE) must be read in light of certain agrarian ideals that were the foundations of life throughout Greek city-states and at Athens in particular. Hanson's book *The Other Greeks* argues that the Greek worldview incorporates both nature and society into an enveloping environment that aids or inhibits action in a very selective way. Human goodness involves the realization of potential that is latent in human character, but the potential for this realization is not wholly under any individual person's control. One develops virtues and vices as a result of how one's environment rewards or penalizes patterns of conduct in a systematic way. There is, therefore, no good person without a good environment. And for the Greeks, a good environment was not a pristine environment but a farm environment.

This type of thought places individuals within concentric webs: family, community, and nature. As described in Aristotle's (384–322 BCE) *Politics*, these webs work as interacting hierarchies to establish feedback loops ensuring that individuals internalize the consequences of their actions into habits of personal character. One does not stand back from a potential impact and wonder how to value it; rather, one sees the whole organic situation as creating more specific value commitments, which are understood as virtues that integrate and preserve the whole. Families provide an environment for the growth and development of children, but communities, in turn, provide an environment that can either help or hinder the proper functioning of family life. Communities themselves take on unique characteristics by virtue of the regional environment in which they exist. In an integrated and healthy moral environment, tensions among family loyalty, citizenship, and stewardship are actually a creative and positive force. They counterbalance one another and prevent the exclusive or obsessive development of any one character tendency over others. A balance or harmony of the virtues signals right action. Decline occurs when otherwise virtuous conduct tends toward excess, veering in the direction of vice.

In Hanson's view, the polis or city-state typical of ancient Greece had a social organization that depended on a type of agriculture that had theretofore not been seen. Relatively small family units formed households, generally supported by family labor and that of a small number of slaves. These household units were mainly self-supporting, but they produced enough surplus for the support of craftsmen and artisans whose skills vastly improved the quality of life (and also made the agriculture itself more productive). Previous agricultures had been organized around large-scale public works for irrigation and the distribution of harvests. They demanded massive numbers of slaves as well as a highly stratified elite to manage the system. The unique mountainous geography of Greece, however, was ill suited to such large-scale, top-down, irrigated agriculture, and the nature of Greek soils and rainfall permitted the cultivation of a broader variety of crops, including olive trees and grapevines. But these tree and vine crops required lifetime investments of labor and maintenance. The farming people (including household slaves) thus developed an interest in maintaining long-term control over their lands that slave laborers in Egypt or China had never experienced.

This was, Hanson argues, the root of solidarity, binding a number of households into those communities that became the Greek polis. Each household had more autonomy than anyone (save the emperor or pharaoh himself) in a top-down agriculture, but each was also highly dependent on the community as a whole. Hanson emphasizes how this interdependence played out in the emergence of a unique military innovation, the phalanx, and subsequently in the emergence of citizenship, relative equality, and limited democracy throughout the Peloponnesian peninsula. The Greek polis; the Greek ideals of citizenship, equality, and freedom; and the Greek conception of morality all rest, in Hanson's view, on the household organization of Greek agriculture. Because ancient Greece is also widely thought to be the birthplace of contemporary philosophy and democracy, it is worth taking some time to examine Hanson's views from a critical perspective. I revisit the Greeks at several junctures throughout the book, examining the warrant and telling of this basic story as it has been developed by both Hanson and others, including the Greeks themselves.

Hanson believes that the political events that spawned the golden age of Athenian philosophy were precipitated by changes in marine technology—by a shift in the way Athens was situated with respect to its biological environment. In the first phase, Athens enjoyed a dramatic economic and military expansion owing to its sea power, but these changes then fed back into the character of the Athenian people themselves. New economic interests emerged. Unlike the interests of those who derived their livelihood and security from the lands surrounding Athens, these new interests derived wealth from trade. Athenians demanded the protection of sea-based trading routes and incessant expansion of the Athenian sphere of influence through military conquest. In response, Athenian moral philosophers attempted to articulate ideals that would express the importance of loyalty to the polis. Hanson argues that key elements in the thought of ancient Greece can be appreciated only when we understand that they were arguments that rest on agrarian ideals.

Agriculture as a Model for Environmental Philosophy

If Hanson is right (and I will eventually argue that he is at least partially right), agrarian ideals are actually implicit in our most venerable sources of ethical thinking. Although philosophies of agriculture are seldom formulated explicitly today, competing philosophies of agriculture continue to be implicit in many if not most of the twentieth-century scientific and policy changes that created the modern world. Like an environmental philosophy, a philosophy of agriculture is a somewhat coherent set of beliefs or principles that express the purpose or guiding vision of farming or animal husbandry—the principal (though not exclusive) vocations associated with food and fiber production. It goes without saying that the purpose of food and fiber production is to produce fiber and food, but the Greeks understood these productive activities to be interwoven with more comprehensive human purposes and social ideals. Furthermore, any productive activity takes place within the context of a social consensus on appropriate rules, constraints, and institutions. Thus for Socrates, Plato, and Aristotle, it was conceivable to propose that human slavery was consistent with one's philosophy of agriculture, but it is not conceivable today.

Of course, few people ever think about what the philosophy of agriculture might include. I first began to think about it when I was asked to teach a course on agricultural ethics in 1982. Not long into my second attempt at the course, a professor of agricultural economics accosted me for what he presumed was my naïve and nostalgic advocacy of family farms. In fact, at that time I had not conceived of agricultural ethics as having anything to do with family farms, and I had developed a course covering world hunger, animal welfare, and the environmental issues associated with agricultural chemicals. But my colleague's too strenuous protest tipped me off. The issue that agricultural economists refer to as "farm size distribution" was and is central to agricultural ethics. It took me many years to knit this insight together with the main themes of environmental philosophy, but I attempt to do it here in the remaining pages of this chapter.

The percentage of farmers among the overall population in industrializing countries has been getting smaller for a long, long time. At the same time, the average size of farms has been growing, whether we measure size in acres or hectares, numbers of animals, or the value of

Two modern phils : Industrial & Agrarian
(production)
↳ sees agriculture
as a social function

the food and fiber commodities produced. These farms have also become much more specialized. Most large farms now produce just one or two things, whereas farms of yore produced a dozen or more crops or animals both for home consumption and for sale. There are exceptions to these trends. Very small farms have actually prospered throughout North America during recent times, although these operations seldom derive all their income from growing crops and raising animals. Nevertheless, the trend toward fewer and larger farms has been a hallmark of industrialization. In addition to his writings on the Greeks, Hanson has written books on this trend in modern agriculture, suggesting that just as the shift away from family farms led to decline in ancient Athens, so it might for us today.

The reason my former colleague cautioned me against a naïve endorsement of small farms is that, in his view, industrialization has forever changed the way we should understand agriculture. He was implicitly endorsing what I call in this book an *industrial philosophy of agriculture.* According to this view, whatever might have been the case in the past, we should now see agriculture as just another sector in the industrial economy. This means that society is best served when farmers, ranchers, and other animal producers make their products available at the lowest possible cost. They should not, of course, impose costs on others to do so. There are still important ethical issues that must be addressed in an industrial philosophy of agriculture, environmental impacts and fairness to workers and animals among them. But we now live in an industrialized world, and perhaps we should simply face up to that fact.

I call the opposing point of view an *agrarian philosophy of agriculture,* although others prefer terms such as *alternative* or *multifunctional agriculture,* and still others associate the word *sustainability* itself with the agrarian way of thinking. This is a view that sees agriculture as performing a social function above and beyond its capacity to produce food and fiber goods such as meat, milk, leather, or wool. The exact nature of these broader social functions may be difficult to specify, and the reasons why we should regard them as ethically significant may seem obscure at first. It will, in fact, take me several chapters to spin out the numerous strands of an agrarian view. Yet it is very clear even at the outset that some people—a minority, perhaps—have very strong feelings both *for* small-scale, traditional or diversified family-style farming and *against* the larger, more specialized farms that are typical of the industrial era.

The strength of these feelings and the intensity with which they are expressed are reason enough to see the opposition between industrial and agrarian views of agriculture as a debate with ethical and philosophical dimensions. It is this debate that becomes the heart of agricultural ethics.

Industrial Agriculture: The Case for Specialization

Perhaps the trend toward fewer, larger, and more specialized farms is a good thing. This is the view of Jeffrey Sachs, for example. Sachs, director of the Earth Institute at Columbia University, is an economist known for his work on poverty reduction, debt cancellation, and disease control for the developing world. Sachs describes the talents of the traditional diversified farmer as "truly marvelous. [They] typically know how to build their own houses, grow and cook food, tend to animals, and make clothing." But he goes on: "They are also deeply inefficient. Adam Smith pointed out that specialization, where each of us learns just one of those skills, leads to a general improvement in everybody's well-being."[4] Farmers who concentrate on growing just one or two crops or raising just one species of livestock can become especially adept at it. They can exploit whatever advantages their soil or weather conditions offer that particular production activity to their fullest. This kind of specialization allows them to produce at the lowest possible cost.

The ethical argument for such specialization is that when goods are produced at the least possible cost, they can be sold at the lowest price. This means that people who eat (all of us) spend less on food, freeing up more of their income for other things, and low-cost food is especially important for those who have the least income. There are thus two ethical arguments at work here: First, selling *anything* for less is good on utilitarian grounds, because when people have more discretion to spend elsewhere, they can allocate their resources to those things that make the greatest contribution to their personal well-being. Technologies that improve efficiency serve the greatest good for the greatest number. Second, selling *food* for less is good on egalitarian grounds, since it is of relatively greater importance to the poor than to the rich. Technologies that reduce the cost of necessities (such as food) are ethically better than technologies that reduce the cost of luxury goods (such as entertainment) because they are especially beneficial to people with lower incomes.

There is a cost to this productivity, and it winds up being borne by those farmers who are slow to utilize the most productive technology available. The price of farm commodities reflects the average costs of all producers. If farmers cannot recover their costs, they do not remain farmers for long. Early adopters of more productive technology have lower average costs but sell at the higher average rate, making windfall profits. But as the new technology becomes the norm, average production costs fall, and prices fall too. Someone who has the new technology can still recover costs, even at the new lower price. They stay in business. Those still using the old technology have costs well above the average. They cannot recover their costs in the new economic environment and eventually go out of business. Who buys their farms? Clearly, it is the early adopters, who enjoyed several years of high profits and now have the wherewithal to snap up these bankrupt farms. Increases in technology thus cause a treadmill effect. The individual farmer must run harder (produce more) to stay in place (recover costs). For the farm sector as a whole, every turn of the treadmill means fewer and larger farms.

If the technology treadmill results in fewer, larger, and more specialized farms, it also results in a general lowering of food prices for consumers. Although the farmers who disappear from farming are the losers, the winners are numerous (all of us), and the comparatively disadvantaged among us win comparatively more. So especially in circumstances in which those displaced from farming can find employment in other fields, the technological treadmill looks like a bargain to development-oriented economists like Sachs. The economic details can complicate the arithmetic of this moral calculation substantially, as I demonstrate in later chapters. Benefits captured by biotechnology companies or the food industry may not be passed on to consumers. Details such as these matter a great deal in any final analysis of the sustainability or moral acceptability of industrial agriculture, but the point here is to stress the underlying ethical logic of the case for specialization.

Notice that this argument does not treat agriculture differently from any other sector of the economy. Specialization in any sector can lower costs. Efficiencies in manufacturing can lower the cost of automobiles or video games. Efficiencies in energy production would be welcomed by all and might be almost as valuable to the poor as efficiencies that reduce the cost of food. More efficient health care technology would, like cheaper food or energy, find moral support on both utilitarian and egalitarian grounds. Policies that prevented the introduction of more efficient technologies in manufacturing, energy, or health care would be suspect.

Have corporations, oil companies, or the health care lobby interfered in the political process to protect their profits? Of course they have. It becomes front-page news whenever this interference is discovered, and congressional committees are convened to stop it. If this is how we react to protecting the economic interests of those who produce health services, energy, or manufactured goods, why would we see protecting the interests of those who produce food any differently?

The argument for specialization applies across all sectors of an industrial economy. If we think that a norm of specialization and encouragement of the use of the most productive technologies should not be applied in farming or livestock production, we are claiming that farmers are a special case. Some reasons for thinking that they might be are discussed later, but it is important to recognize that Sachs's adaptation of Adam Smith creates a burden of proof for those who think that agriculture is different. The view that agriculture is not different from every other sector of the industrial economy sees more productive technology as a good thing on both utilitarian and egalitarian grounds. This is the industrial philosophy of agriculture.

Of course, it goes without saying that there is no true efficiency when there is no true reduction in cost. Lower prices can sometimes be achieved by deferring maintenance or investment costs. This means that these costs will have to be paid sometime in the future, and the lower price does not reflect a true increase in efficiency. Lower prices can also be achieved by forcing costs on third parties. For example, a company can lower its costs by lowering wages and thus sell its products for less, but it is simply the workers, rather than the company, who are bearing these costs. In these cases, lower prices might benefit consumers, but they do not reflect the true costs of production. Considering such cases is a critical part of agricultural ethics, and that is where the discussion turns next.

Industrial Agriculture: The True Cost of Food

Some critics of industrial agriculture argue that the relatively low prices consumers pay for food and fiber goods in industrial societies conceal a host of hidden costs. Sachs praises green revolution technologies that have increased the yields of farmers in India.[5] But Vandana Shiva argues that such calculations neglect the way older farming methods returned nutrients to the soil and maintained its structure. Soil-depleting practices defer costs into the future, especially if rising energy costs also increase the cost of artificial fertilizers. Bill McKibben picks up on the energy theme, noting that the alleged efficiencies in the industrial food system conceal the fact that enormous quantities of fossil fuel energy are used not only for synthetic fertilizers, pesticides, and farm machinery but also for transporting food commodities from distant markets. Our society's reliance on inexpensive fossil fuels has institutionalized a system that is imposing costs on future generations through practices that deplete resources and stimulate climate change.

These points are also noted by Michael Pollan in his enormously popular book *The Omnivore's Dilemma*. Pollan adds the more straightforward point that animal production in the United States and Canada is made to seem cheaper than it actually is by taxpayer-supported subsidies paid to grain farmers. These price-support payments have lowered the cost of animal feed far below the level that would have been established by the economic forces of supply and demand. Other costs take the form of direct harm to public health. Yale professor John Wargo has argued that weak laws regulating agricultural pesticides in the United States have unaccounted costs in the form of long-term health problems and the attendant medical expenditures allocated to addressing them. To the extent that the efficiencies extolled by Sachs depend on tax subsidies or entail costs in the form of harm to health, some of the costs imposed on present-day generations are not reflected in the prices paid by food consumers. They are, in the parlance of economics, *externalities*.

There are also more philosophically controversial costs associated with industrial animal production. Modern feedlots and dairy operations utilize feeding practices that speed weight gain or increase milk production, but at the expense of gastric distress and increased rates of diseases such as mastitis. Modern egg production places hens in crowded conditions where they cannot express their instincts to flap their wings, bathe in dust, or build a nest. Pregnant sows are kept in narrow crates throughout the gestation period, unable to even turn around. Broiler chickens have been bred to have such exaggerated breasts that they suffer from skeletal deformities. Gene Bauer, the founder of Farm Sanctuary, argues that these are costs imposed on the animals themselves and are not accounted for in the prices consumers pay for animal products. Animal biotechnologies have the potential to both mitigate and exacerbate some of these impacts on animals. This book omits any detailed discussion of the argument that animals are moral subjects, although lots of ink has been spilled on this topic by other philosophers. I simply assume that to the extent we regard harsh impacts on animals as having moral significance, these, too, must be counted among the true costs of the way we farm.

The precise way of understanding costs that are not reflected in the market prices of goods is open to a number of different ethical interpretations. The language of cost may suggest a form of benefit-cost weighing that is familiar to utilitarian ethical thinking. Here, benefits from lower food prices might be thought to offset costs, and the crucial ethical questions revolve around the way we estimate the value of costs and the value of benefits and then aggregate them in an attempt to determine whether one outweighs the other. A utilitarian might ask whether the benefits to consumers (especially poor consumers) exceed the costs in taxes or medical expenditures, as well as the costs for future generations or for animals. Other social scientists attempting to take a more ethically neutral stance might say that the problem is one of deciding which trade-offs to make.

But one might also argue that certain types of harm should not be subjected to trade-off thinking. In the libertarian tradition of ethics, harms to health or liberty would be regarded as overriding any benefit-cost calculations. A situation (such as we appear to have now) in which affected parties lack legal rights to prevent such harms would be regarded as morally unacceptable. The libertarian approach to ethics is grounded in a view that social (or governmental) compulsion of individual action can be rationalized only when the person being compelled would actually consent, perhaps in exchange for assurance that government will protect him or her from harmful acts by others. We are justly compelled to respect one another's liberty and property, in this view, but acts of beneficence are morally legitimate only on the condition that they are undertaken voluntarily. All the costs described above would (arguably) qualify as violations of libertarian moral rights, although there are difficult conceptual issues to work out with respect to animals and future generations.

Given the multiple ways of approaching these views, there is more philosophical work to do in specifying exactly how we want to approach the unaccounted for costs noted by Shiva, McKibben, Pollan, Bauer, and Wargo. But this is not the place to undertake a lesson in basic moral theory, so these important issues must be set aside for now. A different philosophical point *is* worth noting. Although this litany of externalized costs serves as an important qualification on the case for specialization, the moral force of these claims is wholly consistent with the industrial philosophy of agriculture. Recall that this philosophy states that we should treat farming just like every other sector of the economy. Certainly we are just as worried about adverse health impacts and unjustified tax subsidies in industries such as energy or manufacturing (where these issues are frequently the subject of moral critiques). Similarly, there is nothing particularly special about agriculture when it comes to costs imposed on future generations. Costs to future generations in the form of climate change appear to be due primarily to transportation and household energy consumption, for example.

Activities such as the use of animals in the entertainment industry (zoos and circuses) or in medical experiments have been the focus of protest by advocates for animal rights. Agriculture is a big user of animals, but the claim that we should account for all the costs of an activity, including those to nonhumans, is consistent with the main thrust of industrial thinking. So all these critiques leveled at industrial-style farming are well within the purview of a philosophy that states that agriculture should be viewed as an ordinary sector of the industrial economy. If there is disagreement between someone like Sachs, who advocates more industrial farming, and critics who seem to want less of it, it is a disagreement about the outcomes that specialization has actually produced. It is, in other words, a dispute about the facts and not about the moral principles we should apply when we think about agriculture.

The Agrarian Mind

In contrast to the industrial view, an agrarian philosophy gives agriculture a moral significance that extends well beyond the way we think of industries such as transportation, manufacturing, or even health care. Here it is useful to return to ancient Greece. The Greek poet Hesiod (circa 700 BCE) saw farming as having a religious purpose, but the religious significance of farming for Hesiod was rather different than it might be for contemporary Christians, Muslims, or Jews. His Zeus was one of several immanent gods, fully present in Hesiod's daily life. The depiction of Zeus in Hesiod's poem *Works and Days* is one of a god thoroughly integrated into nature and the source of all natural unity. The seasons, soil, and water are themselves divinities begotten by Zeus that establish a place for human beings. A key message in Hesiod's poetry is that only farmers dependent on seasons, soil, and water can hope to attain piety or show proper respect to these divinities. Farming is the way human beings justly occupy a place in the divine (that is, natural) order, and it is the gods' intention that this place be fraught with work, toil, and risk. Warfare, violence, and trickery, in contrast, are unjust in Hesiod's poetry because they short-circuit the gods' intended route to material rewards. These human practices will eventually be repaid with misery and loss. Agriculture is thus the singular practice by which humanity makes its way in the world in a pious and morally just manner. It is, of course, important to Hesiod that agriculture bring forth the food and fiber goods that are the focus of industrial thinking, but this is merely the tip of the iceberg in terms of understanding the moral significance of farming.[6]

Throughout history, agrarian philosophies have seen an enormous variety of goods and values stemming from agricultural practice, and they were commonplace in North America until recently. In 1948 political scientist A. Whitney Griswold (1906–1963) found it necessary to devote a book-length monograph to refuting the view that democratic societies are inherently agricultural in their economic organization and political structure. Griswold made Thomas Jefferson into the symbolic progenitor of the myth, although it is arguable that other figures of the time were more committed to it.[7] Benjamin Franklin (1706–1790), for example, argued that farming produced a moral personality more inclined toward honest dealing and loyalty to one's fellow citizens than did the city trades (Franklin was a printer and publisher, himself). The upshot: only a society of farmers can develop the personal habits and virtues necessary for self-rule.[8]

This kind of argument is still with us. We have already considered Victor Davis Hanson, who is reputed to be former vice president Dick Cheney's favorite author. Like Jefferson and Franklin, he has expressed the view that farming is crucial, but in a vein suggesting that present-day Americans' lack of contact with farming has corrupted their political values. In *The Land Was Everything*, Hanson writes that only farmers have a true understanding of how secure property rights lend support to virtues of patriotism and citizenship. Authors on the Left include Brian Donahue, who believes that reconnecting people to the land through gardening and through eating patterns that stress both seasonality and local production is essential to the development of a moral personality that appreciates what it takes to support diverse but culturally integrated and unified communities. Donahue believes that "urban agrarianism" is most critical for the type of political mentality that highly integrated and localized eating and farming practices create. A deep sense of mutual interdependence and common purpose emerges in localities where people interact in the production of food.

Poet, novelist, and essayist Wendell Berry is unquestionably the most articulate advocate of agrarian philosophy in our own time. In *The Unsettling of America* Berry confronts the claims of specialization directly, arguing that the division of labor has created lives whereby people are unable to see the larger wholes in which both human relationships and exchanges with nature acquire their meaning. The fragmentation of contemporary life corresponds to a vision of human beings as "choice-makers" who move from transaction to transaction, evaluating options in atomistic terms, as if choices and the people and places in which they live and work did not form a larger, more integrated whole. In place of this fragmented consumer lifestyle, Berry advocates a return, however partial it must be, to practices embedded in and emanating from a commitment to a given place. For Berry, the communities that have come closest to achieving true community (and true stewardship of the environment) are traditional farming communities. Thus Berry advocates, if not a literal return to agrarian lifestyles, at least the deliberate cultivation of an ethical mentality that locates our ideals of polity, community, and environmental responsibility in agrarian ideals.

Agrarian Philosophy of Agriculture

Notice how criticisms leveled against industrial agriculture take on a different meaning when framed within the context of agrarian mentality. Advocacy of local food is a particularly salient example. In stressing the energy costs associated with the long-distance transport of foods and the role this needless expenditure of carbon plays in global warming, the force of the criticism is to suggest that a more comprehensive accounting of environmental costs associated with industrial farming would produce a different verdict in terms of ethics. This is a perspective that accepts the dogma of environmental impact: Although the low prices of the industrial food system are ethically good, for all the reasons noted by

importance of a local food system

Sachs, there is more to the story. When long-term environmental costs associated with energy consumption are factored into the equation, we see that the cost-benefit ratio is not so attractive. If we are inclined toward a libertarian way of thinking, we might say that these benefits to present-day consumers are being obtained by imposing costs and risks on future generations, which are necessarily unable to give or withhold their consent to this "bargain." Either way, we can generate an ethical critique of industrial food production.

But an agrarian is more concerned with the way a local food system embeds people in practices whereby their commerce with nature and with one another creates an enduring sense of place. In a local food system, even people who buy (rather than grow) most of their food at farmers' markets or through cooperative arrangements encounter the same people repeatedly, week after week. They build bonds with them, and honesty and mutual respect are critical in such ongoing encounters. Furthermore, consumers have contact with the people who grow the food they buy. Consumers become familiar with the rhythm of the seasons, and they learn what grows well under local conditions. They can inquire about the condition of the land and animals under the farmer's care. The agrarian hope is that these kinds of localized transactions will gradually develop into an affection for the people and for the place where one lives, and that through the constant repetition of theses rhythms, this affection, this sympathy, will mature into full-fledged habits of character—virtues, if you will.

The overriding moral concern that emerges from the agrarian mind-set is one focused on the way these quotidian material practices establish patterns of conduct that are conducive to the formation of certain habits. These habits become natural to people who engage in them repeatedly and become the stuff of personal moral character. When such habits are shared throughout a locale, they form the basis for community bonds and become characteristic of the residents. The activities of food production and consumption are strongly tied to repetitive material practice. Furthermore, these localized practices are shaped by tradition and geography, by soil, water, and climate conditions. It is therefore not surprising that moral philosophies focusing primarily on the emergence and stability of virtues, community, and moral character would converge with a mind-set in which agriculture has special moral significance.

Philosophy of Agriculture: Continuing the Conversation

In point of fact, many of the criticisms noted earlier as focusing on the "true costs of food" can be reframed in agrarian terms. Concerns about the long-term fertility of soil and the ecologically adaptive characteristics of plant and animal varieties can be understood as an expression of the stewardship or husbandry that characterizes a well-functioning agrarian economy. To fault industrial systems for paying too little heed to the human practices that safeguard fertility and genetic diversity, as Shiva does, can be understood as a claim focused not on the costs to future generations but on the need to preserve habits or virtues dedicated to land stewardship and animal husbandry. Concerns about the distorting effects of subsidies can be reconfigured as complaints about the way repetitive material practices (the purchase and consumption of food) have themselves become warped by a dysfunctional economic environment.

Indeed, warnings about the dire consequences to those who stray from agrarian habits of character are wholly consistent with the agrarian mentality. Hesiod's poem *Works and Days* is full of warnings for fools who neglect their farms and engage in "grabbing" or indolence. Yet Hesiod was not encouraging his audience to better calculate the true costs of these vices. The entire concept of a rationally calculating, economizing mind-set was wholly foreign to his outlook. Or perhaps we could say that rational calculation would amount to the same thing as "grabbing" for Hesiod. Those who operate outside the place laid for humanity are simply fools. The bad consequences that befall them are marks of their foolishness, events that confirm the flaws of their character. Impacts and outcomes are signs of an inner virtue for Hesiod, not factors to be counted in a rational calculation. The fact that even good farmers can have bad luck—though in their case, bad consequences do nothing to controvert their basic righteousness—proved to Hesiod that calculating costs and benefits has very little to do with morality. Only a grabbing fool would try to outmaneuver the gods! However strange this kind of thinking may sound to contemporary ears, it is worth noticing how Hesiod can predict bad outcomes from bad behavior without suggesting that these bad outcomes are the *reason* for thinking the behavior is bad.

The distinction between industrial and agrarian mind-sets is most usefully understood as a heuristic device that helps us orient ourselves to a more extended and careful inquiry into sustainability and its relationship to agriculture. In succeeding chapters, I revisit several episodes in the dialogue between industrial and agrarian philosophies of agriculture. I gradually expand the intellectual underpinnings of each approach by connecting them with some venerable themes in politics and sociability. My strategy is to allow this initial dichotomy to circle back on itself a number of times, hopefully with growing reach, subtlety, and comprehensiveness. In some iterations of this circle, the debate that seems to be working within the basic philosophical commitments of the industrial world is emphasized. This debate tends to see agriculture as having ethical significance in terms of either environmental or social impacts. Consistent with the dogma of environmental impact, participants in this debate emphasize the way human choices are linked to outcomes, and they tend to understand the ethical acceptability of those outcomes in terms of how they affect health, wealth, and well-being, on the one hand, or the way they affect the freedom or rights of other human beings, on the other. Participants who share a philosophical commitment to the dogma of environmental impact are far from being in agreement about the ethical acceptability of mainstream agriculture as it is practiced today.

I believe that attention to harmful impacts and to the rights of others must occupy a prominent place in our thinking about sustainability. But my larger ambition in this book is to create a philosophical space in which those components of sustainability that are so ably articulated and expressed by others can be augmented by a more ecologically grounded kind of philosophy that I associate with the agrarian tradition. I thus emphasize and at times seem to favor agrarian ideals, even while my own larger philosophy of agriculture holds that we should strive to achieve a conversation or a discourse about the future and about sustainability that accommodates the full range of philosophies and philosophical considerations. Hence, other cycles in my examination of the debate expand considerably on the range of virtues that agrarians might associate with agriculture or farming, and I emphasize how thinking about farming in this traditionally agrarian way has influenced political thinking for the better.

This means that for a few chapters, at least, I veer away from the topic of sustainability as such. First, the industrial and agrarian orientations introduced in this chapter are reexamined as themes in American environmental history.

CHAPTER 2

The Philosophy of Farming in America

Few would dispute that North American agriculture has been moving toward a bipolar organizational structure in the first decade of the twenty-first century. One pole is industrial agriculture, comprising the major agricultural chemical and equipment companies; the principal grain, processing, and packing companies; the major grocery and restaurant outlets; and the largest farm producers. The other pole is often designated alternative or sustainable agriculture, which is a loose network of organic and regional producers, chefs, nongovernmental organizations, and ordinary food consumers. Four or five decades ago, the complex of input companies, large-scale producers, and the food distribution system was regarded as the cutting edge; industrial agriculture was the wave of the future. Today, industrial agriculture is the norm, but sustainable agriculture seems to be gaining on the industrial alternative. Farmers' markets, food co-ops, and community-supported agriculture are expanding. Dozens of books and several new magazines expound on the virtues of the sustainable alternative. However, although sustainable agriculture is growing rapidly, at best it produces only 5 to 8 percent of the food purchased in the United States and Canada. Increasingly, the foundation for this bipolar structure is being characterized in terms of a philosophical dialectic. Industrial and sustainable agriculture are said to represent competing philosophies of agriculture.[1] This chapter traces the intellectual roots of this philosophical dialectic in the North American context and assesses its current state of development.

It is worth stressing that there is a difference between a philosophy of agriculture and an organizational type. In saying that the major agricultural chemical and equipment companies, processing companies, retail restaurant outlets, and large farmers who produce the largest share of the American food supply constitute industrial agriculture, one is stressing an organizational principle. One might also describe industrial agriculture in technological terms: chemical and mechanical equipment tailored to large-scale commodity production and processing. But the aim throughout this book is to articulate the philosophical principles that an industrial organizational structure or technology might represent. The same goes for alternative or sustainable agriculture, a view that I have articulated as a modern form of agrarianism. Many authors have approached the philosophical contest as one-sided partisans. Advocates of sustainable agriculture characterize the underlying philosophy of industrial agriculture in terms of greed and domination, while advocates of industrial agriculture describe the sustainable alternative as arising from nostalgia or xenophobic protectionism. The human tendency to define oneself in terms of what one is against is depressingly evident on both sides.

Both approaches have philosophical resources that can help us understand how agriculture contributes to or detracts from the larger goal of sustainability. Although agrarian views have gained ground in recent years, their philosophical underpinning is far from evident. My fear is that the healthy tension between these two philosophies of agriculture will be subsumed entirely by the industrial model. As noted in chapter 1, even critics of industrial agriculture often resort to industrial philosophical principles to mount their critique. My advocacy of agrarian ideals reflects a situation in which even the friends of sustainable farming practices seem unable to defend them with philosophical principles that articulate their deepest and most enduring significance.

Philosophy of Agriculture in America: A Brief History

As Alfred Crosby teaches us, current agricultural production systems in North America have a European origin, although a number of crops and specific agronomic practices were taken over from Native American peoples. For the first 200 years of European settlement, European-style farming in the lands that now make up the United States and Canada was largely confined to coastal waterways and was designed to support a local population engaged in extractive industries. By 1700, the continent had attracted a sufficient population of European émigrés who understood their society both as an extension of Europe and as a New World. These European residents began to conceptualize agriculture as a strategy for the "domestication" of the continent, which meant displacing native populations and establishing European-style social systems. Don Meinig's cultural geography of New England integrates philosophical themes with more prosaic concerns to trace this history. Expressed as a philosophical ideal, North American society was to be "a city on a hill," a realization of the model to which older European societies had only aspired. But the realization of this ideal emerged through economic and religious conflicts, not to mention conquests, that would hardly bear emulation.

The story of agriculture in North America is difficult to condense without slighting many important dimensions. Here I focus almost exclusively on the political history of the United States. Americans have been embroiled in heated battles for control of the food system for at least 100 years. In one sense, however, the battle can be traced back to the Revolutionary War itself. Hector St. John de Crèvecoeur (1735–1813) was one of the first Americans to write extensively on the philosophy of agriculture. Crèvecoeur was a European immigrant who farmed in New York State. His *Letters from an American Farmer* articulated the view that North America was destined to become a great agricultural society (and by this, he meant a society in the European mold) for two reasons. First, the geographic endowments of North America were neither so mean as to make farming unprofitable nor so generous as to encourage habits of greed or indolence. Second, the personal and economic liberties that characterized American society promoted hard work, innovation, and community solidarity.[2] In other words, the meddling aristocrats—to whom Crèvecoeur was loyal, we might add—were best kept at a comfortable distance.

Though never a revolutionary himself, Crèvecoeur articulated a philosophy that was widely held, and it was gradually turned to the cause of separation from England. The rift emerged in the politics of state formation after independence. Competing visions of economic development promoted by Thomas Jefferson and Alexander Hamilton (1755–1804) prefigured the twentieth-century debate over agriculture and rural society. Hamilton believed that the future of the new republic lay in trade and industrial development, whereas Jefferson favored the strategy of filling the heart of the North American continent with freehold farmers and delaying the creation of an indigenous industrial plant as long as possible. It was in the context of this debate that Jefferson described farmers as "the most valuable citizens" and "the chosen people of god, if ever he had a chosen people." To recount this battle as briefly as possible, Jefferson won. Hamilton was killed in a duel with Aaron Burr, and Jefferson became the third president of the United States.

As president, Jefferson pursued his agrarian vision with the Louisiana Purchase, which doubled the land available for agricultural expansion, and with the Lewis and Clark expedition, which was intended to open these new lands for agricultural settlement. The Louisiana Purchase added more than 500 million acres to the territory of the United States. It was a controversial move. Briefly, Jefferson, James Madison (1751–1836), and others in his party were more disposed to build foreign relations with the French, from whom the lands were obtained, whereas the Federalists were concerned about the likely impact on relations with England and Spain. The controversy also focused on the domestic political future of the nation, and it was here that the influence of agrarian philosophy can be seen. Federalists such as Hamilton were intent on establishing a wealthy and secure leadership elite, much like England's House of Lords, on the theory that wealth would isolate political leaders from the temptation to pursue pecuniary interests at the expense of the public good. In this connection, they urged the creation of an industrial center in New Jersey and recommended that future development of the nation be concentrated along the eastern seaboard.

Jefferson's preferences are clearly documented throughout his writings. He preferred greater democracy and a more diffuse distribution of power. Like the Federalists, he feared the potential of the mob, but Jefferson believed that the risks of mob rule could be significantly curtailed by avoiding the growth of industrial manufacturing and the wage labor associated with it. Jefferson believed that small farmers would be "the most virtuous citizens" not because he had a Romantic vision of noble savages but because he believed that small landholders who invest their time in improving lands for agricultural use are strongly motivated to ensure the stability and defense of their country. Conversely, both owners and workers in manufacturing industries had reason to think in the short term and could pull up stakes and leave, just as many Tory manufacturers had moved to Canada during the Revolution. At about the same time that Jefferson executed the Louisiana Purchase, German philosopher G. W. F. Hegel (1770–1831) was giving lectures at Jena, arguing that nations where agricultural production was organized along the lines of smallholder units were most conducive to the emergence of a collective national identity and virtues of patriotism.

Policy decisions, especially those executed on the scale of the 1803 treaty that produced the Louisiana Purchase, are seldom if ever based solely on a single philosophical rationale. Nevertheless, Jefferson's agrarian views are evident in the reasoning that supported westward expansion of the United States over the industrial development favored by Hamilton's Federalists. Although early-nineteenth-century geopolitics and contrasting views on postrevolutionary France were hardly absent from the debates, there were at least two clear agrarian arguments that favored Jefferson's decision. One was negative. The "mob rule" feared by Hamilton and linked with the French reign of terror was associated with urban industrial workers who not only were vulnerable to the vicissitudes of economic boom and bust but also constituted a ready source of street protests and violent uprisings when employment was short. Jefferson argued that it was better to keep the working classes employed on the farm, where their labors would at least ensure them something to eat and there would be less opportunity for spontaneous rioting. He made this argument initially in the 1781 *Notes on the State of Virginia* (not published until 1787), where he wrote: "It is better to carry provisions and materials to workmen [in Europe], than bring them to the provisions and materials, and with them their manners and principles. . . . The mobs of great cities add just so much to the support of pure government, as do sores do to the strength of the human body. It is the manners and spirit of a people which preserve a republic in vigour. A degeneracy in these is a canker which soon eats to the heart of its laws and customs."

The corresponding positive agrarian theme is sounded in an oft-quoted *Notes* passage—"Those who labour in the earth are the chosen people of god"—and in the almost as frequently quoted 1785 letter to John Jay (1745–1829): "Cultivators of the earth are the most valuable citizens. They are the most vigorous, the most independent, the most virtuous, & they are tied to their country & wedded to its liberty & interests by the most lasting bonds."[3] The subject of the Jay letter was sea power, and the immediate point was to prove that the American states needed a navy to ensure their ability to transport raw commodities to Europe and bring back finished goods. As the previous *Notes* passage shows, Jefferson regarded this prospect as more attractive than bringing the factories to America, and there is little reason to think his view had changed by the time he was supervising the Louisiana Purchase in 1803. But the positive rationale for adding more land (and more farmers) lay not (or at least not solely) in the fact that this would yield more commodities (more "provisions and materials") for trade with Europe. Jefferson believed that tying a person's economic interest to land also cultivated the virtues of patriotism and citizenship. Unlike manufacturers and traders, who during the American Revolution immigrated to Canadian provinces in droves,[4] the farmers' tie to the land ensured a political loyalty that made them "the most valuable citizens."

As a matter of public policy, such views clearly inclined Jefferson toward the Louisiana Purchase and away from developing America's manufacturing capability. As such, the argument that agrarian philosophy influenced this critical land-use decision is relatively straightforward. It is worth stressing the sense in which Jefferson's thinking was oriented toward virtue rather than efficiency or libertarian ideals of property rights. Jefferson was as sensitive to rights-oriented constraints as any man of his time. Yet the reasoning that supported the Louisiana Purchase over industrial development in New Jersey was somewhat more subtle. The purchase was justified not because Jefferson saw immediate use value for the new lands (although he certainly envisioned that they would be farmed) nor because he wanted to protect property rights. Indeed, valuation in either of these contemporary senses was not critical to either of the two agrarian arguments sketched above. Jefferson was thinking about how different ways of deriving one's subsistence—factory work versus farming—would produce habits of virtue (in the form of patriotism) and habits of thought that would incline citizens toward more stable and long-range priorities.[5] However, it is also true that the latter half of the nineteenth century was a time in which cities came to dominate the North American landscape. With the advent of the railroads, agriculture became thoroughly entangled in an industrial web designed to channel inexpensive food to workers in the growing industrial plant.

At this point, the story is picked up in William Cronon's magisterial ecological history of Chicago and the Midwest, *Nature's Metropolis*. If we fast-forward to the last quarter of the nineteenth century and the beginning of the twentieth, we find agricultural politics dominated by a group of interests reflecting the railroads and the major grain companies that worked in concert with capitalists in other industries to assure the availability of cheap food. The rationale was both commercial and philosophical. Railroads made money shipping grain from west to east while shipping manufactured goods from east to west. The factory owners wanted cheap food to supply low-wage employees.[6] Few but the largest farm producers considered themselves to be part of this interest group. The politics of agriculture became defined by the opposition between those who supported corporate interests and those who supported farmers, which in 1900 meant *family* farmers. Arguably, corporate interests were so powerful that they did not need a philosophical rationale, although we should not underestimate the extent to which they saw themselves as justified in broadly utilitarian terms. Industrial growth was providing jobs and consumable goods for a growing segment of the population on the North American continent. With slavery vanquished (regrettably, an episode I must slight in this accounting), America's economic growth made it plausible for egalitarian progressives to see the United States as being on the forefront of progress. Farmers, however, felt themselves to be the losers in this bargain, rationalized by the benefits flowing to the urban poor. On the farmers' side, Jefferson's earlier words extolling the virtues of farm families and the essential link between farming and democracy became the theme.[7]

Although the dichotomy between corporate and farm interests continues to be reflected in political rhetoric to this day, the underlying politics took a surprising turn in the years between 1920 and 1960. During this period, organizers and intellectuals on the Left began to promote the idea that agriculture should be viewed as just another sector of the industrial economy. Politically, this meant that agricultural labor would become organized, and the state would force the owners of land and capital to negotiate with the working class. The state would also regulate agriculture, just as it regulated the steel or auto industry, to ensure compliance with good environmental, public health, and social welfare practices. Such a view was implicit in Left-leaning political theory of the era, which saw industrial technology and the corresponding growth of jobs as progressive. What was wanted was not a return to some earlier technological base but the organization of labor power as a counterweight to the power of capital. The proposal that this kind of thinking could be applied to agriculture may have been made most forcefully by Carey McWilliams (1905–1980), whose book *Factories in the Fields* was published in 1939, the same year as the epic novel of American agriculture *The Grapes of Wrath*. Both books took the stance that they were simply describing facts

on the ground in advocating an industrial vision of agriculture, and that
the Jeffersonian celebration of family farms had become a myth shield-
ing big industrial growers from government regulation.

After World War II, the call to see agriculture as just another sector
in the industrial economy was repeated by A. Whitney Griswold, who
later became president of Yale University. Griswold's 1948 book *Farming and Democracy* presented the argument that the promotion of a
special relationship between land tenancy and democratic or personal
virtue was regressive and would entrench a pattern of low productivity
and poverty in rural areas. Although it is little read today, *Farming and
Democracy* set the tone for agricultural policy in the United States for
the next thirty-five years. By 1960, Griswold's thinking had become the
philosophical underpinning of what we now know as industrial agriculture. Like any other sector of an industrial economy, agriculture must
be organized according to principles of efficiency. Government would
establish ground rules ensuring that fair wages were paid and that health
and environmental costs were internalized; then market forces would
determine which production technologies and management strategies
succeeded under those rules. Although some were not prepared to give
up on the family farm, a generation of agricultural policy specialists presumed that Jefferson's praise of small, family-style farming was passé. In
their minds, good liberals would press forward with a new organization
of American agriculture along the lines of the industrial model.[8]

The Present Day

The philosophy of industrial agriculture was thus the product of the Left.
Its advocates included socialists as well as more moderate social democrats. Virtually no one in the United States or Canada argued for collec-
tivization and government ownership of farms. One reason is that prior
to World War II, the vast majority of American and Canadian owner-
operators had low incomes and were unquestionably part of the working
class. Instead, theorists of the Left first advocated producer cooperatives,
and these were seen as the moral equivalent of labor unions. Both co-ops
and unions would allow economically weak workers to resist the power
of well-capitalized landowners, grain companies, meat processors, and
food retailers. The main task for government policy was to limit the number of farm bankruptcies by enabling the organization of co-ops and also
through direct payments, especially when prices were low. By the 1960s,

a form of political anarchism began to hold sway in Left-leaning views of agriculture. This was not (or at least not generally) the bomb-wielding type of anarchy associated with an earlier time but a mode of thinking that grew out of the era's experimentalism. People would carve out lives largely independent of government's influence and support, first on communes but then, as communal living experiments floundered, through intentional communities in which organic farming and gardening would be prominent ways to promote solidarity.

As Julie Guthman writes in her book *Agrarian Dreams: The Paradox of Organic Farming in California,* the implementation of this experiment became embroiled in the realities of competition, marketing, and real estate. The hippie organic farmers of California may not have intended to get rich, but they had to at least cover their production costs. This put them into competition with large-scale growers and increasingly with one another. Organic standards emerged out of their need to clearly identify the characteristics of their products that attracted buyers; but although the absence of pesticides and other chemicals was certifiable (with difficulty)—a trait that could be tagged onto a carrot or broccoli—political purity was more problematic. Then, owing to the economic success of certified-organic food, the value of organic farmland rose rapidly, especially in the overheated real estate markets of California. Growers who started as Left-leaning anarchists increasingly became libertarians, wanting no interference in their business operations but needing state power to help them protect their property rights in land as well as in the organic standard. If organic production started out as the political Left's critique of corporate agriculture, it never successfully articulated a clear philosophical alternative to the industrial vision.

As argued in the next chapter, industrial agriculture blends libertarian views on property into a broadly utilitarian moral orientation: industrial society is justified in light of its impressive capacity to protect personal freedom and generate benefits for the majority. At the outset, Left-leaning thinkers conceptualized these benefits largely in terms of better wages and higher profits for small-scale, family-owned farms, but the allure of cheap food was also an important part of the utilitarian rationale for the industrialization of agriculture. The benefit of cheap and readily available food for the urban working class would counteract some of the harm done to smallholders who lost farms or workers who lost jobs in the process of mechanizing farm production. Government policy should aim to regulate industry to ensure that the social benefit-cost ratio is as favorable as possible. However, the profound lesson of the American Dust Bowl also made the advocates of industrial agriculture aware of the environmental costs associated with farming. The intellectual approach to environmental impact was also utilitarian: government policies should force producers to internalize the costs of soil erosion or water pollution, and market forces should then allow the appropriate balance between food prices and environmental costs to be struck.

Although this philosophy can be characterized as *essentially* utilitarian, it is fully capable of accommodating the demand to internalize costs to other human beings in terms of rights. If a particular configuration of regulations results in harm to people (through pollution or through the machinations of markets), adjusting those regulations is fully justified—indeed, required—on utilitarian grounds. Since the language of human rights provides an effective way to express the need for such changes, it is easy for those who understand political ideals in terms of human rights to be brought into the industrial tent. For their part, the advocates of human rights can see that the productivity of industrial society benefits people who have historically been among the worst off. Their specific arguments for industrial organization differ from those of the utilitarians, but because human rights are universal—the same for everyone—they have no use for ideals that attribute a special place to agriculture. As such, they, too, are happy to agree with utilitarians in thinking that agriculture is best thought of as just another sector of the industrial economy. Someone with a deep philosophical commitment to human rights would reject the utilitarian argument and substitute arguments that articulate how the governance of agriculture must respect human freedom. But the derivation and justification of these rights have nothing to do with agriculture as such, and the same rights that govern the energy or transportation sector of an industrial economy also govern agriculture.

In the 1960s and 1970s, there was a total inversion of the political-philosophical landscape for the philosophy of agriculture. For the most part, North American agribusiness firms learned that they could live quite happily with the industrial philosophy, despite its heavy reliance on government regulation. Farmers never accepted its commitment to organized labor, but labor has become increasingly less important to farm production as motorized mechanical equipment has taken over much of the work. The labor movement itself seemed to take little interest in the plight of noncitizens who worked the fields planted in vegetable crops, where mechanization had been unable to assert full command. By 1980, industrial agriculture was no longer a philosophy of the Left. It was the preferred view of those who were ideologically committed to neoliberal visions of limited government and free markets, including many people who thought of themselves as liberal Democrats. The interests benefiting from industrial agriculture may have included the urban poor; today, Americans and Canadians spend far less of their personal income on food than any people in human history. But under industrial agriculture, the returns from farm production go to capital rather than to land or labor. Thus, input companies selling fertilizers, pesticides, and mechanical equipment have thrived, while grain companies, meat processors, and food retailers have steadily increased their share of the price paid by food consumers. Although farmers' share of the food dollar has declined, farmers are no longer poor in North America. Most have moved solidly into the middle class, and many are among the wealthiest individuals in their communities.[9] By 1980, then, the idea that farming should be thought of as just another sector in the industrial economy was mainstream and not a prescription for radical reform.

There were certainly points to dispute within this mainstream view. Left libertarian former hippies growing organic specialty crops had little in common with Iowa corn growers. The moderate Left stressed the dark side of industrial agriculture in North America. For one thing, the environmental costs of using fertilizers, pesticides, and other industrial methods gradually became evident. Indeed, Rachel Carson's book *Silent Spring* launched the environmental movement in North America with her exposé of pesticides in 1962. Since that time, awareness of the health and environmental consequences of industrial methods has increased steadily. Organic foods became the alternative, and consumer groups committed to the reduction of chemical use have gained power steadily. However, this consumer-environmental movement has never clearly committed itself to philosophical principles that depart from the utilitarian, Left libertarian premises of the industrial model. Utilitarians, after all, have no difficulty accounting for the wrong associated with practices that cause ill health or that deplete resources needed by future generations. As such, a significant component of the consumer-environmental movement is content to call for the reform of existing agricultural practices within the general utilitarian paradigm of industrial agriculture. As market demand for organic products grows, North American agribusiness is increasingly willing to supply them. We are, in fact, seeing the emergence of organic industrial agriculture in North America: large, well-capitalized firms use organically permitted capital inputs to produce large quantities of organic crops, livestock, and dairy products, which are then marketed through the usual channels of the industrial food system.

Probing for an Alternative

What, then, is the alternative? From a North American perspective, the intellectual and political opportunities for an alternative seem to spring from the original Jeffersonian vision of the citizen-farmer, from the remnants of the small-farm populist movement that has resisted in-dustrialization all along, and from the cultural critique launched almost single-handedly by Wendell Berry in the late 1970s. In other words, a true alternative to the industrial vision must be found in agrarian ideals. Each of these three sources offers philosophical resources for articulat-ing an alternative philosophy of agriculture, and it is worth considering each in turn.

Jefferson was a synthesizing thinker who, along with other Ameri-can colonials such as Benjamin Franklin, John Adams (1735–1826), George Mason (1725–1792), and James Madison, blended a number of themes extant in eighteenth-century European thought to create a unique political philosophy. There is no definitive textual statement of this philosophy, although the agrarian elements of it are succinctly stated in some of the passages quoted earlier. Jefferson offers what we might call the *central agrarian tenet* (CAT): farmers make the best citizens. In sum, the idea was that an agriculturally based economy with dispersed landholdings would moderate some pernicious tendencies of democracy. The long-standing fear (well documented in European political thought) was that democracy would devolve into mob rule, or at least that people would vote themselves benefits but would not be willing to support the taxes necessary to pay for them. Landowners make the best citizens be-cause landed wealth is firmly tied to the interests of the territorial state. The American innovation, made possible in part by technology and in part by the resource endowments of North America, was that almost everyone employed in farming could be a landowner. This would per-mit a much broader participation in governance by small farmers, whose private economic interests were married to those of a stable and self-sustaining social polity.

But it is important to recognize that for Jefferson, there was no reason to see any tension or conflict between CAT and the aggressive pursuit of agricultural efficiency. That tension emerged much later, when the railroads began to exert considerable economic power over small farmers. It spawned the political movement known as populism. American populism shares a great deal with Marxism in decrying the economic logic of capital accumulation and corporate power. But unlike Marxism, it was a movement that arose among American farmers, and since farmers either were or wanted to be profit-seeking landowners, it could not embrace Marxism's critique of private property and the profit motive. Instead, it organized itself around the idea that "big is bad." With this move, small farmers aligned themselves with small-scale entrepreneurs against the emerging trusts and significantly put some conceptual distance between themselves and the more conventionally socialist ideas that (ironically) began to underpin the industrial philosophy of agriculture.[10] Yet, however useful the big-is-bad concept was as an organizing principle, it remained ambiguous. It was readily endorsed by both leftists, who felt comfortable with the growth of industrial technology, and small-scale farmers and local business entrepreneurs, who maintained a strong commitment to the legitimacy of private property. As shown in chapter 1, however, any political philosophy that accepts the legitimacy of technical efficiency in absolute terms will ultimately find a way to rationalize the technological treadmill—the phenomenon that drives small farms out of business and encourages farm consolidation. So as an *agrarian* principle, the idea that big is bad needs a more careful articulation.

One possibility is that big is bad because large bureaucracies have inherent limitations, even when their hearts—if large bureaucracies can have hearts—are in the right place. Large-scale organizations, be they businesses or governments, must organize their affairs from afar. They develop simplified ways of seeing the affairs they must manage, and as a result, they are unable to be adequately responsive to those features that make a given place or situation unique or atypical. Farming, however, is a craft replete with complexity, variation, and peculiarity. Soils can differ from one corner of a field to the next. Each year's weather is a little different. And on top of all that, the current year's farming may be affected in unique and unpredictable ways by specific things a farmer tried in the past. So farming is a task that is poorly done, at least in the minds of agrarians, when working from averages and statistical abstractions. What is more, large organizations are not as attentive to communal needs as are the people on the ground in a specific place. The agrarian communities of the North American heartland were populated by self-reliant farmsteads, but self-reliance should not be understood in the sense of total self-sufficiency. These farm families valued their independence, but independence should not be understood as lacking the need for ties to a broader community. They depended on one another for barn raising and mutual aid, and this help had to be delivered on a timely basis if it was to be of any use at all. Such considerations conspire to support what we might call the *principle of agrarian localism* (PAL). When familiar themes of community solidarity and the enduring value of face-to-face loyalties are added to the mix, one arrives at a principle of political organization that confronts the one-size-fits-all universalism of utilitarian or rights-based ways of understanding civil society in a direct fashion.

Along with CAT and PAL, the third tenet of the alternative view might be called the *great agrarian goal* (GAG). This tenet presumes that some form of self-realization is the driving force behind all forms of voluntary human action and that individuals realize their potential by most fully performing the unique roles that fall to them in the course of a lifetime. The idea that our roles befall us suggests that this ethic of self-realization is quite unlike contemporary ideals of self-gratification, the idea that "the one who dies with the most toys wins." It is not that we *choose* a life plan, as contemporary liberals would have it, and then try to realize that plan. Rather, we find ourselves embedded in situations rich in relationships and responsibilities that determine our possibilities for success and failure in unique ways. A good person is someone who recognizes and discharges the particular duties of his or her particular station in life, realizing him- or herself through the lifelong formation and expression of a virtuous moral character. Few if any of us succeed in every particular, and given the diverse and unique circumstances for moral self-realization presented to us, it would be surprising if we did. It is only within fairly narrow and already well-defined circumstances that we find ourselves needing to make a choice. Quite unlike the utilitarian or rights-theory picture in which a set of universal ethical rules can be spelled out and carefully followed in every case, the GAG is to be as good a person as one can, to live virtuously, and to strive constantly for a form of self-improvement that is open-ended and inexhaustible. Choice becomes morally important, not so much because our choices affect ourselves and others over the short run but because the choices we make today will make us more capable of virtuous action tomorrow.

The main contemporary advocate of the GAG is Wendell Berry, but Berry's argument has precedents in the philosophy of the American transcendentalists Henry David Thoreau (1817–1862) and Ralph Waldo Emerson (1803–1882). Emerson, of course, is the nineteenth century's great prophet of self-realization, writing "Whim" above his door to remind himself never to be caught up in acting conventionally simply for convention's sake. Thoreau famously headed into the woods in his quest for a simple life, but his point was that simplicity opens up a space for greater self-realization. Thoreau and Emerson were both committed to a philosophical program of interpreting spirituality and society in thoroughly naturalistic terms. They believed that instinct, intellect, and institutions such as religion and the family were evolutionary products that took shape during the human species' career as an animal living in constant commerce with nature. The transcendentalists held that the ways of life emerging through industrialization were not suited to the natural capacities and social forms that had evolved when human societies were primarily engaged in pursuits such as farming, hunting, and fishing. Cities and factories were among the chief ills of the industrial age for Thoreau and Emerson. The city dweller and the factory worker did not lead lives that tended naturally toward virtue, and they needed both recreational experiences with nature and models of the naturally virtuous life to aspire toward the fulfillment of human potential.

The farming family was chief among these models. Farming became central for Emerson as his philosophy evolved from an emphasis on language to an emphasis on human productivity. In his early thought, Emerson was deeply influenced by German idealism. He saw nature as standing in need of expression and rational realization through poetic acts. At first, the existential production of the poetic act takes precedence. For Hegel as well as Emerson, poetry realizes the potential for creativity in a form that is closest to spirituality itself. Rather than modeling or mimicking external nature, the poet's art is one of meaning unfolding and looping back on itself through the course of time. The poem must be actively thought, not merely read or recited, and it must be thought sequentially as its verses unfold. In reciting a poem silently to oneself, the transit of one's thoughts is itself the work of art, and in this the romantic idealists believed that the spirituality inherent in nature is most fully realized. But Emerson moved on in his thought and eventually came to see the farmer as more truly expressing the potencies of nature than even the poet. Like the breath with which a poem is recited, the activity of farming is a bodily performance that unfolds over time. But farming's more fundamental engagement with nature makes it more expressive of self and spirituality than mere words, and Emerson came to see farming as having greater exploratory and expressive power than language. Thoreau, too, hoped to engage with flowing time in his aesthetic ambitions, writing in *Walden* that he hoped to "improve the nick of time, and notch it on my stick, too."[11] Like Emerson, he came to see the flow of embodied experience itself as the realization idealists sought in art. He was more cautious than Emerson about farming's power to transform the landscape, however. He advocated a philosophy that Douglas Anderson calls *wild farming*. As an interpretation of the GAG, wild farming calls for attentiveness to wildness, but this is a wildness unlike the celebration of pristine wilderness found in the thought of someone like John Muir. Instead, Thoreau is celebrating a partially civilized wild evidenced in pastures and apple trees, a wild that teaches humanity about nature's pace but nonetheless has a place in human society.[12]

Wendell Berry's celebrated work in the 1970s and 1980s was an updating of the GAG, perhaps marking the first time it was clearly stated as a critique of industrial agriculture. In many respects, Berry was using the same argument made by the transcendentalists. The central agrarian goal is embodied in the way the independent family farm successfully integrates the classical virtues and provides the most reliable environment for the moral development of families and, in turn, of the individual person. The technology of the industrial farm, in contrast, prevents the farmer from hearing nature's feedback and allows the pursuit of excesses that take the form of vice. It has all the faults of employment outside the home, in that it does not instruct the family in the value, nobility, and constancy of work and instead encourages the development of a moral personality structured around consumption and pleasure. Berry's account of the GAG is complex, and his intellectual forebears include not only Jefferson, Emerson, and Thoreau but also Crèvecoeur and twentieth-century figures discussed in chapter 9. In comparison to these ancestors, Berry's writing is singularly poignant and persuasive for readers at the millennium; he is also the first in this line who lived at a time when the approach to farming on which the GAG is based was rapidly disappearing. By 1977, when *The Unsettling of America* originally appeared, industrial agriculture was dominant throughout most of the United States, although industrial farms were and continue to be mostly family owned and operated.

It was not until most of American agriculture was clearly industrial that the philosophy of agriculture built around CAT, PAL, and GAG could be thought of as *alternative* agriculture. Any time prior to World War II, it would have been thought of as the dominant approach to agriculture, and even through the 1950s, 1960s, and 1970s, advocates of industrialization may have thought of themselves as promoting the unpopular alternative. There is little doubt, however, that by 1980 industrial agriculture, founded on a utilitarian philosophy, was thoroughly institutionalized in U.S. and Canadian agricultural research, in the respective agricultural ministries, and in the mind-set of those farmers producing the vast majority of food and fiber commodities. By 1980, alternative or sustainable agriculture was clearly a minority view, promoted mostly by outsiders such as Jim Hightower, Wes Jackson, and Marty Strange.

Philosophical Reference Points for Alternative Agriculture

To the extent that CAT, PAL, and GAG provide a philosophical orientation for sustainable agriculture, it can be described as a form of Aristotelian naturalism. In contrast to utilitarian optimization, Aristotelian ideals of virtue derive prescriptions from a rich description of the relationships binding individual personalities, social institutions, and the natural environment. This view sees morality as a quest to be guided by a conception of how these relationships stand in an ecology that, properly ordered, permits the emergence of virtuous individuals, just communities, and beautiful places. To live rightly is to preserve and promote the integrity of this ecology. Error consists primarily in patterns of excess that throw these relationships out of balance, initiating feedback loops that perpetuate systematic repetitions of unwanted or harmful consequences. It is the feedback rather than the harmful outcome that is the target of moral reform. Because humanity, community, and nature are situated within a complex system of checks and balances, harm to one node of the system reverberates throughout the corresponding nodes. Thus, although CAT, PAL, and GAG might appear at first glance to be anthropocentric principles, the general Aristotelian framework vitiates the distinction between human-centered and ecocentered norms.

Alternative or sustainable agriculture gained its foothold not as a uniquely North American phenomenon but as an international movement focused on alternative farming techniques. Arguably, it emerged from an entirely different intellectual tradition, one that emphasized mysticism and promoted certain dietary regimens as promoting health, despite the lack of any scientific grounding for these approaches. Certainly such currents of thought were gaining prominence in the West at about the same time *Silent Spring* was stimulating a broad reconsideration of industrial farming methods on environmental grounds. As I have argued, those who advocate industrial agriculture have little intellectual difficulty incorporating negative human health impacts into their philosophical framework. As such, the main contested issues associated with the confrontation between industrial agriculture and the international alternative agriculture movement have had nothing to do with the philosophy of agriculture and everything to do with the scientific basis for alleging a risk to health.

The health- or risk-based critique of industrial farming methods has certainly been influential in the United States and Canada. It would be foolish to suggest that consumer demand for organic and health food is based on consumers' attraction to some form of Aristotelian naturalism. Consumers want food that is healthy and that tastes good. Some form of preference utilitarianism is perfectly capable of articulating the ethical prescriptions that can be derived from such consumer demands. The philosophical issues that emerge from this approach are of three kinds. First, there are ethical issues about the legitimacy of certain preferences and whether nonhuman animals or ecosystems have moral standing in the optimizing equation. Second, there are evidential issues about the basis for predicting outcomes and determining when one has enough scientific evidence to warrant the regulation of farming practices or marketing policies that satisfy nonrational consumer preferences. Finally, there are questions of moral economics that govern the weighing of costs and benefits in decision making. These are, of course, the standard issues that emerge from utilitarian moral theory, and their application to food and agriculture does not give them a unique character.

Within rural America, however, the principles of CAT, PAL, and GAG still have their believers. The dilemma of sustainable agriculture in North America is, in some respects, how to marry consumers' self-interested concern about healthy diets to a philosophical vision of agriculture in which this form of self-interest is symptomatic of a hopelessly corrupted social framework, one that has little chance of righting itself so long as people continue to order their lives according to norms of preference satisfaction. In fact, it is my pessimistic view that one of two futures awaits the sustainable agriculture movement in North America. One possibility is that the fixation on consumer health and tasty organic cuisine will win out philosophically, and we will see the emergence of a vibrant but industrially organized sector of agriculture producing the commodities demanded by health-conscious consumers. The other possibility is that the sustainable agriculture community will place its faith in technology (albeit alternative technology), and the philosophical questions will be ignored or minimized. That is, in many respects, the American way. Then, after endless workshops and alternative agriculture fairs, plus much hand-wringing and whining, we will see the emergence of a less vibrant and less profitable but still industrially organized sector of agriculture producing the commodities demanded by health-conscious consumers. In either case, the main part of North American agriculture—at least 80 percent of all food and fiber produced—will continue to use the most cost-efficient technologies, including chemical inputs and genetic engineering.

I think this is a bad thing, and I have two basic reasons for thinking so. First, although I do not think the kind of Aristotelian agrarianism I have described here is an adequate philosophy of agriculture, I am committed to a general philosophy of agriculture that would extend and be inclusive of this tradition. Second, for reasons that Aiden Davison has articulated well in his book on sustainability, I believe that the industrial model of agriculture embodies a form of cultural and political one-dimensionality that crushes human creativity and promotes an unsatisfying portrayal of human potential, social purpose, and the meaning of the natural world. Davison rejects all formulations of *sustainable development* in favor of what he takes to be the broader and more open-ended ideal of *sustainability*. Caught in the trap of development theory (as shown in chapter 9), sustainable development—perhaps like the industrial philosophy of agriculture itself—sees human making and doing narrowly, in terms of satisfying existing wants and needs. It provides no resources for examining the question of what we *should* want or what needs will actually turn out to be most satisfying.

Still, we should not write off the critical and conceptual resources available within an industrial philosophy of agriculture. Agrarian agricultures of the past may have instituted well-defined social roles that gave people a sense of their moral possibilities, but it is not clear that these are the roles we want to endorse today. Some of these roles involved rigid gender stereotypes, and the long-lived agricultures of ancient Egypt and the Greco-Roman world would have been impossible without some form of bonded labor (that is, slavery). The tradition of political ideals that has given us a rich notion of human rights provides crucial philosophical resources with which to combat these forms of human injustice. The utilitarian philosophy found its original expression in eighteenth-century England, primarily as a way to overcome the hidebound conservatism of landed elites that was preventing the reform of traditions and policies that endorsed the subjection of women and condemned many to a life of poverty and deprivation. We will need the vocabulary of rights and utility to formulate any adequate discourse on sustainability.

In short, agrarian ideals today are threatened equally by industrial farming practices and by a narrowed philosophical vocabulary. Even opponents of the industrial system of organizing society seem committed to the moral and political ideas that gave rise to the industrial world. This is not entirely a bad thing, because those ideas helped end slavery and moderate oppressive systems in humanity's past. But there are resources in agrarian ideals that can help us in our pursuit of sustainability. With this in mind, we set CAT, PAL, and GAG aside as we search for more inclusive and more adequate expressions of agrarian ideals. The first task is to see how competing philosophical principles inform competing visions of agriculture's future.

CHAPTER 3

Political Values and the Future of U.S. Agriculture

In 1988 I contributed to a policy briefing book for mainstream agriculture leaders in which I warned them against trying to "bar the door, barricade the windows and attempt to hold on to what power [mainstream agriculture] has to dictate the agricultural policy debate," although I also conceded that they could expect to achieve many of their immediate political ends if they did just that. In the intervening decades, farm groups have begun to appreciate that others will insist on having their say. The U.S. Department of Agriculture's creation of a certified-organic label, the rise of retailers (such as Whole Foods and Walmart) that have developed sustainability standards for their suppliers, and pressure from companies such as McDonald's that have promoted similar standards for animal welfare, have made mainstream agriculture keenly aware that times are changing. Meanwhile, some civil society groups such as the Humane Society of the United States have decided to go "around" the political process, which they see as still controlled by traditional large-farm interests. They have utilized lawsuits and ballot initiatives to mandate changes in agricultural production systems. And, of course, books such as *Fast Food Nation* (2001), *Food Politics* (2002), and *The Omnivore's Dilemma* (2006) have brought food and agriculture into the national consciousness.

Traditional agricultural interests played on the sympathies of Americans for decades, quoting Jefferson and voting subsidies for themselves. But the stark contrast between the rural idyll and the contemporary reality of American agriculture has finally begun to dawn on citizens plagued by recalls of meat, ecological dead zones due to selenium concentrations or nitrogen fertilizers, and threats of mad cows, bird flu, and cloned animals. The path being followed by mainstream agriculture is increasingly seen as one fraught with risk. At the same time, mainstream farmers have never done better economically. Policy decisions to draw down global stocks of grain pushed prices for all commodities to record levels in 2007. Some U.S. corn growers reaped windfall profits for crops diverted to ethanol production, although the long-term future of this application is still very much in doubt. Are we destined for "food wars," where sustainable and mainstream agriculture are opposing forces? And do developments such as organic food and best-selling food authors actually contribute to a more sustainable society in the sense that I have been urging? That is, does eating local, organic, or fair-trade food communicate a symbolic sense of agrarian ideals that can draw on our national heritage and unite us into a people? Arguably, there are not just competing interests and practices but competing visions of American agriculture.

Two Visions of American Agriculture

Industrial and agrarian philosophies can be projected into future scenarios of the American food system. In the first scenario, we see the completion of an industrial transformation of our food system, a process that has been under way for several centuries. But it is important to recognize at the outset that the industrial agriculture of the future will differ in important ways from the industrial agriculture that today's food activists campaign against. In this scenario, food and fiber producers still organize their time and resources in response to consumer demands, but these demands have become much more diverse. Whereas yesterday's food consumers responded only to price, convenience, and appearance, tomorrow's consumers also want attributes such as humanely raised, locally produced, and fairly traded. Industrial farmers are happy to supply such products, so long as they get paid for it. Nor does this vision of industrial agriculture necessarily mean huge, corporate-owned farms. Some producers in this scenario operate on a small scale, growing crops or raising animals to supply high-value niche markets or high-end specialty stores located in wealthy suburbs. In these locales trends change rapidly, and consumers are willing to pay for high quality and timely delivery of unusual products. But other producers are still growing large volumes of traditional commodities for consumers who still want low prices above all else. They are also growing new biomass commodities that may be processed by genetically engineered microbes into animal feeds, industrial products, and transportation fuels.

Both types of producer engage in businesses that were not typical of farming in America's past. For example, our small, specialized producers market their products through special subscription services and sell over the Internet. For the convenience of their customers, they may stock housewares or offer entertainment services, such as an opportunity to watch cheese being made over a Webcam. Our large commodity-oriented food producers might also operate supporting enterprises that use their farming skills. They may have small conversion facilities on their farms that allow biomass conversion to fuel, or they may be planting special cover crops that neutralize greenhouse gas emissions, collecting a check from a company that sells carbon offsets. Both types of producers are much more sensitive to environmental issues than were farmers of the past. The Internet sales of the small farmer are designed to have a low carbon footprint, for example, and the large farmer has come to realize that the payments she receives for environmental services have more than replaced the old-fashioned commodity subsidy payments her father got back in the bad old days.

In this vision of agriculture, communication is largely a process of reading market signals and responding to price changes. This is true both for consumers, who signal their displeasure by spending their money elsewhere, and for producers, who respond to projected demand by deciding whether to use their resources to plant tomatoes or stock up on gingham dresses to sell over a Web site. The rural landscape is not a prominent feature of this industrialized agriculture. Some commodity-oriented producers still have open fields, but others (especially animal producers) have production facilities that look more like a light manufacturing facility than a traditional farm. The farmstead may be an assemblage of metal buildings for raising poultry and livestock or for storing feeds and other supplies. A few of the high-value production facilities look like farms of the past, but much of this work is done in plastic-covered Quonset huts and carefully managed hydroponic greenhouses. Nor do many of these producers—large or small—feel the need to live on the premises. Workers and owners alike may live in houses or apartment blocks from which they commute to the farm by car or bus. Instructions to workers are sent by e-mail, and night guards keep the premises secure in their absence.

The second scenario for American agriculture is more consistent with the vision of Thomas Jefferson than that of Earl Butz (1909–2008), the former secretary of agriculture famed for telling producers to "get big or get out." But my version of this scenario is not really Jeffersonian in the sense that everyone is honest and fair and democratic opportunity is afforded to the poor and the uneducated by offering them land. In my scenario, we still have a rural landscape populated by farms that Jefferson would recognize as such. The people who farm this landscape still live in the country. They own or lease this land, and they expect to make their full livelihood off it. They may or may not have several employees, and they may utilize various forms of land tenure, but they expect to stay on this land all their lives, and they make their decisions accordingly. They think of their farms as home, and the geographic scale of their farming operation is keyed to that way of thinking. Above all, they continue to refer to the farm as a place—as in "the old home place"—and they are aware that life in a place requires one to be attentive to its particularities, its proclivities, and its demands.

Tomorrow's agrarians—if I may call them that—are not simple-minded rustics or latter-day hippies. They have accepted a variety of regulations that restrict pollution and that match the scale and character of their operations to both ecological and cultural expectations. They may, for example, accept that farmers in this region have always stacked hay in a particular manner and endeavor to continue that practice. If they are indeed self-reliant, they are not really wholly independent monarchs of their own domain. These farmers are more professionalized than yesterday's, and they might even be licensed and organized into professional associations. They participate in standard-setting processes that apply to many aspects of their operation and their products, including not only approaches to maintaining soils and producing healthy foods but also compliance with local traditions. Rules for developing an appellation for wine or cheese production are one example of such standards, but they can be applied equally well to landscapes. For instance, areas in Austria already specify the shape and density of haystacks in order to preserve the aesthetics of distinctive local places.

Many future farmers will have dropped out of organic certification programs because their customers trust them to do what is right. The costs of certification for such farmers can be ignored, for consumers know who they are and do not require a third party to verify that their farming has been done well. These farmers have some form of direct marketing, be it a local farmers' market or farm stand or some high-tech system that involves advanced electronics. Others expand their relationships with consumers in creative ways. Many embrace an educational mission to the broader public by supporting activities such as farm vacations for families and on-farm learning experiences for youth.

In this scenario, many farmers are linked to groups of food consumers through community-supported agriculture (CSA) organizations, where members pay a subscription fee and receive a share of the farm's produce. Members may also come out to the farm and contribute a day or two of work every season. The farms are sites for cooking and canning lessons and places where farm rituals such as hayrides and corn mazes are made available to the wider community. Kate Clancy has written about the wide array of models CSA can take, and there is quite a bit of variety in my vision as well. But I exclude from this vision the limited-subscription service whereby a box of food gets picked up at the shopping mall parking lot. A deeper and more enduring interpersonal connection between farm and table prevails here. Like Clancy's ideal CSA participants, mine do not insist on eating fresh fruits and vegetables out of season. Their participation in the food system (whether through a CSA organization or otherwise) teaches them both what to expect from farming and what is truly good food. These better-informed food consumers take farm vacations; they send their teenagers to summer camps conducted on farms and ranches where campers learn the principles of ecological food systems (while acquiring an acquaintance with hard work, as well as a good tan).

From Vision to Philosophy

Of course, the agriculture of the twenty-first century may be well on its way to resembling both these scenarios, though at different locales. The industrial scenario dominates in some regions, and the more community-oriented agrarian scenario is beginning to take hold in rural areas along the urban fringe. But there are limits. It is difficult for both to coexist in the same place at the same time, and they seem unlikely to thrive under a single set of agricultural policies. The industrial vision depends on an open market structure that signals producers what to supply. Rules for grades and standards are enforced strictly, but these may be unnecessary and even contrary to the closed contracting typical of a CSA. For its part, the community-oriented approach may involve local zoning that gives citizens some say about what happens in their particular region. Such zoning rules might stipulate that no genetically modified organisms can be grown or, once again, impose standards for those pesky haystacks. ⌐Although local rules allow producers and consumers in a region to pursue compacts for mutual benefit, they balkanize markets, making it very difficult for an industrial food system to operate.⌐

The fact that these two visions of agriculture may need different policies and may issue out of different mind-sets points us back to agrarian values and agrarian ideals. My two visions of agriculture reflect different philosophical understandings of what the agrifood system should do for us as a society. In that sense, these two competing scenarios are intended to illuminate the food wars. To develop a fair comparison of the underlying philosophies, I have tried to sketch scenarios that express optimistic but not unrealistic versions of each philosophy. Combatants in the food wars would probably not be inclined to such a charitable rendering of their opponents. But there are undoubtedly combatants out there who see some of the more attractive features included in my industrial scenario as part of the agrarian vision, and vice versa. My hope is that readers can find something appealing in both visions. As such, it becomes important to think about how philosophical values inform these visions.

Actually, both scenarios are based on certain core commitments reflected in agrarian thinking, and both also reflect larger philosophical orientations to the political process. The tenets of both industrial and agrarian philosophy have acquired somewhat distorted interpretations throughout the history of American debates on agriculture and land use, and these interpretations can affect the policy process in ways that their original advocates may not have intended or foreseen. Here it is useful to examine how some adaptations of traditional agrarian thinking have become wedded to the industrial vision, while others support a more community-oriented ethics and thus truly represent Jefferson's bequest. The two ideals I most associate with the industrial vision are private property rights and efficiency. Although it is difficult to select only two ideals that underlie the agrarian vision, for parity's sake I emphasize stewardship and self-reliance in the analysis that follows.

Most agrarian ideals have been generalized and detached from the agricultural context throughout the long debate over the proper structure and organization of society. That is certainly the case for property rights and efficiency, and slightly less so for stewardship and self-reliance.[1] American farmers have always endorsed a strong commitment to private property and to the promotion of efficiency. Indeed, some sort of stable claim to control the use of land is essential to agriculture. As philosopher Jean-Jacques Rousseau (1712–1778) illustrated in his book *Emile,* one cannot expect one's potatoes to grow if one cannot be assured that someone else (in his case, the gardener at Chenonceau, the château where he was living at the time) will not come along and dig them up. The Western tradition of private property has been thoroughly intertwined with shifting agricultural and land-use practices over time. It is in this sense that private property represents an agrarian ideal. Efficiency is less securely tied to agriculture, although as historian Samuel P. Hays argues, Americans who have promoted the conservation of American lands have traditionally campaigned against waste and idleness, creating a "gospel of efficiency" that rationalized the draining of swamps, the tilling of fields, and the widespread conversion of natural areas into agriculturally productive landscapes. Here I sketch brief treatments of the way these ideas inform a political theory.

The Case for Property Rights

When agricultural producers (who are often landowners) insist on the inviolability of private property, they are calling on a philosophical tradition with a long and distinguished pedigree. Property rights usually protect four dimensions of the owner's interest in land against interference from others, including the state itself. First, the landowner may permit or exclude others' use of the land. Second, income (or other benefits) derived from the land accrue to the owner or to a beneficiary designated by the owner. Third, the owner decides how the land will actually be used (out of many possible uses). Finally, the owner may dispose of the land through sale or gift under any terms acceptable to him or her (and to the contracting parties). Two philosophical traditions have been used to invoke moral support for a landowner's maintenance of this bundle of rights. One looks ahead to the ideal of *efficiency,* and the other stresses *noninterference.*

The principle of noninterference implies that neither another person nor the state itself may abrogate the rights conferred on owners in each of these four respects. The personal interest of property owners may rest on nothing more philosophically grandiose than a desire to do what they want. Being able to do what one wants (rather than what someone else wants) has a simple, straightforward, commonsense name: *freedom.*

As such, the complex philosophical tradition supporting property rights makes frequent appeals to principles of freedom or liberty. The contemporary political movement that places the greatest emphasis on freedom in the form of noninterference is called *libertarianism*. But freedoms can be of different kinds. When President Franklin D. Roosevelt (1882–1945) promulgated the idea of four basic freedoms, he included a notion of "freedom from want." But if I have a right to be "free from want," then making this freedom meaningful surely implies that someone, possibly the government, has a duty to secure my needs. Governments gain the means to secure one person's needs by taxing someone else. To libertarians, taxation is interference in property rights that can be justified only when the direct interest of the person being taxed is at stake. Some governmental activities such as maintaining a police force or providing for national defense can probably meet that test, but libertarians have been loath to recognize securing someone else's freedom from want as a legitimate governmental end. Programs that call for a taxpayer-financed expansion of government are clearly *not* what libertarians have in mind by *freedom*. Their notion is limited to those freedoms that can be understood as noninterference in an individual's ability to act.

Being free to do what one wants with one's own property does not extend to someone else's property. As such, it is useful to be a bit more specific about what is meant by freedom or liberty as it relates to property, and focusing on noninterference does this. When property owners assert the rights of exclusion, profit, disposal, and transfer as they relate to land, they are relying on a principle that blocks or overrides actions taken by others that might interfere with the exercise of those rights. Importantly, the principle of noninterference overrides the cost-benefit style of public decision making in all but the most extreme cases. Owners are not required to calculate which use of private land would be most beneficial to society as a whole, nor are they bound to make the wisest use of their land with respect to their own self-interest. Owners decide— arbitrarily, if they like. Period.

But contrary to this, Eric Freyfogle, a law professor and self-professed new agrarian, has argued that the finality implied by this picture of property rights provides a deeply mistaken portrait of property law. In the first instance, he points out that property law recognizes principles and situations that constrain an owner's rights. In cases in which a person's use of property violates the noninterference rights of another, for example, the state is obligated to intervene to prevent this harm. Such intervention is a function of police power. Police power merely ensures that the moral principle of noninterference extends to everyone. It is thus philosophically consistent with the strongest imaginable conception of the moral foundations of private property rights. However, as Freyfogle notes, courts have changed their minds over time about what constitutes an actionable harm to others, and with this change, the scope of private property has waxed and waned. Have you been harmed if your neighbor decides to build a skyscraper next door, obliterating your view of the scenic sunset? This is not a question that the principle of noninterference can decide all on its own. Rather, it depends broadly on our collective understanding of what we mean by *harm,* which in turn depends on prevailing attitudes about how land should be used. In a world of people who are focused primarily on using their land to make a buck (arguably, the agrarian past was such a world), scenic views may not count for much. But when most landowners are thinking of property in terms of a place to live and not a place to work, the understanding of harm may work out differently.

Eminent domain is another principle limiting private property rights. It limits the fourth dimension of an owner's rights by allowing the state to take property (with compensation) without the owner's prior consent. Such takings can occur only when significant public benefits are at stake. But Freyfogle notes that the courts' willingness to invoke eminent domain has also waxed and waned. Here, what seems to change over time is our collective sense of when a public benefit is truly significant. Historically, lands have been taken to build roads, and the rationale has focused on economic development. Freyfogle argues that our growing understanding of the ecological and environmental fragility of our public land base is providing an increasingly more persuasive rationale for invoking both police power and eminent domain to prevent destructive land use, whether that land use is dedicated to agriculture or not. With eminent domain, the moral principle of social efficiency—a calculation of total social benefit—is allowed to override the principle of noninterference. Not surprisingly, these are some of the most hotly contested actions that state and local governments undertake.

Is there any reason why the nonfarmers among us should be willing to extend the strong protection of noninterference in property rights to agricultural lands? When upward of 85 percent of the American population were farmers, it may have been plausible to see the preservation of all four dimensions of property rights in land as serving the common people. But now that less than 2 percent of us are directly involved in farming, one could just as easily regard this type of private property argument as a vestige of America's past. It is therefore worth noting the view that property rights actually protect even more fundamental liberties, such as the right to life, to personal security, and to freedom of conscience. All of us feel a sense of ownership and accomplishment in our work. If another person takes or destroys our work with no compelling reason, it is natural to feel harmed and wronged. Furthermore, this sense of harm attaches to one's very person. It is not just "stuff" that has been taken or damaged; one's very self has been harmed. Similarly, one depends on the security of one's possessions in conducting one's daily affairs. Uncompensated loss of one's possessions compromises the ability to pursue one's goals.

Yet surely Freyfogle is correct here. Although the philosophical case for a broad commitment to property rights remains strong, it does not necessarily support the notion of absolute noninterference that many landowners like to claim. Land uses that result in the emission of odors or pollutants violate the noninterference rights of neighbors. At most, the libertarian case for property rights establishes a burden of proof rather than an absolute protection: those who wish to curtail farmers' property rights must produce morally compelling reasons for doing so. When a particular use causes demonstrable environmental harm or poses a risk to others, that burden of proof can easily be met. Thus, although private property is an agrarian ideal that continues to influence our understanding of agriculture, property rights in agricultural lands are not absolute. They can and should be overturned when harm to others or significant public benefits provide compelling reasons to override the presumption of noninterference in the landowner's rights.

The Case for Efficiency

As we saw in chapter 1, economists such as Jeffrey Sachs often justify industrial agriculture in terms of its efficiency. Being efficient is, in popular parlance, the opposite of being wasteful. Efficiency is, in this sense, the personal virtue conveyed in slogans such as "Waste not, want not." Who would argue *for* waste? Other things being equal, it is always good to conserve resources rather than to waste them, and the key resource in the history of agriculture has probably been the farmer's time. But Sachs has something a little more complex in mind. The efficiency of a particular work process can also be expressed by the following equation:

$$\text{Efficiency} = {}^{\text{Benefit or gain}}\!/_{\text{Expenditure, loss, or cost}}$$

Mixing up notions of expenditure, loss, and cost in this way will annoy economists, who take pains to differentiate these ideas, but a loose representation of the ratio is sufficient for present purposes. The efficiency of a work process is the ratio of benefit to cost. The farmer's time spent working (or goofing off) is an expenditure or cost, as are obvious things such as seed, fuel, or fertilizer that actually cost money. The obvious benefits are the income the farmer gets after selling a crop, but there may be subtle benefits if the farmer makes improvements to the land that increase its value. Therefore, failing to make sure that one maximizes the amount of benefit in the top half of the ratio, given a certain expenditure, is just wasting one's time or money. But the technical expression of efficiency has come to stand for much more complex as well as questionable ideas in debates over public policy. Efficiency seems to demand that the farmer get the greatest total production from the resource base (including personal labor). Although this might be translated as simply "avoid waste," the calculation of efficiencies too often neglects long-term consequences and almost always leaves out costs that must be borne by neighbors, food consumers, and future generations.

Partially in response to such problems, agricultural economists have promoted a more comprehensive approach to efficiency. True efficiency should include costs, losses, or expenditures incurred over the long run, especially if they must be paid by parties other than the farm decision makers themselves. By the same token, if there are benefits that accrue to others off the farm, these should be included in the efficiency measure. Using a richer notion of efficiency can test our belief that industrialization is efficient. When food production industrializes, small farms are consolidated into larger operations, permitting the use of larger machines or increasing the productivity of labor or management. This is clearly efficient from the perspective of the industrial operator because there is greater production per unit of cost, but what about the costs borne by the farmers who lose their farms and must find alternative work? Clearly, they have experienced losses that the industrializing producers are unlikely to include in their own calculations. Although a comprehensive notion of efficiency would include these costs, it also must include additional benefits. For example, if the industrial farm produces food more cheaply, consumers benefit. Because there are more than fifty American consumers for every farmer, small benefits to consumers add up quickly, and the total benefit to consumers may more than offset the costs borne by farmers who leave their farms. Thus, an individual farmer understands efficiency as an admonition against waste, but social efficiency means that society (that is, all of us) gets the best benefit-cost ratio from farming, once the costs and benefits of all affected parties are considered.

Although individuals want to pursue their personal goals efficiently, efficiency as such does not tell us what those goals should be. We rely on our individual values to set those goals, and then we allocate our time and money to achieve them. But as we move to a notion of social efficiency, the argument is different. "Making the most efficient use of society's resources" can be interpreted as a comprehensive goal for society that reflects the assumption that the individual members of society are acting on their own in pursuit of individual goals. Utilitarian philosophers coined the expression "the greatest good for the greatest number" to reflect this social goal. Each of us chooses from the array of goals out there to pursue whatever rocks our personal boat. To the extent we get what we want, we gain a little, but sometimes we lose. In many cases, individuals' goals are incompatible with one another. My goal may involve entertaining people by playing my guitar, but since I am not a particularly talented player, others may not see it as entertaining. A utilitarian resolves this by saying that my frustration or personal loss is outweighed by the satisfaction of others who do not have to put up with my poor guitar playing.

The picture has gotten a bit more complex, because we now have to weigh one person's satisfaction against another's disappointment. At this point, mathematical approaches to maximizing satisfaction break down, and we find ourselves in the realm of pure philosophy. But several plausible arguments have been put forward. One is to assume that whenever people are making voluntary exchanges, both parties benefit. Voluntary trades are then assumed to move us closer to the most efficient allocation of society's total resource base. Another assumption is that when workplace efficiencies are going up, prices are generally coming down, which means that each of us gets a little more than we did before. This has made economists like Sachs sanguine in equating social efficiency with a general trend toward economic growth, so long as individuals remain free to expend their increasing incomes on whatever helps them achieve their personal goals. However, there are problems with this general picture.

Instead of actually measuring efficiency as a ratio of total social benefit to total social cost, the argument for efficiency has been reinterpreted as a general endorsement of the allocation of society's resources by means of voluntary trades among individuals—that is, transacting in unregulated markets. But of course, the trades one is willing to make depend heavily on whether one is rich or poor, well-informed or not, or powerful or vulnerable in other respects. This leads to a second and more philosophically damning problem. Good economists have long recognized that social efficiency depends on the initial distribution of resources and the specific system of property rights that fixes the rules for trade. That is, if we achieve social efficiency by eliminating waste in the way our society utilizes resources, it seems reasonable to define *efficiency* as "putting resources to their most valued use." So if someone, call her Ariel, is willing to pay more to use a given resource than someone else, call him Akbar, who currently controls the resource, we increase social efficiency when Ariel and Akbar make a trade. Restricting such trades is inefficient, and this kind of thinking quickly ratchets up into a general defense of free markets.

I develop the critique of this view at some length in *The Spirit of the Soil*, but a summary may suffice here. For the first point, notice that Ariel's willingness to pay for Akbar's resource depends on how much money she has to begin with. If she is wealthy, she may be able to offer considerably more for the resource than if she is poor; if she is wealthy, her offer may represent a relatively trivial desire for the resource, whereas if she is poor, she may be unable to satisfy even very important needs. So basing our concept of social efficiency on what people are actually willing to pay for the use of a resource represents a persuasive interpretation of efficiency as a moral ideal only if we are already convinced that the relative distribution of wealth is itself morally just. Few would argue that it is, and I am not among those few. The second point holds even if the distribution of wealth is not a problem. The trades that Ariel and Akbar are able to make depend greatly on the rules for holding, controlling, and exchanging the resources in question. Although the free-market philosophy sounds a bit like "no rules," it actually presumes that police and the courts can be called on to enforce a fairly extensive set of property rights.

For example, Ariel cannot simply wait until Akbar is not looking and then use the resource however she pleases. That is not considered a trade, and the police or courts can be called in to get Akbar some compensation. Or perhaps she *can* simply take it: if the resource is a bicycle and Akbar lives in my neighborhood, leaving such tantalizing property unattended is generally regarded as a sign that you don't want it anymore. Calling the police does no good at all. As we have already learned from Freyfogle's remarks on property, the rules for controlling and using resources such as water, fresh air, and sunshine are constantly evolving, and under some configurations of these rules, simply taking the resource *is* considered fair game. The point here is that once the rules are set in a particular way, we can make sense of social efficiency in terms of allocating resources to their most valuable use because we gain a measure of relative value from the trades or exchanges people make. But if the rules are different, people make different trades. In my neighborhood, leaving a bicycle unlocked indicates that the owner does not value his or her control over its use, but in a neighborhood with better police protection, an unlocked bicycle might remain secure for weeks. These behaviors that are putative indicators of the most valued use are wholly contingent on the rules for appropriating and exchanging the resources in question. This means that our behavioral approach to efficiency is comparatively useless for telling us what those rules ought to be: we can't appeal to greater efficiency (in this sense, at least) as a rationale for changing property rights. As such, social efficiency is hardly what it was initially pretending to be—a comprehensive moral principle for social policy. As noted, good economists know this. Not all economists are good, however, and laziness in our use of the word *efficiency* has allowed some rather mindless notions to influence our thinking on social policy far too much.

Property, Efficiency, and the Industrial Vision of Agriculture

The values of property and efficiency are deeply ingrained in the American psyche, and they have a place. Arguments that appeal to property or to efficiency make important moral claims that should never be taken lightly. Nevertheless, we have seen that both these notions have taken on somewhat distorted forms that overreach the commonsense rationale they might have enjoyed in years past. In particular, it is important to see how recent claims about property and efficiency are intertwined with one another. Sophisticated measures of social efficiency always presume a given set of property rules. Change the rules, and you change the allocation and disposal of resources that turn out to be efficient. Neither set of rules nor the results they cause are more or less efficient than the other; they are just noncomparable. At the same time, a defense of property rights that calls attention to our need to control our possessions or be compensated for our work attains much of its persuasive power from the fact that our current system of exchange has made us dependent on particular types of possessions and particular forms of work. Change that system, and that dependency might change, too. It is difficult to generate an argument for radical alternatives within a philosophical framework that relies heavily on ideals of private property or social efficiency. In fact, as we have seen, property rights and efficiencies are interdependently defined and interpreted. Once we have a clear set of property rules, we can interpret efficiency in terms of exchange behavior that is consistent with those rules. Once we have a functioning economy, we can interpret freedom in terms of our ability to choose.

Nevertheless, property and efficiency remain important ideas for constructing an argument that articulates what is truly good about industrialized agriculture and why it might be preferable to a more community-oriented vision. The agriculture we have in the United States today evolved in a political environment that placed great emphasis on property rights and efficient production. As defenders of mainstream, large-scale farming are quick to point out, the result is that Americans spend far less of their disposable income on food than virtually any other people in history. For their part, opponents of large-scale commercial farming can note the recent evolution in food consumers' tastes. An industrially organized agriculture is very responsive to consumer needs, as long as consumers have money to spend. Consumers who want standardized commodity goods can get them, but consumers who demand higher-quality goods can get them, too. When people show that they are willing to pay for fairly traded coffee or humanely produced eggs, the industrial system will adapt to that taste. *

The philosophical principles underlying the industrial vision are not wholly without resources for policy-guided social change. Producers in the industrial vision are free to use property however they see fit, but this is subject to two constraints. First, as already noted, if they want to survive in the business climate of the twenty-first century, they will have to use their land and resources to produce goods that twenty-first-century consumers want to buy. This is nothing new. Second, they will have to observe the principle of noninterference in the rights of others—a principle that supplies a fair amount of moral muscle to the industrial vision. On this point, things have changed, just as Freyfogle notes. People live closer together. Production technologies such as pesticides and fertilizers are now known to have harmful off-farm effects. Today's farm producers may have been slow to acknowledge these changes, but their own commitment to the principle of noninterference may eventually force them to recognize the legitimacy of rules that protect the environment. An industrializing agriculture may have caused these harms to the environment, but an industrially organized agriculture will be capable of responding to these regulations, producing things people want to buy, and eventually passing the costs on to consumers themselves.

One can also use broad arguments from efficiency to support this kind of change in an industrial system. The calculation of efficiency should include all costs and benefits, so if an agricultural system is imposing costs on future generations or on the environment at large, there is a philosophical case for reforming the rules so that producers have to include those costs in their decision making. Costs (and benefits) that have not been reflected in decision making are called *externalities*. The push for a more inclusive and complete characterization of efficiency thus provides a rationale for adjusting the market structure so that property owners are not free to impose costs on others. Here the libertarian notion of noninterference conspires nicely with the utilitarian conception of social efficiency to provide a one-two philosophical punch for political reforms that are much more cognizant of externalities that harm human health and the environment. This does not mean that it is easy to measure these harms, and there is still the practical problem of reaching a social consensus on when harm has occurred.[2] Nevertheless, these practical problems can all be addressed within the framework of philosophical principles that have guided the industrial conceptualization of agriculture for at least fifty years.

The environmental responsiveness of industrial agriculture is particularly important to the idea of sustainability, for some combatants in the food wars may be inclined to think that the agrarian vision is preferable on environmental grounds. The word *industry* connotes smokestacks, toxic waste dumps, noxious fumes, and general environmental degradation, but these effects were associated with manufacturing and chemical industries that arose when environmental impact was unregulated. Whereas manufacturing was associated with pollution, small-scale farms were considered to have either negligible or invisible effects on the environment. Yet a watershed populated by 1,000 farms with 100 animals each results in the same amount of manure deposited into the environment as one populated by 10 farms with 10,000 animals each. What is more, small farms may lack the economies of scale to employ the most effective means of containing, processing, and recycling the waste. Arguably, the big guys can better afford the technology needed to minimize environmental impact in the future, although this also depends on how the animals are actually situated on the land. In either case, the principles of industrial agriculture insist that all producers, big or small, internalize the external costs their methods impose on the environment. These principles cut no slack for the little guys simply because we like their old-fashioned barns. There is thus much to be said for the industrial vision of agriculture. An advocate of sustainability does a disservice to environmentalism if the case for an industrial agriculture is taken too lightly. So what *can* be said for the agrarian vision?

The Challenge for Agrarian Virtue

President Theodore Roosevelt echoed Jefferson's praise for farming when he wrote, "If there is one lesson taught by history it is that the permanent greatness of any State must ultimately depend more upon the character of its country population than upon anything else. No growth of cities, no growth of wealth can make up for a loss in either the number or character of the farming population." Roosevelt the warrior might have been calling attention to the fact that military and economic greatness depends on a nation's capacity to produce enough food to support manufacturing and armies, but his emphasis on the word *character* suggests otherwise. For both Jefferson (200 years ago) and Roosevelt (100 years ago), the notion that farming—at least the right kind of farming—produces character was commonplace. Country people were thought to possess virtues essential to the conduct of statecraft and democracy. These virtues were not produced by formal education or by reading philosophical books, nor even by religious devotion, which urbanites shared with rural folk. Farming itself was thought to form the character of rural people.

But this was not just any kind of farming. It was the kind of farming being done throughout New England and across the American Midwest in the latter half of the nineteenth and early part of the twentieth centuries. It was a kind of farming that had come somewhat later to the American South, with the breakup of large plantations that resembled the latifundia of southern Europe and Latin America. It was a type of farming that was being somewhat spottily replicated in California and the American West, where smaller ranches and farms were interlaced among extremely large haciendas, large fruit orchards, and other farms that employed many hired laborers. Roosevelt and others like him believed that the family-owned and -operated farms common at the turn of the twentieth century reinforced the acquisition of a virtuous moral character. This was one reason for public policies that favored this particular social form and protected small farmers from predatory practices on the part of land speculators, lending agencies, and large grain companies. Although resentment toward financial interests and corporations is familiar enough in the present day, the idea that support for a particular way of structuring production could be justified because it produced virtue is almost wholly foreign to the political discourse of the twenty-first century.

In the aftermath of the civil rights movement of the 1960s and subsequent social movements stressing women's rights and gay liberation, American liberals developed a moral vocabulary built around claims of rights and justice, on the one hand, and domination and resistance, on the other. This vocabulary is often at odds with arguments stressing property rights and efficiency, but most of the moral ideas pervasive in the political life of the early twenty-first century continue to promote an ideal of individual autonomy. Like noninterference, autonomy is an expression of freedom, but autonomy means that an individual can formulate and pursue a personally chosen life plan, that the individual is not forced to accept life goals or values imposed by others. In contrast to noninterference, the principle of autonomy produces morally compelling arguments for a fairer redistribution of property and economic opportunity with respect to minorities and victims of past discrimination. The principle of autonomy can also be somewhat reconciled with notions of social efficiency. Indeed, the utilitarian support for free markets and voluntary exchanges relies on the belief that each individual is the best judge of what is good or bad. This belief echoes much of the sentiment behind the principle of autonomy.

Arguments that stress the formation of character have seemed out of step with the liberal causes that brought a vocabulary of rights, justice, and autonomy to the forefront. Arguments based on a conception of the virtuous person often select a particular exemplar and then proceed by asking, "What would that person do?" Since exemplars have often been white males, this mode of argument has had little appeal to feminists or advocates of civil rights. Arguments based on the moral character of a particular exemplar can be made to suggest that each person has a "natural" place or role in society. But the natural places and roles of repressed people are contrary to the aspirations of women, racial or ethnic groups, and gays who are seeking new places and new roles. People such as former secretary of education William Bennett have argued for the importance of virtue and have celebrated folktales that reinforce uncontroversial virtues such as truth-telling or keeping promises, but they have also been associated with political groups that defend a status quo that has pushed too many people to the margins of modern societies. Although the advocates of virtue have celebrated the family, church, and ethnic communities that provide a milieu for character-building life experiences, they also seem bent on rolling back progressive social reforms that liberals have accomplished since World War II. For their part, social conservatives have been reluctant to scrutinize the arguments that link these institutions to the formation of moral character, preferring to rely on vague threats of moral decay.

All this means that the current cultural climate is somewhat hostile to the conception of agrarian virtue that underlies the agrarian vision of twenty-first-century agriculture. Today it is hard to defend a vision of farming that relies primarily on its salutary effects on moral character. Such claims are met with justifiable suspicion from every side. "Emotion!" says the scientist. "Reaction!" says the liberal. "Nostalgia!" says the free marketeer. Even the social conservative is unlikely to welcome an argument that ties virtue to farming. Yet I will argue that what is most compelling about the agrarian vision of American agriculture is that we can see how it might promote the acquisition of sound moral character for everyone, not just farmers.

The tradition of philosophy that dates back to Aristotle holds that a concept of human virtue is the touchstone for moral and political philosophy. One needs a just society because justice is instrumental to virtue, not the other way around. Aristotle famously thought of the virtues as a mean or balance point situated between two extreme character traits where a person falls into vice. Courage is a virtue, but too much courage becomes the vice of foolhardiness, and too little becomes cowardice. The virtues are not absolute standards or rules that stipulate specific conduct but conceptions of moral aspiration that regulate one another in a kind of moral ecology. Society is thus the ecosystem of virtue. In a just society, the expectations and approval of one's neighbors and peers are applied to many aspects of one's conduct. These multiple ways in which one might win praise or approbation condition one toward the virtuous mean.

Aristotle was no agrarian in the American sense. He thought that those who labored with their hands would be forever deprived of the opportunity for learning and contemplation that was necessary to acquire human excellence. By Roosevelt's time, this aristocratic ideal had faded. Born to a wealthy family himself, Roosevelt felt the need to go out to the American West and work in cattle ranching to acquire the character traits that would make him suitable for leadership. By his time, the ordinary farmer or rancher was thought to live in a society that was more conducive to virtue than Aristotle's own. Farmers needed to work with their hands to produce commodities so that they could live; they could not be lazy. But in the world of the farm, the virtue of industriousness did not spill over into the vice of greed. Rather, it was checked by the virtue of stewardship, for greedy farmers depleted the soil, undoing themselves in the process. Farmers also needed to be self-reliant. Dependency was a vice that could be ill afforded on the farm, but the virtue of self-reliance did not spill over into selfishness because farmers depended on good neighbors to help with occasional chores such as barn raising or when illness struck. Farm communities thereby became microclimates of virtue, where virtues such as hard work, stewardship, and self-reliance were prevented from becoming obsessions.

Any reasonable account of virtue demands that we ask how the material conditions of life reinforce the moral balancing act I have just described, and that is a very long story indeed. But two points are important here. First, people living under social and material conditions conducive to virtue should tend to be virtuous. This does not mean that they are all virtuous or that they are virtuous all the time. Even more significant, it does not mean that they can articulate a coherent statement of key virtues. Virtues are often embedded in habits and daily practice, rather than being something people talk about. But if this type of moral philosophy has any force at all, we must be able to discern some conception of virtuous moral character in their habits and behavior, and they must possess some means of determining whether conduct in a given situation is consistent with the habits characteristic of virtue in their social milieu. Second, even those who do not actually live under the material and social conditions conducive to the acquisition of virtuous habits can come to an understanding of virtue when such a society is taken to be a model. This is why agrarianism lives on in the poetry and literature of the agrarian idyll. One might argue that we still use nineteenth-century farm communities as models. They appear repeatedly in the stories we read to our children. This means that it is at least possible for a virtuous community to produce virtue in a vicarious manner. Its moral importance becomes symbolic and extends far beyond its actual existence in space and time. The emphasis is less on agrarian practice than on agrarian ideals.

Stewardship, Self-Reliance, and the Agrarian Vision

The best argument for the agrarian vision described at the beginning of this chapter is that it serves as an ecology of virtues, a generator of values that structures, ennobles, and gives purpose to life, not only for farmers but also for the vast majority of participants in the food system. It makes humanity's dependence on nature and natural systems more obvious, not only for those who grow the crops or tend the livestock but also for community members who get a chance to see this activity and interact with it in recreational and educational settings. In these respects, it promotes the virtue of stewardship for nature throughout society. Stewardship means using nature for human flourishing rather than preserving it in a museum, but it also implies a fine appreciation of the constraints implicit in the ecosystems where human life exists. This is not the kind of human-centered or instrumental valuation of nature decried by many environmental philosophers and activists. Far from seeing nature as something to be deployed or mastered, the agrarian steward looks to nature for a sense of place, an understanding of the underlying structure that informs personal values and gives meaning to human life. The virtue of stewardship thus stands in some contrast to the liberal idea that we should, as autonomous individuals, be able to choose our life goals.

Agrarian stewards allow nature to have a strong voice in choosing our goals for us.

This vision of agriculture helps people discover and develop the virtue of self-reliance as well. This is obvious enough for farmers. Self-reliance is perhaps the preeminent small-farm virtue. But others are able to see how life is made from the earth. Farm experiences show that we must work to make the food that makes our bodies, and they show that agriculture involves production, not just consumption. The virtue of self-reliance is a habit of personal initiative but also a habit of relying on one's experience rather than on conventions. Acts such as eating and cooking in response to seasonal variations can encourage both traits. In a community-oriented vision of agriculture, the potential for unrestricted growth of wants and egomania is also held in check by placing the habit of self-reliance firmly in a social and ecological context. Thus stewardship places a check on self-reliance, and self-reliance prevents stewardship from becoming too convention bound, too closely tied to a traditional practice that may cause one to miss subtle changes in the social or natural climate. Clearly, these virtuous habits are not universally inculcated in everyone who participates in my agrarian vision of agriculture, but perhaps the vision itself can spark the creation of virtues in the hearts of many who do not farm at all.

The agrarian vision also promotes social solidarity, because even self-reliant stewards experience setbacks and tragedies. In a liberal society, financial and personal setbacks might leave an individual bereft. This is often the proximate cause for relocation. But in the agrarian vision, producers are committed to making their living from their land. The fact that land cannot be relocated leads farmers to recognize the mutual self-interest in solidarity. Ironically, it is also the agrarian and not the industrial vision that promotes the virtue of industry—simple hard work. On the traditional farm, the link between work and reward is visible even to young children. The consequences of lassitude are learned early, with chores tailored to a child's ability. Yet unlike the urban household in which income is everything, the farm is a place where the performance of chores actually makes an immediate and visible contribution to family well-being.

It is also useful to contrast how property and efficiency are realized in the agrarian vision. In the industrial vision, we think of property in terms of noninterference and of efficiency as a ratio of benefits and costs, a measure of social welfare. There is little place in this vision for notions of virtue. Yet in the agrarian vision there is still a place for property and efficiency, though both become related to moral character. Property plays a role in self-reliance, for without a secure place to plant one's potatoes, self-reliant initiative is moot. But the self-reliant steward accepts constraints on what may be done with property: land must be treated with respect and with consideration for posterity. Efficiency is, of course, a minor virtue on its own in the agrarian vision, because too little efficiency is the vice of profligacy or waste. Yet in the agrarian vision, a single-minded focus on efficiency makes one penurious and shortsighted. Avoiding waste may be at the heart of good husbandry, but the virtue of efficient farming is still held in check by other considerations.

The fact that property and efficiency have a place in the agrarian vision but not the reverse is itself significant. The industrial vision shows a tendency toward a kind of moral reductionism whereby only a few moral principles become decisive and the full range of moral considerations that have informed human societies since antiquity is ruled out of bounds. The moral pluralism of the agrarian world means that it is often difficult, if not impossible, to legislate morality abstractly or in advance of encountering the specific context in which a problem needs to be solved. But this does not mean that there are no moral standards at all. The overall stability and interactivity of agrarian virtues provide a basis for moral decision making when habits fail us or come into conflict. Thus, we might regard the fact that the agrarian vision allows many sources of moral wisdom to remain in play as a kind of virtue in itself. Rather than becoming reductive and exclusionary, the agrarian vision remains open to a broad range of ethical considerations, traditions, and forms of thought.

Yet the agrarian vision I have sketched for the twenty-first century is not that of nineteenth-century America, much less that of Jefferson's Monticello. The patriarchal system that dominated the nineteenth century has waned, and my agrarian vision must make room for the social progress achieved in recent decades. One additional difference is that the twenty-first-century vision does not imagine 80 percent of our population living on the land, at least not full time. People may spend some time on the land, but it will be more like Roosevelt's foray into cattle ranching: a brief education in virtue. Farmers may even derive some of their income from providing this service. But this means that rural communities must be open to everyone, to people from diverse backgrounds and walks of life. Another important difference is that farmers will not rely strictly on property rights and God's provenance to maintain the social and material conditions that are crucial to the ecology of virtue. Social policies and community covenants (those Austrian haystacks, yet again) will help ensure that the interdependence between town and country and among neighbors can thrive. Similarly, they may ensure that technology does not undercut social institutions.

Making such social institutions into a carefully thought-out component of rural life is a change from America's past. But perhaps it is a less dramatic change than those of us who imagine that past from the distance of a century or more might imagine. Creating community has always been work, and it is work that was often done by women in America's past. It is yet another signal of our debility when imagining an ecology of virtue that this work would be undervalued and erased in the current climate of ideas. The new vision will not attempt to keep women in "their place," but neither will it obscure the contributions to community solidarity and the gender-oriented virtues that have characterized past ways of life. The work of community building cannot be omitted from the tasks we all undertake in a sustainable twenty-first-century society. Tomorrow's agrarian agriculture will be different from that of our past, and it will be better for its commitment to a conceptualization of virtue that is liberated from the patterns of discrimination and domination implicit in the agrarian lifestyles of Roosevelt's era, as well as Jefferson's.

From Visions to Sustainability

I have offered two scenarios for tomorrow's agriculture and sketched some moral and political arguments in support of each. Both visions appeal to important moral ideas, but although there is little immediate danger that property and efficiency will disappear from America's moral vocabulary, the discourse of virtue is not so secure. There is little danger that the agrarian vision of agriculture will overrun the industrial one, but the risk that the reverse will happen is great. We have seen how easy it is for consumer interest in healthy, organic, humane, or even fairly traded foods to be incorporated into the industrial vision. We cannot assume that the rise of interest in eating ethically will necessarily point us

toward an agrarian agriculture. So it becomes incumbent on us to consider more carefully whether the connections between agrarian ideals
and sustainability actually provide reasons to encourage the emergence
of an agrarian food system.

Making the case that an agrarian system is the more sustainable one
involves some big tests. Not the least of them is whether it will produce
enough food. Yet the question of how much is enough depends partially
on having a vision in mind at the outset. Will the Chinese, the Russians,
and consumers in Africa and the Middle East need large quantities of
American commodities? Or will they, like the Europeans, the Southeast
Asians, and the Latin Americans, join the ranks of exporters? Will people continue to feed large quantities of grain to animals in order to maintain diets rich in animal protein, or will health and ecological concerns
change the way we eat? Most critically, will the answers to these questions be determined solely by market forces operating within the current
global division of property rights, or will we think deliberately about
our needs and consumption patterns, evaluating them in light of how
our agriculture affects our quality of life? It may well be that allowing the
industrial vision to prevail in only a small part of the United States could
meet all these bulk food needs.

The question of which vision, or what combination of visions, is most
compatible with sustainability remains. A complete evaluation requires
the more careful examination of sustainability presented in subsequent
chapters. For now, we should note that achieving a sustainable food system will require us to develop arguments and reasons for preferring one
vision over the other. We should not simply assume that family farms
promote environmental quality or that family-values arguments are the
stalking horse for people who fear social change. What is more, the arguments for property rights and efficiency have validity, and they have
shaped our social and political transformations for at least 200 years. I
have only begun to stake out those arguments by suggesting how claims
about noninterference and social welfare might be reshaped by reconsid-
ering an ancient way of thinking about work, about nature, and about
the communities in which we live.

CHAPTER 4

The Moral Significance of Land

A *Lesson from* The Grapes of Wrath

We have seen how the industrial philosophy of agriculture emerged as a philosophy of the Left, only to become reconciled to the middle of the road. This chapter uses the novel *The Grapes of Wrath* and the political events of the Great Depression to explore the links between political philosophies of the Right and Left, on the one hand, and the moral significance of land, on the other. The way John Steinbeck (1902–1968) used character studies and dialect, as well as the aesthetic effect of his celebrated intercalary chapters, accounts for much of the critical debate over *The Grapes of Wrath,* but it is the events of the novel that are of primary interest here. As liberal activist and commentator Carey McWilliams documented in 1942, Steinbeck did not distort the conditions facing refugees from family farms when they reached California in the Depression years. Despite the outcry of those who found the book too hard on the good citizens of California and Oklahoma, the fictional Joad family encountered obstacles that were real enough and encountered by many in both places. Like McWilliams's widely read books *Factories in the Field* and *Ill Fares the Land,* Steinbeck's portrayal of the Joad family in California can be interpreted as a Left-leaning critique of private property and of the labor relations spawned by a system of private property. Or it can be read as insight into why the rural working class resisted the leftist vision and drew on a rather different way of understanding land.

The philosophical themes of the novel line up with some of the main approaches to contemporary social ethics: libertarianism, egalitarianism, and utilitarianism. On one level, there is a dispute over land use, and each approach offers principles and arguments for resolving the dispute in one way or another. At a deeper level, there is the philosophical issue of whether mainstream political theories provide more or less adequate measures of agriculture. Here I map the path from practical issues of land and labor policy to fundamental philosophical debates. This mapping of the connection between values and policies suggests one way to express the leftist view of California agriculture: the migrants should have abandoned their libertarian values when they became wageworkers; they should have switched to some form of radical egalitarian or utilitarian outlook. Although Steinbeck's personal sentiments seem clearly aligned with this view, the book also provides a basis for understanding the lead characters as deeply resistant to all the options available in this three-way characterization of political ideals. In fact, a close examination of the mentality and material circumstances of Steinbeck's characters suggests a fourth philosophy of agriculture—one that is agrarian in nature and quite unlike the options found in contemporary political theory. Failure to recognize the agrarian view amounts to a silencing of the rural working class.

Literature is, in one sense, an apt forum for articulating a person's perspective and moral orientation. Steinbeck's description of life-as-lived opens the way for readers to develop empathy with the characters and for the work they did before leaving for California, as well as after they got there. It is as if the reader sees things as the characters see them, as if one could "try on" the characters' values as one would put on a suit of clothes. One limitation is that novels (and films) seldom provide a venue for the sophisticated development of basic philosophical ideas. Advocates of the political philosophies discussed in this chapter will not be satisfied that they have been developed adequately or treated fairly. The point, however, is to understand how Steinbeck portrayed the mentality of the characters in *The Grapes of Wrath,* especially with respect to their moral orientation toward land. This becomes relevant to sustainability because it illustrates why rural people like the Joads might feel unsympathetic to the basic vocabulary of contemporary liberalism. If people fail to connect with the most basic formulations of a political ethic, they are unlikely to move on to a more complex treatment. More significantly for the overall theme of this book, if an agrarian approach to the moral significance of land contains the germ of a philosophy for sustainability that can be generalized beyond the worldview of the rural working class, then the repression of agrarian political values deprives all of us of a crucial philosophical resource.

⚹ *The Grapes of Wrath* as Political History

The basic story of *The Grapes of Wrath* will be familiar to those who have read the novel or seen the film directed by John Ford (1894–1973) and starring Henry Fonda (1905–1982) as Tom Joad. Tom returns home after being paroled from prison, where he had been serving a term for manslaughter. He finds his family in the process of being evicted from the farm they once owned. Typical of many Great Plains farmers, the Joads lost title to land they most likely purchased from speculators, but until Tom's arrival, they had continued to live and farm under a tenancy arrangement with the bank that foreclosed on their original mortgage. The Great Depression is the backdrop for the novel, when foreclosures were common across the United States. But as residents of the Great Plains, the Joads are also victims of an ecological disaster. A combination of soil-drying drought and high winds has ruined the land, creating the Dust Bowl and causing crop failures throughout the 1930s.

Evicted from their tenancy lease, Tom and his family migrate to California, where they hope to resettle and find good-paying work harvesting fruit and vegetables. The Joads' flight on Route 66, the highway that brought refugees from the panhandles of Texas and Oklahoma to the Imperial Valley of California, makes up nearly half the novel. They experience a series of setbacks that reinforce both the family's solidarity with other displaced migrants and their alienation from property-owning classes. When they arrive in California, the Joads find the cornucopia of fruit and vegetable production they expected, but they are excluded from the jobs they hoped to find. The family sinks lower and lower. Family members die or steal away in the night, abandoning those who remain to the downward spiral of poverty, homelessness, and hunger. Tom Joad commits his second killing at a demonstration led by labor organizers protesting the wages paid at an orchard where the family has found temporary work. The orchard owners' hired thugs assault Casy, the family's onetime preacher and, for some readers, the Christ figure of the book.[1] Tom comes to his aid. Wanted both for parole violation and for murder, Tom is forced to abandon the family. The book ends with the Joads thoroughly broken and distraught, living in abandoned railroad cars amid the squalor of flood and famine.

Steinbeck explores the relationships among social roles (owners, tenants, wageworkers, employers, and businessmen) throughout the book by articulating how these roles are reflected in peculiar ways of seeing the events of the 1930s. In episodes with used car dealers, café owners and wait staff, and large-scale California farmers, the incentives of a profit-seeking economy bring people into conflict with traditional ways of life. Chapter 14, for example, notes that the new tractors have broken the land and cast its people on the road, then concludes with this passage: "If you who own the things people must have could understand this, you might preserve yourself. If you could separate causes from results, if you could know that Paine, Marx, Jefferson, Lenin, were results, not causes, you might survive. But that you cannot know. For the quality of owning freezes you forever into 'I,' and cuts you off forever from the 'we.'"[2] Steinbeck's litany of names in this passage connects the American and Russian revolutions and signals a conceptualization of political ideologies that was even starker in the 1930s than it is today.

The Grapes of Wrath is widely accepted as a literary classic, but it is also criticized as offering a romanticized portrait of the American working-class people it depicts. Edmund Wilson (1895–1972), for example, called it "mere sentimental optimism." Those who defended the novel read it as an allegory for the Israelites' exile in Babylon or, alternatively, Christ's message of redemption—sentimental, perhaps, but not merely so.[3] In either case, the characters of the novel endure a trying time in which selfishness gives way to altruism and to a sense of the greater whole. However, Wilson articulated the final judgment that many liberals would make. McWilliams and others had been arguing (persuasively, for many intellectuals) that California agriculture was being conducted on an industrial model and that agricultural workers would be exploited until they embraced a combination of unions and government regulation. To readers in 1939 who were familiar with that debate, Steinbeck's novel was wishy-washy. Passages in which the novel's characters recognize their interdependence are ambiguous. The embrace of the factory-worker class mentality is never explicit. The lingering notion is that if each individual would simply embrace altruism, all would be resolved. That lingering, implicit theme is what made the book seem so sentimentally optimistic to those who were trying to bring factory-style organized labor to the fields of California.

The Great Depression was, of course, the preeminent crisis for the U.S. economy. Along with McWilliams, Steinbeck took the disenchantment with capitalist values that was widespread among 1930s literary intellectuals beyond familiar urban settings. *The Grapes of Wrath* probes the internal contradictions of rural life in industrialized society. At the time of its publication, the harsh treatment of the Joads was taken to be its primary moral message, and sympathetic readers were likely to regard such treatment as typical of that extended to the working class in town and country. However, the story line in *The Grapes of Wrath* typifies economic events that affected farm families throughout the twentieth century, not only in the Dust Bowl years but also when the fortunes of urban workers were cresting. Steinbeck infuses the Joads' story with social and political observations that raise fundamental questions about private property, public policy, and class-consciousness. The book is a general critique of Depression-era capitalism, on the one hand, while it picks out themes unique to agriculture, on the other.

Chapter 5 of Steinbeck's novel provides an illustration of the tension between these two themes. It begins with a discussion of tractors. Once owner-operators, the Okies (now merely tenants) continue to farm the land as if it is their own, using traditional methods and family labor. But the farms do not pay, so the owners are consolidating their holdings and paying wages to the drivers of large equipment that cannot be operated efficiently on smaller tracts. As the chapter begins, the tractor driver is described as one who "could not see the land as it was" and who "loved the land no more than the bank loved the land." As the chapter progresses, the driver acquires a name of sorts (Al Davis's boy) and is discovered to be a local boy forced by economic circumstances to take work demolishing the life's work of former friends and neighbors. When Al Davis's boy takes a break for lunch, he talks with the nameless Oklahoma farmer about to be run off the land. In these passages, Steinbeck underlines the perceived futility of resistance to the owners, first articulated by the boy and then accepted by the farmer, who wants to know, "Who do I shoot?"

This episode is handled a little differently in the film, which followed publication of the book by only one year. There, the chapter is scripted as a flashback narrated by the Joads' neighbor Muley Jones, who lost his own farm before the story begins. In both book and film, Tom and Casy encounter Muley in an abandoned farmstead. Although most of the dialogue from chapter 5 is retained in Muley's flashback, the "Who do I shoot?" part of the conversation takes place between Muley and a man in a convertible who has come to tell him that he is being evicted. Muley threatens the tractor driver in the next scene of the film but backs off when he learns that the boy is a local. Muley is disheartened to find that

Al Davis's boy has turned against them, but he realizes that this is not the person to shoot. Ford's subtle transformation of the narrative makes it more plausible to see Muley's threats in the context of resistance to capitalism. The man in the convertible looks very much like someone from the bank. But Steinbeck's own rendering reminds us that rural folk like Muley might well have been prepared to shoot interlopers of all kinds.

In the film version, the tractor driver's inability to "see the land as it is" also becomes wholly implicit, if not absent altogether. The tension between the incompatible mentalities of the farmer and the tractor driver is muted. Arguably, that tension is more effectively communicated in the Dust Bowl documentary *The Plow That Broke the Plains* (1936) by Pare Lorentz (1905–1992). Lines of machinery march surrealistically across fertile plains resplendent with grain, leaving parched earth and dust in their wake. The narrator in Lorentz's film is able to comment on the effects of machinery in a manner that would have sounded sanctimonious coming out of Muley's mouth. These themes are important because *The Plow That Broke the Plains* preceded both book and film by several years. They also illustrate how Ford's film, extraordinarily faithful to the book in many respects, obscures the ecological dimension of the actual historical causes as well as Steinbeck's portrayal of the Okies' political mentality. Land that should not have been plowed at all was broken first by the farm families and then turned to dust by large-scale plowing.

It is also worth noting how another filmmaker of the period handled the tractor driver issue. Noted French surrealist Jean Renoir (1894–1979) made a few Hollywood films in the late 1930s and early 1940s, including *The Southerner*. The film was based on *Hold Autumn in Your Hand*, but it owes more to Renoir's politics (and Hollywood aesthetics) than to the George Sessions Perry (1910–1956) novel. Renoir's title character, a distraught Depression-era farmer, plays several scenes with his wage-earning brother-in-law, who is employed in a factory far from the farm. Renoir has the two allude to *The Grapes of Wrath* in one scene when the farmer says that if things don't work out, he will either head west or get a job driving a tractor. Taking neither of the alternatives available to Tom Joad or Al Davis's boy, Renoir's farmer sticks it out against the odds. He does so partly because the brother-in-law helps the family make it through a rough spot. Whereas Steinbeck uses his tractor driver scene to expose a rift between the poor dirt farmer and the wage-working tractor driver, Renoir plays up solidarity among all members of the working class.

A Philosophical Interlude: Libertarian and Egalitarian Ethics

The events of *The Grapes of Wrath* turn on the uneven contest between the itinerant Okies and the various representatives of the property-owning class they confront. The bankers and large California farmers get no sympathy from Steinbeck, but the events of the novel demand that we understand their worldview. That worldview comes directly from the seventeenth-century British philosophy typified by John Locke, although any twentieth-century American would certainly recognize it in the work of Robert Nozick (1938–2002) and other libertarian thinkers. The central ethical concepts are personal liberty and property rights, both of which are understood as embodying the principle of noninterference.

A philosophy that specifies ethical conduct in terms of noninterference demands that we do nothing to violate the liberty or meddle in the affairs and property of another person. Acting ethically means respecting constraints defined by the rights of others. Acting within one's rights (which is to say, voluntarily) to benefit another is permissible, even praiseworthy. But violating another's rights even to avoid serious harm is not allowed. One cannot require another person to act in a beneficent manner, since to do so would be to interfere in that person's affairs. That is why beneficent actions must be voluntary. Rights of noninterference protect personal security (one may not kill, threaten, or harm another person), liberty (one may not restrict freedom of speech, religion, or assembly), and property. Since there is no basis for requiring a person to act to obtain the best (or even a good) outcome, the choice of what to do with property is solely the prerogative of the property owner. Interference in the disposal of property is also understood as a violation of the property owner's liberty, since only by holding property rights can one maintain oneself as a free person. This is the neoliberal or libertarian system of social ethics. It construes ethics as a set of side constraints that remove certain options from consideration altogether (those that interfere with others' liberty and property); however, the decision maker is entirely free to choose—on a whim—from those that remain.

There are episodes in *The Grapes of Wrath* in which hired bullies violate the Okies' constitutional rights of free speech and assembly. No libertarian would excuse this, but much of what happens in the novel is consistent with the demands of libertarian morality. Economic practices such as farm evictions, exorbitant prices charged to transients, and the manipulation of wage rates in California do not violate liberties as libertarians construe them. Indeed, any public policy intended to constrain such practices would probably violate the property rights of the bankers, business owners, and large farmers. Although property owners do not appear as developed characters in the book, their libertarian values— their belief in ownership—are the obvious target of Steinbeck's spleen.

If libertarians are the bad guys, who are the heroes? If we read the novel as a Depression-era political tract, the leaders of socialist reform movements such as End Poverty in California (EPIC) come to mind. EPIC was organized in the mid-1930s by novelist Upton Sinclair (1878–1968), who mounted a campaign for governor. The most straightforward philosophical interpretation of this movement is egalitarian. Egalitarianism is a philosophy that insists on supplementing individual liberties and property rights with the guarantee of certain key opportunities. Opportunity rights include the provision of things such as health care, education, and technical training. The taxation of wealth necessary to guarantee these rights for all is not regarded as interference in the use of one's property. Depression-era egalitarians were, perhaps, more likely to insist on the equal distribution of wealth than are contemporary liberals. Yet the idea that a just society tends to equalize life chances by providing the poor with skills, knowledge, and health—which are the basis of opportunity—has endured. An egalitarian would argue that the rights of the Joad family had been systematically violated throughout their lives. A just society would provide them with life chances more equal to those of the property-owning class. Among the many who initiated an egalitarian attack on private property in the eighteenth century, Jean-Jacques Rousseau is probably the best remembered. A highly sophisticated version of this philosophy is associated with the recent work of John Rawls (1921–2002).

This is, of course, an oversimplified statement of the contrast between libertarian and egalitarian philosophy. Yet Steinbeck had something like this in the back of his mind, as did any number of enlightened intellectuals in the Depression era. The most obvious philosophical reading of *The Grapes of Wrath* is as an extended case study in social injustice, with the Joads gradually acquiring the class-consciousness that places them in solidarity with wageworkers. According to historian Charles Wollenberg, Steinbeck felt that the emergence of a white American workforce in California would disarm the racist proclivities of the state's labor politics.

Wollenberg reports that Steinbeck hoped the theme of white domination would be transformed into one of class conflict, mediated by organized labor and government intervention. It is also this obvious interpretation that Wilson derided as sentimental optimism.

Although passages such as the one referring to Paine, Marx, Jefferson, and Lenin clearly support the obvious reading, others, such as the tractor driver episode, do not. Steinbeck correctly perceived that all of agriculture, and especially that on the Great Plains, was beginning to look like the large-scale monoculture of California that he knew well. Popular opinion blamed individual farm failures on bad luck and bad management. Firms in every industry were increasing in size; agriculture appeared to be just another instance of "bigger is better." Many viewed the Dust Bowl as merely a particularly dramatic example of this phenomenon, and farm failures were widely thought to be the result of a natural disaster or a punishment from God—not surprising in the Bible Belt regions of the South most dramatically affected. It was not until after World War II that farm failures were widely seen as a sign of fundamental problems in the nation's agricultural economy. Steinbeck's own account stresses environmentally harmful technology (tractors) and bloated markets. References to natural disaster or divine retribution are relegated to the Okies' self-perception of their plight; they never accrue to the narrator's point of view.

✗ *The Grapes of Wrath* as Economic History

The economic structure of U.S. agriculture (the relative size distribution of farms, patterns of ownership and land tenure, relative percentage of off-farm income, and so forth) has undergone a dramatic transition since 1900. At the beginning of the twentieth century, approximately 70 percent of Americans lived on farms. At the beginning of the third millennium, the number stands at 3 percent. Although many forces have influenced this transition, the unwanted loss of a farm home through bankruptcy and eviction—the events that befall the Joads—has not been atypical. Many more families abandoned farming voluntarily when they saw that such a fate lay in store. The economic forces and events that precipitated the Joads' plight are not recounted in the novel, but with a little help from historian Donald Worster's environmental history of the Dust Bowl, we can identify two ideas from economic theory that explain what might have happened in a way that is entirely consistent with Steinbeck's text.

The Joads once owned their land, mortgaged it, then lost it to the bank. Why were they unsuccessful? The first concept for analyzing this question is the technological treadmill. They may not have been particularly bad farmers; they may simply have slipped off the technological treadmill. As Worster recounts in his book *Dust Bowl: The Southern Plains in the 1930s*, farming of the Great Plains began mostly in the 1890s, when innovations in farming systems made methods of dryland cultivation possible. It then expanded with the introduction of motorized tractors that had the capacity to work larger and more recalcitrant tracts of land. Worster also mentions the introduction of disc plows, which chopped the ground up more finely than the moldboard system of sodbusting. These new technologies allowed Great Plains farmers to participate in agriculture's "golden era," a time when prices were high due to disruptions in world grain supplies associated with World War I. But while technologies that allow the expansion of agricultural production or that increase its efficiency benefit a few farmers over the short run, over the long run they fuel a process of bankruptcy and ruin. This is true even without the environmental consequences of damage to fragile soils.

Economists generally credit Willard Cochrane with the analysis of the treadmill, although Karl Marx articulated the basic idea 100 years earlier. What is more, Franklin D. Roosevelt used the treadmill terminology in commenting that farmworkers could no longer count on being able to work their way up the ladder to eventual farm ownership.[4] Whatever the origins, the key to the treadmill is that improved farm technology, often portrayed as a blessing to farmers, does not actually benefit farmers at all. Rather each new innovation upsets the existing structure of agriculture and precipitates a new round of foreclosures and consolidation.

The economic logic goes like this: Agricultural technology increases farm productivity. New seeds and farming tools make two seeds grow where one grew before. But the demand for food is more sharply limited over the short run than is the demand for more durable goods. People only eat so much. There is little expansion of demand when prices go down. More production lowers prices *and* farm profits. Farmers must then run faster (that is, produce more) just to stay in place (maintain a steady income). Much of North American agriculture was mechanized for the first time from 1910 to 1925. Tractors and mechanical harvesters increased farm productivity in Canada and the United States. The increase in output was a boon to farmers in the years that farm exports went to feed a war-torn Europe. Eventually, however, European farmers returned to their fields. North American farmers who had accumulated debt to purchase land and equipment were caught in a spiral of falling prices. Mechanization became widespread, and productive capacity exceeded demand. Land from failed farms was bought by larger farmers or by land companies, either of which could consolidate their holdings to make the use of expensive mechanical equipment more cost-effective.

The second idea from economics is that of the prisoner's dilemma, borrowed from game theory and rechristened "the tragedy of the commons" by ecologist Garrett Hardin (1915–2003). The prisoner's dilemma models economic circumstances in which it would be irrational for individuals acting on their own to undertake actions that would clearly have the best outcome for everyone. The idea here is that each individual user of a commonly held fragile resource has no incentive to conserve. Indeed, individual conservation practices turn out to be doubly costly. An individual sacrifices the extra income he or she would make by exploiting the resource over the short run, while the actions of others deplete the resource anyway, negating the long-run savings that conservation is intended to bring about. Although everyone would be better off if (almost) everyone took a conservationist approach, doing so is irrational from the perspective of an individual resource user.[5]

As Worster notes, Great Plains farmers plowed lands that had never been plowed, exposing dry soils to wind. In this circumstance, farmland lost fertility whether someone else's dust covered the land or the topsoil blew away. Farmers had no incentive to conserve the fertility of their lands by cutting back on their plowing. To do so would have meant forgoing the windfall profits of the golden years when North American farmers were selling everything they could to Europe. Thus, the new mechanical technologies had two kinds of harmful impact on farm families. One was the slow death of the cost-price squeeze, as the treadmill turned one rotation after another. The other was the collectively irrational neglect of conservation in which individual farmers were forced to participate.

When the events of *The Grapes of Wrath* are interpreted in light of these two economic concepts, it becomes clear that the Joad family is the victim of property rules that make cooperation difficult and public policies that promote the development and spread of production-enhancing technology. The socioeconomic analysis suggested by the treadmill and the prisoner's dilemma supports the egalitarian interpretation that Steinbeck seems to favor. If the Joads were just incompetent or unlucky, their plight would not serve as an object lesson for social reform. Because their situation can be understood as a policy failure, government intervention is justified.

✳ A Philosophical Interlude: Egalitarian versus Utilitarian Ethics

At this juncture it is important to draw out a philosophical distinction that is not developed in the novel. The socioeconomic analysis of Great Plains agriculture can be given two different ethical interpretations. One draws on the egalitarian ideas already noted. Since the Okie farmers are not responsible for their plight, and since others benefit from it, there is, to the egalitarian, an obvious sense of unfairness and injustice in the events of the novel. The egalitarian response would be to supplement the world of noninterference rights (the world portrayed in *The Grapes of Wrath*) with a system of justice ensuring basic needs and opportunities for advancement for families like the Joads.

However, the economists and social scientists who originated the socioeconomic analysis of the Dust Bowl would be more inclined to offer a utilitarian interpretation. Put simply, a utilitarian evaluates any practice or public policy in terms of the utilitarian maxim: policy should promote the greatest good for the greatest number of people. For the utilitarian, the good consists in improvement in or detriment to the welfare of the individuals affected by the policy. To call for the greatest good is to say that one should adopt policies that maximize the total satisfaction and well-being of all affected individuals. If we are to understand the ways social critics might evaluate *The Grapes of Wrath*, we must not neglect the utilitarian alternative.

For a utilitarian, the property rules and public policies of the Joads' world are wrong because they produce less than optimal outcomes. The treadmill–prisoner's dilemma analysis shows that there are better alternatives, at least in theory. An agreement, contract, or government regulation that limits production or increases conservation would make more people better off. The utilitarian approach to policy is typified by eighteenth-century political philosopher Jeremy Bentham (1748–1832). Hardin is only one of many scientists who have applied a straightforward utilitarian approach to natural resource policy. The reasoning is quite simple: if a pattern of use depletes a renewable resource, it cannot be construed as the greatest good for the greatest number. For Hardin, this is all that needs to be said about the ethics of land use. We should use the tools of ecology and social science to predict the outcome of each proposed land-use policy, then enact the proposal that promises to produce the best consequences. Scientifically trained people populate the administrative agencies of government, and they are likely to evaluate proposals for policy change in utilitarian terms.

One of the great strengths of the utilitarian approach is that it provides a way to interpret the environmental devastation associated with the Dust Bowl in ethical terms. Theories of rights do a poor job of stipulating moral imperatives in circumstances in which the cumulative impact of individual actions causes resource depletion or environmental destruction. Each individual action contributes very little to environmental impact. The focus on fairness or liberty fails to raise concerns about the total environmental impact of many individual actions, each of which might be entirely consistent with fairness or liberty when considered in isolation. The utilitarian approach thus provides a way to articulate a moral theme that *is* present in Steinbeck's novel: the environmental devastation of the Dust Bowl is a moral wrong perpetrated by people who could not see how their actions contributed and who could not have acted differently.

However, utilitarianism seems to permit costs imposed on one person or subgroup when they are offset by even greater benefits to the population as a whole. Furthermore, there is no reason why one subgroup (such as women, minorities, or the poor) would not be cast in the losing role on a regular basis. Accordingly, it is not necessarily true that a utilitarian ethic would justify government services and regulations to help the Joad family keep their farm. Consolidation might yet turn out to be the optimal strategy for limiting production and controlling erosion. The utilitarian argument on farm foreclosures depends on facts, not on claims about fairness. This is the dimension of utilitarian thinking that egalitarians such as Rawls have found unacceptable. For them, the goal of equalizing life chances should predominate.

Rights philosophy places all its emphasis on the structure of society, on the rights and institutions that constrain (and enable) individual action. The libertarian does not justify this structure in terms of the costs and benefits it produces but instead singles out whether the structure itself is consistent with the principle of liberty, of noninterference in each person's actions. If rights and institutions fail to produce the best consequences, so what? As Nozick has pointed out, the libertarian is under no obligation to choose so as to produce a particular pattern of consequences, be they optimal for society as a whole or optimal for the worst-off group. A libertarian would be hostile to government intervention to reverse the socioeconomic consequences of the treadmill and the prisoner's dilemma because no one is interfering with the Okies' freedom to make choices that lead to these consequences. Furthermore, using public funds and government authority to reverse these consequences *would* interfere in the liberty of farmers and taxpayers alike.

Many (perhaps most) egalitarians would respond to this libertarian argument by suggesting that a just society guarantees opportunity as well as liberty. As such, they would argue (as suggested earlier) that the basic structure of society should include opportunity rights as well as rights of noninterference. It is thus possible to interpret libertarians and egalitarians as being focused primarily on the rights that are protected in the basic structure of society. In this, they agree with each other against utilitarians, who believe that only the public welfare matters. Indeed, most political philosophers of the twentieth century would be inclined to analyze the social ethics of the Dust Bowl and the California migration in terms of the libertarian, egalitarian, and utilitarian philosophies that have been described thus far.

The Agrarian Worldview of the Joads

Steinbeck's research for *The Grapes of Wrath* retraced the Okies' path in reverse direction. He began with the violent confrontations at California orchards that serve as the climax for both *The Grapes of Wrath* and *In Dubious Battle*. He then wrote a series of articles for a San Francisco newspaper based on interviews he conducted with refugees and staff at a government relief camp that became the basis for the book's account of "Weedpatch" (curiously rechristened "Wheatpatch" in the film). The character Jim Radley is based on Tom Collins, the real-life manager of the camp Steinbeck visited. To complete *The Grapes of Wrath*, he supplemented these California experiences with several months of traveling with Okie refugees along Route 66 and a briefer visit to the devastated regions of the Dust Bowl itself. Steinbeck's respect for his characters in

The Grapes of Wrath is evident when compared to his treatment of the migrants in his newspaper articles.[6]

The Okies' experience was shaped by the agricultural methods then in use at both ends of Route 66. Throughout this journey they encounter working people of all kinds: auto mechanics and waitpersons, as well as other refugees from the Dust Bowl. The characters in the novel thus provide multiple perspectives on the events of the 1930s. These multiple ways of framing the moral issues posed by *The Grapes of Wrath* provide the underpinnings for interpreting the novel as a moral critique. On one level, it is a call for government intervention as a brake on the interests of capital. On another level, it places both economic interests and moral beliefs into complex ecological relationships in which no one form of moral discourse rises unequivocally above all others.

It is hard to miss Steinbeck's own voice calling for an egalitarian interpretation of events in passages such as the Paine, Marx, Jefferson, and Lenin text quoted earlier. Nevertheless, Steinbeck never suggests that the Joads themselves see things this way. Even as farm tenants, the Joads retain a self-understanding as yeoman farmers, individuals who produce the means of their own sustenance under conditions of economic independence and personal autonomy. Although they do not own their land, they are still *of* the land. The agrarian ethic of the yeoman farmer entails a resolution of the tensions between self-reliance and community, between stewardship and exploitation of the land. These tensions are resolved by an overriding commitment to make one's life at a particular place. When abstract ideals threaten this commitment, it is the place, the farm, and the land that must prevail. Because the Joads are of the land, in their own minds at least, they inherit a system of social arrangements shared by others with whom they are placed. They have moral relations with specific individuals, and these relations are fixed by geographic parameters. Everyone is tied to land, and not just any land but the land on which they live and farm. By investing their labor and their very being into the improvement and conservation of a particular place, farm people also fix their social milieu. For the most part, farm people interact with the same individuals over a lifetime. Factors such as heredity, debt, personal history, and personality structure the moral relations among rural people in very particular terms that vary from one person to the next.

This way of understanding moral relationships is quite unlike the pattern developed in philosophies that build on rights or welfare consequences. Liberal and neoliberal political theories tend to presume that morality and justice depend on characteristics that can be applied universally to all persons and in any situation. It is the specificity of the people to whom reciprocal moral relations are owed that animates the agrarian vision. What is more, unique personal and role-dependent aspects of a person's identity must be recognized for these moral relations to become effective. In stressing reciprocity and recognition, the agrarian way of understanding moral relationships also gives rise to a conception of community as a group of specific individuals pursuing life at a particular place. It is each individual's commitment to the place that binds them together as a community, not an abstract commitment to others' rights or welfare.

Under such circumstances, the Joads and their neighbors can understand the moral dimension of their social life in terms of loyalty to place and loyalty to those other individuals who have demonstrated the most loyalty to that place in their own affairs. As such, rural people bond together when it comes to barn raising and responding to adversity, and in doing so they recognize one another in ways that establish reciprocal obligations that make life at a given place possible and even rewarding. They do not do this because neighbors have a *right* to expect this, nor because cooperation is sometimes more efficient. Instead, they do it simply because they *are* neighbors and because they recognize one another as such. Furthermore, this is not a loyalty to the ideal of neighbors in general but a loyalty to the particular individuals who stand in a neighborly relation to one another. Choices are not generalized in terms of rights or consequences; they are seen entirely in light of the need to satisfy sometimes conflicting duties acquired through personal relationships. After they leave Oklahoma, the Joads must sell their labor on the flooded California labor market, and they are itinerant, without place. But does this new situation occasion a transformation of their self-image?

In literal economic terms, the Joads have become proletarians when they arrive in California, even if they were not already in Oklahoma. Despite the agrarian nature of their employment, migrant laborers may represent the purest form of proletarian wage laborers that existed in twentieth-century America. With only their unskilled labor to sell, and with no other visible means of security or support, the link between hard work and sustenance is far more tenuous than it ever was on the farm. In this new situation, work is not done at the discretion of the worker, and wages are often an inadequate and unreliable source of income. One would expect the Okies to lose first their self-respect and then their sense of being Jeffersonian citizens as they are subjected to this unrelenting competition with one another for marginal jobs. As the families move west, a political liberal would hope that a form of class-consciousness would take the place of agrarian ideals.

Steinbeck depicts the socioeconomic circumstances of the Joads' class transformation quite clearly. As the families move west, the practice of establishing reciprocal duties among known individuals erodes. It becomes clear that each member of the family will be in an increasingly weaker position to repay moral debts to others as time goes by. Furthermore, the itinerant nature of their lives and employment constantly places them among strangers. Eventually, the sense that these strangers will one day be neighbors must begin to fade. As main characters are drawn into circumstances that should lead them to adopt egalitarian ideals, minor characters are drawn into a libertarian ethic that stresses the protection of property rights and denies any but voluntary, charitable duties to aid the poor. Yet the accompanying psychological transformation of the less fortunate characters is never fully realized.

Although characters such as Jim Casy and Tom Joad come very close to embracing a radical egalitarian worldview and a socialist politics, a twinge of place and person-bound morality remains. Tom commits his second killing at least as much from a personal loyalty to Casy as from an enlightened interest in class politics. The famed "I'll be there" speech spoken by Henry Fonda in the John Ford film is perhaps the most enduring political symbol of *The Grapes of Wrath*, and it is taken from the novel word for word. Although Tom Joad expresses solidarity with working people everywhere, the philosophical grounding of this solidarity remains ambiguous. Is it because Tom has come to see politics as a competition of class interests, or because he has learned that the world is a much bigger place than he once thought?

The other family characters such as Ma, Pa, and the younger children do not, on my reading, ever entertain an ethic of class conflict, much less accept one. It is impossible to avoid the conclusion that Steinbeck was rooting for a radicalization of the Okies' moral sensibility. At the same time, the ambivalence with which he viewed radical politics is even more apparent in his novel *In Dubious Battle,* where socialist agitators appear first as heroic figures but end up as men who lack a crucial capacity for human feelings. Though hardly conservative, Steinbeck seems unable to give up entirely on the work ethic of the yeoman farmer. As such, Steinbeck's socialism and his critique of private property are at war with his commitment to an ideal of place-bound morality.

Of course, agrarianism is not without a philosophical pedigree. The notion that morality could be rooted in the work experience of rural people occupied an important place in the thought of Jefferson, Emerson, and Thoreau. The farm family is blessed because each member occupies a social role that makes their interdependence easy to see. This philosophy stresses the particular rather than the universal. The individual is linked to the moral community by an extensive network of ties to specific others, family members, neighbors, and even businessmen in the nearby town. Anyone committed to such a philosophy will resist attempts to render these relationships in abstract or general terms. Such moral relations depend not only on the specific people who occupy these roles and on the history of their life together but also on the placement of these people around the permanent, stabilizing place that is the farm itself.

Agrarianism is an ethic of place, and the Joads are out of place in California. Their personalized ethic of agrarian reciprocity is unable to function in a wage-labor environment. The socialist agrarian reformers of *In Dubious Battle* exploit the migrants' sense of personal, place-bound community, attempting to use it as a substitute for class-consciousness. For their part, the property owners can rely on the Okies' commitment to place as a substitute for a true ethic of property rights. Steinbeck might have used his platform to characterize the Okies as dupes and their agrarian ethics as self-deceiving ideology. Yet *The Grapes of Wrath* always returns to the agrarian framework for its most authentic and poignant portrayals. The book closes not on a note of class-consciousness but on an act that conveys deep moral conviction, without implying any larger view of class interests or rights. Rose of Sharon, herself in wretched circumstances having lost the child she would suckle with her milk-laden breasts, responds to a particular person, known face-to-face if not by name. She fulfills that person's need for sustenance, a need claimed not by right or commitment to the greater good but because he and she are people in the same place, at the same time.

sense of identity/place

Ethics, Agriculture, and Rural Americans

The philosophical contest for the hearts and minds of rural Americans continues today. On the one hand are those who would cast them (for good or ill) as libertarians, primarily interested in private property. On the other hand are those who continue to characterize the rural poor as victims of race, class, and gender discrimination. Socioeconomic transformation in rural America since the 1930s tends to support such a dichotomous analysis of rural politics. Since World War II, farm income has improved steadily. Farmers are no longer among the worst off in rural communities; they would clearly be considered middle class in the vast majority of cases. It is easy to see how the comfort farm owners derive from their land could lead them to favor a strong ethic of noninterference in an individual's right to use and dispose of property however he or she sees fit.

This ethic would still be opposed to the egalitarian's commitment to the poor. It is just that farmers are no longer poor themselves. The rural poor are landless people who do farmwork or who work in rural industries such as meatpacking, construction, or transport. They are the heirs of the California Joads, and as such, they can be expected to articulate political ideals in terms of either rights-based or consequentialist versions of egalitarian political philosophy. As with Steinbeck, liberal analysts continue to search for class-consciousness among the rural poor. Deborah Fink's ethnography of Iowa meatpacking workers is an example. Fink takes pains to point out that farmers are no longer emblematic of the rural working class. Yet like Steinbeck, Fink must end with the admission that her subjects do not see themselves playing the role that liberal egalitarianism has prepared for them. In their own minds, at least, they are making a life at a particular place and will submit to whatever it takes to do so. Even workers in Iowa who are far from home maintain a sense of identity and personal loyalty to a specific place, often in Mexico, from whence they came.

Even more pertinent is the way Worster challenges the claim that Dust Bowl refugees could have been motivated by any genuine sense of place. His *Dust Bowl* provides detailed studies of Cimarron County, Oklahoma, and Haskell County, Kansas, where farm families suffered fates similar to that of the Joads. The book's analysis of the cause and consequence of dust storms provides the basis for an ecologically and

economically enriched understanding of the events that is missing from
Steinbeck's novel, although Worster endorses Steinbeck's portrayal of
the human drama as essentially accurate. Yet Worster argues that those
who participated in the industrial-style farming sweeping across the
Great Plains were motivated by an industrial vision and the dream of
expanding profits far more than they were by any agrarian philosophy.
He questions whether families like the Joads could have experienced an
authentic sense of place, noting that their milieu was one of chain stores,
store-bought bread, and Coca-Cola. They depended on oil deliveries provided through a transportation and communication network that made
them part of a regional economy wholly unlike that of agrarian villages
from days past. Based on his interviews with Dust Bowl survivors and
research from documentary sources, Worster recounts that their attitude
toward the land was one of ambivalence and disappointment, reveal-
ing "how inchoate was their sense of place." Worster concludes that the
real lesson of the Dust Bowl was actually not learned by the Okies. "By
the end of the thirties they found themselves still unable to accept their
part of nature on its own terms, to regard its limits without apology, and
to shape their culture by its imperatives and not by those of capitalist-
consumer drives. Their eyes were still on the far horizon, and their feet
were not planted firmly on the ground."[7]

Yet Worster also quotes a number of respondents and sources who
reject being cast as either entrepreneur or proletarian. Perhaps like Steinbeck himself, Worster is convinced that Marx got something right and
that liberal political theories such as egalitarianism or utilitarianism
provide the best means at our disposal to articulate it. But also like Steinbeck, Worster is confronted by voices who reject this vocabulary, falling
back on agrarian themes. What are we to make of the resiliency of place
in the moral mentality of rural Americans? One possibility is to trace it
to cultural causes, to Jeffersonian agrarianism and its continuing resonance. As historian Ruth Cowan relates in her *Social History of American
Technology,* the U.S. labor movement was most successful in urban areas
where factory workers were European immigrants of relatively recent origin. In Europe the working class never had any expectation of ascending
into property ownership, and they were not tempted by political ideologies that gave credence to the legitimacy of property. In nineteenth-
century America, wage work was generally viewed as temporary, something one did only long enough to get a stake and buy a place of one's

own. Although FDR and Steinbeck alike declared this hope obsolete in 1937, it is a portrayal of the rural personality that has reverberated throughout popular culture ever since.

Philosophically, *The Grapes of Wrath* leaves us to ponder whether agrarianism offers something that is missing from libertarian, egalitarian, and utilitarian political philosophies. Indeed, the agrarian mentality shares certain characteristics with communitarian moral thought, which often draws on agrarian metaphors—native soil, rootedness, and organicism.[8] Such an interpretation would portray rural politics as embroiled in a philosophical debate among what are arguably the four most prominent approaches in contemporary political theory. It is best to be cautious here. Libertarian, egalitarian, and utilitarian philosophers might be justly angered by the simplistic characterizations of each philosophy offered above. However, it would be a far greater distortion to equate the communitarian philosophy advocated by people such as Michael Sandel or Charles Taylor with the agrarian mentality and moral universe of the Joads. As such, this theme must be left undeveloped in the present context.

Returning to *The Grapes of Wrath*, we can now read the novel not merely as conveying a message about economic events but as a discourse that places various forms of political philosophy into dialogue with one another. We can summarize this dialogue with a matrix, a philosophical depth chart, if you will. The novel portrays three interest groups clearly: property-owning bankers; class-oriented social reformers; and, caught between them, the Okies, lost in a world of wage labor but with their agrarian moral sentiments intact. We can add a fourth group that reflects the treadmill–prisoner's dilemma analysis in utilitarian terms. Members of this group might argue their case by noting that the Dust Bowl was an ecological disaster that left human misery in its wake. I take the liberty of calling them "environmentalists" because the interest they represent is an interest in maintaining the integrity of the Great Plains ecosystem. All four of these parties are in contention over land use. Land is the contested good that sits at the top level of the philosophical depth chart.

Each interest group interprets the moral significance of land differently. For the bankers, it is property. For the reformers, it is an opportunity to work and prosper. If the land does not secure these opportunities, another social institution will have to. Ecosystem advocates see the costs of environmental degradation as externalities, as consequences that are not accounted for when individuals in a prisoner's dilemma situation act

	Party 1	Party 2	Party 3	Party 4
Contested good	Land	Land	Land	Land
Interest group	Bankers	Reformers	Environmentalists	Okies
Moral significance of land	Property	Opportunity	Externality	Place
Principle	Liberty	Equality	Efficiency	Recognition
Philosophy	Libertarianism	Egalitarianism	Utilitarianism	Agrarianism
Contributors	Locke Nozick	Rousseau Rawls	Bentham Hardin	Jefferson Berry

A philosophical depth chart for *The Grapes of Wrath*.

only on the basis of rational self-interest. For most of the main characters in *The Grapes of Wrath*, land is a place to live. Moving a notch deeper, we can see that each of these interpretations is principled. One might justify a property rights view in terms of liberty or rights of noninterference, or an opportunity rights view in terms of fairness or equality. The environmentalist is simply seeking a more efficient use of resources, while the Okies interpret the moral significance of place in light of reciprocities that are geographically based. Their interactions with the land and with one another create identities that must be recognized in their uniqueness. Moral identity cannot be inferred from universal abstractions. I have already given names to the systematic philosophical approaches that ground each of these principles, and I have had occasion to mention some of the philosophers and social critics—both historical and contemporary—associated with and contributing to each. Though they may seem to be interested solely in fundamental philosophy, they have created argument forms that animate our most practical public debates.

The philosophical depth chart can be misleading if it is taken to reduce debates in political philosophy to simple conflicts of interest. And as Worster reminds us, the entire picture is misleading if we take it to represent facts on the ground in the 1930s too literally. Instead, the depth chart is intended to illustrate how concrete policies and the principled arguments that interested parties make to influence policy can be linked to established philosophical traditions. Any policy analysis that does not consider the full range of philosophical traditions ignores key burdens of proof that are demanded not only by interested parties but also by the philosophical perspective on political life they represent. This means that, ironically, liberals who insist on debating worker interests in light of libertarian, egalitarian, and utilitarian concepts may actually be depriving rural workers of a voice that, if not wholly authentic (as Worster tells us), is still the voice with which they choose to speak.

Of course, when it comes time to actually set policy, one may judge one or another of these philosophical approaches to be correct and choose accordingly. Alternatively, one may try to fashion some compromise that leaves each interest partially satisfied (which means that each principled philosophy is at least partially violated). In other words, laying these conflicts out in tabular form does not resolve the issues of property rights, class-consciousness, and sustainability. Nevertheless, there has been a marked tendency for liberal critics of industrial agriculture to stick to the spectrum of ideals available within liberal philosophy. They are anxious to link farmers' interests to libertarian individualism in the case of large property owners or to more Left-leaning ideas of exploitation and workers' rights in the case of smallholders. Yet it seems that any approach to rural development and the plight of the rural poor must accommodate all four of these orientations, not just the first three. To do less is to deprive rural people of the moral vocabulary in which they express their moral identity. It casts them as actors in a social drama that does not speak to their interests, as they understand and choose to express them. And it is contrary to the spirit of liberalism to deny the working class their chosen voice on putatively liberal grounds.

[At the same time, in recognizing the agrarian alternative, we are able to see putatively conservative tendencies in rural America as being grounded in something other than a libertarian conception of property rights. It is certainly true that many rural Americans have favored a self-image of rugged independence, but it does not follow that they are thoroughgoing libertarians. Indeed, unlike libertarian property rights, the agrarian conception of living on the land entails an obligation to help neighbors in their time of trial. And whereas libertarian property rights protect the transfer of ownership to a bank or to corporate owners through the legal processes of foreclosure, an agrarian protests that these acts threaten rural communities. Bankers and corporate officers will not show up with a casserole when Ma takes sick, nor will they be there to participate in barn raisings and other community projects.

If allowing the Joads to speak in their own way makes a liberal reading of *The Grapes of Wrath* more difficult, we can now see the dimension
of Steinbeck's novel that his contemporaries dismissed as "sentimental
optimism" in different terms. Whatever political views Steinbeck himself
might have had (and they were assuredly Left-leaning, if also devoutly
anticommunist), his respect for the Okies and for their story prevented
him from placing liberal rhetoric in their mouths. Arguably, this complexity enriches the book, and it certainly makes it more appealing as an
object lesson on the mentality of rural Americans. At the same time, *The
Grapes of Wrath* clearly shows that living under a regime of agrarian ideals does not mean that one is living sustainably. This is Worster's main
point: the putatively place-based values of people in Haskell County,
Kansas, did not keep their environmentally exploitative farming practices in check. Nevertheless, the moral complexity of an agrarian view
may be just what we need to think more carefully about sustainability.
It is with the thought that agrarian ideals may represent a resource for
considering sustainability (albeit one that needs revision and refinement)
that we leave Steinbeck and the Joads in Depression-era California and
strike out for a more environmentally adequate account of agrarian localism and the celebration of place.

CHAPTER 5

Farming as a Focal Practice

Albert Borgmann developed the ideas of focal things and focal practices in the final stages of his inquiry into the failed promise of technology. His book *Technology and the Character of Contemporary Life* is a philosophical study of why life in modern society has become so disjointed, frenetic, and unsatisfying, despite the hope of previous generations that science and technology would free humanity for more satisfying and ennobling pursuits. Focal things and focal practices encompass a broad array of objects and activities that give meaning to people's lives. They are capable of addressing the failure of technology because they unify and harmonize fragmented experiences into a more satisfying whole. They do this because they overcome technology's tendency to overwhelm us with consumable commodities, goods whose sheer commodiousness undercuts the ends to which consumption is intended to be a means. Writing before the fall of the Soviet Union, Borgmann stressed the point that fragmentation is not solely a product of capitalism. Citizens of socialist and capitalist societies alike feel trapped in an order of life dictated by the terms of technological production, distribution, and consumption. A careful and philosophically informed appreciation of focal things can, Borgmann thinks, end this entrapment. Only then can technology truly serve the ends worthy of human lives.

Borgmann's analysis of focal things originated in reference to technology, but it also applies to land. The deeper philosophical meaning of agrarian ideals can be articulated when farming and what Borgmann calls "the culture of the table" are understood as focal practices, as established habits of living that impart broader meaning and purpose to people's lives. This is not to say, of course, that everyone should farm. As in previous chapters, we must understand agrarian ideals partially as symbols or narratives that provide guidance for sustainability. So it is partially in the contemplation of farming that the notion of focal practice is fulfilled. But it is also true that everyday habits and practices matter a great deal. This is where Borgmann's culture of the table, introduced in his book *Real American Ethics,* complements the contemplation of farming and completes sustainability as a set of practices in which everyone can actually engage. This is also how popular social movements associated with eating locally and organically grown food or shopping at farmers' markets can be integrated with agrarian ideals. The notion of focal practice is thus central to the entire argument of this book.

Focal Practice and the Commodification of Life

Borgmann tells us that "a focal practice, generally, is the resolute and singular dedication to a focal thing. It sponsors discipline and skill which are exercised in a unity of achievement and enjoyment of mind, body, and the world, of myself and others, and in social union."[1] Borgmann develops the idea of focal things in contrast to commodities, and he sees the failure of technology consisting in the commodification of focal things. The terms *commodification* and *commoditization* have been used widely, broadly, and interchangeably in social theory for a long time. They often convey a vague sense of disapproval with very little exposition of what commodification is, the mechanisms by which it is alleged to occur, or the rationale for regarding it as a bad thing. In some cases, the term refers to the way goods once reserved for exchange through gift or patronage come to be bought and sold on markets. Or it may be a pejorative reference to things that an author thinks should never be bought and sold: human affection, bodily organs, and sexual favors come readily to mind. Human capabilities such as skills, labor itself, or, more recently, courteous or friendly behavior (referred to as "emotional labor") can become more or less valued and traded through market relations. As Borgmann notes, economists who see the expansion of market relations as a good thing hardly ever use this term.

In *Technology and the Character of Contemporary Life,* the theme of commodification is introduced as a function of the device paradigm, another of Borgmann's wonderfully evocative conceptual inventions. As an example of the device paradigm, Borgmann contrasts the hearth with the modern central heating system. Both technologies provide warmth to an interior space, but the hearth does so in a manner that centers and directs a wide variety of materials and social practices. The hearth must be tended frequently, requiring attentiveness and monitoring from the occupants of the space. The radiant heat it provides lends an implicit ordering to the space within a domicile, so that people congregate around the hearth for warmth. Fuel for a hearth must be gathered long before it will be needed for warmth, thus making the hearth and the need for warmth a continual presence in planning and decision making. Partly as a consequence of all this, the hearth also becomes a focal point for gathering and sociality, and it becomes incorporated into other activities such as cooking and household chores. The hearth is thus what Borgmann calls a *focal thing*, and the heat it produces is but one of many products yielded by the material practices of tending the hearth.

The central heating system, in contrast, yields heat as a good deliverable on demand and without the entanglements and inconveniences of constant tending or year-round planning. This is, Borgmann allows, a good thing, but it comes at a price: that is, the central heating system is in no sense a focal object that can serve as a commanding presence in home life, centering and ordering activity while availing sociality and purpose to daily practice. The central heating system is a device that delivers heat as a commodity, a relatively detached and isolated good that is obtained not by activities that integrate the social group occupying a domicile but by monetized exchanges that require people within the household to earn income in employment outside the home. Thus, commodities are goods that have been detached and isolated from a richly interwoven nexus of material practices that integrate social groupings such as a family or a household, giving meaning and purpose to the work involved in obtaining necessities and indulgences alike. Commodities are obtained by activities that require little or no involvement or personal investment, activities such as handing over one's credit card or flipping a switch. The idea that life is gradually emptied of meaning and richness as it becomes taken over by devices and commodity goods has been a persistent theme in Borgmann's philosophy.

Real American Ethics develops this theory of commodification by teasing apart the processes of developing goods that can be traded in markets from aspects of the device paradigm that emphasize the decline of meaning, purpose, and quality of life. Transformations associated with the marketization of goods and social relationships are designated *economic commodification*, while transformations that reduce the richness of everyday life are referred to as *moral commodification*. These overlap in many if not most cases. In the case of the central heating system, home heating becomes an economic commodity purchased through transactions with utilities and heating companies. It is a moral commodity, in that it has been disconnected from the focal practices that center and provide meaning to household life when heat is produced by the hearth. Borgmann goes on to illustrate how the design of private and public spaces can both facilitate and resist moral commodification, referring to the home architecture of Thomas Jefferson and Frank Lloyd Wright and providing a particularly effective discussion of the minor league baseball park in Missoula, Montana.

In summary, Borgmann understands commodification as the transformation of focal things and practices into devices. Technology has failed humanity, he argues, because it has fallen into the device paradigm, where a "successful" technology is viewed exclusively in terms of its ability to make life easy by making goods available without entanglements and nuisances. This is often associated with an economic transformation: goods and activities once thoroughly embedded in institutions such as family or village life become available to any buyer who can pony up the seller's asking price. Borgmann is less interested in the fact that the goods and services produced by devices are bought and sold than in the effect they have on family or village life. Focal things and focal practices may be inefficient means for producing a simple thing such as home heating, but they have a hidden value in the way their pursuit creates meaning and substance as a by-product. A world dominated by devices is ultimately a world without meaning, a world in which lives seem empty and shallow. *no focal practice?*

Farming as a Focal Practice

How do food and farming fit into this picture? Any demonstration that farming is a focal practice would be an example of what Borgmann calls "deictic discourse," a conversation or description that unwinds at its own time and pace, that is responsive to idiosyncrasies of context, and that cannot be controlled in advance. Although Wendell Berry is a master at deictic discourse on farming, Gene Logsdon's book *At Nature's Pace* is another example, and one more poignant than anything I can offer here. Although it is presumptuous and misleading to summarize Logsdon in a few sentences, I can say that his account reveals farming to be a set of practices and techniques that have evolved in response to a specific place. Good seed, for example, takes on its genetic characteristics as a result of having been planted in and harvested from the same soil, year in and year out. The traditional barn "has evolved through centuries of experience."[2] Farming, then, is "the resolute and singular dedication" to land—and not just to land in the abstract but to the specific land on which one farms.

One might, of course, be dedicated to a place without farming it. Many people are dedicated to the preservation of natural or historic places or to the beautification of their homes. Although these kinds of dedication might also constitute focal practices as Borgmann conceives of them, farming unifies "achievement and enjoyment of the mind, body, and the world" in a way that preservation and beautification cannot. Farming is and has been throughout history the preeminent practice by which human beings bring forth the sustenance of their lives (we might also include hunting and fishing). Farming is productive and reproductive of human life. Farming must, of course, be supplemented by skills and crafts that are not part of farming per se, but building, toolmaking, and the martial arts do not center, order, and unify "myself and others" in the way farming does. As Borgmann writes, "It is certainly the purpose of a focal practice to guard in its undiminished depth and identity the thing that is central to the practice, to shield it against the technological diremption into ends and means. Like values, rules and practices are recollections, anticipations, and, we can say now, guardians of the concrete things and events that finally matter."[3]

Farming demands the engagement of mind and body with the world. The evolution that Logsdon praises is a mindful and social process whereby individuals and social groups evolve a way of being, of continuing to be, that is attuned to, in Thoreau's words, the expectations of the land on which they are situated. On the traditional farm, everyone depends on everyone else. Fields must be tilled and animals must be fed. Milk must be made into butter and cheese; crops must be planted and later threshed. Cows, pigs, and chickens must be slaughtered and rendered. These practices establish roles for each member of the farm family and, in some communities, for designated individuals or family groups who become butchers, millers, or wheelwrights or who take up some other task that complements farming activities. There is no formula for these roles; every farm, every farm community, is different. The differences reflect different soils, different microclimates, different neighbors, different histories, and different social institutions. In every case, however, focal practices evolve under the weight of feedback mechanisms and impressive object lessons that communicate the interdependence of people with one another and with the land.

In traditional farming, farmers who are not attuned to the unique characteristics of their situation or not singularly dedicated to the pursuit of livelihood that is farming's central norm fail. Communities that are not organized around the needs and capacities of their farmers fail. Those that are successful truly "guard in its undiminished depth and identity" the dialectic that arises between land and livelihood. This dialectic is perilously vulnerable to the diremption of which Borgmann speaks, where sustenance becomes the end and land a mere means. Clearly fishing unifies the practices of many coastal villages in a similar way, as it did for the North American tribes who followed the salmon and for others who adopted the buffalo as a focal thing, engendering a way of life highly attuned to nature and unsurpassed in freedom. The centrality of farming, as opposed to these other focal practices, is contingent on the actual history of European civilization, as well as on its role in providing life and livelihood. Farming represents a particularly significant focal practice because the history of European civilization is, in crucial respects, a history of the spread of European plants, animals, and farming techniques across the entire expanse of temperate zones on our planet.

Farming's Fall from Grace

Borgmann's early work cites Wendell Berry, but wilderness recreation and sports activities figure most prominently in his discussions of focal practice. David Strong also emphasizes the saving character of wilderness in developing Borgmann's ideas. Perhaps it is because we fancy ourselves as coming from a pretechnological past and heading into an uncertain technological future that these wilderness ideals can be linked so readily to salvation, recovery, and sustainability. But the farm occupies a similar place in the imagination. Strong cites Berry's discussion of plow horses to illustrate focal things, but to contemplate how farming could save us from a life without meaning, it may be necessary to recall how farming itself has fallen into the device paradigm.

The fall of farming is documented in rather Borgmann-like language throughout Berry's own writings. Berry emphasizes the seductive nature of modern farm technology in offering relief from toil. Industrial technology offers easy solutions to past problems of farm production. If soils are poor or if insect or rodent pests are an annoyance, a package of chemicals can be pulled off the shelf of the local co-op. Farm machinery relieves the drudgery of farmwork. Tractors can be well utilized when farmers standardize the size and shape of fields, and the time of plant maturity has also been standardized through crop breeding. Berry laments the farmer's loss of contact with the land that results from farming behind the windshield of the computerized and comfort-controlled modern farm tractor. The result is that land is replaced by a version of the device paradigm. Land is now merely one of many purchased inputs. Land is reduced to its chemical and physical characteristics, which are bought or leased along with machinery, seeds, and chemicals. Land as place recedes, and with it, perhaps, the social and moral connections to nature and to community that gave land its focal character.

Berry's vision of farming can be contested. His reference point is farming as it was done in North America from European settlement until approximately World War II, but there are few generalizations that hold true over such a broad swath of time and geography. Berry is thinking of a form of community and family-based farming that still exists in many parts of the United States and Canada, but one that is unarguably on the wane. We must allow him a bit of latitude in his agricultural history, and I will not pick nits here. It is important to remember that there is little constancy in the way land reveals itself as a focal thing. Land is also a focal thing in feudal and plantation agriculture, for example, but in a manner quite unlike Berry's vision. Yet whether one examines the transition away from the manorial systems of old Europe, the plantation systems of the American South, or the family farms that were common throughout Europe and North America in 1900, the way one tells the story is crucial to its moral lesson. Berry's critique selects one dimension of that history, to be sure. A different history might stress how agrarian ideals become implicated in the exploitation of race, class, and gender. Such a history might be useful for moral evaluations stressing human rights, human welfare, or the domination of marginalized groups. In contrast, Berry's history shows us why industrial farming offers far less than these earlier forms in terms of its capacity to "guard in its undiminished depth and identity the thing that it is central to."

Which history is better? Which history is true? In another context we might well ask whether industrial agriculture is more or less repressive than admittedly repressive manorial and slave-based systems or family farms with rigid gender roles. These are appropriate and wholly legitimate moral inquiries. They might lead us to revise and update the characterization of libertarian, egalitarian, and utilitarian lessons we derived from *The Grapes of Wrath*. But these questions, important as they are, must be deferred in the present context. In contrast to these moral inquiries, Berry, Borgmann, and Strong are urging us to pay attention to the disappearance of place, the dissolution of community, and the dissipation of human virtue. Perhaps the liberation we associate with industrial society compensates for these losses in some sense, but we cannot even raise that question until we understand that these losses have occurred and begin to value them appropriately. Farming has a history in which the focal character of land has plasticity subject to biological, technological, and economic constraints. The circumstances of nineteenth- and early-twentieth-century farming in most of North America were conducive to farming as a focal practice. Because many people farmed under this regime, virtually everyone had only a few degrees of separation from the land. Farming can, under those circumstances, be a focal practice for society as a whole. It unifies social practice even for those who do not farm. Contemporary industrial agriculture is not conducive to farming as a focal practice. Borgmann's device paradigm coupled with Berry's account of agricultural technology gives us the words to explain why.

Industrial Agriculture and the Device Paradigm

Farming in the industrial age becomes thoroughly preoccupied with devices that stand between person and task, person and land. John Steinbeck anticipated this aspect of the device paradigm when he wrote that the tractor prevents its driver from "seeing the land as it is." Since Steinbeck's era, precision farming connects tractor devices to detailed information about fields through computer records and GPS devices. This technology can improve management practices and reduce environmental impacts, since chemicals are applied in measures precisely calculated to soil conditions at a specific location in the field.[4] Yet this combination of technology is also a classic example of Borgmann's device paradigm. Like the central heating unit, precision farming solves problems that hitherto required a significant amount of skill and effort. Whereas "knowing one's land" was once a critical element of good farming, any idiot with a GPS device can buy the management skills associated with precision farming. This kind of commodification weakens farmers' self-reliance and deepens dependencies on the farm input supply industry.

In a preindustrial dairy, the farmer knew each cow as an individual and addressed the animal's health and productivity as a focal practice. In fact, the size of a traditional dairy was constrained by the farmer's ability to manage complex information. The more cows a farmer had, the more things there were to remember or record with pencil and paper. The traditional dairyman or -woman had a number of tools—feed rations, forage management, nutrient cycling, genetics, and veterinary medicine among them—to employ in successful dairying. Even by 1950, however, some of these tools had become rather device-like, animal drugs being a prime example. Yet most still required skill and judgment in their application, as well as a resolute dedication to the animals. In an industrialized dairy, cows wear bar-coded ear tags that are read by a computer as the cow walks through the automated milking stall. Drugs and feed rations are metered by the computer, and milk production data are recorded automatically. When a cow ceases to be productive, the computer marks it for culling. Only the number of gigabytes limits the computer's "husbandry." The farm and the cow as focal things recede behind a veil of devices that manipulate animals, feed, and manure in the economically efficient production of milk.

One might even say that the philosophical history of farming came to an end with industrial technology. From the beginnings of agriculture until the present age, changes in culture mirrored changes on the land. Human communities that depended on agriculture formulated basic patterns of thought and practice within the technological parameters of survival through farming. For many—including many among the elite classes—much of their waking lives was spent in attentiveness to the land and in the direct application of hand tools to land, crops, animals, and the focal things of household life, including the hearth. The shift from itinerant cropping or pastoralism to permanent agriculture was an existential change involving a transformation of the daily texture of individual and communal life. The shift from feudal and manorial agriculture to family and then capitalist production was also a transformation of an entire civilization's way of being. The very essence of human life consists in the passing moments of a person's lifetime. When innovations such as the moldboard plow or the shift from fallowing to forage crops restructure the way time is passed, people—who and what they are—become transformed in a way that has the deepest possible spiritual significance.

According to Norman Wirzba, embodied experience suffered from centuries of neglect due to the influence of the mind-body dualism of René Descartes (1596–1650). Only in the twentieth century did philosophy and theology begin to recover a renewed understanding of the whole person. Wirzba believes it is only natural that we should now return our attention to agrarian themes. In an age when innovations such as the computer have introduced enormous changes in the way many people pass their hours, it is all the more tempting to ignore the body, to imagine "being" as a scene played out by flashing lights before a disembodied mind. But in the agrarian world, throughout every episode of technological transformation, physical work on the land dominates human experience. Virtually everyone *feels* the give-and-take between land and food production in their bones. Philosophical conceits identifying self with mind and denigrating the body do not cut deeply in such a world. Yet how isolated are we from that give-and-take today? The story of humanity's being as told through changes in physical work regimes—historically, farmwork— appears to have ended in our era.

If we accept Berry's telling, the historical development of farming reached its apogee under early capitalism and at a time when the Industrial Revolution was well under way. The farming he praises is undercut by a gradual transformation and commodification of agriculture. Farming's capacity to unify the world and to guard its essence has been drastically reduced. Today, farming might be focal in the way that running or golfing might be focal—as a hobby or life activity for a few. It no longer seems to possess a focal power to unify society and culture.

The Culture of the Table

To Borgmann's credit, his critical discussions of modern life have always been accompanied by concrete suggestions for reform and positive action. Previous writings discussed participation in sporting activities, wilderness hiking or camping, and musical performance. In *Real American Ethics,* Borgmann adds a discussion of "the culture of the table" to that list. He suggests that becoming more deeply involved in the preparation and consumption of one's food can serve as an antidote to the spiritual alienation rampant in contemporary American life. This means, at a basic level, simply learning to cook and appreciate good food, but Borgmann sees these steps as significant because they open the way to further engagements of an extraordinarily diverse sort. Dining with friends and family grows into a rich form of sociability. Cooking grows into a craft with true elements of art. The thoughtful procurement of food and food ingredients links one with farmers and vendors in a social interaction that invites the exchange of ideas, recipes, and expressions of appreciation and mutual interest or suggestions for further interaction; it also initiates a deeper connection with nature. The culture of the table leads to new understandings of seasonality and can bring a richer understanding of place through knowledge of local foods.

The culture of the table is a direct link to sustainability and agrarian ideals. As popular authors such as Michael Pollan have argued far more effectively than I can, some of the lost richness we associate with an agrarian past might be recaptured by more resolute and attentive practices in our purchase, preparation, and consumption of food. In this connection, it is helpful to frequent farmers' markets or find other ways to interact face-to-face with people who produce food. This kind of mindful practice multiplies its benefits several times over. For one thing, it may actually make it economically feasible for at least a few farmers to live up to Wendell Berry's ideal. Buying directly from farmers vastly increases the share of the food dollar that winds up on the farm. But what you can learn from even a brief encounter with farmers will be far more valuable. With a little luck, you may brush up against someone who is actually living out a life premised on self-reliance and stewardship.

At a minimum, you will learn what is in season, for farmers are not shipping produce in from Chile or China so that you can eat fresh tomatoes in the dead of winter. Learning what is in season is the first stage of reconnecting with natural cycles. Learn to look forward to those tomatoes that are available only in late summer or those peaches that are available at different times in different regions. Anticipation and patient waiting themselves become a form of resoluteness that guards the ability of these foods to bestow joy, meaning, and grateful appreciation on those who eat them. I am not a zealot about this, by the way. Have a winter tomato or two. Once focal anticipation of seasonal foods has become part of your being, they will only serve to heighten your appreciation for foods more authentically expressive of time, place, and the person who grew them.

There will likely be some nutritional and health benefits as well. Pollan tells us to eat around the edge of the grocery store where most of the fresh meats, vegetables, and dairy products are found. Avoid the center aisles, home of highly processed and often the most fattening foods. As Joan Dye Gussow has long argued, a diet of whole foods—foods that have not been cooked, dehydrated, or otherwise dismembered before they get to your kitchen—will likely repay dividends to your health. This has now become standard dietary advice, and there is little point in repeating it ad nauseam. Perhaps I shouldn't mention it at all. Although I certainly have no desire to prevent people from eating healthily, my primary message is that obtaining and eating foods should be seen as an intrinsically valuable and meaningful aspect of one's life. Stressing the health angle may put too much emphasis on a derivative value.

A more extended set of focal practices allows one to encounter new foods and new ways to prepare and enjoy old foods. During the last several decades, Americans from all social classes have become aficionados of numerous global cuisines—Chinese, French, and Italian being almost universal. Most of us have gone further, encountering mole sauces, pad Thai, sushi, falafel, souvlaki, and delicacies associated with Latin America or Africa. All this is well and good, but at the same time, the American diet has become radically attenuated in terms of the whole foods that most people recognize and prepare. This makes us less self-reliant, less knowledgeable about what does and could nourish us, and less competent in the kitchen, an area of the house where opportunities for focal practice abound. Frequenting the farmers' market is a step toward curing that deficiency, and signing up for a community-supported agriculture project almost forces one to do so.

It is also true that simply talking about the culture of table can have edifying results. A discussion of *Real American Ethics* at the April 2007 meeting of the American Philosophical Association illustrated the philosophical and ethical potential of these connections. A member of the audience speculated that the culture of the table represents an elitism in Borgmann's work, suggesting that the meal a poor family in New York City eats at McDonald's may be very rich in symbolic engagement, a rare opportunity, and one that should not be denigrated.[5] Borgmann's verbal response defended his focus on the middle class in articulating his view of food culture and focal practice. It is clear that Borgmann's intention is to provoke a personal response from his readers—readers who are, in turn, members of an economic class in which consumption activities are often a response to advertising or other forms of cultivated demand.

Are Focal Practices Elitist?

Borgmann's introduction of the distinction between economic and moral commodification is intended to distance his core argument from Left-Right political dichotomies and Marxist discussions of commodification. His response to the individual who saw elitism in his position echoes that goal. Borgmann and I share a deep belief in the need to consider more carefully real things, material practices, and the way tools and techniques alter them. We agree that a large part of the social theory devoted to commodities and commodification has neglected the philosophy of technology. But there is also an important sense in which technology *is* implicated in the spread of market relations that has been a focus of Left-leaning social critique, and it is important to understand why.

We can disambiguate aspects of the device paradigm by noticing that a new technological device or means can also change the alienability, rivalry, and exclusion cost of goods and services that people need. *Alienability* refers to the way goods can be separated one from another or from the person of their creator. For instance, recording technology allows a musical performance to be alienated from the time and place in which it originally occurs, and this creates a new kind of good that can potentially be sold. *Rivalry* refers to the way goods have incompatible uses, forcing people to the market to buy them more frequently. The creation of so-called terminator seed, which can be used to grow a commodity crop but not saved and replanted next year, is a classic example of a technological transformation that increases the rivalry of goods. *Exclusion cost* is simply the cost of keeping others from accessing a good. Fences are the classic technology of exclusion, and better locks or better means of encoding an electronic file lower the cost of excluding others from using the goods protected by these technical means.

Such changes can and do contribute to what Borgmann calls economic commodification, the process of marketization whereby greater portions of our lives become regulated by monetized exchange relations. They do this in numerous ways, but a few points will suffice to establish the general idea. First, only alienable goods can be bought and sold in cash transactions that are the paradigm of commodity exchange. There are complex relations of reciprocity in all human encounters and institutions. But a simple cash sale implies that when the requisite sum of money is handed to the seller and the good is handed over to the buyer, the transaction is finished. Each party has total control and use of what they have obtained through the exchange. This cannot happen if the good being sold is somehow tied to the person of the seller or to other things that are not subject to the terms of the exchange. Making one good separable from another makes it possible for the first good to be bought and sold in situations in which the second good is not. Second, people who have goods that can be used over and over or in multiple ways do not need to obtain new goods. Rivalry affects a potential buyer's need to participate in market exchange. A farmer who can either plant a seed or eat her seed need not return to the market next year when the new crop is ready to set. The terminator gene forces farmers into seed markets when it is time to plant. Third, goods with high exclusion costs tend not to be bought and sold simply because if one cannot limit others' access to these goods, people have no incentive to buy them.

Borgmann's contrast between the hearth and the central heating system illustrates these three concepts. Both produce heat, but heat from the hearth is bundled with numerous other goods, as well as some nuisances. The hearth heats the space inside a traditional home, but it also provides an organizing center to household activities. Some have argued that the hearth's ability to order and structure the attention of family members has now been taken over by the television set. The hearth also provides heat for cooking and drying the laundry. In homes with central heating systems, these goods are no longer bundled together. The hearth also ties heating to work activities such as cutting wood or shoveling coal. The technology of the central heating system allows one to alienate space heating from cooking and clothes drying, as well as from the structuring of household life. These have now become totally distinct goods, and the work that procured them has been replaced by anything that brings in money. Furthermore, heat for cooking, clothes drying, and space heating is now consumed in each separate use and is not transferable from one task to another. The modern home owner must go to the market (that is, pay the utility company) for each of these distinct and vital uses of heat. Finally, the technology for delivering electricity or natural gas for a central heating system makes the provision of heat a good with low exclusion costs. This means that it is not very costly for the owner of the gas or the electricity to control who has access to it. In contrast, the owner of a woodlot might find it difficult to control others' access to firewood, whether on his own lot or elsewhere. Such an owner might need expensive fences or night guards to keep out trespassers and would likely rely heavily on support from the sheriff or police. And firewood is often widely available for the taking, in any case. The technology of modern utilities replaces the need for laws and police to exclude unauthorized use. Electricity and natural gas are available *only* as commodity goods that can be obtained by purchase in a market.

In an example such as the central heating system, there may appear to be a tracking relationship between technological devices and economic commodification, but this is not always the case. A technology such as the Internet may reduce rivalry and raise exclusion costs, meaning that goods such as musical recordings, images, and texts posted on the Internet are often bought and sold much *less* frequently than they were in the past. But as Borgmann himself notes in a brief response to critics, this does not mean that surfing the Internet becomes a focal practice. In fact, the most important thing about the way technical change affects economic commodification is that such changes typically escape the political process, where democratic control and deliberative debate might raise questions about their impact on our character and quality of life, as well as more conventional political concerns such as rights and distributive justice. Unlike technical changes, changes in law and policy are much more likely to be viewed as political and to become the focus of deliberative debate.

I do not think we can dispense with the old debates between the Right and the Left quite as handily as Borgmann appears to think. The idea that efficiency is a social desideratum—perhaps the only truly social desideratum—continues to be extremely influential in American thought, despite withering philosophical critiques from the likes of Alisdair MacIntyre and Charles Taylor. It was resisted by earlier theorists such as Marcel Mauss (1872–1950), who argued that social realities were much thicker than advocates of efficiency suggested, and the attenuated notion of subjectivity implied by the rationally optimizing decision maker was a distortion. This critique was represented as Marxist when it went on to claim that such distortions were particularly useful to the forces of capital, which sought an expansion of the market model in the hope of economic gain. Today this critique is an important part of the resistance to globalization, and those who have a dog in that fight would do well to familiarize themselves with the account of commodification Borgmann has been developing for the past twenty-five years. To the extent that food system activism, the revival of farmers' markets, and eating locally are seen as elements of that resistance, the culture of table is relevant as well.

None of this implies that we should chide a resource-challenged family that elects to have an outing at McDonald's. Indeed, it is not the *occasional* meal (understood here both as marking a particular occasion and as comparatively infrequent) that is the problem for rich or poor. The food culture problems of depressed urban areas have more to do with a lack of access to fresh fruit and vegetables or, indeed, to any reasonably priced source of ingredients for a healthy diet. Within this context, frequent rather than occasional fast-food meals may be economically rational. Nevertheless, it is not as if residents of the food deserts that dot the inner core of many American cities are expressing autonomous preferences when they eat multiple meals a day at chain restaurants. Inner-city residents eat cheap, fast foods that are high in fat and sugar but low on both nutritional and cultural scales, and Borgmann's comments on the culture of the table are, again, relevant. Unlike the suburban readers for whom *Real American Ethics* was written, residents of the urban core often lack effective opportunities to make healthier and more appealing choices. What is more, the vending machines that dispense empty calories in poor neighborhoods or schools exemplify how the culture of the table is displaced by the device paradigm. But all this is less a refutation of the value Borgmann associates with the culture of the table than a reminder of the way economic opportunity and moral commodification are sometimes (but not always) linked.

Embodied Being

All the themes discussed above converge in an important set of philosophical ideas. Much of the science being done at the beginning of the twentieth century was grounded in a cluster of philosophical assumptions about subjectivity, knowledge, and the structure of human experience. Stated succinctly (and therefore loosely), scientists thought of themselves as knowing subjects, as receptors of data. Metaphors dating back to the ancient Greeks suggest that the mind is like a movie screen on which images are projected. What we "see" or "hear" is not real but merely images or "sensory data" reflected back into the mind from the real world. But who or what "sees" these mental images? Well, "I" see them, and "you" see them, but we can't be talking about you and I as embodied beings if we are talking about sensory data playing about in our minds. So to complete the metaphor, there must be something corresponding to the "I" that sees or hears, and this is what intellectuals refer to as the "subject," the spectator position implied by the metaphor of mental life as a kind of picture show.

Descartes made modern science possible by inventing a dualistic theory of reality in which ideas are in the domain of subjects (that is, minds), and physical properties are attributed to objects, or things in the material world. Subjects are the "I" or ego behind "I think" or "I see." Objects are things having a spatial existence. But Descartes' understanding of "space" was quite different from our discussion of "place." A mathematical genius, he invented the Cartesian coordinate system consisting of the x-, y-, and z-axes. It was a quantification inspired by the "empty box" idea that artists had long used to create perspective drawings representing three-dimensional objects on a two-dimensional surface.

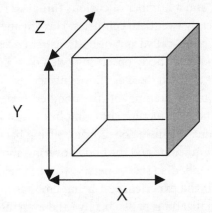

Descartes' coordinate system and the artist's empty spatial box.

The resulting quantification of the "extendedness" of things was quickly identified as an essential characteristic of real things in the material world. In addition, it is possible to stipulate a fourth axis representing time, so that physical reality can be understood in terms of a four-dimensional space-time nexus, permitting a similar quantification of the movement of things through space over time. That is, motion can be represented as a change in the coordinate position of an object as the entire three-dimensional coordinate system representing space progresses on the temporal axis from time t_1 to t_2. The picture show has become a three-dimensional moving image. The properties of things that can be mapped into Cartesian space are understood as primary and "objective"; other properties, notably color, taste, and odor, are secondary and exist not as features of the thing per se but within the perception or mind of the viewing subject, hence "subjective."

In this model, for us to know something directly through experience means that sensory data relating to that thing have been projected into our minds. If we really are just our minds, just subjects that receive sensory data from the world, then our bodies are not really part of us in any deep sense. Now, this could be an attractive conclusion, given certain religious orientations related to the soul and to life after death. The human body is understood as a kind of technical apparatus that supports the soul, the subject, during a time on earth and then falls away after death. The mind, the soul, the subject is thus what Gilbert Ryle (1900–1976) calls "the ghost in the machine." But the model does not hold up very well under critical scrutiny, and a number of curious things were noticed in the late nineteenth and early twentieth centuries. Has anyone ever *had* a disembodied experience? So-called out-of-body experiences are described as if one were in a *different* body observing one's own body, sometimes from a vantage point characterized as "hovering above." The out-of-body experience is thus *not* an example of *dis*embodied experience. The old metaphor of the mind as a picture show implies that a little embodied person—a homunculus—is inside one's head, sitting back and watching the show. But the homunculus and the body hovering above retain all the ways in which being embodied shapes perspective and field of orientation. In fact, it seems as if the experience of being embodied is carried over into artists' conceptualizations of perspective and even into philosophers' understanding of the "subject." So a growing number of philosophers and scientists began to take bodies much more seriously and to develop notions of experience and knowledge that corresponded to the idea of human experience as fundamentally and irreducibly embodied.[6]

John Dewey (1859–1952) came to regard Descartes' notion of space, which he saw as essential to modern physics, as an abstraction. Its validity lies in the way modern physics has provided a coherent theoretical understanding that is broadly applicable to a large number of concrete situations. Modern physics and the Cartesian projection of spatial objects are both true because there is a correspondence between the projections or predictions that each makes possible and the world as human beings experience it. In that sense, the Cartesian concept of space is testable and holds up very well. But this provides no basis for thinking that space is real and place is just a figment of the imagination, a projection of disembodied subjects. Notions of place also hold up quite well in their ability to organize experience and help us get around in the world. And accepting embodiment and the realness of places does not imply a rejection of truths derived from modern science. Space and place are alternative ways to describe the world. Within the specific contexts in which they are deployed, each is useful, and each can describe the world as it truly is.

Embeddedness

This line of thinking led to the reconceptualization of ideas that are directly relevant to sustainability and agrarian ideals. If people are bodies rather than disembodied subjects, there is every reason to believe that embodied experience situated in specific contexts or at specific places is significant and worth looking into. A line of thought prior to this reconceptualization and dating back to Thomas Hobbes (1588–1679) suggested that "self-interested behavior" is a universal feature of human subjectivity. That is, human beings understood as disembodied subjects have a consciousness or mind structured by the pursuit of self-interest. As discussed in chapter 7, Hobbes stressed the notion of self-interest in his political theory. When married to Descartes' dualism, self-interest becomes a pervasive feature of subjectivity. In fact, it becomes the essential feature of subjectivity in much the way extendedness becomes the essential feature of things in the world. And indeed, a generalized notion of self-interest was central to the development of economic theory. But what if self-interest is actually a fairly specific way in which human action is oriented in certain situations? What if there are other situations in which self-interest does not come to the forefront? Perhaps self-interested behavior is characteristic of people who inhabit settings where trading for advantage is habitually ingrained. But what if people living in different types of social worlds have consciousnesses with very different structures?

This question was probed by a number of theorists, including Marcel Mauss, who studied forms of gift exchange in archaic societies, and economic historian Karl Polanyi (1886–1964), who studied the transformations in work rules and rural practices that opened the way for the Industrial Revolution in England. Both began to speak of an alternative to the modern way of being in terms of *embeddedness*. The idea here is that goods and practices we think of as being up for grabs and available for sale or trade based on self-seeking advantage were simply not thought of in that way in earlier societies. Something as straightforward as wheat or rye grain might be thought of as belonging to a local village not so much in the conventional economic sense of ownership but in the sense of being appropriately situated at a given place and thus unavailable for trade on markets in other places. To be sure, English farmers who grew grain on plots they owned or farmed on a share basis had been able to sell or barter this grain at least as far back as the thirteenth century. Grain was, in that sense, an alienable good. But it was not technologically feasible for farmers to sell their grain much beyond the confines of the villages where it had been grown. As roads and canals were built, they were increasingly able to alienate these goods from local markets, that is, move them away from the local village in search of a better price.

As British labor historian E. P. Thompson (1924–1993) recounts in a famous article called "The Moral Economy of the English Crowd," the practice of alienating goods from local markets resulted in food riots in many English villages. Villagers felt that farmers' long-standing right to sell their grain was being abused when the grain was removed from the locale where it had been grown. This disembedding of a good once locally embedded by the technical difficulty of moving bulky sacks of grain was a technological commodification. The English Crown eventually had to intervene on the side of those who wished to seek better prices for their grain, and Thompson portrays this intervention as a fundamental step along the road toward capitalism. But villagers and farmers no longer see grain growing in a field as a focal thing that unites and solidifies their communal interest and fate. Grain is now a commodity good, and the social relations among farmers and other villagers are determined by the facts of monetized exchange. In this new world of exchange relations, it is possible that a different kind of consciousness, one characterized by self-interested behavior, would begin to emerge.

The Curious Place of Place

The old idea of subjectivity is still very influential in the way our social science conceptualizes place. A literature has developed around the idea that people associate positive feelings with specific locales, and those feelings translate into a willingness to expend resources or make sacrifices to preserve, maintain, or gain access to those locales. Here the notion of place is used to acknowledge that specific environments exhibit features that differentiate them from other environments. These unique characteristics afford a basis for valuations that can motivate conservation practices, create expectations about the use or purpose of biological and mineral resources within the environment, and cause social conflict when plans for development or appropriation of the environment threaten the values associated with a sense of place. A variety of techniques have been developed to measure sense of place values, drawing on the full range of social science methodologies. What the vast majority of these methods share is the presumption that "sense of place" is an affective response that humans associate either with specific locales or with locales of a certain kind.[7]

The literature of rural studies sees place identities as social constructions that are rhetorical products of various discourses conducted in connection with the control, utilization, or representation of certain locales. Paul Cloke, for example, suggests that characterizations of rural areas in terms of place are constructions that deploy the normative connotations of being "in" or "out of" place to reinforce racial exclusion. This line of thought is situated within a recent intellectual tradition that has attempted to displace conceptualizations of nature that rationalize practices of exclusion or marginalization in the countryside. Still more broadly, this literature has deconstructed the long tradition of idyllic rhetoric that has been used to portray farms and rural areas as possessing or promoting virtues that distinguish them from the evils of the city. The methodological deployment of social construction stresses the way these conceptualizations are themselves products of discourse, hence their contingency.[8] Significantly, this tradition utilizes the linguistic formulation *rural space* as the unmarked, neutral, or noncontingent term. Thus values associated with the characterization of any given rural space in terms of place become the product of discourses that construct this space in terms that favor the interests of specific parties. In either case, place is a function of sensory and linguistic representations. Space—the underlying reality—is represented as place by subjects who experience a given spatial locale in association with certain cognitive or emotional affects, on the one hand, or through the interpretive filter of certain discourse practices, on the other. Place is thus dependent on the cognitive processes of subjects. Place exists only in the mind, in the experiences and practices of perceiving or discoursing subjects. It is a secondhand copy of actual spatial locations mediated by cognitive or linguistic processes. Although these social science literatures are not explicitly committed to the claim that space is real and place is not, they do accept the assumption that the physical and biological sciences yield objective accounts of events occurring in time and space, whereas affective and linguistic representations constitute a subjective and somewhat sketchier domain, existing either privately in the mind or nowhere in particular. The contrast between the robust objectivity of space and the sketchy subjectivity of place puts "placial" attributes into a familiar kind of ontological dependency.

This contrast between place and space has also been the focus of philosophical discussion, although an almost opposite conclusion was reached. Edmund Husserl (1859–1938) concluded that the very idea of space is a derivation from geometry handed down from ancient Greece and further abstracted by Descartes, who introduced the three-dimensional system of algebraic axes.[9] The Greek conception derives from Pythagoreans and especially Plato. Pre-Socratic thinkers understood being or existence in terms of enduring or persistent presence. Existent beings are present over time. But as both Heraclitus and the Velvet Crush observed, nothing really stays the same; everything flows. Thus Plato argued that it is not the physical things before us that are enduringly present but their geometric forms. Martin Heidegger (1889–1976) argued that the erroneous translation of this doctrine into Latin by neo-Platonists rendered Plato's doctrine as a theory of ideas, creating the philosophical mistake that in turn created modern science. The notion that ideas are enduringly present before an incorporeal, atemporal subject (God, perhaps?) suggested that sensory ideas could be fleetingly present to human subjects. Whether Heidegger was right about the neo-Platonists, knowledge and reality were seen to cohere in ideas, a doctrine that became deeply entrenched during the medieval period, when academic disputes were settled by simply lining up the number of authorities that could be cited on either side of an issue.[10]

Dewey also campaigned tirelessly against Cartesian dualism and against what he called the "hypostatization" of subjectivity. In philosophy, *hypostatization* refers to the error of seizing on some abstracted feature of a thing or situation and taking that to be its essence. Thus the "subject" comes to be thought of as the essence of mentality or personality. In Dewey's case, hypostatization often carries the connotation of *hypostasis* in the medical sense: a blockage caused by a slowing down of blood flow. In real life where the blood is flowing—that is, in embodied and embedded situations—it is entirely appropriate to refer to various aspects of a situation as "objective" or "subjective." Indeed, doing so facilitates our ability to address practical issues immeasurably, and especially in cases in which modern science can be employed to address a difficulty. But those social sciences that have utilized useful abstractions to undercut equally legitimate understandings of embodied being, embeddedness, and place do us a disservice. Notions of space and Cartesian dualism are, in fact, the results of a particular intellectual history. Although any given work of history reflects the historian's subjective view, history itself is not a product of subjectivity. History is real.

Embodied Being, Embeddedness, and Place: All Together Now

We are not Cartesian subjects or ghosts in the machine. We are embodied beings. Our experience in twenty-first-century America is one of living in a commodified world, a world where we interact with one another by making constant trades. This commodification is the product of our material practice: we live in a world of devices rather than in a world of focal things. As such, the habit of looking after our own interests has become ingrained in us. Given that, it is natural that we might come to see ourselves as efficiency-maximizing subjects, choosing from an array of possible futures in the same way we might select from an array of candy bars displayed on a store counter. Given that, it is not even unusual that we might think of the store counter itself as a kind of three-dimensional movie image being projected before us. But in fact, the counter is a place, and if we are looking at candy bars, our bodies are in that place. And the place fixes and determines our experience, not the other way around. An earlier generation of humans almost certainly experienced the places where they lived and worked quite differently. Embedded within those places were a host of goods and other people, and the ways of comporting oneself with respect to those goods and people was almost certainly a function of what was proper at a given place and time.

In contrast to the geometer's understanding of space, place is an element in the horizon of actual embodied human experience. An experience is generally if not always *of* a place, and its temporal occurrence is *at* some place. Place is thus a component of the "worldedness" of our ordinary, common lives; we inhabit or visit places, and the places where we work, play, and live constitute our experience of the world. Place is thus a characteristic of the lifeworld, while space is a characteristic of objectively present reality. Twentieth-century German philosophy and sociology introduced the term *lifeworld* to indicate the domain of life-as-lived experience and to distinguish it from conceptualizations of spatial reality necessitated by the formulas of the physical sciences.[11] Within both phenomenological and critical theory traditions, many theorists shared the goal of questioning both dualist and materialist ontologies that assign a privileged status to the notion of space.

This is the philosophical tradition in which Borgmann's work on focal practice is situated. It is therefore not surprising that many of the focal practices Borgmann describes are tied to specific places. This is even truer of Strong's adaptation of Borgmann's philosophy, which focuses not on the idea of wilderness but on specific wilderness places, such as the Crazy Mountains in Montana. Farms, too, are places, as are the farmers' markets and kitchens where we might practice the culture of the table. To allow these places to speak to us, we must simply relax back into our bodies and feel what it is like to be in them. An intellectual model that defines place in terms of subjective affect or subjective discourse is unlikely to help us here. The social science that interprets place this way is taking us in the wrong direction. Researchers interested in how a sense of place might contribute to sustainability need to find a different approach.

It may seem odd that old philosophical errors could be threatening our ability to live sustainably. I do not want to make too much of the philosophical odyssey that has occupied the last part of this chapter. These controversies have brewed for centuries, and discussing them at greater length would only confuse and frustrate some readers needlessly. Furthermore, there is no chance that mine will be the last word on the matter. Thus, in closing, let us return to the central point. In a commoditized world, a world dominated by the device paradigm, it is not surprising that we see ourselves as self-interested optimizers. That is the moral burden from which we must be relieved. To be saved is to see ourselves as embodied beings and to become reembedded in a thick network of focal practices situated in focal places among focal things. Solidarity and self-reliance will come as naturally in that world as our habit of self-interested optimization is in ours. That is the promise of the agrarian ideal. But what does this have to do with sustainability? To answer that question, we must first consider the ideal of community.

CHAPTER 6

Food and Community

Albert Borgmann's "culture of the table" is offered as a practical way for present-day Americans to begin recovering a deep and sustaining moral meaning in their common lives. Food can be a focal thing in Borgmann's sense when it becomes the centering orientation that holds a number of meaning-giving activities together, providing coherence and purpose to our lives. These activities certainly include at least some dimensions of gathering, preparing, and eating, although I want to include elements of farming as well. Borgmann himself starts with the meal. As a focal practice, eating should be at the heart of our personal and communal identity, at least when we are actually doing it. This does not mean that one thinks mindfully about chewing and swallowing or even that one takes special care to savor and contemplate the flavor or texture of each bite. Becoming a gourmet might be part of making food a focal thing, but Borgmann has other things in mind: eating simple meals with friends; taking the trouble to set an inviting table; setting aside enough time to enjoy both food and company; preparing a dish rich in family or personal meaning, then sharing the story along with the meal.

On the "gathering" side of the culture of the table is selecting what one eats with care. Some might go so far as to grow it themselves, while others might develop personal relationships with farmers or grocers. Not all farmers and grocers will be receptive to personal relationships, of course, but that is part and parcel of what Borgmann means by focal practice. Focal practices integrate people in bonds of community, if not friendship, because they require us to take some trouble in our interactions. Our commerce and exchanges with others go well beyond the commodity form, where cash payment for the asking price exhausts everything the buyer and seller need to know about each other. The fact that few of us would think of obtaining food as a form of gathering actually tells a story. In the modern world, we obtain food but we seldom gather it.

I have alluded to some of the new and revitalized social forms that make it more feasible to practice the culture of the table. They include farmers' markets, co-ops, and community-supported agriculture. For example, a "cow share" consists of people who share ownership in a cow, generally to get around health regulations that prohibit the sale of raw milk. There are also buying and cooking clubs, where busy people form partnerships. They might buy in bulk or pool resources to make a special trip to some distant locale to gather a special item. They might work together to prepare a special meal or take turns preparing meals in a single kitchen and then distribute those meals to several households. Such practices accommodate tight schedules that make the culture of the table difficult, but if done well, eating can become a focal practice even for people whose work lives leave them without the time or energy to prepare a good meal every day.

My interest in this chapter is the way making food a focal thing seems to involve the formation and maintenance of community (what I mean by community will, I hope, become clear by the end). Some people take it for granted that community is a good thing, worth building and rebuilding, but I must begin by acknowledging that the very idea of community can be problematic. This chapter thus provides a little appetizer and salad before actually getting to the main course.

A Little Philosophy

One hundred years ago, it would have been completely natural for anyone with an interest in ethics to take the importance of community for granted. That consensus broke down in a number of ways and for a number of reasons throughout the twentieth century, but I will spare readers the detailed detour into the history of ideas. Given our abiding interest in environmental values in this book, it is possible to short-circuit the long version of the story by starting with a question: where do environmental values come from?

As noted back in chapter 1, the most common answer to this question has been that they come from human beings. Natural resources (or simply the environment) are valuable because human beings need them to accomplish things they want to do. This answer is not only anthropocentric (it presumes that environmental values derive from human needs and goals); it is also instrumental: it is through furnishing means to other human ends that nature has value. But what are those ends? If we are concerned with ethics, we probably want to recognize some ends as being more worthy than others. There is, again, a common answer to this question. Human beings derive feelings of pleasure, satisfaction, happiness, or well-being from some experiences or events, and they suffer pain, anxiety, distress, and ill-being from others. These affective psychological or emotional states are the ultimate source of value in the universe. Although many philosophers (including me) would reject this statement as a final basis for ethics, it is a good starting point for reviewing the ethics of the environment.

One route to environmental ethics has been to argue that nonhumans have psychological and emotional states too. Animals deserve moral consideration because, like humans, they have minds. If we take the satisfaction or distress of all minded creatures to have moral significance, then we have direct moral duties to nonhuman animals. What is more, on this basis, many parts of nature, such as nonhuman animal habitats, have added instrumental significance. That is, an ecosystem or environment might be valuable not only because humans find pleasure or satisfaction in it or because they need it to live but also because woodchucks, wildebeest, and wolverines derive mental satisfaction from living there. One can go a long way toward developing a robust environmental ethics with this way of thinking, and it is one way of developing a nonanthropocentric view without having to challenge the idea that values have their ultimate source in the minds of creatures.

But lots of environmentalists see things very differently. It is not simply that habitats are valuable because they create positive feelings in people and other animals; the earth is valuable *in itself.* Nature has intrinsic value, not just instrumental value for minded creatures. Richard Sylvan (1935–1996), one of the founding figures in environmental philosophy, developed an argument for this view in one of the first philosophical papers devoted to environmental themes. Imagine, he suggested, that you are the last person on the planet. Is it okay for you to destroy natural ecosystems simply for your own amusement? Assume, in other words, that no other human minds will experience distress. Does this make destruction of nature a morally acceptable act? Many people think not, and this, Sylvan argues, implies that they think of nature as having more than instrumental value for humans. They think of nature as having intrinsic value. Ever since Sylvan made this argument, environmental philosophers have tried to develop an account of intrinsic values in nature. Often their strategies involve identifying sources of order or organization in natural systems and attributing intrinsic value to those sources of order or to the systems themselves. As we saw in chapter 1, this line of thinking can lead to the dogma of environmental impact, but for now, we will turn in a different direction.

A Kantian Approach to Intrinsic Value

None of this suggests that the idea of community would be important in environmental ethics, but one widely read environmental philosopher, Mark Sagoff, has a view that involves community in a fundamental way. Sagoff describes himself as a Kantian. By this he means that his entire philosophical approach to environmental issues relies on philosophical doctrines established by Immanuel Kant (1724–1804) in three books published between 1781 and 1790. The first doctrine holds that scientific forms of inquiry into the causes of things cannot, by their very nature, ever be the basis of values or support judgments of value. Kant's argument is developed throughout a long and notoriously difficult book, and I have no intention of becoming embroiled in this aspect of Sagoff's view here.[1] Note that anyone inclined to think that the psychological or emotional reactions of conscious or minded beings are the ultimate source of value in the universe would probably agree with this position, but that is not what is important about Sagoff's view in the present context.

The second doctrine is that logically rigorous introspection can give us absolute certainty with respect to our moral duty toward other autonomous beings. Lots of philosophical apparatus is needed to specify what an autonomous being is, but the concept clearly covers adult human beings with normal mental capacities. Kant did not think that it included nonhuman animals, but this point, like Kant's views on causality, is neither here nor there in the present context. What matters for Sagoff is that laws, regulations, and moral prescriptions that address harm to people through pollution or environmental degradation rest on a secure, if wholly anthropocentric, basis. Science is useful in helping us see how other people can be harmed, and in this way, science is important for environmental ethics and policy. But *harm* implies a value judgment that science cannot supply. In the case of harm to other human beings, the value dimension comes from commitments we must make if we are to reason ethically in a logically consistent manner.

But unlike some anthropocentrists, Sagoff also thinks that we *do* have duties to preserve nature in the form of national parks and forests, wilderness areas, wildlife species, and natural habitats, and that we have such duties because these things have intrinsic value. Since Sagoff's views on the limitations of science seem to rule out the possibility that we could discover intrinsic value through empirical inquiry, where does the intrinsic value of nature come from? Sagoff believes that Kant answers this question in his third book in the series, *The Critique of Judgment.* Many philosophers read this as a work on aesthetics in which Kant tells us how we develop standards of good taste in music or paintings. A judgment of quality in art implies more than just "I like it." It implies that anyone who participates in the music or art community can recognize and appreciate a quality piece, even when it does not appeal to their personal taste. Works of art are said to have intrinsic value; their value does not lie in the pleasure they give us. Indeed, it is we who should strive to develop good judgment so that we can appreciate this value, even when it does not elicit a feeling of pleasure or satisfaction.

In a similar way, we can and do extend notions of aesthetic beauty to nature. Just as it would be wrong for the last person alive to wantonly destroy the *Mona Lisa* or Picasso's *Guernica,* it would be wrong to destroy natural things that have qualities of beauty, dignity, or nobility. This is exactly what Sagoff means when he says that wilderness areas or endangered animals have intrinsic value. It is a meaning that is fully consistent with Sylvan's "last person" argument for intrinsic value, but it is very different from those who would reach a nonanthropocentric ethic by finding some feature in animals, habitats, or the environment at large that is the source of their intrinsic value. It becomes possible to speak about intrinsic value in nature because communities of nature lovers, environmentalists, or perhaps just plain citizens can appreciate the intrinsic value of an undeveloped seashore even when they have no personal interest in going to the beach.

Value and Community

[handwritten annotation: Community = ability to communicate with one another]

This may be a persuasive account of intrinsic value and aesthetic judgment, but it presents an interesting problem for moral ontology. Where do these values come from? Evidently not from the paintings or musical performances themselves. No description of their natural properties will ever produce a value judgment. Nor do they come from the pleasure that aesthetes take in them. For one thing, noting such pleasure is just stating an empirical fact about aesthetes. If Kant's first critique is correct, simply stating facts about human beings can never form the basis for a value judgment. For another thing, the whole point of these judgments of taste lies in the way they transcend the taste of any individual, reflecting the collective or communal judgment of the whole. So here we have a value that seems not to come from any kind of mindedness, except insofar as we would be comfortable talking about the community itself as forming some kind of mind.

Philosophers of the nineteenth century were extremely comfortable with this kind of talk. After Kant, Hegel rather famously took issue with Kant's claim to have founded our duties to autonomous beings based on rational certainty. He was more comfortable with the idea that even our obligations to other people reflect a kind of community consensus based not on logic but on the actual historical evolution of European society. Later Hegelians such as T. H. Green (1836–1882) and F. H. Bradley (1846–1924) developed ethical systems that seemed to take expressions such as "the spirit of the people" or "the spirit of the times" with utmost seriousness. [They tended to characterize human beings' moral insight as having a limited and fallible capacity to partake in flashes of this transcendent spiritual consciousness, as someone might take a sip of water from a flowing spring] In such instances, the individual mind achieves momentary harmony with the greater collective mind. And of course, the *transcendental* in the transcendentalism of Emerson and Thoreau may have implied something similar in their thinking.

For a lot of reasons, this kind of robust idealism waned throughout the twentieth century. Fascist and Soviet communist abuse of phrases such as "spirit of the people" was not the least among them. Within the social sciences, one wave of thinking stressed methodological individualism, or the dogma that all value statements must be definable in terms of the psychological states of individual minds (individual persons). Other than the aforementioned political abuses, little argument was ever given for this dogma. What is more, it makes mincemeat of the very idea of taste in art. And as contemporary environmental philosopher Bryan Norton has argued, this dogma has been nearly as destructive in our political lives as were the collectivist abuses it was invoked to counter. Another wave of social theorists takes the view that, like the word *nature,* *community* is simply a social construction. This means that there is no "there" for either of these words. Rather than referring to anything, both simply reflect patterns of linguistic practice and, as such, appear to be totally up for grabs. Powerful actors impose a particular way of talking and thinking about nature or community, but these patterns simply reflect the political and economic aims of those actors themselves. We would be wise, in the view of this social science, to be skeptical of any normative or ethical claims advanced on the authority of the community.

Sagoff himself rejects the robust nineteenth-century conceptions of community. He follows Wilfrid Sellars (1912–1989) in wanting to take our moral ontology "back to Kant." I am uncertain enough about Kant to be cautious in attributing anything I say here to him.[2] Like the social constructionists, Sellars views the relevant understanding of community as a reflection of linguistic practices. Unlike them, he does not think it possible to get "outside of language" in order to make comments on it, and consistent with remarks on subjectivity in the preceding chapter, he is skeptical of Cartesian dualism. Here is a very rough sketch of his approach: Linguistic competency (for instance, the ability to speak French or to converse about theories in particle physics) implies a group of people who share relevant language abilities. These abilities are elastic; they assume the shape they have through usage. Ideas about particle physics change in part because of the way people in the linguistic community of particle physicists talk to one another. Linguistic competency is also implicit in thought itself. At least some aspects of thinking involve talking silently to one's self, and here people think in the languages they have acquired by interacting with others. In Sellars's view, having linguistic competency and being willing to follow the basic rules of conversational practice are components of our ability to think. Even thinking thus implies a minimal notion of community.

This minimal notion of community can form the basis for a conceptualization of intrinsic values in nature, as well as taste in art. Once one has learned the language of a given community, one gains a sense of what can be said without challenge, explanation, or elaboration, as opposed to expressions or assertions that must be defended or translated. Within any linguistic community, intrinsic values are those that can be asserted without challenge. Values themselves are simply expressions voiced in the optative mood (Would that Jones were here) as opposed to the declarative mood (Jones is not here). Within a linguistic community where people know Jones and what it would mean for current projects if she were here, everyone understands whether the speaker is simply expressing a personal preference (I wish Jones were here) or making a claim that others in the community recognize as intersubjectively valid (Irrespective of my own preferences, it would be a good thing if Jones were here).

Sellars's approach to ethics and values implies that many ethical commitments are deeply entrenched in the way members of a linguistic community communicate. The Jones example shows that it is very difficult and confusing to stand back from a conversation and try to analyze what is going on (and if you think that's bad, try reading some of Sellars's work). But when people inhabit their language rather than trying to step out of it and examine how it works, things go relatively easily. People who are interested in or committed to sustainability quite naturally talk to one another about what is important in the environment. Environmental values are intrinsic values when no member of this linguistic community challenges them. Thus, members of the Whooping Crane Society do not challenge one another to produce a reason or justification when one of them sighs, "Would that whooping cranes be saved!" (This example comes directly from Sellars.) Challenging that claim signals that one is *not* a member of the community. Any challenge to a communally held (that is, intrinsic) value must be followed either by a search (perhaps futile) for some larger, more encompassing intrinsic value or perhaps a slow indoctrination into the ways and practices of whooping crane lovers that ends with community enrollment. Or the challenger may simply exit the community.

Notice that Sellars's approach to values does not require us to say anything about anyone's feelings or preferences. Valuation may or may not have a psychological or subjective dimension, but Sellars's analysis of intrinsic value does not involve any discussion of beliefs or desires, and it does not involve any reference to a Cartesian subject that possesses beliefs or desires. Rather, it focuses on a practice: using a language. Sellars is not a behaviorist in the old-fashioned sense of denying that anything mental happens at all. His view leaves open the possibility that someone might say to himself, "I don't give a hoot about whooping cranes." But someone who thinks that thought might not be challenging the intrinsic value of whooping cranes, even privately. The example of art can help illustrate this point. As a member of the linguistic community of art lovers, one can accept the greatness of Picasso's *Guernica* yet not care for it all that much. To know that *Guernica* is a great painting is to understand a community-based standard and accept that standard as constituting good taste. But one's personal preference may be for paintings of big-eyed children by Margaret Keane. In making intrinsic value a matter of linguistic or communicative competence, Sellars and Sagoff rely on the way linguistic practices bridge public practices of speaking or writing, on the one hand, and saying something to oneself (thinking), on the other.

Norton arrives at a similar conclusion through a different route. Norton disdains the phrase *intrinsic value* and denies the Kantian separation between science and value judgment. Norton's book *Sustainability: A Philosophy of Adaptive Ecosystem Management* begins by observing that environmental policy making often founders on scientists' inability to overcome differences in perspective that are the result of the disciplinary jargon in which they speak and think. Norton says that philosophers' unique contribution to environmental policy is transforming these different modes of thinking and talking into ordinary language. Only when scientific terms and findings can be stated in language accessible to all do we have any hope of agreeing on environmental goals. Norton makes this argument very early in his book, and readers may not appreciate its significance. Although it is obvious that policy makers and politicians must translate scientific findings into something that approximates ordinary language, Norton is claiming something more. He, like Sagoff (and Sellars), argues that participation in the process of language building through ordinary conversations and debates actually *creates* a form of public, intersubjective value that goes beyond individual preferences. When scientists carry on isolated disciplinary conversations, they create value commitments, but the language in which these conversations occur precludes more broadly shared understandings. Because the conversations about ecology, economics, toxicology, and public health are all distinct, each with its own technical vocabulary, there is little basis for the creation of shared values. So, unlike Sagoff, Norton sees the activity of science as deeply embroiled in values talk. Like him, however, Norton sees environmental values as reflected in the linguistic practice of a community.

All manner of shared meanings and experiences can create limited and overlapping communities of speech and practice in this sense. Environmentalism, for Sagoff, does best when it aligns itself as much as possible with very broad sources of community. He argues that national heritage and cultural identity are foremost among these, so we can cultivate a sense of environmentally oriented community by visiting shrines and monuments (which appear frequently in the titles and text of Sagoff's articles) and by making a pilgrimage to Yosemite or Yellowstone. In situations of conflict, we can build narrow and local sources of community through dialogue, discussion, and debate. This leads both Sagoff and Norton to agree that participatory methods of environmental decision making are critical for environmental ethics. Or more broadly, we can conduct a more open conversation through our arts, our political campaigns, and, indeed, our philosophy. All these humanistic activities build linguistic (and practical) capacities in which some form of community is implicit.

One abiding idea of agrarian thought is that food practices—Borgmann's culture of the table—are a potent source of community in Sagoff's sense. This means that community is not solely about linguistic competence; shared experience matters as well. Worries about social construction or the multiple, contested meanings assigned to community abound in the respective social sciences where food and food practices have been studied. These worries have a place, but they must be set aside in the present context. We cannot escape our language to develop a master theory of constructed subjectivity any more than we can escape eating to understand food. An effective culture of the table can be served by environmental philosophy only when we inhabit our own language as Sagoff (and Sellars) would have us do, hoping to discover sources of community not only in our speech and writing but also in material practices that build both connections and barriers among potential neighbors and fellow travelers. It is in this spirit, then, that we return to food.

The Community-Food Connection

Connecting food with community is actually a commonplace. A community event without food is rare, and the bonding people experience when sharing food and drink underwrites a number of diverse human institutions. The family table, dinner and a movie, the church supper, the wedding banquet, and the business lunch are icons of sociability, each centering on a meal but implying distinct forms of common interaction and shared meaning among human beings. Thanksgiving dinner is one of the most richly symbolic meals for Americans, reenacted annually as a performance of community on many levels. Partaking in this annual meal links people to friends and family, as it ties us to those who have gone before. As a national celebration, Thanksgiving commemorates the encounter between Native Americans and European settlers in a mode that promised a new community emerging out of distinct traditions, even as it celebrated the Pilgrims' success in reestablishing their religious community on new soil. If the encounter between Europeans and Native Americans was not so happy in its particulars, this need not cloud Thanksgiving's positive vision of community that the sharing and blending of new and old foods, strange and familiar traditions, portend. All these symbolic sources feed into Borgmann's culture of the table, but where do these values come from?

The sociability that occurs in connection with food has an anthropology and a sociology, but does it have an ontology or an ethics? Let us begin with anthropology in search of philosophical significance. Claude Fischler's work provides a promising start. Fischler's social psychology assigns food consumption to the realm of "magical thinking," which he derives from Marcel Mauss. Magical thinking is a form of metonymy that permits a number of translations and identifications. The part is seen not simply as signifying but also as functioning for the whole. Another element is a presumptive contagion whereby intimate contact transfers properties from one entity to another. For example, with magical thinking, eating lion meat transfers the properties of the lion to oneself—but not only the properties, because these function as the lion itself. Thus, one who eats lion *is* a lion—or, as the saying goes, you are what you eat. Fischler claims that this aphorism might as well be taken literally as far as food choice goes, and especially with respect to explaining reactions that give rise to food scares and risk preferences.[3]

The expression *food scare* indicates a phenomenon of widespread public concern, usually short-lived, that arises in connection with bad news about some aspect of the food system. Food scares precipitate an unusual degree of media coverage, immediate alterations in the pattern of food purchases, and dramatic responses from government officials. For example, the deaths of three children who ate undercooked hamburgers from a Seattle fast-food restaurant in 1993 received national press coverage. This coverage led to a spontaneous drop-off in business for Jack in the Box, as well as U.S. Department of Agriculture and Food and Drug Administration food safety initiatives to limit the risk from consuming the virulent *E. coli* O157:H7.

Although one can debate whether the public and government response to *E. coli* O157:H7 met minimal standards of rationality, Fischler's work relating risk to magical thinking is intended to illuminate cases in which events that cause a full-blown food scare in one population cause barely a ripple in another. Genetically engineered crops and mad cow disease are regarded as specters of decay and pollution in Europe, but neither has engendered comparable outrage or policy responses in the United States. Fischler's analysis is that food has a cultural valence in Europe that it lacks in America, that dietary threats are, in a European context, threats to culture and community, whereas they are seen as public health issues, pure and simple, in North America. The differential status of American and European links between food and community is both suggestive and puzzling, but for the time being, I want to probe the positive association between food and community further.

Fischler grounds his claim that at least some cultures associate food with magical thinking on the work of Marcel Mauss, the French anthropologist best known for his 1925 book *The Gift*. Mauss analyzed the Native American potlatch, among other gifting practices, to evaluate nonmarket methods of redistributing food, clothing, and other necessities of life. His analysis contradicts the view that wealth acquisition and accumulation are virtually universal attributes of human nature. Instead, Mauss argues that it is far more likely for human communities to engage in ritualized forms of gift exchange as a way to establish loyalty, indebtedness, and reciprocity. Although the archaic societies that Mauss studied engaged in limited trading activities, where exchange might be negotiated on a value-for-value basis, these activities were typically conducted with persons from outside the community nexus. Community bonds were generally coterminous with exchange relations conferred through feasts, ceremonial sharing of goods, or contributions of labor. These gift relations created expectations of mutuality, to be sure, but the terms of reciprocity were never subject to the truck and barter that is typical of trade.

Metonymy is present in gifting, according to Mauss, for the gift of food or housewares signifies a pooling of the entire community's assets. Although day-to-day control and dispersal of these assets might continue to rest with a chief or headman, the gift exchange performs the dual function of providing secure material subsistence for the entire population of the community and signifying an underlying mutuality of interest and ownership of consumable goods. The centrality of food in any subsistence society means that gifts of food are among the most common and most important in underwriting community solidarity, but Fischler's work on food goes beyond Mauss in attributing an additional layer of magic to the sharing and mutual consumption of food.

Because food is taken into the body and becomes incorporated into body tissue, it is possible, Fischler asserts, to understand "You are what you eat" as a literal truth. Our bodies, at least, are largely composed of what we have eaten. This fact licenses a reconciliation of the archaic, magical thinking with the standpoint of modern natural science. The identification of self and food is born in the magical modes of contagion and metonymy but can be translated into chemistry and biology as the modern scientific account of eating, digestion, and cell replacement. Fischler cites many instances in which this translation is made felicitously, such as when nutritional scientists rail against "junk food" by equating the being of a person with what that person eats. The moral: don't be junk.

The Moral Ontology of Eating

Once translated from metaphorical aphorism into biochemical equivalence, the claim that one is what one eats can be translated again at the level of social psychology. Here, the sharing of food associated with food festivals, community feasts, and potluck dinners underwrites a commonality of being at the deepest ontological level. If I eat what you eat, then we are materially of the same substance. If I am what I eat, and you and I eat the same thing, then metonymically, I am you. Or better, we are we, because each of us is what we have eaten. To offer the other one's food is to invite the other into a commonality of bodily being. When two or more partake of the same meal, their bodies carry forward a communion of physical substance that is real, even by the exacting standards of the natural sciences.

Of course, one should not be too hasty in presuming that sharing the foodstuffs from which bodies are constituted cannot be thought to promote or underwrite the forms of commonality associated with political or moral community. The blood and soil rhetoric of national identity rests in part on an alleged connection to the homeland. This connection is established through inhabiting the places of one's home country, and the community is built through mutual familiarity with the haunts and rambles of a given geographic region. But it is also true that soil contributes to national identity through the cultivation (literally) of a national cuisine. In eating the foods and drinking the wines derived from one's home soil, one accumulates a base of experience that, like the haunts and rambles, binds one to one's countrymen through common memories. That the commonality of memory is reinforced through a commonality of the physical substances of which the bodies of fellow citizens are composed can only strengthen the sense in which soil, along with blood, is a contributing element in the formation of common bonds.

Blood and soil nationalism may not provide the most hopeful model for community in the twenty-first century, but linking memory to the physical constitution of the body in this way provides a metaphysical hypothesis that can serve as a starting point for understanding the link between food and community. Given the literality with which being and eating are equated in this hypothesis, one should not presume that either Fischler or the various dietary advocates he cites intend a metaphysical claim. In fact, Fischler's tactic of explaining the equation of food and being in terms of metonymy and magical thinking suggests quite the opposite. People act *as if* they think the food they eat can turn them into the things they have eaten. They act *as if* eating the same thing can make them members of a common body in a literal sense.

Yet the *as if* here goes beyond what is claimed for ordinary metaphors or figures of speech. How far beyond? That seems to be the question posed by an inquiry into the moral ontology of food and community. The blood and soil conception of community suggests that there is a dual linkage. Communities of memory are reinforced by communities of the body. People who are communally integrated because they share common memories of a certain sort are doubly integrated because their bodies come from the same source. Such people are mutually constituted at both the physical and the mental level. The strongest sense in which this dual constitution can be rendered metaphysically is identity: you are what you eat. Yet it is precisely this strong sense of constitution in terms of identity that seems to go far beyond what is meant by ordinary metaphors.

One reason this metaphysical hypothesis goes too far is that what unifies in this sense also divides. To eat differently is to *be* different, to be made of different stuff. Dietary practice becomes a form of "other-ing," a practice of differentiation. Indeed, religious dietary practices have at various times been construed in precisely this sense. Articulated as ritual practice, dietary rules prevent the religiously observant from com-muning at the table of the nonbeliever. These rules for eating and other-ing take many forms. For observant Jews, a kosher table reinforces the boundaries of the religious community, effectively creating a space of daily practice into which others may be invited, though on a nonrecip-rocal basis. The faithful may share their table and may dine with non-Jews whenever kosher has been kept, but they may not consume the food that marks the non-Jew as other. They may not accept the invitation to partake in the other's traditional cuisine. In contrast, the host of Chris-tian communion is traditionally made available exclusively to confessed members of the faith; the other is excluded from the community of the faithful.

Practices of differentiation on the basis of diet thus lend themselves to forms of political and social differentiation and exclusion. Though not necessarily a bad thing, some forms of exclusion deny political rights. States commonly base regulatory policies on widely accepted food be-liefs. In the United States, for example, meat from dogs or cats violates U.S. Department of Agriculture standards for "safe and wholesome." People who do not share this cultural norm are effectively prevented from traditional food practices that may be important to their commu-nity life. Related issues of the right to determine one's dietary practice can be seen in the development of market standards for foods that are organic or that have not been genetically modified.[4] Even more serious forms of exclusion may occur when food practices become one element in a widespread system of differentiation whereby people from exclud-ed social groups are denied access to credit, business opportunities, or needed information. Here, there is likely to be a divide between com-munities that is reinforced in many, sometimes subtle ways. The legacy of blood and soil conceptions of community has been to foster ethnic hatred, to rationalize wars of expansion and conquest, and to justify theft of property, murder, and genocide. Although dietary practice is but one element in the broad pattern of differentiation that supports such forms of exclusion, these examples illustrate why we might worry that a strong identification between being and eating goes too far.

The Ethics of Eating Together

Insider-outsider conflicts associated specifically with food can arise in more prosaic circumstances as well. Those who mark themselves as "other" by what they do or do not eat may be denied ordinary opportunities for expression, inclusion, and social interaction. Vegetarians choose not to consume meat for a variety of personal, prudential, aesthetic, and moral reasons. This choice can easily create problematic circumstances of "othering." Announcing that one is a vegetarian may prevent one from participating in group or family bonding rituals, from the backyard barbecue to the traditional wedding feast. The popular film *My Big Fat Greek Wedding* makes light of just such a situation and also illustrates how attitudes of generosity can mitigate the tension felt in such circumstances, but the outcome is not always so happy in real life. Many who make this lifestyle choice receive little support from friends and family. Vegetarians commonly find themselves in both public and private settings where little effort is made to accommodate their diet. Some are subjected to hostility, ridicule, ostracism, and, in extreme cases, deliberate attempts to subvert their dietary values that rise to the level of cruelty. And when the balance tips so that vegetarians are in the majority, the carnivore can expect similar practices of exclusion.

What is happening here? If there is any truth to what has already been said about food and community, the social tensions involved in planning a common meal reflect alternative conceptualizations of the metaphysics of community. On the one hand, a strongly multitextured view of community might see community bonds resting on relationships that cut across many ontological domains. Members of a community share common memories, common rituals, common traditions, and even a common biological constitution. Eating together is a practice that unites all these ontological realms. The offer to share one's table with another is thus rich in community significance. It is not so difficult to see why refusal of this offer can be taken as an affront, especially when the refusal arises from moral righteousness. On the other hand, if community is largely a matter of mutual recognition and hope, it may be more important for the host to configure a meal in a manner that anticipates and respects the dietary preferences of the guest. Here, food preferences are seen as a matter of personal taste. They make an individual distinctive and unique. Community arises from sharing knowledge about one another's individual personalities and from developing practices of mutual respect.

A vision of community that emphasizes recognition and accommodation of difference may call for a somewhat different understanding of food and dietary practice. Rather than seeing food consumption as something that binds or separates people, an individual's ability to control what he or she eats may be seen as something approaching a natural right. People should be free to adopt standards for what they eat based on autonomy. For some, eating might be seen as a health practice that depends on individual factors such as level of activity and genetic predisposition. For others, it might be seen as a matter of economics, aesthetics, or convenience. As Wittgenstein wrote, "I don't care what I eat as long as I eat the same thing every day." It might even be a matter of ethnic or family tradition, but here, participation in these traditions is seen as a product of autonomy. The particular foods that individuals eat may matter greatly to them, but food plays a role in community only insofar as community consists of practices that recognize and respect individual autonomy.

Food Communities and Agrarian Ideals

It seems unlikely that many people have explicitly articulated conceptualizations of community like the ones sketched above. At best, such notions of community are implicit, pragmatic dimensions of their ways of life. Yet most people have fairly definite habits with respect to food. Most people eat several times a day, and most people negotiate meals in common with others on a routine basis. Food habits are both social and cognitively available for discussion or reflection. Eating together is something that people know how to do, and they can talk about it as well. As such, my hypothesis on the metaphysics of food and community can now be revised: food habits are the material practices in which implicit and philosophically complex conceptualizations of community reside. Or, to reverse the grammar, environmental community emerges as the implicit meaning of food consumption. Community exhibits a diversity of form and content that reflects the diversity of human dietary practice. This diversity has the capacity to unite and to divide, and it carries contradictory impulses that can emerge as social conflict. This is not to say that community resides only in the material practices of food habits, but the ubiquity and frequency of these habits suggest that we should not overlook them when thinking philosophically about community.

Eating or not eating and sharing or not sharing food are material practices within which community is implied or denied. The meal is the earthly home in which the spiritual value of community dwells on a daily basis. Community may have its forays into formal politics or social activism, but the habits of the table provide these forays with the patterns of interaction that ground them in quotidian practices. Arguably, it is these relatively unreflective daily routines that make more philosophically and politically potent notions of community possible. That is the hypothesis on which this inquiry into the metaphysics of food and community comes to rest. Although I cannot regard the hypothesis as proven, I suggest that it illustrates a form of common commerce among people and with the soil that might well underwrite an understanding of community that gives rise to intrinsic value in just the way Sagoff suggests. This portrayal of embedded community among people and with the earth is an ideal: we sigh and say, "Would that such a thing were here." As an ideal, it is its very distance from our daily reality that infuses it with moral force.

Like Jefferson's farmer-citizen, the local food community represents in ideal form a mode of practice that expresses our hopes. At the same time, since it is an ideal expressed as a mode of practice, it suggests that those who engage in the practice will more or less realize these hopes regardless of the interests or beliefs that may have led them to engage in the practice. Ethics is, in this model, less about doing things for the right reasons (as many contemporary ethicists assume) than it is about seeking convergence between practices that can be broadly (even unreflectively) motivated and practices that seem to have some hope of expressing and realizing aims that are, for now, specified in highly idealized terms.

In Jefferson's time, ideals converged around a mutual hope for the stability of a self-governing republic. Though it may seem remarkable to us now, Jefferson was able to express (and, arguably, substantially achieve) that hope through agrarian ideals. Jefferson was not particularly worried about environmental as opposed to political sustainability, though he did write that the earth is given to present generations in usufruct, suggesting that he may have had some insight into the hopes and needs of future generations. It is only in our own time that it has become necessary to formulate ideals that express our hope for the fate of the earth itself. The ideal of a local food community is a very new kind of agrarian ideal. At best, it anchors our hope by expressing (and, through material practice, cultivating) the first-person plural perspective that both licenses the use of words such as *we* and *our* and orients hope toward the sustainability of the soil, the earth, that binds our practice together.

This is not a sufficient articulation of sustainability, although this understanding of community through material practice may well be a necessary component of any future agrarian ideal.

CHAPTER 7

Why Philosophy Matters for Agricultural Policy; Why Agricultural Policy Matters for Sustainability

Agricultural policy encompasses diverse laws and administrative procedures that have been developed for the governance of agriculture. First there are very broad laws and regulations that govern the full range of productive and commercial activities, although these laws sometimes make important exceptions for farms and farming. The constitutional ban on the restriction of interstate commerce, for example, has important implications for the governance of agriculture, in that it prohibits states or counties from passing laws that make it impossible for farmers from other parts of the country to sell their products in a given locality. Environmental and labor laws also apply to agriculture, but many of these laws have been written to include agricultural exceptions. Though we should not forget these important framing elements when considering the governance of agriculture, they are not the main focus of this chapter.

In the United States, the main instrument of farm policy is a recurring law (passed approximately every seven years) that authorizes programs to support farm prices, conservation activities, and a broad range of agricultural research, as well as pay for key food and nutrition programs. This law has had many actual names, but it is always referred to colloquially as the "farm bill." In addition, a host of state and local laws govern land use and promote activities such as state agricultural extension services, which provide advice and assistance related to growing crops, raising animals, and processing, preparing, or consuming food. Much of the public debate over agriculture concerns agricultural policy as defined by these laws. When Michael Pollan wrote his 2008 article "Farmer in Chief," putatively a letter to then–presidential candidate Barack Obama calling for a renewed focus on local food and better nutrition, he was thinking about agricultural policy in exactly this sense. In fact, the details of these laws do not concern us here. The goal of the chapter is to articulate the philosophical reasons why we even *have* such a thing as agricultural policy.

Although it is impossible to survey all the reasons why agriculture is valued by us as individuals and as a society, we can identify four general ways that our food and fiber system takes on importance. First, as consumers of food and fiber, all people depend on agriculture for sustenance. Beyond the obvious fact that everyone eats, many derive their livelihood from producing, distributing, and preparing food and clothing. Although we are accustomed to thinking of farming as a rural activity practiced by few, between 20 and 30 percent of American livelihoods are tied to the agrifood system. Second, agriculture is intimately tied to both human health and environmental quality. What we grow and, in turn, consume affects our bodily health; where and how it is grown affects land and water and, in turn, the habitat for wild plants and animals. These first two reasons seem to be Pollan's primary focus. Third, agriculture is a critical component of homeland security and our relationships with other nations. Years of food surplus have led most Americans to take food security for granted, but international trade in food commodities is an important component of American foreign policy and a major part of how we appear to others. This concern seems to be the one Pollan is arguing against. Fourth, the cultural traditions of American agriculture have lent a moral and aesthetic importance to family farms and ranches, to rural landscapes, and to the ways of life we associate with them. Farmers have a symbolic and political significance that far exceeds their actual numbers. Strangely, these are themes that Pollan ignores completely.

It is very likely that anyone asked to rank these four reasons in terms of their importance for sustainability would list them exactly as I have here and would rate the fourth—agriculture's symbolic or cultural importance—much lower than the other three. Pollan seems to think that trade and political symbolism have come to dominate agricultural policy at the expense of food and health. But my approach to sustainability begins with the fourth and seemingly least important dimension of farming—ironically, the one that Pollan seems most anxious to dismiss. As critical as livelihoods, personal and environmental health, or international relations might be, there is really no obvious sense in which thinking philosophically about agriculture or farming itself is the source of values we associate with it in these three dimensions. We might well say that manufacturing, engineering, or medicine matter because each contributes to livelihoods, affects personal and environmental health, and plays a role in our security and relationships with the rest of the world. Surely the sustainability of our society depends on robust manufacturing, technology, and medical sectors, and it is not unreasonable to think that the agrifood sector contributes to sustainability in similar ways.

These general reasons explain agriculture's place in industrial policy, but there was (once upon a time) a rationale for an American way of life that attached peculiar significance to agriculture and rural life, a political rationale for agriculture as such. It is echoed in recollections of the "Jeffersonian ideal" and the "rural idyll" and in nostalgia for family farms and small rural towns. As noted already, agrarianism presumes that farming or ranching has special moral and political significance. Agrarian ideals assert that the activity of farming confers unique characteristics on the people and communities that practice it. Throughout history, agrarian ideals are the reasons public policy has made special concessions to farmers and rural communities. Thus, an agrarian philosophy is implicitly committed to a vision of sustainability that goes beyond sustaining livelihoods, sustaining personal and environmental health, and sustaining our national security and standing in the world. The agrarian's view is that agriculture is unlike manufacturing, technology, or medicine, although what makes agriculture different from other sectors of the economy varies from one agrarian thinker to another. My complaint about Pollan is that he is, in the end, just another industrialist. What we need is a revival of the agrarian way of thinking about agriculture.

Jeffersonian Agrarianism: A Reprise

Thomas Jefferson is easily the most emblematic figure, if not the patron saint, of an agrarian mentality. As noted in chapter 2, this reputation rests largely on a few quotations that have been recited repeatedly by political orators, agricultural activists, and policy analysts, although in the last case, the citation is as likely to be disapproving as not. One, from Jefferson's *Notes on the State of Virginia* (1781), describes "those who labour in the earth" as the "chosen people of god," though it immediately adds, "if ever he had a chosen people." Jefferson continues, "Corruption of morals in the mass of cultivators is a phaenomenon of which no age nor nation has furnished an example." Another more widely quoted passage is from a 1785 letter to John Jay, in which farmers are described as "the most valuable citizens . . . tied to their country & wedded to its liberty & interests by the most lasting bonds."[1]

Although political orators might mention Jefferson for any number of purposes, two stand out. First, the ode to farmers is frequently cited in tributes to family farmers and their way of life. Jefferson is recognized in such contexts as a wise man who understood farming in a deep way and as the founder of a cultural tradition that set the United States on the road to a prosperity that has become threatened in recent years. The alternative reading is that the passages express a "myth" that has hindered policy development. In these contexts, Jefferson is at best the first in a long line of astute politicians who cynically play to the farm audience with empty rhetoric, or he is an archaic and outdated grandfather whose prescriptions for public policy were long ago rendered obsolete.

But the actual story is a bit more complex. Both passages were written before Jefferson became president, but they reflect a point of view that he brought into office in 1801 and was widely understood by the framers of the U.S. Constitution. Since Plato, political philosophers have recognized that democracy's potentially fatal weakness lies in the tendency of citizens to press for policies that benefit them personally while shirking responsibility to support policies in the public interest. If given the chance, people will vote for benefits but defeat the taxes needed to pay for them. Eighteenth-century political debates in England and America turned on how to resolve this problem. Jefferson's political ally James Madison is credited with leading the push toward constitutional features such as the bicameral legislature and separation of powers, both intended to curtail the human tendencies that create inherent weaknesses in democratic society.

Alexander Hamilton and John Adams were political opponents of Jefferson and Madison who believed that the United States should follow the English pattern and instate a republic whose leaders were drawn from the wealthier classes. The view promulgated by their Federalist Party presumed that the English House of Lords, composed of gentlemen farmers whose interests were tied to the preservation of their landed estates, moderated irresponsible initiatives coming from the House of Commons. The idea is that wealthy landowners make a strong connection between their personal economic interests and those of the state. The Federalist Party advocated a similar political structure to inoculate the nascent United States of America from the threats of an irresponsible mob. Jefferson, however, noted that in the United States it was yeomen, rather than gentlemen, who occupied the land. These small farmers could be relied on to temper tendencies toward irresponsibility as readily as the rich. Hence, Jefferson's praise for farmers is specifically tied to the role they play as citizens.

Jefferson's vision of agriculture and his view of its importance for democracy remain sources of moral wisdom and political vitality. Nevertheless, Jefferson is erroneously identified as the philosophical founder of the agrarian ideals we associate with farming's cultural, moral, and historical value. Beyond the passages quoted, one searches his letters and speeches in vain for a lengthy articulation of agrarianism as a political philosophy. The cited quotations are therefore less relevant to the continuation of an agrarian political tradition than many contemporary commentators seem to think. At the same time, Jefferson's savvy political understanding of the link among individual economic interest, political sustainability, and the virtue of citizenship makes him much more germane to our contemporary situation than his detractors are willing to admit.

Agrarian Ideals and the Rural Idyll

How, then, can a particular type of agriculture and a particular configuration be thought of as valuable and relevant to sustainability? One common picture evokes the idyllic nature of rural livelihoods, which are said to provide an almost ideal way of life. Living in the countryside is contrasted with cityscapes portrayed as dirty and mean. Even Jefferson's agrarianism presumed that living conditions in urban areas tended to be very bad for the working class. Word of mouth could spread quickly in these close quarters, making mob rule most apt to arise. And is it not in cities that merchants and manufacturers most readily exploit the poor or spoil the air and water with smoke and waste, then seek political concessions from local governments that depend on jobs to stay in power? In contrast to this picture, uncounted novels and poems have celebrated the rural idyll, which portrays rural life as a form of pastoral bliss, with carefree living and blue skies. The rural idyll is more evident as a term of art in British literature than in American arts and letters, but the ideas are not unfamiliar.

It would be extremely naïve to accept an idyllic picture uncritically. Rural areas have historically housed a greater proportion of the poor than have cities, and many literary idylls portrayed a lifestyle that few yeomen or peasants could even imagine. But one important theme can be isolated from the rural idyll that *is* true to life: rural people do not farm, ranch, or engage in other forms of renewable resource production with the same attitudes or ends in sight that characterize the working-class urbanite's view of a job. They do not do it simply to earn a living or to return a profit on a business investment. They value the farming life; it is not simply a means to an end. Although there are exceptions, this is almost unquestionably true for many farmers and ranchers, and it partially explains why farms continue to operate despite a lower return on time and money invested than the prevailing wages paid for comparable labor in urban settings. This is, of course, not a sufficient condition for seeing agriculture as a special case. The same thing could be said of many occupations in American society, including the arts, the ministry, and (arguably) teaching.

It is necessary to give reasons that extend beyond the pleasure or subjective preference of individuals who make lifestyle choices to farm or live in rural areas if one is to defend the claim that the rural idyll should be reckoned with in considering sustainability. Such a defense can be sketched by examining two distinct ways in which the farming way of life is thought to be valuable by the people who live it. In one version of the idyll, farming is said to be a generator of good character and moral virtue. In another, farming is tied to democracy through a quasi-populist argument whereby farming families are emblematic of "the people" a democracy is intended to serve. These lines of thinking recapitulate themes that were first introduced in chapter 2, but here I emphasize two contemporary voices.

Farming and Moral Virtue

As we have already seen, the idea that farming is an intrinsically valuable way of life is both central to agrarianism and subject to multiple expressions from different points of view. If Jefferson is thought to be the patron of agrarian political philosophy, poet and essayist Wendell Berry is surely the contemporary touchstone for one of the most persuasive articulations of agriculture's moral value. Like agrarianism itself, Berry's work is not easily summarized. The synoptic statements made here summarize a longer discussion of Berry's ideas in my book *The Spirit of the*

Soil, but there is no substitute for direct acquaintance with what the man has said in his own voice.

In a long series of essays and novels, Berry argues that the personal virtues needed for human fulfillment are frustrated by the fragmentation of city life. Most Americans work to provide income that is used to support families and leisure activities that have no purpose beyond the satiation of pleasurable experiences or the signaling of social status. Children in American homes have no role in maintaining the household and, as a consequence, experience themselves either as a drain on their parents' lifestyle or, worse, as the central focus and purpose of the household's existence. In contrast, the farm family has a unified sense of purpose, simultaneously satisfying both physical and spiritual sustenance. There is an important sense in which the whole family farms, not just the head of the household. As such, the farm household is a unified social ecology unto itself that requires an economic as well as a spiritual contribution from each family member. In turn, performing these functions confers value and dignity on everyone in the household. Family and leisure exist within the integrated nexus of work and rest, each bestowing meaning on the other.

Berry also describes farming as a form of work that brings the individual into intimate commerce with nature. This commerce or interdependence with the natural world is most evident to members of the farm family in the unyielding character of their daily labor. Farmers must, he thinks, embrace toil and shun narcissistic pleasures. The traditional agrarian ideal of industriousness has vitality on the farm that it lacks in the urban setting. Nature can be a generous benefactor for those who are willing to put in the labor needed to enjoy her blessings, but woe be unto the indolent. Virtues such as industriousness and stewardship thus complement each other in the farm setting, and these virtues are the hard-won lessons of having one's future depend on how well one works with nature today. At the same time, a good farmer is constantly experimenting, constantly on the lookout for new approaches, new forms of feedback from nature. Consequently, creativity is a farming virtue as well.

Hard work, self-reliance, and openness to alternatives are keys to Berry's vision of farming, and these values are also central to his philosophy of the moral life. Farming practices that relieve drudgery, make the farmer dependent on credit or government programs, or limit decision making by stipulating a specific regimen are thus to be regarded with suspicion. Indeed, Berry is sharply critical of many changes in twentieth-century agriculture precisely because they tended to erode the quality of life he finds essential to the moral purpose of farming. The farm life is valuable, then, to the extent that daily tasks of farming reinforce and reproduce the character traits that Berry associates with a life worth living. Though it is possible to imagine other walks of life where these virtues would be rewarded, as a matter of history, it is through farming that humanity has come to know and appreciate them.

Farming and Democracy

Links between farming and democracy are often made in reference to Jefferson, but there are a few contemporary voices worth noting as well. Jim Hightower is one of relatively few authors who have revived this form of the rural idyll in recent years. Hightower is a political activist and radio personality associated with the left wing of the Democratic Party. He served a term as the elected Texas commissioner of agriculture in the 1980s and is a frequent commentator on agriculture and agricultural policy. As sociologist Fred Buttel (1948–2005) writes in his short history of alternative agriculture, Hightower became well known for his book *Hard Tomatoes, Hard Times,* a critique of the way publicly funded agricultural research promotes industrialization and fails to support small-scale farmers. Hightower's basic political philosophy is articulated in the book *Eat Your Heart Out.* Like Berry, he celebrates the hard work of the farm family, but Hightower focuses more on the farmer's role as an entrepreneur who declares independence from big business and wage labor. Hightower identifies farming as one of the few careers available to independent-minded individualists today, and it is a profession open to people with relatively little formal training and few specialized skills.

The claim that agriculture is a form of self-employment open to many is important to Hightower's understanding of the political value of the family farm. A society where economic opportunity is limited to the wealthy and well educated is no democracy for Hightower. Even well-paid upper-middle-class executives work under the supervision of bosses. There is thus a sense in which people in these well-paid positions lack the independence of mind that democratic society demands. Theorists since Plato have seen the tendency to use hard-won resources irresponsibly as an inherent weakness in democracy. The self-employed are thought to be a countervailing force to this weakness because they have developed a form of self-reliance that appreciates the precariousness of being responsible for one's own living. Having a place in the social order where the "little guy," working largely independently and definitely not as an employee of others, can make it economically is thus essential to the preservation of free thought and unfettered political action. This is not, in Hightower's thought, a form of anticapitalism. Indeed, a society lacking in such opportunities becomes vulnerable to radicalism, anarchy, and revolution. Capitalist democracy depends on maintaining entrepreneurial opportunities for all citizens.

Hightower is a self-avowed progressive Democrat, and although he has supported many liberal social programs, he sees agriculture as the primary bulwark that shields capitalism from socialist critiques. The socialist decries the economic weakness of those who work for wages and calls for the government to step in on the worker's behalf. But if one has a choice about whether to work for wages or work for oneself, one attains a means of resistance. Historically, the Homestead Act of 1862 gave everyone in America a way to do just that by choosing to farm rather than choosing to work for wages. Agriculture is thus the place (or at least a key place) in society where entrepreneurial opportunity can be preserved, even for poor and relatively uneducated people. In short, the fact that a poor person can take up farming has assured the legitimacy of American political institutions. Farming is a way to provide for oneself and one's family without working for wages and is thus an outlet for those who might be unable to start a small business or factory of their own. It is therefore a moral and political imperative to protect this outlet and to ensure that there is at least one refuge in the American economy where even the poorest can be their own bosses.

In this, Hightower's view updates a nineteenth-century philosophy that was especially influential in rural areas. It stressed the average citizen's need to be protected from powerful business interests in general and farmers' vulnerability to gouging by railroads and trusts in particular. This populist version of the rural idyll led to the formation of farm-based political movements such as the Grange and ultimately to political reforms during the presidency of Theodore Roosevelt. The importance of family farms as entrepreneurial units provided a rationale for farm cooperatives, where many independent owner-operators organized into large purchasing and marketing units that could fend off the economic power of grain companies. In the late twentieth century it also provided a rationale for many farmers to explore organic production, farmers' markets, and experiments such as community-supported agriculture, where consumers buy subscriptions from farmers and share some of their financial risk.

In the present context, Hightower's populism is most significant because it provides an alternative to the deeply moral agrarian ideals espoused by Berry. Hightower's emphasis on political themes and economic power may be more resonant with some of the economic realities in contemporary farm life. Stressing entrepreneurship rather than backbreaking sweat and toil may allow even comparatively large farmers (who are often family farmers in the true sense of the word) to climb down from the air-conditioned cabs of their four-wheel-drive, GPS-guided tractors and onto the political bandwagon for agrarian ideals. This version of the rural idyll portrays farming as a way of life that is deeply involved with resistance to the corporate middlemen, the railroads, grain companies, and banks that have traditionally been portrayed as enemies of the farmer. Populist agrarianism, in other words, may have more political bite than the deeply philosophical, almost religious agrarianism associated with Berry.

Agriculture as a Symbol

Wendell Berry's agrarianism has clearly struck a chord with many of his readers, regardless of whether they came from or currently reside in the countryside, much less whether they derive their living through farming. Even though Berry's vision of agriculture is far removed from that lived by the vast majority of American producers, his version of the rural idyll undoubtedly expresses beliefs that are shared by many Americans, both on and off the farm. Similarly, Jim Hightower's populism resonates with many descendants of farm families long after they have left the farm. In linking economic opportunity to independent-minded entrepreneurial initiative, he sounds another theme that appeals to many. There is no shortage of young people hoping to live out his version of the idyll by starting small, selling in farmers' markets, and living on the land.

This suggests that the visions articulated by Berry and Hightower have a kind of value apart from their ability to actually generate the virtues they extol. It may not matter so much whether farming really produces industrious stewards and integrated families. It may not matter so much whether farming really provides an outlet for independent-minded individuals who want to be their own bosses. What may matter instead is the resonance these versions of the rural idyll have for so many people who will never plant a pea, slop a hog, or load the pickup with fresh-picked raspberries at five o'clock in the morning in order to be at the farmers' market for setup at seven. Now, I must stress that I am not dismissing the possibility that actual work practices in farming (or even eating) might be capable of generating moral virtues. Rather, I am suggesting that the rural idyll's resonance among nonfarmers is important for sustainability above and beyond farming's actual ability to generate and safeguard moral or political virtues.

Even if one doubts the substantive versions of the rural idyll offered by Berry and Hightower, one must admit that the family farm is deeply significant for American history. It provided the backbone of American economic and cultural life for more than 200 years. Even if the agrarian ideal is no longer valid, it was surely valid once, or at least so we all believe. Even if one does not have to be a farmer to learn independence and self-reliance, the heritage of the family farm is one of the ways we remind ourselves of these virtues. Even if most of us will never farm beyond the backyard garden plot, the story of farming that lives in the rural idyll serves as a way to pass along our moral and political commitments. Thus, the rural idyll becomes a theme in children's literature, in films and novels, and throughout cultural life as a whole, continuing to serve in symbol what it once served in fact. In much the way the previous chapter discussed eating as a source of community solidarity, the rural idyll becomes a myth that serves as part of the backstory for twenty-first-century America.

The symbolic value of agriculture may seem like a fairly weak factor in sustainability. Although it is far from obvious how symbolic values ought to be accommodated in our public policy, it would be a mistake to dismiss them out of hand. The farms of the agrarian ideal form part of the cultural heritage for many Americans. It is difficult to parse the way real-life agriculture should be related to its symbolic counterpart, and equally difficult to imagine how we can measure this symbol's contribution to the sustainability of our collective life. And how can our public policies address something as nebulous as cultural heritage (if indeed they should)? The fact that we lack a clear response to these questions might be relevant to any detailed discussion of the farm bill, but it should not be allowed to make us think that symbolic values are somehow unimportant simply because they are difficult to understand. They may be vital to our feeling of community and common purpose, and a failure to address them seriously could haunt our pursuit of sustainability in ways that are impossible to predict.

Mark Sagoff has argued that symbols such as these are the only ones capable of binding a people into a true political community. Sagoff denigrates appeals to the utility of the natural world in his environmental philosophy. He argues against the rationales that economists have attributed to "natural capital," "biodiversity," or our "willingness to pay" for nature preservation. Instead, he believes that we must cast aside attempts to make us think we *need* nature. It is only when we can unite around our monuments and our dedication to sacred places simply because we love them that we attain self-understanding of ourselves as a political community. It is thus the symbolic dimensions of nature that are, for Sagoff, most essential to the sustainability of political life, to our ability to think of ourselves as forming a "we" that is capable of acting in the community's interest.

If Sagoff's reasoning on the environment can be extended to agriculture, it suggests that of the four reasons for thinking that agriculture matters (livelihood, health, security, and what I call here "beauty"), only beauty has the ability to unite us. In this statement, I augment remarks on food and community from the previous chapter with an explicitly political notion of community that is more directly relevant to public policy. Accordingly, it is the cultural and symbolic components of farming that are critical to sustaining our commitment to communal life. If community is something we want to sustain, if sustainability has anything to do with reproducing and reinvigorating our ability to live and work together, we neglect this symbolic dimension of agriculture at our peril. The stories we derive from idylls as told by Berry, Hightower, and countless others contribute to our sustainability by making us into a "we." Without that, no conception of sustainability is achievable.

I do not want to deny the importance of agriculture for livelihoods, personal and environmental health, or national security and foreign relations simply to stress the significance of the symbolic. I admit that agriculture is important to sustainability for a variety of reasons. What is more, those whose livelihoods derive from working in the food system may express a legitimate sense of impatience with starry-eyed recitations of cultural heritage and symbolic values. The further question, then, is how should such disparate values be weighed against one another, and how should each be reflected in our national, state, and local policies or in our business and consumption practices? For now, I focus on government. One way to view the policy process is to understand it as a balancing act: the producer's interest in income is weighed against the environmentalist's interest in conservation, for example. The alternative advocated by Sagoff is to see politics as an attempt to achieve a common vision of the good society, so that sustainability for all is not sacrificed to the private goals of individual citizens. Each of these two general philosophies has strengths and weaknesses, and it is useful to see how each relates to debates over agricultural policy.

Public Policy and Competing Interests

One vision of civil society is that of a tenuous peace imposed on naturally contentious individuals by the power of the sovereign and the rule of law. English philosopher Thomas Hobbes offered one of the most influential and long-lived statements of this view in his book *Leviathan* (1651). This philosophy does not deny that opportunities for cooperation and mutual satisfaction of wants exist. Indeed, the reason why it is rational, over the long haul, for individuals to accede to sovereign power rests in the benefits of cooperation. Nevertheless, the inherent competitiveness that exists between and among individuals acting in their own self-interest is thought to be so great that, were it not for government's ability to resolve disputes among competing parties, society would degenerate into a war of all against all. This was a very realistic vision for Hobbes, who lived through the English civil war and the subsequent rule of Oliver Cromwell (1599–1658). His understanding of the sovereign was also literal, meaning the living person of the king. Subsequent thinkers in this tradition of political philosophy have broadened the notion to represent the abstract notion of state power, but they have retained Hobbes's notion that the sovereign power—the government—must maintain an absolute monopoly on the use of coercion and violence to force cooperation.

In this vision, rational individuals recognize that their long-term interests should lead them to favor organized and peaceful activity; however, their short-term interests and the lack of trust in others prevent long-term voluntary cooperation. One cannot ever sleep in such a world for fear that one's property will be taken by an opportunistic neighbor. The justification for government is therefore to bring about the state of affairs that everyone rationally desires by instituting laws, the police power, and a system for adjudicating disputes (the courts). That is, government is justified by the fact that every rational person wants this system to come about. Later theorists fashion this rational desire as a form of hypothetical consent. The role of government consists in defining and enforcing the laws and policies that mitigate the centripetal forces that persistently threaten to turn this competition of self-interested parties into the chaos of a totally disorganized state of affairs, hardly deserving of the name "society." Subsequent political theorists have debated how far this role extends, but many believe that this picture places sharp limits on how far the government can legitimately interfere in an individual's private affairs.

This vision of competing interests is clearly relevant to the problems of sustainability, just as it is relevant to agricultural policy. In the simplest case, producers and consumers of food and fiber are wedded to each other by the laws of supply and demand. But they are wedded in a way that creates an intrinsic conflict of interest on matters of price and income. A rather stylized account of the competing-interests picture has this conflict being resolved in a natural and voluntary fashion by the unfettered operation of the free market. But even the freest market operates against a background of property rights and exchange rules imposed by the government. Previous chapters have examined the way important elements of our current views on property rights and the role of government were deeply influenced by agricultural conflicts taking place in Hobbes's England.

Sticking to our own time for now, we can see that this vision of competing interests and the role of public policy becomes more pertinent as different types of interests are added to the picture. Whatever we think about markets resolving the conflict between producer and consumer, for example, it is not at all clear that we should allow markets to establish how safe our food should be. Producers have an incentive to improve food quality to the extent that doing so is reflected in the price they receive, but if they are simply self-interested economic maximizers, they have no reason to produce food with no pesticide residues or microbial contamination unless they are getting paid for it. Consumers have an incentive to buy quality products up to the limits of their ability to pay and to discriminate the differences, but the trade-offs of the market may result in some (or even all) people consuming food that is unfit, either because they cannot afford better or because they cannot recognize better quality. One cannot see bacteria or pesticide residues by examining a carrot or a banana at the produce counter. Regulations addressing food safety and quality—including rules that provide for the labeling of traits that consumers desire—can then be introduced as a government solution to this conflict between the interests of producers and consumers.

The point to stress here is that regulation is seen as justified because of the inherent underlying conflict of interest. In some cases, everyone wins from the regulation: farmers get higher prices when a carrot is labeled "organic," and consumers get the quality they want. In other cases, the government simply decides how an irresolvable trade-off of interests is to be settled: workers may face higher risks from handling pesticides that degrade quickly, but the risk to consumers is reduced. The framework of conflicts and mechanisms can become very complex. The policy maker attempts to develop solutions that benefit the largest possible number of people or that offer incentives to soften the implicit coercion of regulations introduced to resolve a conflict. Often enough, conflicts are real and unavoidable. This trade-off framework then becomes the only viable model for policy analysis. However, there are alternative understandings of public policy that describe politics as a way to arrive at a shared conception of the common good.

Public Policy and the Common Good

One weakness of the previous view is that all values relevant to the policy process tend to be defined as expressions of individual self-interest. Furthermore, individuals' motives for pursuing interests arise purely from self-regarding desires. Individuals never really act with regard for others in this model. Even someone who seems to be doing something to benefit others is really doing it for selfish reasons—for status or to make themselves feel good—or so the story goes. Such individuals participate in a political process exclusively to advance their self-regarding interests and satisfy their own subjective desires. Although this picture of the self-interested individual was taken for granted in the economics and political philosophy of the late twentieth century, it was being viewed with increasing skepticism by century's end. And there have always been thinkers who understand politics in a fundamentally different way.

In fact, one interpretation of Socrates, the figure often placed at the beginning of the Western philosophical tradition, sees him as a vigorous opponent of the idea that people enter politics only to advance their personal interests. Although Socrates never denied that people do in fact use government to pursue personal interests, he rejected the notion that this is a philosophically adequate picture of the underlying purposes of political debate. The ancient Greeks understood the essence of politics to lie in the dialogue between two opposing points of view. Socrates and later Plato insisted that this process of dialogue implies the existence of an overarching form, a "right answer" that in some way transcends the personal interests at stake. Here, a person enters politics because he or she desires to become sensitive to and appreciative of the broader needs of the community as a whole. The individual does this by stating his or her own reasons for advocating a policy, to be sure, but this is followed by careful attention and response to an opponent's reasons for advocating an alternative. This process of growth and moral development takes place simultaneously in the consciousness of the individual and in the cultural orientation of the community itself.

Another of Hobbes's presumptions, that all values can be defined as expressions of individual interests, was criticized by Jean-Jacques Rousseau. Rousseau believed that some values actually bind individuals into a community, creating society as an entity that has an existence beyond that of a group or a crowd. Such values simply cannot, by their very nature, be sought by individuals. The value of preserving and fostering a neighborhood, a town, or a city is not, in this view, reducible to the subjective preference that each self-interested individual has for a secure and stable social environment in which to pursue personal goals. Rousseau's book *The Social Contract* (1762) argues that truly self-centered individuals would never be willing to contract into a state. Instead, the formation of community requires that individuals be able to recognize and desire a common good, an idea that transforms them from a collection of "I's" into a "we." This is, of course, the idea that Sagoff associates with environments and places that are loved and cherished, places that people preserve because they value them simply for what they are.

The symbolic value of agriculture clearly qualifies as one of these common, unifying goods, but the other ways that agriculture matters for sustainability, such as homeland security and international relations, can also be understood as a common interest in a similar sense. Food security involves the preservation and advancement of a common fate. It is a fate we share as a people, to be sure, but it is also a fate that we impose on others. Far from the simple addition problem implied by compiling each person's interest in trade or personal security, an adequate conception of agriculture's role in global markets involves the way the United States is seen as a nation and as an agent in determining other nations' ability to feed their peoples. This, in turn, reflects on the way Americans are seen by others, creating a cultural identity that each American must inhabit in one way or another. As anyone who has traveled abroad knows, one does not control this identity, nor is it determined by the values that individual Americans express or the actions they take when pursuing personal goals in the global arena.[2]

These departures from the competing-interests picture painted by Hobbes complement one another. Through the process of communal and individual growth implicit in Greek philosophy and developed explicitly by Rousseau, society develops a common identity—a "we"—and expresses its general will. But to hold this view of political community does not mean that one places faith in politics to achieve an expression of the general will. Indeed, the political process does not always—and perhaps does not often—serve the formation of this common identity or allow us to perceive a common good. Sometimes a compromise between conflicting interests may be the best that can be achieved. For someone like Sagoff, however, who advocates this more complex and idealistic picture of politics, it is simply wrong to presume that the purpose of political life has been fulfilled when a bargain has been struck. Rather, it has failed.

Perhaps this is the connection that makes Jefferson's famous quotations on farming relevant to agriculture today. In identifying a link between farming and citizenship, Jefferson was trying to resolve a conflict between individual interest and the common good. Agriculture was morally significant for him because it represented a unique marriage of personal and national interests. Jefferson's solution to this philosophical dilemma may not be applicable to our contemporary attempt to understand sustainability, but his commitment to resolving the political tension between public and private good is still vitally needed. The closing decades of the twentieth century saw a rebirth of social and political philosophies aimed at restoring a capability for public dialogue oriented not simply toward resolving conflict but toward developing a sense of shared destiny. *Habits of the Heart* (1986), by R. Bellah and coauthors, documents the American yearning for a sense of community and place.

Robert Putnam's *Bowling Alone* popularizes the idea of *social capital* as an expression intended to capture this sense of common purpose. Although the obstacles facing those who want to engage in and maintain a public dialogue on the role of agriculture in our conception of the common good remain formidable, the trend represented by these two books (among many others) suggests that it may be time to try.

Reconciling Philosophy and Policy for Sustainability

This chapter has taken two cuts at the problem of understanding how agriculture matters to sustainability. The first identifies the philosophical rationale for agriculture's role in public policies directed toward achieving a sustainable world. This rationale emphasizes the symbolic contributions of farming to our culture over the actual material functions of agriculture. The second contrasts two ways for approaching the role and purpose of government and the policy process. One reflects the individualist tradition in political thought, and the other stresses notions of community and the common good. From the first cut, it is clear that the philosophical underpinnings of our agricultural policies continue to rest at least partially on a vision of political purpose and cultural heritage that goes well beyond that held by many economically and ecologically oriented analysts of agriculture. This vision may be well served by an industrial philosophy of agriculture. From the second cut, we see that there is a long-standing philosophical tradition of taking this vision seriously and that this tradition is enjoying a revitalization in American public life.

This public, common, and occasionally symbolic understanding of why agriculture matters to sustainability makes agricultural policy a subject of interest for all of us, a topic for common political debate and not simply an enclave for agricultural interests. From the perspective of the common good, the question of who promotes agrarian values in the political realm is inconsequential. It is more important how agrarian ideals and the rural idyll play a role in defining our common struggle and how they provide a mirror in which our hopes and dreams are reflected. What is important is preserving their meaning rather than negotiating a deal among conflicting interests. This is not to say, of course, that public policies' consequences for the welfare of individuals or for the environment are unimportant, nor does it deny that deals will be or should be made. Rather, my point is that the philosophical aims of our agricultural policies should include the derivation and regeneration of agriculture's symbolic contribution to our common interest and to the public good. Our farm policies will, of course, continue to be influenced by the need to placate special interests, but it is no justification of a policy, as a Hobbesian might have had it, to say that it balances the interests of various constituencies.

This is a significant claim. Agricultural policy has been seen as the special preserve of institutionalized groups of producers, their organizations, the agricultural service industries, and civil society groups that have bargained with them over issues such as nutrition and access to food for the poor. These players in the farm policy game may well be reluctant to abandon the interest-balancing paradigm for the policy process. It has served them well, particularly given the erosion of farm power that has occurred as fewer and fewer people live on farms. Traditional farm groups are besieged by new and unpredictable political forces impinging on the time-honored turf of the farm bills that come before Congress at seven-year intervals. In fact, Pollan's 2008 essay was a follow-up to what he regarded as the failed politics of the 2008 farm bill. He was calling for a new way of understanding agricultural policy that involved seeing it as a "food bill." His point was that consumers have interests that run counter to the special interests of farm groups, and as such, they should start paying attention to farm politics.

Not surprisingly, Pollan's interventions were not welcomed by mainstream farming organizations. In a similar vein, my claim that we should think of how farming contributes to our sense of common identity and purpose will probably seem threatening to them. Farm groups might ask, "Wouldn't Thompson's view further erode the power and influence of traditional agriculture over the policy issues it has come to regard as its own?" Questions like this make *sustainability* a dirty word in some quarters of mainstream agriculture. It is clear that the traditional conglomerate of agricultural interests will not cede control of the full agenda for agricultural policy anytime soon. But Pollan's approach, which reinforces an interest-based conception of politics by calling for renewed attention to consumers' interests, might also reinforce the industrial philosophy that sees agriculture as one sector of the economy among others.

In fact, a view of agricultural interests as national and common ones, rather than special interests, could lead to more favorable outcomes for farmers and farm groups as well as for consumers. Given the shifting climate of agricultural policy issues, traditional mainstream agriculture seemingly has two options. One is to accept that the context for agricultural policy has changed and that Michael Pollan's writing is evidence that many people who once ignored agriculture are now paying attention. These new faces can be engaged as partners in articulating a clearer understanding of agriculture's role in the pursuit of sustainability. The alternative for big agriculture is to hold out against any attempt to redefine the terms of the policy debate for agriculture and to focus efforts on lobbying the congressional and administrative decision makers who have been captive to agricultural interests in the past. This alternative puts mainstream agriculture on a collision course with food consumers, just as Pollan believes.

But it is possible to go further. Our agricultural policies need to be founded on a conception of sustainability, and that conception of sustainability needs to include an understanding of how agriculture contributes to the common good. Agriculture both contributes to and must be governed by principles of sustainability. At the same time, individual farmers must not be sacrificed to unrealistic and sometimes contradictory conceptions of a sustainable society. This is the challenge that Americans face today. It is one that requires a renewed commitment to moral seriousness. Agriculture matters to sustainability in many ways, but one is that farming can be a source of ideals that produce and inform our understanding of sustainability in the way moral seriousness requires. In that spirit, our inquiry into sustainability begins in earnest.

CHAPTER 8

Sustainability and the Social Goals of Agriculture

In a 1983 essay on research and development policy, agricultural economist James T. Bonnen states: "Changes in society's values and social agenda, in part the consequence of externalities to agricultural policy and production, will remain an important source of disequilibria. This will require not only social science, physical and biological science, but also humanities research on the ethical and value choices that must be made." Bonnen's view was particularly enlightened and prescient not only for its recognition of the importance of ethics and values in technology policy but also for his suggestion that the humanities could and must contribute to what we now call "sustainability science." Many social and natural scientists who are inclined to agree with Bonnen might still think of values and ethics as arising from the misty depths of individual subjectivity, a region so alien to the methods of economics and physical sciences that we might as well call on the humanities, perhaps as a last resort. Although the overall purpose of this book is to respond positively to this call for a humanities approach to the question of sustainability, the message of this chapter is that even philosophers would do well to notice the account of agriculture we derive from the social sciences in order to understand sustainability.

Agriculture is a human activity that takes shape through interaction with nature and with the rest of the society in which it is practiced. All but the most rudimentary of human societies have had an agricultural component, and even hunter-gatherers practiced forms of environmental management, whether they were consciously aware of doing so or not. Although the practice of agriculture is a virtually universal component of all human societies, the purposes, goals, and adaptations that a given society is able to achieve through agriculture are quite variable. If we are to say anything helpful about the agrifood system's contribution to sustainability, we must have a clear sense of the possible purposes, goals, and adaptations it makes available. We must also understand that the goals of the agrifood system may not be mutually compatible or mutually shared by all Americans. The likelihood that we will perceive agriculture's role differently is what Bonnen refers to as "the ethical and value conflicts in the choices that must be made."

The thesis of this chapter combines two themes. First, the notion of moral value or duty derived from an introspective look at our own thought processes provides an inadequate basis for understanding the sense in which sustainability is a social goal. The focus here is on social goals rather than sustainability as such, and I examine how the agrifood system can be seen to have social goals. Second, an analysis of the social goals for any social subsystem, such as the agrifood system, depends on a comprehensive understanding of the natural and social systems in which human activities are practiced and reproduced. An analysis of sustainability demands a systems perspective. My strategy for elucidating the concept of a social goal is to review a series of proposals for stipulating social goals for agriculture. The first is drawn from the pathbreaking work of William H. Aiken (1947–2006), one of the first academic philosophers in the contemporary era to devote serious attention to agriculture. The second is drawn from a stylized neoclassical interpretation of the agricultural economy. These two approaches are compared to Thomas Jefferson's understanding of the relationship between agriculture and democracy. It is on the basis of this comparison that we are able to move toward a second thesis, providing an ecologically informed conceptualization of social goals that addresses some of the deficiencies in Jefferson's model that are obvious from our vantage point in history.

The Concept of a Social Goal

The subject of goals for agriculture was Aiken's contribution to "Agriculture, Change and Human Values," an important conference held in 1982 at the University of Florida. The conference itself was a watershed event. Richard Haynes, later the founding editor of *Agriculture and Human Values* and longtime editor of the *Journal of Agricultural and Environmental Ethics,* convened an extraordinary collection of intellectual lights from a wide array of disciplines. Aiken was known then as one of the leading thinkers on the moral problems associated with world hunger.

His conference paper began by recognizing that one goal for agriculture is profit. People who farm must more than cover their costs, at least on average. But he quickly moved on to consider the sustainability and environmental safety of their production practices. In addition, the combined output of all agricultural producers must be capable of meeting the needs of the human population and serving a just social order. Aiken argued that these goals are of greater moral significance than private profit. After reviewing all these possible goals, he concluded that meeting human food needs is the overriding moral goal of agriculture. Each of the other goals is legitimate to the extent that it is compatible with and actually serves the overriding goal of meeting human needs. Profitability can be assured, according to Aiken, by the right combination of subsidies and incentives to coax farmers into practices that satisfy human needs. Profitability is not a worthwhile goal in and of itself.

The rationale for Aiken's ordering of goals appears to be based on a straightforward principle for ordering rights and duties described by Henry Shue: one right or duty is more basic than another whenever the moral benefits of the second can be extended to all people only after the first right has been secured. For example, a right to life is the most basic right of all. It is more basic than the right to an education, because one must be alive in order to be educated. The principle of basic rights holds that a society should not go about securing the right to education for a few until it has secured more basic rights for all. In like manner, the right to subsistence food is more basic than the right to profit monetarily from one's activities. Wealth could be rendered meaningless by famine. Thus, society should secure rights of economic opportunity only if the right to food has been secured for all. Environmental pollution or resource depletion presents more of a challenge for Aiken's approach, since it is less clear how these practices involve the violation of an individual's right to life. Nevertheless, it is quite plausible to prioritize goals of environmental quality somewhere between immediate threats of starvation and more comprehensive notions of social justice, leaving the right to personal opulence as the least basic of all.

If this is a fair summary of Aiken's reasoning, he offers exactly what Bonnen was asking for: a method for resolving ethical and value conflicts in the choices that have to be made. Aiken also produced a number of more extended discussions of world hunger and of the environmental impacts of agriculture as examples of priority setting for agricultural goals. His rights-oriented approach clearly provides a logically consistent way to structure and organize a number of important moral considerations. It is most effective when comparing rights and duties that can be specified as obligations that one individual owes to another. Thus one person would have a right to pursue a high standard of living only insofar as that pursuit does not preclude him from fulfilling duties to secure more basic rights for others. For example, a farmer has the right to apply chemicals that increase the farm's profitability so long as doing so does not violate the more basic rights of others to health and safety. Aiken's essays on agriculture and the environment deny that this condition is satisfied. Here, Aiken is applying a principle of basic rights in much the way that the principle of noninterference (discussed in chapter 3) might preclude agricultural practices that cause harm to others. In comparison to noninterference, however, the basic rights approach also entails the duty to do things for others (such as securing their right to food) who are less well-off than oneself.

So given Aiken's rights-based approach to social goals, agricultural producers' goals are to enhance their own quality of life while at the same time fulfilling basic requirements of moral responsibility to others. This applies to all of us; it is not unique to farmers or ranchers. As such, Aiken's moral goals emerge as a set of standards for any intentional action undertaken by a human agent. Like many others, he is hoping to reform agriculture by expecting it to live up to the principles of the industrial creed. His priority rule provides the individual moral agent with a way to rank each of his or her actions and intentions in a moral hierarchy. Environmentally safe production, for example, is specifically described as a goal that should be achieved by having each farmer perform this ranking after being informed of the toxic properties of agricultural chemicals. Achieving environmentally safe agriculture, then, is accomplished as the collective result of every farmer acting morally, which in Aiken's view means acting in conformity with this principle of basic rights.

Some of the goals Aiken assigns to agriculture are less amenable to this model of individual moral obligation, however, and sustainability is a case in point. When Aiken states that sustainability is a goal for agriculture, he means that the entire system for producing and distributing agricultural commodities should be organized so as to minimize the consumption of natural resources. An individual farmer can set the goal of minimal consumption of natural resources, but this will not make a meaningful contribution to the total sustainability of agriculture unless many other farmers act in the same way. In identifying sustainability as a moral goal, Aiken quite properly draws our attention to the vulnerability of the agricultural ecology and suggests that unsustainable practices are wrong because they upset the natural balance. They create dangerous dependencies on fragile processes (such as soil renewal) and potentially scarce resources (such as water). These dependencies can jeopardize the stability of civilizations and the livelihoods of the people who rely on agriculture to serve their basic needs. Yet Aiken's method for prioritizing goals demands that a social goal be ultimately reducible to statements of duty or obligation owed by one individual to another. Aiken thus has a philosophical problem: he must account for an individual producer's obligation to practice sustainable agriculture.

Aiken struggles directly with this problem in an essay entitled "Ethical Issues in Agriculture." Here he describes sustainability not as an obligation the farmer owes to specific individual others but as an obligation owed directly to nature itself. In this essay, Aiken draws on what were, at the time, new ideas in environmental ethics that emphasize a nonanthropocentric intrinsic value approach. The basic idea is a search for philosophical methods that extend the scope of moral obligation beyond duties owed to other living human beings. In this connection, Aiken discusses duties owed to nonhuman animals and to the ecosphere itself. The farmer's duty to practice environmentally conservative agricultural methods then becomes a consequence of the duty to respect and preserve the natural world. Yet Aiken retains his method of prioritizing duties in this essay, making duties to the ecosystem less basic than duties to secure the survival of other human beings. He concludes, however, that these duties have priority over one's right to pursue profits. Thus his approach to sustainability is still consistent with the basic rights model for stating and prioritizing goals for agriculture.

Yet this adaptation of the basic rights model places a severe burden on the principle that is intended to resolve conflict among competing goals and values. When the ecosystem and nonhuman animals are left out of the picture, it seems somewhat reasonable to insist on a stepwise pursuit of goals that are deemed "more basic" when they serve as prerequisites to the enjoyment of more refined moral goods. But this stepwise approach yields no obvious order of ranking between human rights such as life and liberty and nonanthropocentric goods such as animal welfare or ecological balance. Why is it that a cow's or a pig's well-being can be sacrificed to preserve human life, but the integrity of an ecosystem cannot be sacrificed to raise farm income? It is possible to pursue answers to this question that tie ecosystem integrity to the preservation of human life, but that is not what Aiken or other environmental philosophers of that era had in mind. Ultimately, this ranking just depends on the intuition that the role of a pond or a woodlot in providing habitat for wildlife is "more basic" than a farmer's pursuit of profit. In this respect, Aiken's attempt to stipulate sustainable or ecologically sensitive agriculture as a duty that individual farmers owe to nature strains credulity. The more general problem is that the framework of obligations owed by one human being to another fails to elucidate why holistic outcomes matter morally. Such outcomes are the consequence of the systemic causal interaction of myriad individual acts, rather than direct outcomes framed as conscious intentions.

The production choices of individual farmers are certainly relevant to the overall sustainability of the agrifood system, and later chapters examine this relevance in more detail. Nevertheless, it is false to suggest that the actions of a single producer make a great deal of difference either way. As the discussion of the American Dust Bowl in chapter 4 shows, individuals acting rationally can collectively produce calamitous environmental consequences. Individual farmers or ranchers who choose sustainable methods may perform an act of moral courage, but they also commit a rather subtle logical fallacy if they think that they have adopted sustainability as a personal goal in the morally relevant sense. Their actions and intentions cannot achieve the goal of sustainability in the way that offering hungry people a hot meal accomplishes the goal of meeting their basic needs. Nor does the fact that individuals acting conscientiously have adopted resource-conserving agricultural practices tell us why that is the right thing to do. It is not their conscientiousness or their intentions that make sustainability into a social goal; nor are conscientious intentions either necessary or sufficient conditions for making an agriculture sustainable. One must understand sustainability at the level of the entire system in order to understand it at all. Moral philosophies that derive accounts of value and moral justification from the conscious goals that human agents have in mind when they undertake an action— that is, from the reasons they give for doing it—are severely handicapped in accounting for social goals.

An alternative account of goals thus becomes necessary. This does not mean that people cannot be "for" sustainability in the same sense they are "for" the Atlanta Braves or "for" a given candidate for president. In some sense, it is correct to point out that all goals seem to depend on people having feelings or hopes that incline them in a certain direction. But this is not the same thing as having a reason for doing something. One might attend a game because one is "for" the Braves or cast a vote because one is "for" a given candidate, but these actions are at best only indirectly related to the victory—the ultimate goal that one is "for." In fact, no single member of the Braves, much less a fan in the stands, can bring about the victory. It is a team accomplishment. In a somewhat similar way, sustainability is not a goal that any individual can bring about by acting or living in a particular way. It is a goal for society as a whole. Societies, however, are not moral agents, nor do they intentionally follow a course of action in pursuit of some good or to fulfill some duty. Ecologically sustainable agriculture is a goal that is best expressed not as a duty intentionally pursued by individual producers but as a pattern in the operation of the social and ecological system that encompasses both producers and consumers of agricultural goods. It is, in precisely this sense, a social rather than an individual goal. Powerful and insightful as Aiken's approach is for prioritizing agricultural goals, its reliance on individual rights and duties limits its applicability to the goal of sustainability.

The Market Analysis of Social Goals

The philosophical problem raised by social goals is associated with methodological individualism in the social sciences. As Bryan Norton describes it, this movement arose especially among American social scientists who were appalled by the way individual rights were abrogated in the name of social good by repressive regimes of the twentieth century. Adolf Hitler (1889–1945) and Joseph Stalin (1879–1953) justified horrific programs of extermination on the ground that doing so served an abstract conception of the social good. One version of methodological individualism arose in response to these horrors of collectivist movements, holding that social goals are fictions and that only actual goals pursued by living, breathing human beings in their intentional, goal-directed behavior have any legitimacy. As Norton notes, this doctrine has pernicious applications in environmental philosophy, where it has been used to vitiate the validity of attempts to protect and preserve ecosystems, habitats, and natural monuments. Oddly, however, the neoclassical economic paradigm favored by many methodological individualists is itself a fine source for articulating a coherent notion of social goals.

Neoclassical economic theory provides a model of producers and consumers interlinked through laws of supply and demand. Supply and demand operate through a market. The abstract idea of an economic market is a generalization of what happens in real markets that still exist in many parts of the world. Local farmers congregate in a central location, displaying their wares. Buyers—both consumers and merchants—examine the offerings, tendering money for lots of beans, peas, melons, meat, eggs, or fish, sometimes talking the seller down from the original asking price. The market for corn that exists in industrialized nations is an amalgam of technology (railcars, elevators) and institutions (grading mechanisms, the Chicago Board of Trade), but it still allows producers to seek buyers for their goods. As individual producers determine what things to offer and buyers budget their resources to discipline their desires, the market—the invisible hand—guides the final outcome by establishing prices that reflect the willingness of all parties to make an exchange. Markets perform this aggregation function more or less effectively, depending on a host of factors, but my purpose here is not to offer a thoroughly realistic or critical treatment of economic exchange. My point is this: because neoclassical economic theory yields a set of standards by which we can judge how well this system is operating, it provides a basis for identifying social goals for the system's performance. As Adam Smith noted, these are not the same goals that bring individual buyers and sellers to the market. Individuals may not have any preferences in terms of how they would like to see the market perform; nonetheless, their ability to satisfy their conscious goals can be materially affected by the way the market does perform.

Neoclassical theory can be extended in ways that specify a large number of social goals. Economists generally shy away from actually advocating these goals. The point of their analysis as they understand it is simply to point out the consequences of organizing a market system in one way rather than another. Two goals that are easy to bring into a discussion of ethics can also be described in fairly nontechnical terms, but unlike my economist friends, I do not demur to the use of "shoulds" and "oughts" in describing them. When functioning properly, the market should assure that the things people want and need to live are available because there are economic incentives for producers to supply them. We can call this the productivity goal of the neoclassical model. Second and correlatively, markets should direct investment toward the mixture of enterprises that best satisfies the aggregated demands of consumers. This is the efficiency goal of markets. I admit that my terminology is loose, but the terms *productivity* and *efficiency* are so badly abused in contemporary usage that there can be little harm in abusing them a little more here.

[Agricultural productivity is a social goal for an industrialized society because people need the food and fiber commodities that agriculture produces, and because industrial societies are organized so that the majority of people are in no position to produce food and fiber goods for themselves.]Although all of us want to eat, no one in an industrial society needs to set food production as a personal goal to accomplish this end. This is true even for farmers, who may buy all the food they eat from the local grocery, just as I do. Farmers and ranchers may produce food and fiber because they feel a moral duty to prevent starvation or because they hope to sell it for a profit. For my part, I may walk down to the delicatessen and buy an olive-pimento cream cheese bagel because I want to put some money in the pockets of farmers, about whom I care deeply, or simply because I'm hungry. In the market system, it makes little difference what the intentions of individual buyers and sellers might be. The social goal of productivity depends on how well all these exchanges are coordinated through the market mechanism.

[However, agricultural productivity would not be a social goal in a society in which agricultural commodities are not exchanged.] In a society in which everyone is a subsistence farmer, everything really does hang on individual intentions, as well as a bit of luck. Industrial society functions only because people are able to obtain the food they need at the restaurant or grocery store, and these retailers are able to provide food only because they can buy it, through a complicated system of middlemen, from farmers and ranchers who represent a fairly small proportion of the population. The division of labor in industrial society is possible because market structures assure the production of food needed throughout society in a way that releases a substantial number of people for pursuits other than farming. Modifications of our social

organization that are intended to achieve moral goals such as poverty reduction, distributive justice, an end to hunger, or environmental
protection may reasonably be expected to retain the general division of
labor that frees a large portion of the population from farming. Now,
I am not really contradicting Aiken's views on profit here, although
my emphasis is decidedly different. When he argues for "subsidies and
incentives," he is arguing for government actions that are focused on
what I call the social goal of productivity: ensuring that farmers have
the economic incentives they need to produce. I don't think that farmers
necessarily need to have people's basic rights in mind when they make a
decision about what and how much to plant, and I'm not sure that Aiken
thinks so either.

The question of efficiency is a little trickier. As we saw in chapter 3,
technical economic definitions of efficiency are somewhat variable. What
I have in mind here is that the productive resources of society can be ar-
ranged in a number of ways that might result in enough food being produced, but we want more from our agrifood system than simply enough
food. Seventeenth-century philosopher John Locke gave a commonsense
formulation of agricultural efficiency in his discussion of property rights
in his *Second Treatise of Government:* "he that encloses land, and has a
greater plenty of the conveniences of life from ten acres, than he could
have from an hundred left to nature, may truly be said to give ninety
acres to mankind: for his labour now supplies him with provisions out
of ten acres, which were but the product of an hundred lying in common."[1] Locke's claim may simply be that agriculture makes more efficient use of land than does scavenging from land left in its natural state,
although it is likely that there was something a little more complicated
going on. Locke wrote at a time when English farmers were phasing out
the practice of growing a crop on a plot of land, then leaving it fallow
for a relatively long period. While lands were fallow, the practice was to
treat them as a commons for livestock grazing. The new system involved
planting forage crops instead of leaving a field fallow, which could support a larger number of both people and animals. But animals had to
be kept off the land, or the forage crop would be destroyed; hence farmers were literally enclosing their lands with fences and walls to prevent
other people's animals from destroying their crops. Transitioning to this
more efficient system was a personal goal for individual farmers, who

had larger quantities of salable commodities, but it was also a social goal to the extent that, in Locke's words, it gives "ninety acres to mankind."

Efficiency is a hotly contested social goal because it has been defined in so many different ways. In Locke's passage, the efficient use of land is at issue. Historian Gilbert Fite advises that in North America, getting the most out of land has never been as important as the efficient use of labor. In the age of climate change, energy efficiencies have become newly important, and radical economist Michael Perelman writes that with regard to energy use, American agriculture fares poorly in comparison to less labor-efficient agricultural systems used in nonindustrialized settings. To serve as an ethically defensible social goal, an efficiency measure must reflect all the resources that go into agricultural production, but there is a logical problem, for one cannot optimize more than one variable at once. Cost efficiency may be one means of trying to reflect each of these notions, but as already discussed, it can be notoriously difficult to internalize all the costs. This criticism seems to be what Aiken has in mind when he writes caustically, "Efficiency in agriculture rests on one idea: Does it pay?" Resource economist Sandra Batie notes that permanent soil or water loss is not something that farmers pay for when they put the crop in the ground; hence it may be left out of cost efficiency calculations. Cost efficiency presumes that money is an adequate proxy for a diverse set of variables, but as noted before, good economists know this simply isn't true.

I should stress again that I am not defending an inadequate measure of efficiency in place of more substantive environmental criteria. I have already remarked more critically on efficiency in chapter 3 (as well as in *The Spirit of the Soil*). My point here is that for all its flaws, the neoclassical economic model provides a better conceptual account of social goals for agriculture than does Aiken's hierarchy approach. It does so because the distinction between productivity or efficiency as a social need and the individual goals farmers set for themselves is very clear. Productivity is a social goal because it addresses food needs while freeing a lot of people from the necessity of making food production a personal goal. Farmers are interested in producing food for a totally different set of reasons. There are some economic conditions in which high individual production goals help a farmer stay in business, but that is not always the case. In *The Spirit of the Soil* I write about religious motives for wanting to produce especially large or fecund crops, but these motives are not very directly related to productivity as a social goal. Indeed, a single-minded emphasis on maximizing yields might well defeat the attainment of productivity as a social goal, and the same can be said for efficiency.

A market analysis shows why productivity and efficiency become social goals for agriculture, but not because of what agriculture is as a human activity. Something similar might be said of the trading of pencils or shoes in markets. Beyond Aiken's wholly legitimate point that food is a basic human need, if there is any sense in which agriculture makes unique contributions to the workings of society—contributions not shared by the pencil or shoe industries—the market analysis is sure to miss them. Neoclassical theory achieves explanatory power precisely because its simplifying assumptions focus on production and exchange characteristics that apply to all forms of economic activity. Agricultural economics has documented a number of characteristics, such as "asset fixity," that make it more difficult for farmers than for other types of producers to back out of an investment when the market signals that they should. Still, the economic approach must be augmented if we are to understand social goals that derive from the kind of activity that agriculture itself is.

The Political Goals of Agriculture under Jeffersonian Democracy

Thomas Jefferson's views on the moral virtues of farming are part of the stock rhetoric on American agriculture, and it is worth repeating him. He states in his *Notes on the State of Virginia:* "Those who labour in the earth are the chosen people of god, if ever he had a chosen people, in whose breasts he has made his peculiar deposit for substantial and genuine virtue. . . . Corruption of morals in the mass of cultivators is a phaenomenon of which no age nor nation has furnished an example."[1] The 1785 letter to John Jay adds, "They are the most vigorous, the most independent, the most virtuous, & they are tied to their country & wedded to its liberty & interests by the most lasting bonds."[2] As noted earlier, these passages can be used to praise or condemn virtually any development in American agriculture, although they are best read as clues to Jefferson's views on the relationship between farming and citizenship. Nor is it clear that the contemporary tendency to read the passages as praise for family farms and condemnation for large-scale commercial farming was ever part of Jefferson's intent. Jefferson himself farmed on a very large scale. In this chapter, however, I follow Wendell Berry's interpretation of Jefferson, and I do not attempt to square his reading of the Sage of Monticello with my own.

Writing in *The Unsettling of America*, Berry ties the citations on the virtues of farming to Jefferson's conviction that democratic liberty is not only a human birthright but also a right to be protected and cultivated through education and moral development. In this connection Berry writes, "to keep themselves free, [Jefferson] thought, a people must be stable, economically independent, and virtuous . . . [and] he believed . . . that these qualities were most dependably found in the farming people." According to Berry, the "lasting bonds" Jefferson mentions in the letter to Jay go beyond those of economics and property and are derived from the effects of farming and farm life on the development of moral character. Berry quotes Jefferson on industrialists to contrast his views on the hortatory effects of agriculture: "Jefferson wrote: 'I consider the class of artificers as the panderers of vice, and the instruments by which the liberties of a country are generally overturned.' By artificers he meant manufacturers, and he made no distinction between labor and management. . . . [The quote] suggests that he held manufacturers in suspicion because their values were already becoming abstract, enabling them to become 'socially mobile' and therefore subject preeminently to the motives of self-interest."[3] Berry thus finds the farm to be a superior environment for the cultivation of a moral sense, and the occupation of the farmer to be a superior activity for the development of moral virtues. Recall from previous chapters that these themes represent key agrarian ideals. Here I stress how they are expressed as social goals for agriculture.

One social goal implied by Jefferson's view was particularly relevant to his own political milieu and was discussed at some length in chapters 2 and 7. Jefferson and the other founding fathers recognized the challenge of binding self-interest to the social good, opening up the possibility for a broader conception of national interest. In this connection, it is important to notice that Jefferson's agrarian comments are about statecraft, rather than agriculture. They presume that an economy based on small yeoman families occupying the land will be superior to one in which individual self-interest is tied to movable and consumable assets. The farmer is tied to the land. His economic livelihood is bound to the security of his lands—a theme stressed by Victor Davis Hanson in his discussions of ancient Greece. What is more, the farmer must find some common compact with his neighbors and take an interest in the long-term stability of society. [The virtues of honesty, integrity, and charity promote a stable society, and in Jefferson's context, they are virtues wedded to the farmer's self-interest.] A manufacturer (as well as factory labor) is not so firmly tied to a particular place. The artificer, to use Jefferson's term, can spoil the air, exploit others, poison the wells, and then pick up his assets and move on down the road when the business environment becomes hostile. Pertinently, a "hostile" business environment is one in which people are demanding that external costs be internalized. There is thus a more natural fit between the individual farmer's interest and that of society as a whole, and there are a number of permanent tensions between the interests of an individual businessman and those of the nation. Jefferson was no particular enemy of industry, but through this rationale he was nonetheless able to portray the encouragement of farming as a contributor to an important social goal for the emerging nation: a unified and stable economy.

Wendell Berry is arguably more interested in a different set of virtues. His point is that the farmer must be adept at a variety of skills. This fact requires the farmer to appreciate the complexity of nature and the need for flexible and diverse approaches in coping with challenges. The farmer thus incorporates one aspect of the civil society—strength through diversity—in his or her personal character. The manufacturer succeeds not through this kind of diverse self-reliance but by specializing, by learning how to do one thing better than anyone else. Berry thus lays heavy stress on specialization in his critique of modern agriculture.

What happens under the rule of specialization is that, though society becomes more and more intricate, it has less and less structure. . . . The community disintegrates because it loses the necessary understandings, forms and enactments of the relations among materials and processes, principles and actions, ideals and realities, past and present, present and future, men and women, body and spirit, city and country, civilization and wilderness, growth and decay, life and death—just as the individual character loses the sense of responsible involvement in those relations.[4]

In emphasizing specialization as the curse of modern society, he may be making an argument along the lines of Albert Borgmann's view of the device paradigm. Both describe a tragic irony inherent in the promise of technology. As devices become specialized and reliable, the need for diverse, integrated skills and social relationships recedes. As people become less reliant on both personal and collective capabilities that afford flexible and ingenious (though often laborious) responses to adversity, they gradually lose their sense of community and place.

The loss of these capabilities—these virtues—may be a key to the unsustainable nature of contemporary life. An inability to appreciate and cultivate capabilities of personal and group self-reliance may eventually contribute to the erosion and destruction of the very devices that have replaced the practical self-reliance we associate with the yeoman farmer. Personal and community self-reliance was generated by the daily household activities of eighteenth- and nineteenth-century farm life. According to social historian Ruth Cowan, the term *husband* derives from the traditionally male role of looking after the household, caring for and tending to the land. He derived this name from the house (*hus*) to which he was bonded. The housewife and husband both worked the land, hence the term *husbandry* for what we later came to call farming. Their household security depended on working together and *husbanding* their resources. The success of the household depended on a complementarity between these gender roles in order to complete a set of diverse but well-defined tasks. Cowan writes:

Buttermaking required that someone had cared for the cows (and this was customarily men's work), and that someone had either made or purchased a churn. Breadmaking required that someone had cared for the wheat (men's work) as well as the barley (men's work) that was one of the ingredients of the beer (women's work) that yielded the yeast that caused the bread to rise. . . . Women nursed and coddled infants; but men made the cradles and mowed the hay that, as straw, filled and refilled the tickings that the infants lay on. Women scrubbed the floors, but men made the lye with which they did it.[5]

Cowan concludes this discussion by noting that, before industrialization, survival required that each household contain individuals of both sexes to perform the requisite gendered tasks. The farmstead thus represented a system of focal practices whereby a form of household (not individual) self-reliance was generated by the essentiality of constant and reciprocal interaction with others of the opposite sex. In the household systems of Jefferson's era, gender defined fundamentally different but equally vital and complementary social roles. Today, by contrast, Berry argues that the chief requirement of a household is simply cash income—a need that can be satisfied only by activity outside the household.

This more detailed picture of the historical context makes it apparent that self-reliance and community solidarity could readily be identified as social goals for agriculture. We can also see why productivity and efficiency would not have been understood as social goals. To be sure, Jefferson was keenly interested in farm productivity, and producing the food needed to sustain the household has always been a goal of agriculture, but in Jeffersonian America, these were not *social* goals. With upward of 80 percent of the population living in farm households, producing enough to feed the family was a critical household goal. But it is precisely because these families were feeding themselves that there was no need to understand agriculture as an activity that must be organized and maintained in a way that secures the structure and sustenance of society at large. Those not actually employed in farming could be fed by the surplus generated through the activity of the majority, who thought of producing the way any producer thinks of it—as an activity intended to serve personal ends. In a similar fashion, self-reliance involved a kind of commonsense efficiency, but these efficiencies were household rather than social goals. The spirit of community solidarity and household self-reliance were both personal and social goals. They were traits that all citizens in the new republic needed to have for nation building to occur. And such traits could be acquired through the experience and example of agriculture.

This vision of agriculture's role in forming the American character was shared by several generations of American leaders. Abraham Lincoln (1809–1865) established the U.S. Department of Agriculture, which he called "the people's department," and he said of farmers, "no other human occupation opens so wide a field for the profitable and agreeable combination of labor with cultivated thought, as agriculture."[6] Philosopher and poet Ralph Waldo Emerson also praised farmers, saying, "that uncorrupted behavior which we admire in young children belongs to him . . . the man who lives in the presence of Nature. Cities force growth and make men talkative and entertaining, but they make them artificial."[7] Teddy Roosevelt has already been quoted as noting that a nation depends "more upon the character of its country population than anything else."[8] If the experience of the Jeffersonian household is so fundamental to the formation of the American character, what are we to think of ourselves? Are we consigned to the lot of Emerson's urbanite—talkative and entertaining but hopelessly superficial?

Some interpreters of contemporary American culture take their concern for the moral character of people quite literally. Berry concludes that the urban experience is incapable of instilling the crucial virtues of solidarity and self-reliance, and he particularly laments the fact that the modern agricultural university has transformed the farm itself into a domain overrun with technological devices. But despite my promise to let Berry have his own version of Jefferson, I cannot resist pointing out that this is a distortion of the social character of Jefferson's vision in an important sense. Jefferson no doubt thought that the life experiences of the American farmstead were capable of inculcating key virtues, but he was also aware that the countryside was full of scoundrels seemingly lacking in any virtue whatsoever. His "Farm Book" contains many passages describing cantankerous neighbors in rather unflattering terms.[9] Nevertheless, the ideal of yeoman agriculture could model key virtues required by the nation as a whole. Jefferson observed that other occupations, notably education, could serve as models for essential virtues as well. The teacher modeled self-discipline and respect for truth, and these virtues were also necessary for the new republic to succeed. Agriculture happened to play an especially pivotal role because community solidarity and household self-reliance were needed to coordinate an emerging, pluralistic society that had to acquire a sense of self-identity and independence from Europe. Jefferson understood that these needs would evolve as the nation matured.

As such, the mere fact that most Americans no longer live on farms is no reason to give up entirely on Jefferson's vision of agriculture's moral purpose. The idea that agriculture has to serve as a moral example seems pretty old-fashioned in today's world. What is more, the patience of today's farmers, agricultural researchers, and agribusiness employees must wear thin when they are told they must be moral saints, exhibiting virtues of solidarity, self-reliance, stewardship, faith, hope, and charity in an economic environment that is very much like that of any other business. Understood as moral duties that the rural folk must perform for the salvation of our urban population, the Jeffersonian ideals are absurd. Yet the key point is that acquiring this set of virtues can still be understood as a social goal, even as a component of sustainability. As I have intimated several times, these virtues are now displayed more prominently in our literary and artistic representations of farming than they are in mainstream farming itself. Some of the alternatives emerging in the food system—community-supported agriculture, slow food, and "local-vores"—may revitalize the sense in which agriculture serves to cultivate virtue. What is critical in the present context is the way the Jeffersonian ideal illustrates a social goal for agriculture, as distinct from the productivity and efficiency of other sectors in the industrial economy.

Sustainability as a Social Goal

It is possible that agriculture and the entire agrifood system can serve a wholly new social goal in the future. A properly functioning food system could serve as model for sustainability itself. Participating in a well-integrated agrifood system could give everyone a vantage point that relies on a set of practices and institutions that renew themselves in economic, ecological, and social terms. If the operations of this system are sufficiently accessible and transparent to food consumers, obtaining and eating food could become a practice that reminds people what sustainability means in a substantive sense. Subsequent chapters develop this theme in more detail. Yet it is clear that neither Jefferson's agriculture nor the agrifood system as it currently functions serves this goal. As such, I close this chapter with some reflections on what is needed to achieve a more comprehensive understanding of the social goals we might associate with some future agriculture.

In his 1972 book *Small Is Beautiful*, E. F. Schumacher (1911–1977) argues that too much emphasis on productivity and efficiency has led us to lose sight of agriculture's broader purposes. Like Berry, Schumacher laments the phenomenon of specialization and the emphasis on cash income that it brings. He describes "the philosophy of the townsman," who interprets the failure of many small farms as evidence that agriculture is merely a "declining enterprise." The main focus for Schumacher is the proper use of land, and his intention is to demonstrate that economic values have undercut agriculture's traditional land ethic. The main danger of our time is "the townsman's determination to apply to agriculture the principles of industry." He condemns those who see agriculture as essentially directed to the production of salable economies and writes:

A wider view sees agriculture as having to fulfill at least three tasks:
   —to keep man in touch with living nature, of which he is and remains a
   highly vulnerable part;
   —to humanize and ennoble man's wider habitat; and

—to bring forth the foodstuffs and other materials which are needed for a becoming life.

I do not believe that a civilization which recognizes only the third of these tasks, and which pursues it with such ruthlessness and violence that the other two tasks are not merely neglected but systematically counteracted, has any chance of long-term survival.[10]

Schumacher thus sees social goals for agriculture that extend well beyond productivity and efficiency and that connect directly with the sustainability of society.

Aldo Leopold, the man many point to as the model of an environmental philosopher, was also a critic of productivity and efficiency. He describes an ethical sequence through history whereby humanity has come to understand the difference between social and antisocial conduct more clearly. He cites the abolition of slavery as a great example of progress in this sequence. Leopold argues that slavery ended only when we learned that other human beings should not be thought of as forms of property. The buying and selling of property, he writes, "is a matter of expediency, not of right and wrong." Leopold thought the next stage in humanity's moral development would involve a similar move in which land would no longer be thought of simply as property.

Land, like Odysseus' slave girls, is still property. The land-man relation is still strictly economic, entailing privileges but not obligation. The extension of ethics to [land] is, if I read the evidence correctly, an evolutionary possibility and an ecological necessity. . . . All ethics so far evolved rest upon a single premise: that the individual is a member of a community of interdependent parts. His instincts prompt him to compete for his place in that community, but his ethics prompt him also to cooperate (perhaps in order that there be a place to compete for).[11]

For Leopold, as for Jefferson, community solidarity is a social goal that brings into focus how we are dependent on one another for the independence and liberty an individual receives from living in a free society. Leopold is especially clear that this interdependence includes the natural world.

Leopold and Schumacher teach that economic goals need to be moderated by a clear-headed appreciation of our dependence on natural systems. Both authors think that the pursuit of productivity and efficiency can lead to the abuse of natural resources and the degradation of natural systems. Now there is a sense in which economic relations serve quite well to communicate our dependence on natural systems: as natural resources become scarce, their price goes up and our ability to afford them goes down. In the case of foodstuffs, however, demand goes down only when the population decreases, and this, as Thomas Malthus (1766–1834) observes, is achieved primarily through human misery and vice. Any population thus needs to establish not only adequate production of foodstuffs but also a margin of safety if it is to put the brakes on human misery. This margin of safety is, in an economic sense, an inefficiency. It is a waste of resources that might be put to a different use, and indeed, they will be put to another use if falling commodity prices are allowed to drive down farm production. If this margin of safety reduces human misery, however, it secures one of the main social goals articulated for the welfare state. I am not against reducing human misery.

Yet at the same time this margin of safety protects us from the tragedy of famine and malnutrition, it isolates us from the feedback mechanisms that inform us when our vulnerability to breakdown in the agro-ecosystem is increasing. Under such circumstances it is possible to become oblivious to our general dependence on nature as well as on the people who cultivate natural resources to fulfill society's needs. I am keenly aware that many millions of people in the world do not exist within this margin of safety, and even in the United States, hundreds of thousands live in food-insecure circumstances. These facts make the typical American ignorance of our dependence on farming all the more tragic, especially in light of many Americans' blissful ignorance of the ecological stresses and economic injustice that perpetuate global hunger. As Aiken's comments suggest, a common philosophical response to hunger has been to stress liberal values of human rights. My point here is that such claims must not be advanced as if there will always be enough to go around, as if selfishness is the only moral problem. A global food system must be a sustainable food system, and if we are to pursue this goal democratically, people need to have some conception of what that involves.

Schumacher and Leopold also teach that our agriculture must find new ways to establish lines of feedback on our use and abuse of natural resources, and these new ways must kick in well before the Malthusian controls of famine and warfare. This lesson is especially critical as we try to move a larger portion of the global population into food-secure circumstances. This new goal for agriculture is a consequence of the agrifood system's thus far only partial success in achieving productivity and efficiency goals. It is, as Leopold thought, a modification of Jefferson's bequest, the old Jeffersonian conception of community. We must become cognizant of our total community, and this means not only our fellow citizens in the United States and abroad but also our communion with the natural environment. We must find a way to become self-reliant, which now means being responsible for moderating our use of economic and natural resources through a process of deliberative social self-control.

Self control is important

CHAPTER 9

The Road to Sustainability

What do we mean by sustainability? The words *sustain* and *sustainable* are common terms. Some time back I recall pundits on the national news proclaiming that the rise in residential home values was "not sustainable." They did not have to define this term. We all knew what they meant, and since the collapse of the U.S. mortgage industry in 2007, it is clear that they were right. The word *sustainability*, however, is sufficiently nonstandard that it is not included in the dictionary supplied with my word processing program (though I doubt this will continue to be the case for long). It was only a few years ago that long-winded debates over the meaning of *sustainability* were commonplace in scientific circles. Disputes frequently ended with everyone concluding that the term was meaningless. Today these debates have been replaced by attempts to develop standards that would allow vendors to advertise products or services as conforming to norms of sustainability. Thus, although the exact nature and contours of sustainability are still unclear, there now appears to be widespread agreement that the word must mean something.

In this chapter and the following two I develop the idea that sustainability is an essentially contested idea. That is, like our ideas of democracy, justice, truth, and reality itself, there are competing philosophical visions of sustainability and a seemingly endless number of fine points on which even those who are in broad agreement can differ. This is not, however, a reason to think that sustainability is meaningless. On the contrary, as with our ideas of democracy, justice, truth, and reality, the contested nature of sustainability is a reason to think that it is philosophically important. My own philosophy holds that the family of meanings I define in terms of *functional integrity* comes nearest to a satisfactory framework for thinking about sustainability, but my own philosophy also holds that appreciating the dialectical nature of contested concepts comes before choosing up sides and arguing for one of them. I thus move slowly toward my preferred vision. In this chapter I explore how sustainability came to be so important.

The Brundtland Report

In 1987 the World Commission on Environment and Development, under the leadership of former Norwegian prime minister Gro Brundtland, issued a report entitled *Our Common Future*. The original language of the United Nations General Assembly resolution establishing the Brundtland Commission called for "long-term environmental strategies for achieving sustainable development to the year 2000 and beyond."[1] The report defined *sustainable development* as development that "meets the needs of the present without compromising the ability of future generations to meet their own needs." These words are perhaps the most frequently quoted characterization of sustainability. The Brundtland Report is, in fact, a watershed for the very idea of sustainability. Although (as the 1983 UN resolution itself indicates) people were talking the language of sustainability well before 1987, *Our Common Future* established a framework and goals that made compliance with its characterization of sustainable development a desideratum for all manner of public and private activity.

Yet the significance of the Brundtland Report did not depend on a particularly sophisticated or well-worked-out conceptualization of sustainability. The quotation above is about as far as the authors of the report went in specifying the meaning of the word. *Our Common Future* attained importance because it represented a new consensus on the way environment and development would be connected in international affairs. The Brundtland Commission had the good fortune to issue its report less than two years after Mikhail Gorbachev became general secretary of the Communist Party of the Soviet Union. Within a few years of its publication, the USSR had collapsed altogether, and the old model of developing nations as client states for the Great Powers became permanently passé. The degree to which *Our Common Future* offered a new way to conceptualize relationships between developed and developing states can be grasped by contrasting its rhetoric to that of another international commission whose report had been issued only seven years earlier.

The Independent Commission on International Development, led by former German chancellor Willy Brandt, issued a report entitled *North-South: A Programme for Survival* in 1980. Any comparison of the Brandt and Brundtland documents must begin by noting their similarity. Both attempt to establish an agenda for multilateral foreign relations among developed and developing states. Neither offers specific policy proposals. The topics covered in their pages are virtually identical: population, food and agriculture, energy, renewable resources, trade, and disarmament. Both reports should be read as attempts to place these topics on the table for international relations, and both implicitly endorse the view that such topics had been neglected in a world where global politics was dominated by a contest between the United States and the USSR. It is in light of these overall similarities that the rhetorical differences between the Brandt and Brundtland reports are so striking.

As implied by its title, the Brandt Report presents recommendations within a framework that implies a division between North and South. North-South relations are characterized in terms of southern dependency on northern industrialized economies. The dependency is multifaceted. Southern economies revolve around the supply of raw commodities to northern manufacturing and service sectors. Finished goods are sold back to the South. The South is thus dependent on the North for its markets and for the supply of industrial products. This pattern of trade is said to defeat capital accumulation in the South and slow the development of industries that would allow trade to take place on a more equal footing. The Brandt Report stresses the developed-country responsibilities created by this dependency and also uses the language of rights that may be claimed by individuals from developing countries against the governments of the developed North.

In stipulating responsibilities owed by governments of the developed world, the Brandt Report also implicitly extends rights held by the citizens of developed nations to noncitizens in the developing world. The ground for this move consists in the dependency relations created by the terms of commerce, as well as the history of colonialism and European expansion. The theme becomes explicit in Brandt's introductory remarks, where he writes that the process of restructuring relations between North and South

has to be guided by the principle of equal rights and opportunities: it should aim at fair compromise to overcome grave injustice, to reduce useless controversies, and to promote the interlocked welfare of nations. . . . A right to share in decision-making processes will be essential if the developing countries are to accept their proper share of the responsibility for international political and economic affairs. It is this right which nourishes the aspirations of developing countries for a new international order, and these aspirations will have to materialize if relations are to be placed on a new basis of confidence and trust in international cooperation.[2]

The language of rights and responsibilities in this passage is characteristic of the Brandt framework. The reference to a new international order similarly reflects claims of distributive justice levied by people in the South against the developed North.

The Brundtland Report is notable for the near total absence of rhetoric claiming rights and imposing responsibilities. Its title, *Our Common Future*, reflects a shift from claims of the South against the North to a framework in which mutual interest is the baseline. The document begins with a lengthy section discussing common concerns. The section headed "Equity and the Common Interest" is especially notable. The text begins not by noting responsibilities for the redistribution of wealth or for meeting the needs of the poor but by noting that "ecological interactions do not respect the boundaries of individual ownership and political jurisdiction." The section continues by describing a series of collective-action or "prisoner's dilemma" type problems associated with the management of resources. In contrast to the North-South dichotomies of the Brandt Report, the Brundtland Report says: "It is not that there is one set of villains and another of victims. All would be better off if each person took into account the effect of his or her acts on others. But each is unwilling to assume that others will behave in this socially desirable fashion, and hence, all continue to pursue narrow self-interest." It is only at the close of this section that equity finally makes an overdue appearance: "An inequitable landownership structure can lead to over exploitation of resources in the smallest holdings . . . monopolistic control over resources can drive those who do not share in them to excessive exploitation of marginal resources. . . . As a system approaches ecological limits, inequalities sharpen."[3] Throughout the section, equitable distributions of power and resources are consistently discussed in terms of their contribution to collectively irrational outcomes, to situations in which the structure of choices available to individuals precludes them from reaching solutions that are in the interests of wealthy and poor alike. Within a few years, the phrase *new world order* would be deployed by President George H. W. Bush to reference not redistributive responsibilities but the final victory of capitalism.

Our Common Future makes interests, rather than rights and responsibilities, the basic concept for motivating multilateral attention to its agenda of concerns. Peoples of the developed and developing world are portrayed as having common interests they cannot satisfy because the social institutions for cooperation are, in their present form, dysfunctional. Although the document notes that there will be winners and losers in specific instances, it stresses that common collective interests are being sacrificed by the existing pattern of international relations. It then presents roughly the same agenda of items for negotiation submitted in the Brandt Report less than a decade earlier. This time, however, they are not claims levied by people wronged by virtue of economic dependency or the legacy of colonialism. This time they are topics for negotiation with the idea of achieving common interests. It was in this general context that the Brundtland Commission's ideas on sustainable development were received.

Sustainability after Brundtland

The publication of *Our Common Future* is thus a signal event in the way processes of development affecting weakly industrialized nations came to be conceived. Suddenly it became important to have a conception of sustainable development that could be operationalized in development planning and project design. Legions of resource and development economists leapt to the task, producing a plethora of technical measures to specify sustainability in a manner consistent with existing economic concepts. Working from a framework of development economics, David Pearce, Edward Barbier, and Anil Markandya were among the first to hit the ground with a coherent approach. They first utilize conventional measures such as per capita income, improvements in public health and nutrition, measures of educational achievement, and the equitability of income distribution to define what they call a "development vector." They then suggest that "*sustainable* development is . . . a situation in which the development vector D does not decrease over time."[4] Robert Costanza utilizes tools from resource economics to approach sustainability. His definition is simple: a sustainable system is a system that survives or persists. What resource economics can do to help society persist is to apply a variety of techniques for assigning values to natural resources and eco-system services that are not subject to market pricing mechanisms.

Indeed, models began to proliferate. In 1995 the World Bank published a lengthy technical report surveying the literature on these new economic approaches to sustainability. The editors summarize these definitions and measures as representing three distinct conceptual approaches to sustainability. First are what they call the "input-output" views. Here, ecosystem processes are presumed to exist in a steady state, supplying various raw materials for development processes. Factors that might lead to a decrease in well-being are presumably due to either the exhaustion of nonrenewable resources (such as oil) or economic policies and institutions themselves (an area in which a wealth of mutually incompatible economic tools has been vying for decades). The second group of approaches involves a so-called capital or stock view. These are derived from works that treat both natural resources and ecosystem processes as forms of capital that are themselves drawn on to produce goods and services for economic exchange. Just as an investor hopes not to squander financial capital with foolish investments, society should be cautious about conserving natural capital. Economist Herman Daly is prominently associated with this group of models. The last group of models covered in the World Bank study is described as taking the "potential throughput" view. These models emphasize the use of renewable resources (such as fish in the sea or agricultural crops) within the limits of the ecosystem's ability to regenerate them through a series of natural cycles.[5]

The most enduring definition of sustainability by an economist was offered by Robert Solow in a lecture delivered to commemorate the fortieth anniversary of Resources for the Future, a Washington, DC, environmental think tank. Solow develops an economic analysis of the way reproduced capital can substitute for the declining stock of an exhaustible resource. *Reproduced capital* refers to wealth gleaned through production, then reinvested in new technology or manufacturing capability. The intuitive idea is that future generations can enjoy a quality of life comparable to (or better than) that of present generations, despite the fact that exhaustible resources (such as fossil fuels) become more scarce as they are consumed. In one sense, Solow is telling us that it is possible to satisfy the conditions needed for constant acceleration of the development vector even while the stock of exhaustible resources declines. Thus, as long as wealth is reinvested in productive capability, the Brundtland criterion (economic development that meets the needs of the present without compromising the needs of the future) can be met. This general approach to sustainability has been referred to as *Solow sustainability* or *weak sustainability*. In contrast, *strong sustainability* requires a commitment to maintaining stocks of natural resources, a view originally associated with the work of Daly.[6]

Ecologists were also very busy in the wake of the Brundtland Commission's reformulation of international politics, though they were a bit slower than economists to embrace the goal of competing to specify the concept. The journal *Ecological Applications* published a symposium on "Science and Sustainability" in 1993. The lead article by Donald Ludwig was somewhat skeptical and bore the title "Environmental Sustainability: Magic, Science and Religion in Natural Resource Management." Ludwig returned a few years later, however, with an article cowritten by Brian Walker and C. S. Holling. They begin by describing the concept of system resilience using the example of a block of wood floating in water. Perturbations to the block displace it only so long as physical force is actually in play. When force is removed, the total system of the block afloat in water returns to its original parameters. The system is resilient. This article goes on to specify a set of equations that might be used to characterize the concept of resiliency in ecosystems and suggests that this could be a useful approach to the problem of sustainability.

It was Ludwig's coauthor Holling who arguably became the foil to Solow. Holling begins with the assumption that sustainability for a species or an ecosystem depends on the interaction of elements functioning at many scales. A relatively small number of controlling processes within the interaction of these elements results in self-organizing systems, systems that can be reproduced and rebound from many if not most shocks or stressors that come from the larger environment in which interactions occur. Sustainability thus refers to the stability or resilience of these self-organizing systems, which Holling finds present not only in natural ecosystems but also in human-dominated ecosystems and, indeed, within society itself. The approach of tying the concept strongly to the ability of a self-organized system came to be known as *Holling sustainability*. Recent debates on sustainability compare Solow sustainability and Holling sustainability, with some disagreement as to whether they are compatible.[7]

The technical detail in these various economic and ecological models is mind-numbing. My point in discussing these few examples is simply to document the diversity of approaches that followed the Brundtland Report. A volume entitled *A Survey of Sustainable Development: Social and Economic Approaches*, published in 2001, exceeds 400 pages. By the mid-1990s, a substantial literature had already developed around the problem of sorting through the multiple definitions and concepts of sustainability. These comparisons often note that any defensible approach to sustainability needs to address economic viability, environmental impact, and social acceptability, but the recitation of alternative models often becomes soporific itself. More than one reader has told me that my own treatment of these problems in the final chapter of *The Spirit of the Soil* is an excellent cure for insomnia. In the next chapter, I offer a (hopefully) more stimulating framework for grasping the main philosophical points of these alternative approaches to sustainability. But first I want to reverse direction and look at some patches of the road to sustainability that had already been traveled when *Our Common Future* appeared.

Sustainability before Brundtland

By 1984, economist Gordon K. Douglass had published a collection of essays entitled *Agricultural Sustainability in a Changing World Order*. Douglass proposed that advocates of agricultural sustainability tend to cluster around three discrete themes. First is an emphasis on food sufficiency: to be sustainable means that an agricultural system can feed the human population, whatever other costs it might entail to the environment. Second is what Douglass calls ecological integrity, or farming with an emphasis on minimizing the long-term depletion of the soil, water, and genetic resource base. Those focused on the third theme stress community, with a strong emphasis on rural social vibrancy. Douglass calls this social sustainability. Each merits some elaboration and discussion.

"Feeding the world" had long been a mantra for mainstream agricultural science, and in the 1970s it became an explicit ambition of large-scale commodity agriculture. President Richard Nixon's secretary of agriculture, Earl Butz, advocated using "food-as-weapon," by which he meant that the West's capacity to produce prodigious amounts of grain could be used to political advantage through programs designed to meet the food needs of poor people in developing nations. He coupled this with an injunction for farmers themselves to "get big, or get out," meaning that very large, industrially organized farms would be the source of this production. Although Butz himself was not one to use the word *sustainability* in the same sentence as *farming*, his vision of agriculture's contribution to sustainability is one that dates back at least to Thomas Malthus's notorious *Essay on the Principle of Population*. It is obvious that people must eat to live, so if any human society is to be sustainable, its people must be sustained by daily bread. Malthus had prophesied that growth in the human population would tend to outpace growth in agricultural production. Hence, a sustainable human population would necessarily be one that either found some means to check population growth or achieved sustainable numbers at the price of perpetual misery in the form of starvation or wars fought over agricultural resources. The food sufficiency view thus sees agriculture as necessary for the sustainability of human civilization. Indeed, the imperative of food sufficiency is thought to be overriding. Food trumps or outranks the desire for luxury goods, which may include environmental amenities as well as leisure consumption. Some who adopt the food sufficiency point of view may follow Malthus in thinking that elements of social justice, such as the right to health care or education, and a fair distribution of life's opportunities are also luxuries available only to those who have solved the hard problems of daily survival. The Malthusian race between population and food sufficiency is the underlying tension in this view of sustainability. Many people who take this view, including many mainstream agricultural scientists, see the last 100 years as a defeat of Malthus's principle made possible by an all-out campaign to use technology to increase and stabilize agricultural yields.

There are, however, important skeptics among agricultural scientists. Most notable is Lester Brown, who has devoted a lifetime to Malthusian calculations and whose books such as *Who Will Feed China?* question whether agricultural science can continue to win this race. Brown is credited by some as having coined the phrase *sustainable development*, and his questioning takes on many dimensions. One is that as people become wealthier, per capita caloric consumption increases with a shift toward diets rich in animal protein. As such, the need for increasing agricultural productivity actually grows *faster* than human population. Furthermore, Brown notes that the putative success of agricultural science in sustaining the human population has actually been built on a number of resource-depleting production practices. Chemical fertilizers and pesticides accumulate in the environment, with long-term effects on both human and environmental health that are only now being realized. Mechanized irrigation technologies often draw on nonrenewable underground water supplies, and declines in soil fertility from intensive cropping amount to a form of mining. It is Brown's kind of thinking that Douglass sees as representing ecological integrity.

Brown's emphasis on broader environmental impacts reveals that the ability to produce food depends on maintaining the integrity of the natural resource base. A view of agriculture that considers only year-to-year yields in cereal crops or animal protein fails to recognize that a unilateral focus on feeding people day to day can actually result in farming methods that are not sustainable over the long run. In the ecological integrity view, it is agriculture itself that must be sustainable. It is not simply a matter of agriculture making society sustainable by ensuring that there is enough to eat. According to ecological integrity, a truly sustainable agriculture is one that operates within the natural hydrological cycle as well as the earth's ability to regenerate fertile soils. Even subtler processes may be at work in the regeneration of genetic diversity.

Douglass's third paradigm—social sustainability—calls attention to the need for vibrant rural communities. It relies heavily on work done by Walter Goldschmidt, who studied two towns in California's San Joaquin Valley in the 1930s and 1940s. One was surrounded by many relatively small and diversified farms operated with family labor, and the other was set amid a few very large monoculture operations typical of what we now call industrial agriculture. Goldschmidt's study, published in 1947 under the title *As You Sow,* found that the community dominated by large commodity-oriented farms had difficulty maintaining basic infrastructure in the form of schools, public health, and municipal services, whereas the rural community consisting of small family-based operations had a thriving infrastructure and a rich communal life.

Douglass's 1984 book also came on the heels of a lawsuit over the University of California's participation in the development of a mechanical tomato harvester. It was a large and expensive piece of equipment that could not be efficiently utilized by small growers. The availability of the mechanized harvester, along with some key legislation on migrant labor, precipitated the rapid concentration of California's tomato industry. Hundreds of relatively small-scale farms were consolidated (through sale and bankruptcy) into a few dozen between 1968 and 1978. This concentration in the tomato industry led many to remember Goldschmidt's work and to conclude that the machine would indirectly cause a decline in the rural communities where dozens of tomato farms had been replaced by one or two.

The scale-increasing effects of new technology, along with Goldschmidt's work, led advocates of social sustainability to conclude that the industrial systems favored by advocates of food sufficiency were the opposite of a sustainable agriculture. Thus, social sustainability was closely tied to California in 1984, although the general phenomenon of larger and more specialized farms displacing smaller, more diversified farms has been repeated in many places. Oliver Goldsmith (1730–1774) lamented a similar decline following the widespread adoption of enclosure methods in English farming with his poem "The Deserted Village" (1770):

Ill fares the land, to hast'ning ills a prey,
Where wealth accumulates, and men decay;
Princes and Lords may flourish, or may fade:
A breath can make them, as a breath has made;
but a bold peasantry, their country's pride,
When once destroyed can never be supplied.

The point behind social sustainability suggests that a certain type of farm structure—small-scale, diversified, family-operated farms—is more conducive to sustaining viable rural communities than is a farm structure consisting of industrially organized farms producing commodity crops. Here, as in the case of food availability, it is agriculture (though now a specific kind of agriculture) that is sustaining society, as opposed to being something that must itself be made sustainable.

Thus, well before the publication of *Our Common Future*, there was a robust and complex discussion over sustainability as it should be understood with respect to agriculture. Douglass's three-way approach was fairly influential for a while within agricultural circles, but it was soon overwhelmed by the flurry of models and methods that crowded the literature in the wake of Brundtland. In the next two chapters I build on Douglass's work far more than I do on that of the World Commission on Environment and Development. Yet first it should be recognized that much water had passed under the bridge before *sustainability* became a buzzword for agriculture sometime in the 1970s.

Before Sustainability

As noted earlier, popular appreciation of the environmental impact of agricultural chemicals can be traced to Rachel Carson's *Silent Spring*. Carson collected both scientific and anecdotal evidence of the effect the bioaccumulation of agricultural pesticides (especially DDT) was having on wildlife. Some scholars cite her book as the beginning of the environmental movement. Yet within agriculture itself, there was an even older tradition of what we would today call ecological thinking. Liberty Hyde Bailey (1858–1954) advocated a norm of "permanent" agriculture, by which he meant farming methods that maintain fertile soils and viable crops in perpetuity. Bailey was unarguably the most famous agricultural scientist of his era. He promoted outdoor "nature study" as a form of general education and developed a philosophy that saw the land itself as a locus of moral duty.

In the United States and Canada, Bailey's lessons on permanent agriculture were reinforced by the Dust Bowl, the result of wind erosion that took on continental proportions between 1930 and 1936. Soil scientist Hugh Hammond Bennett (1881–1960) diagnosed the source of this environmental catastrophe as patterns of overcultivation that depleted soils on the Great Plains, leaving them with weakened texture, or tilth. When denuded of plant growth after harvest, these lands were vulnerable to the dry winds that blackened the skies of North America, depositing ruined soil in huge drifts and leaving lands totally unfit for farming. Bennett created extensive programs of soil conservation and worked with popular author Louis Bromfield (1896–1956) to promote an approach to farming that anticipated many elements of what Douglass would refer to as the ecological integrity approach to sustainable agriculture.

In his time, Bromfield was a widely read novelist and well-known Hollywood screenwriter. His book *Early Autumn* won the Pulitzer Prize in 1926. Movie stars Humphrey Bogart and Lauren Bacall were married on his Ohio farm in 1945, and the event was covered in *Life* magazine. He was compared to writers such as William Faulkner and Ernest Hemingway, although his relative obscurity half a century after his death suggests otherwise. Bromfield's writings range from spy stories with exotic locales to agrarian novels that celebrate country life, the virtues of farming, and the sense of community associated with small-scale rural communities. Two of his later works, *Pleasant Valley* (1945) and *Malabar Farm* (1948), still bear reading for students of agrarian thought. These quasi-autobiographical books include rich portraits of real and legendary personalities from the Mansfield, Ohio, region, interwoven with stories of Bromfield's attempts to reclaim his farm and resuscitate his soils.

Bromfield used his celebrity to promote Bennett's conservation reforms both among farmers and throughout the general population in the 1940s. Famous visitors to Malabar Farm would be expected to pitch in with farm chores, sometimes manning the farm stand where Bromfield peddled jellies and fresh farm produce in the summer months. Large farm fairs were conducted to demonstrate the advanced farming techniques Bromfield had adapted from Bennett, and Bromfield's rhetoric celebrated an agrarian ideal in opposition to the industrial style of farming that was taking shape after World War II. Pesticides such as DDT had been developed as battlefield technologies, and the capacity to produce them in quantity had been created as a national defense imperative. This effectively subsidized the development and infrastructure for pesticide technology. Bromfield advocated what he believed to be a more natural approach, but he was not totally opposed to chemicals. Indeed, he admits in *Malabar Farm* that he was unable to make a go of the grass-fed livestock methods he had advocated only a few years earlier, reverting to the production of fodder crops.

Although Britain never suffered an agricultural environmental disaster on the scale of the Dust Bowl, parallel developments in the United Kingdom led to the founding of the Soil Association by Lady Eve Balfour (1899–1990). Drawing on the work of Sir Albert Howard (1873–1947), the Soil Association began to promote the extensive use of composting for developing soil tilth and eschewed the use of synthetic chemical fertilizers. Howard served in a series of agricultural posts throughout the British Commonwealth and was president of the thirteenth session of the Indian Science Congress in 1936. His work in India emphasized the improvement of composting techniques already in widespread use by Indian farmers. The Indore method—Howard's approach to composting—stressed the storage of animal manures in slatted bins to accelerate aerobic decomposition and to facilitate mixing with soil and vegetative waste. Howard believed that composted manure was superior to synthetic fertilizer for plant nutrition by virtue of its ability to foster the growth of soil microbes. He stressed the mycorrhizal association between soil microbes and plant rhizomes, small horizontal offshoots from the plant's principal root structure, believing this to be an unappreciated source of plant nutrition.

In contrast to Howard's faith in composting, the agricultural science of the 1930s emphasized the stimulation of plant growth through the copious administration of ammonium sulfates. The increased yields for most agricultural crops subjected to this treatment led plant physiologists and farmers alike to conclude that any nutritional benefits being sacrificed through their neglect of the mycorrhizal association must be negligible. Furthermore, the capacity for ammonia production had grown significantly. Facilities developed for the production of explosives for World War I were converted to the production of artificial fertilizers in the 1920s. With chemical fertilizers cheaply available, scientists who were trying to revitalize agriculture during the years of the Great Depression quite naturally advocated the chemical approach in lieu of slower and less certain composting, and farmers who were desperate for access to the most efficient methods were quick to oblige. Thus the chemical philosophy of agricultural technology pioneered by German chemist Justus Liebig finally won out over biological philosophies stressing organic unity or soil health.[8]

Howard was not convinced. He began to argue that neglect of the mycorrhizal association accounted for an overall deterioration in plant health, a decline that is passed on to animals (including human beings) that feed on these weakened plants. For evidence, Howard cited plants' vulnerability to fungal and microbial diseases or insect pests, and he drew support from a dubious theory of disease being promoted by a British medical doctor named J. E. R. McDonagh (1881–1965). At the same time, Howard lambasted what he took to be an ill-considered reductionism in the agricultural sciences, arguing that proper agricultural research needed to be conducted under realistic conditions—preferably on a working commercial farm. Howard's views became the basis of organic approaches promoted by the Soil Association in the United Kingdom and by the Rodale Institute in the United States.

Howard's references to "soil health" were far too reminiscent of the élan vital (or life force) that had been one of Liebig's primary targets in the nineteenth century. What is more, his reliance on McDonagh did little to win friends for organic farming in agricultural universities and scientific societies. Writing in the *Quarterly Review of Biology*, one reviewer had this to say of McDonagh's "unitary theory of disease":

The result is a vague farrago of opaque terminology whose meaning (if any) it is almost impossible to interpret. The biochemical, microbiological, and clinical material seem almost equally meaningless.

Some purveyors of eccentric literature are able to make their claims superficially plausible, even if they reason very loosely from very dubious assumptions. Thus it is sometimes interesting to read works which attempt to prove that the earth is flat, or that all civilizations originated from the continent Mu which later sank into the Pacific Ocean. Other eccentrics are merely tiresome and dull. It is the opinion of the reviewer that this book falls into the latter class.[9]

Howard's belief that rhizomes engage in a unique association with soil microorganisms, however, was not quackery. This mycorrhizal association was, in Howard's view, the ultimate source of plant health, but synthetic chemicals tended to destroy microorganisms and weaken tilth. Howard also believed that this health would be passed on to animals (including humans) that consumed healthy plants and that returning animal manures to the soil through composting established a cycle that would make farming truly permanent. Thus, the idea of systemic or holistic health was the driving value in the British organic movement. Howard's ideas were brought to the United States by J. I. Rodale (1898–1971) and became the basis of work at the Rodale Institute in Emmaus, Pennsylvania, that continues to this day.

On the European continent, a somewhat similar approach developed in connection with the philosophy of Rudolf Steiner (1861–1925), an Austrian who emphasized the role of intuition and imagination in his thought. Soil was conceived as a living organism. Healthy soil would support plant growth without artificial amendments, and healthy plants would resist pests and promote health in the animals that ate them. Thus, though different from Howard's approach in its philosophical underpinnings, Steiner's approach was similar in emphasizing soil health through composting, forswearing the use of chemicals, and linking soil, plant, and animal health in a cyclic fashion. Steiner was a scholar of Johann Wolfgang Goethe (1749–1832) and had a strong interest in Goethe's scientific writings and his theory of archetypes. In the nineteenth century, Goethe had been claimed by advocates of the life force, but his scientific views were eventually deemed untenable by twentieth-century standards, however much he continued to be admired as a polymath and for his literary accomplishments. Steiner's writings and teachings fall almost entirely outside the accepted boundaries of academic philosophy as understood both in his lifetime and in recent years. He became associated with followers of the Russian psychic Madame Helena Blavatsky (1831–1891), modifying her teachings and leading a breakaway group called the Anthroposophical Society.

In the year before his death, Steiner delivered a series of eight lectures on agricultural methods and supervised some limited agricultural trials. Steiner provides no details about the source of his approach to agriculture. Some of the specific techniques appear to have been handed down to him from farmers he knew as a youth in eastern Austria and what is now Croatia. Yet the text of Steiner's lectures implies that his agricultural methods could be derived from anthroposophical principles stressing cosmic forces that permeate the universe. Consistent with Steiner's reputation as an esotericist, comments and questions from the audience suggest that he was simply able to intuit his agricultural principles by virtue of his general wisdom and spiritual excellence. Steiner's agriculture involves methods for creating a series of preparations that are applied to crops or crop manures in homeopathic doses. These preparations are themselves formulated from organic materials such as dung or plant and insect parts, then composted according to detailed procedures that involve burying at specified depths and at times and places determined by lunar phases and planetary alignments. Steiner's background; his interest in mystical intuitionism; his implicit alliance with vitalism, teleology, and other discredited scientific approaches in biology; and his opaque references to cosmic forces all tend to discredit his legitimacy as a scientifically informed theorist of agriculture. Yet Steiner's preparations have attracted a worldwide following among organic farmers who refer to his methods as *biodynamic farming.*

Biodynamic farming as practiced today generally meets organic standards, but not all organic methods meet the standards proposed by various national biodynamic agricultural associations. In fact, the contemporary biodynamic approach does not stipulate the use of Steiner's preparations, even though some biodynamic farmers continue to swear by them. Instead, present-day biodynamic associations emphasize the organic unity of the farm, encouraging farmers to make their own fertilizer by keeping animals. They derive principles of organic unity from the ideal of a diverse, integrated farm having both crops and animals, much like those of Steiner's youth. For example, biodynamic farmers do not use more fertilizer on any given plot of land than would have been produced by growing fodder crops on that land and feeding it to animals. Biodynamic associations stress the uniqueness of each farm, implying that uniform standards may not be appropriate, but they also encourage farmers to live fully in the organic spirit, including participation in activities intended to promote the biodynamic way of life.

Although Howard and Steiner developed specific techniques for improving soil fertility that continue to be widely used by organic farmers, both became associated with ideas that were rejected by the scientific establishment in their lifetimes. In fact, only recently have agricultural scientists begun to take organic methods seriously. They have been spurred in part by the evident success of contemporary organic methods, by rising consumer demand, and by the recognition of environmental problems associated with chemical methods. As historian Frank Uekoetter notes, "Promoting a plurality of opinions, and of approaches, is an important contribution to the quest for an agriculture that is both productive and sustainable. . . . And researchers should not be discouraged by the fact that there is no Liebig quotation to legitimate this endeavor."[10]

Back to the Present

From Bailey to Bromfield and across the ocean to Howard and Steiner, these figures represent only some of the better-known names who advocated an environmentally sound and ecologically enlightened approach to farming decades before we began to talk about sustainable agriculture. Organic and biodynamic farming methods will be familiar to many people involved in alternative agriculture today. Bailey, Howard, and Steiner each used language suggesting that soil is a living thing to promote their vision. Bailey went so far as to say that humans have a moral obligation to the earth, to the nonhuman world, by virtue of its standing as a holy thing. Bailey's ideas would, in fact, have a substantial influence on Aldo Leopold, who is celebrated today for advocating that land has a moral status beyond its simple legal standing as property.

It is difficult to say how seriously or in what philosophical vein we should read this talk of the earth or soil as a living thing, having a moral standing all on its own. Steiner is often read as meaning this in a totally literal way and as having deep insights into mysteries that have eluded science. But caution is warranted. On the one hand, Steiner's milieu included philosophers such as Henri Bergson (1859–1941), who posited an élan vital, an impetus in nature that drives both evolutionary change and human creativity. It also included respected biologists such as Hans Adolf Driesch (1867–1941) and Johannes Reinke (1849–1931), who rejected the mechanism implicit in Darwinian evolution and Liebig's biology. What is more, agriculture played a comparatively minor role in Steiner's intellectual life. He was far more occupied with the development of educational theories intended to stimulate interest and spark creativity in children by cultivating their imaginative abilities. On the other hand, Steiner himself claimed to base his systems on clairvoyance, and it is difficult to avoid the occultism that pervades much of his writing. Distinguishing those aspects of Steiner's agricultural theories that simply represent patterns of thought typical of his time but quite unlike our own would require a systematic study of his entire system of thought.

Bennett and Bromfield were also wont to reference soil and the earth as a living system, but here it seems to be a case of pure metaphor. Bennett was, in fact, a mainstream agricultural scientist who did most of his work through the U.S. Department of Agriculture. His publications include highly technical tracts on soil classification and soil physics. He was an authentic conservationist, but his work does not evince the disdain for chemical amendments that one sees in the writings of Howard or Balfour. For his part, Bromfield comes off as a wholly secular commonsense conservationist, quite willing to try anything in a spirit of curiosity but not inclined to endorse metaphysical explanations too seriously. He was no zealot and countenanced some sparing use of chemicals. In *Malabar Farm* he notes reluctantly a shift toward more specialized monocultures on his own farm, noting that he simply could not make the diversified model he had promoted in his earlier work pay off in the real world of Ohio agriculture.

In fact, serious philosophical inquiry into the deeper ontological commitments of figures such as Bailey, Howard, or even Steiner may be pointless. In calling for their contemporaries to view the soil as a living thing, and in saying that humans should adopt an attitude of ethical responsibility to the land itself, they were indicating courses of conduct intended to counteract the pervasive and mindless disregard they saw undercutting the sustainability—the permanence, to use Bailey's word—of farming systems being used even in the first half of the twentieth century. They stand as models, but not as models to be emulated slavishly. Their ideas set us on the road to sustainable agriculture, but pursuing that road requires some innovations of our own.

CHAPTER 10

Sustainability as a Norm

As noted in the last chapter, defining the phrase *sustainable development* became important for integrating environmental issues into international political relations after the Brundtland Report. Yet a robust debate over the meaning of *agricultural sustainability* preceded the Brundtland Report. This debate had been going on for perhaps a decade before *Our Common Future* was published in 1987, if one focuses narrowly on the use of the word *sustainable* to characterize an agricultural practice. But if one thinks broadly enough to encompass ideas about making agriculture *permanent* or *resilient,* the beginnings of the debate can be pushed back to the early decades of the twentieth century, if not further. Yet these preliminary discussions left us with no clear statement of what it means for a given practice to be sustainable.

In this chapter we finally make some progress toward linking sustainability and agrarian ideals. As we have seen throughout, agrarian ideals are normative. Sometimes they articulate aspirations for human practice and for the human species that are appropriate for integration with the natural world. Sometimes they emphasize character traits or virtues such as citizenship, industriousness, stewardship, and even freedom; other times agrarian ideals specify social forms such as community, nation, or democracy. In every case, agrarian ideals advocate, urge, and recommend. They say how people *should* or *ought* to behave, or they express goals that human communities *should* or *ought* to achieve. In the Brundtland Report, sustainability is also normative. It is a statement of how states ought to configure their international relations with environmental issues in mind. But when we say that something is or is not sustainable, it is not obvious that we are always making a normative statement. How, then, does sustainability relate to norms, morals, or political ideals?

Sustainability and Systems

Just yesterday I read in my local newspaper that the new Catholic bishop for the Lansing Diocese would evaluate the sustainability of several local parish churches. Like speculating on the sustainability of real estate values, this natural way of talking about sustainability makes it sound as if the question of whether something is sustainable is pretty straightforward and factual. But in *The Spirit of the Soil* I argue that the factual question "Is it sustainable?" implies a systems orientation. Asking whether something is sustainable always implies that a number of elements are interacting in a regular, continuous, or ongoing manner. The question becomes answerable only when one can assess the relevant system of human practices and natural processes. In the case of real estate values, that system includes both the real estate market and the lenders that write mortgages. In the case of Lansing churches, it includes at least current and prospective church attendance and the various sources of financial support on which the parish and the diocese can draw. Other types of systems might be identified globally or at the level of a farmer's field, or they might be limited to the systematic interaction of nutrients and microorganisms in the rhizosphere—the soil surrounding a plant's roots—which appears to be critical to plant growth.

In some familiar cases, the system in question may be obscure. If we ask how food sufficiency is related to sustainability, a straightforward answer might be, "Food sufficiency is critical for the sustainability of the human population." But there is a little ambiguity in this answer. Sometimes to sustain a person simply means giving him or her enough to eat, and *sustenance* often simply means *food*. But even here there are systems at work. In the case of an individual sustained by daily bread, it is the human body—a living system of interacting parts—that is sustained. In the case of a population, it is an exceedingly complex system of human reproduction, family life, and the global system of agricultural production and trade. Even if we say that the human population is being sustained, there is actually a system of interacting elements implicit in the way we evaluate whether a given level of human population is sustainable or not.

Sustainability implies that the system in question supports the continuance of the practice, the institution, or the phenomenon in a roughly stable state, although it is possible to conceptualize systems that are in constant yet orderly states of change. We can then at least define sustainability in the negative: if a given practice contributes to a collapse of the system, it is not a sustainable practice. Collapse here means a sudden and irreversible disruption of the pattern of interaction among system elements. The important empirical question for sustainability is whether the practice or phenomenon is compatible with continuous (or cyclical) reinforcement or reproduction of the underlying system. But readers may notice that phrases such as "roughly stable," "orderly change," "pattern of interaction," and "reinforced or reproduced" are actually very difficult to pin down. As such, there is a nagging tendency for discussions of sustainability to rely heavily on examples, in which case it is often surprisingly easy for people to agree on what sustainability means. The cases of real estate values and the Lansing Diocese attest to this.

Another way to approach the factual or empirical dimension of sustainability is to ask whether the relevant system is highly vulnerable to internal or endogenous threats. The distinction between endogenous and exogenous threats is critical to questions of sustainability. It would be silly to suggest that a given church in the Lansing Diocese is unsustainable because it is vulnerable to being hit by a meteorite or a nuclear holocaust. When we ask about the sustainability of something, there are always lots of ways that it could stop, decline, change, or cease to function as a result of something totally outside the relevant frame of reference. There is a nonzero probability that the earth will be hit by a comet and fracture into pieces sometime in the next 100 years, but it would be silly to argue that our current systems of agriculture are unsustainable because they would not survive such an impact. Thus, questions about the sustainability of some practice or phenomenon are almost always asked with some rough and ready assumptions about where the boundaries of the relevant system lie. However, the question of whether a threat is internal or external depends on how people conceptualize (often implicitly) the system of interest. And that conceptualization itself can change. It is unlikely that people would have considered climate change an internal threat until fairly recently, yet it is now seen as a consequence of human activity. Our implicit system borders have shifted before our very eyes.

One of the reasons that conversations about sustainability end in confusion is that people assume that everyone has the same frame of reference, when in fact they do not. When we speculate on the sustainability of real estate values or of the Lansing Catholic Diocese, it is obvious that we are talking about two different systems. When Gordon K. Douglass collected authors to write about agricultural sustainability in 1984, it turned out that some of them were talking about a fairly complex global system that sustains human population; others were talking in general terms about the biological systems that reproduce soil nutrients, microorganisms, tilth, and water tables wherever agriculture is practiced; and still others were talking about the sustainability of rural communities in California. Douglass gave each of these conversations labels: food sufficiency, ecological integrity, and social sustainability, respectively. The recognition that agricultural sustainability could be parsed in these three distinct ways was a revelation to many readers of *Agricultural Sustainability in a Changing World Order.*

Parsing Sustainability

Douglass's introduction to the book recognizes that the workings of sustainability are somewhat different in each of these three cases. Food sufficiency is understood largely as a complicated accounting problem: how many people, how much food? Ecological integrity is much more focused on the dynamics involved in reproducing an ecosystem, whether that system is a watershed or a farmer's field. Social sustainability, in contrast, is focused on achieving certain kinds of desirable political goals: rural community preservation, but also fair treatment for small farmers or farmworkers displaced through technologically induced changes in the structure of agriculture. Not only do these three conversations focus on different underlying systems; they seem to be approaching the evaluation of sustainability in conceptually different ways.

In fact, Douglass recognizes that thinking of sustainability as an accounting problem can be adapted to a wide variety of questions. Indeed, attempts to estimate the global supply of petroleum are paradigm examples of an approach that involves a variety of techniques for estimating how much of a given resource is available and the rate at which it is being consumed. Given these estimates, calculating sustainability becomes straightforward. A given practice (a petroleum-based global energy system, for example) would be sustainable (that is, could be continued) for X number of years, depending on what values are assigned to the estimates. One can solve for X and find out how long the practice can continue; or one can stipulate X and work backward to figure out how total supplies or rates of use must change in order for a practice to be sustainable for a given period.

It is also possible to perform more complex calculations. Total global energy use, for example, can be conceptualized as a problem of estimating total global supply, which includes not only petroleum but also natural gas, firewood, and other potential sources such as hydroelectric generation, wind power, and so on. Then one estimates the rate of consumption, which, given economic growth and development, is actually a rate of *increase* in energy consumption. The potential for conservation (use of less energy) can also be factored into this equation. Petroleum is a finite resource; it will eventually be exhausted. A pattern of energy use sustainable for 100 years would require the gradual replacement of petroleum with other resources, and this system of equations (or model) can provide insight into how various replacement strategies might interact.

Now, this portrayal conceals some extremely difficult scientific problems related to generating the estimates, but it is nonetheless a conceptually accurate (if superficial) description of how sustainability is actually approached when thinking about energy and many other nonrenewable resources. It is not fundamentally different from the way experts in agricultural productivity and human population dynamics approached the question of food self-sufficiency in Douglass's volume. Thus, there is a general view of sustainability here that might be called *resource sufficiency:* a practice is sustainable if the resources needed to continue it are foreseeably at hand. Some system of interacting elements is implied by the phrase "needed to continue it," and one must get into mathematical models and complex calculations to arrive at rates of consumption (or growth in consumption) and rates of supply (or growth in supply). But conceptually, this is still just accounting.

Ecological integrity, in contrast, seems to be stressing something else altogether. The ecologists who contributed to Douglass's book were not estimating the amounts of this or that available in various ecosystem processes. Instead, they were developing models of how ecosystems are reproduced (or changed) through a series of natural cycles. Plants undergo a period of growth in the spring, making protein available for herbivores whose numbers grow, making food available for carnivores that keep the herbivores from browsing plants so extensively that they fail to set enough seed to allow them to overwinter. If these elements are in balance, the whole process starts over the following spring. Although the individual plants and animals are different, the ecosystem has been reproduced over the annual cycle.

Again, this is a very simple-minded account of interactions in a wild ecosystem, but what is important to notice is the way it focuses on interactions among what are taken to be the main elements of the system (in this example, plants, herbivores, and carnivores). The ecological model shows how individuals in each of these groups interact so that there is continuity of the overall system, even though the individual plants, herbivores, and carnivores die. Threats to this system arise through interactions that are out of balance. Elimination of predators is a famous example drawn from the work of Aldo Leopold, who recognized that far from making more deer available to hunters, the killing of wolves actually destroyed the integrity of the wildlife ecosystem. With no wolves to prey on them, the deer population explodes, but the deer browse too heavily on the available plant life. When there is nothing more to eat, there is a crash in the deer population, resulting in far fewer deer to hunt than when human hunters shared the field with wolves.

Although Douglass did not notice it, the idea of system integrity can be applied fairly broadly. The 2007 crash in real estate values is a case in point. The real estate market in the United States depends on the availability of home mortgages. Americans who buy houses have historically financed around 75 percent of the purchase price. The availability of funds for these home mortgages depends on other home buyers repaying their loans. However, in recent decades an underlying market for mortgage securities developed, creating a segment of the mortgage industry that realized profits by writing loans and selling them to other financial institutions. As long as home values were increasing and foreclosures were few, this was a fairly low-risk investment. But as lenders became more interested in making money by selling mortgages and less interested in writing loans that would actually be repaid, they began to write larger and riskier loans.

It took some time for this vulnerability in the home-finance system to become evident. With more loans being made, more homes were sold. With more buyers in the market, home prices increased rapidly. This brought speculative buyers into the market, many of whom took out these risky loans. Eventually, enough people could not repay their loans, making credit harder to get, thereby reducing the number of buyers and leading to a rapid decline in home values. This, too, has a systematic effect. People who owe more than their homes are worth repay even fewer loans, and the cycle of downward value intensifies. It is thus fair to call the emergence of secondary mortgage markets a failure in the underlying integrity of the financial system that supported residential real estate. Since this is not an ecosystem, it is not ecological integrity that failed here. Let's call it *functional integrity*. A large class of sustainability problems can be understood in terms of threats to or failures in the integrity of the functional systems on which they depend.

What about Douglass's social sustainability? In the previous chapter, I stressed the way Walter Goldschmidt's work on the economic viability of farm communities informed thinking on sustainability. Arguably, this could be analyzed as another example of functional integrity: in communities with a few large farms, income is unevenly distributed among the population, making it difficult to support basic infrastructure. But Douglass's contributors who focused on small farmers and farmworkers who had lost their jobs after industrialization would be more inclined to articulate sustainability as a straightforward problem in social justice: to say that a practice is unsustainable is to say that it is socially unjust. Here it seems as if one has made a straightforward normative claim rather than a statement about how the world is. This raises the larger question: how should we understand sustainability as a norm?

Sustainability and Moral Norms

When people inquire into the sustainability of some institution or pattern of events, they are usually inquiring about something that matters to them (or to someone of interest). The question of sustainability is generally asked about something that human beings value, strive for, or hope to attain. Thus, although we need strategies for determining whether something is sustainable in yes-or-no terms, we ask the question in the first place because it is closely aligned with moral or prudential goods, responsibilities, and goals. All these considerations suggest that we should not imagine a sharp line separating the fact and value questions involved in pursuing a sustainable society. Human perception often blurs the line between facts and values. The ability to frame any question generally involves at least a quantum of normativity, as there must be *something* at stake in asking a question, no matter how trivial.

In the examples discussed above and in the preceding chapter, the moral importance of inquiring into sustainability is fairly obvious. Sufficient food for the human population? Lives are at stake. The integrity of agricultural ecosystems? We need those systems to work in order to produce food. The quality of life in rural communities, or fair wages for rural workers? These are, on the face of it, moral notions. The same can be said of sustainable development—an idea that, by emphasizing development, ties sustainability to a long-established if also long-contested social goal. Nevertheless, it is possible to go too far in linking sustainability with moral considerations. Because we would like to continue to possess the goods we value, and because we aspire to certain goals, we are easily inclined to think that only good things *should* be sustained. In *The Spirit of the Soil* I argue that we should not simply incorporate traditional moral and societal goals or values into our idea of sustainability. If we already know what we mean when we say that something is unjust or morally wrong, we add nothing to that meaning when we also call the unjust or wrong practice unsustainable.

To be sure, we lecture one another this way all the time: "This behavior just cannot continue!" (Although the smart alecks being lectured may be saying to themselves, "Why not? I can keep it up indefinitely!") We need to tolerate this kind of loose talk on sustainability, but we have many examples of societies that tolerated widespread abuses of human rights yet endured for centuries. Marcel Mazoyer and Lawrence Roudart provide a fascinating ecologically based account of agricultural systems that have supported human civilizations since the beginnings of agriculture. By far the longest-lived of these is the Egyptian system, which relied on careful management of the annual flooding of the Nile River. It persisted for almost 7,000 years before siltation and population growth resulted in a decline in its productivity. Yet at its peak, this system depended on the enslavement of the vast majority of the people it supported! Certainly anyone who tended to equate sustainability with social justice or with the quality of life in the community would be strongly disinclined to judge the Egyptian system of slave agriculture sustainable. Nevertheless, it seems that we can learn something about sustainability by studying Egyptian agriculture. Here is a system that functioned for a very long time. Do we have a dilemma here?

I do not believe this dilemma is very deep. We have to tolerate a fair amount of ambiguity in the way the word *sustainability* is used, and as the next chapter makes very clear, sometimes we should tolerate uses that equate "That's unsustainable" with "That's unjust" or "That's morally wrong." But we would not have invested the effort to understand the scientific underpinnings of sustainability if there were no empirical questions to be answered. Conceptualizations in terms of resource sufficiency and functional integrity give us ways to assess sustainability that are distinct from a simple judgment of approval or disapproval. They approach sustainability as a factual issue: is it sustainable or not? In *The Spirit of the Soil* I argue that this should be the primary way we understand sustainability, but we should not understand it simply as a factual concept. Whether seen in terms of resource sufficiency or in terms of functional integrity, sustainability indicates a possible state of affairs that we understand as a social goal. We can (and should) ask whether this state of affairs obtains in fact, but by seeing it as a goal, as a morally or politically desirable state of affairs, our interest in sustainability is much more than a matter of scientific curiosity. In previous work I said that we should see it as an "add-on" goal, one that applies when important moral and political criteria such as freedom and justice have already been met. In the following chapters I take a small step away from that view. But first it is important to see how the possible states of affairs indicated by resource sufficiency and functional integrity get conceptualized as norms.

Sustainability as Resource Sufficiency

The basic idea behind resource sufficiency could not be simpler. One can tell if a practice is sustainable by measuring the rate at which resources are being consumed, then multiplying the rate of use by the time frame over which the practice is to be sustained. If current or foreseeable supplies meet or exceed the calculated amount, the practice is sustainable. Using this simple idea as a policy tool involves extensive data collection and elaborate mathematical models to estimate current or foreseeable supplies (stock) and the potential rate of use (flow). As noted above, these models allow one to estimate how long a practice is sustainable. Models become complicated because for some key goods—fertile soil, for instance—stock and flow are dynamically interrelated. Given a long time horizon, natural processes of soil formation will build fertile soils. There is thus a base rate of increase in the stock of fertile soil. But some farming practices consume nutrients and others cause erosion, two ways to "consume" fertile soil. This consumption of soil can be modeled as a rate of depletion, and one can develop resource sufficiency models that determine how long soil-depleting farm practices can continue.

The permanent agriculture advocated by Liberty Hyde Bailey envisions farming methods that do not consume fertile soils faster than they can be built up. The soil conservation work of Hugh Hammond Bennett developed means to augment natural processes of soil formation and to slow rates of consumption through specific farming practices. If the rate of soil loss—the rate of use—can be brought below the rate at which the stock of fertile soils is replenished, the answer to the "how long?" question becomes "forever." One hastens to add that forever is a long, long time. There will undoubtedly be other processes at work that challenge any given farming system's longevity, but the conceptual point still holds. It is, in principle, possible to envision sustainable agriculture as a permanent practice, that is, as a practice operating well within the ecological dynamics that build the stock of resources needed for farm production. The ability to conceptualize sustainability in this way, as existing within natural constraints, is an important source of insight into what sustainability might mean for civilization as a whole.

Of course, not only civilization as a whole but also current farming practice consumes a number of goods that are not being replenished at all. Water stored in ancient aquifers such as the Ogalalla is one example, and fossil fuels used for farm equipment and in the manufacture of fertilizers and other farm inputs are another. If we are to extend the ideal of permanent agriculture to our conception of sustainability, we will need to conceptualize our consumption of nonrenewable resources over an indefinitely long time horizon. One can begin to accommodate this kind of thinking by picking a time horizon—say, fifty years—and using resource sufficiency models to estimate how stocks will be affected. For critical resources—those that will be dramatically affected over fifty years—one can calculate the rate of decline in use that must be achieved to make the practice sustainable. Perhaps this decline can be brought about by substituting other more abundant resources, by introducing conservation practices, or by developing technology that utilizes resources more efficiently.

The potential for such adaptations is implicit in Robert Solow's thinking on sustainability, as well as in models that address global responses to greenhouse gas accumulation and climate change. Economist Julian Simon became well known in the 1980s for his view that science and technology would provide a virtually unlimited ability to compensate for declining resources. More recently, futurist and inventor Raymond

Kurzweil has sounded this theme. Supreme confidence in technology might lead one to presume that there is no need to worry about the consumptive use of renewable resources either. More ecologically oriented authors such as Herman Daly, David Pimentel, and Miguel Altieri make just the opposite assumption about our future ability to develop substitutions for natural resources that become depleted. One's faith in technology has a dramatic influence on the emphasis given to conservation and reduced consumption in reaching the balance needed to achieve resource sufficiency into the indefinite future. Thus the debate over resource sufficiency tends to be one between those who are optimistic about the potential for substitutions and new technologies and those who are not.

Both groups, however, are likely to agree about the moral basis for making adjustments that bring current practice into accord with resource sufficiency. As Jeffrey Burkhardt has argued, the moral obligation to adjust current practice and to plan for sustainability "derives from a general obligation we have to respect and secure the rights of future generations."[1] Environmental philosophers have debated how we should understand moral obligations to future generations for more than thirty years. Derek Parfit formulates some of the most enduring puzzles in his book *Reasons and Persons,* where he argues that a concern for posterity becomes embroiled in paradoxes of moral mathematics. On the one hand, we increase the total amount of future satisfaction simply by increasing the number of satisfied people. This suggests that we should think about resource sufficiency in terms of the maximum carrying capacity of the earth. Until that carrying capacity is exceeded and the quality of life drops to a point at which life is not worth living, we should be answering the question "Enough for whom?" in terms of the largest number of future people possible. On the other hand, Parfit notes that almost no one endorses this result, believing that it would be better to limit human population growth and provide a better quality of life for a smaller number of people.

Burkhardt was one of the first authors to discuss some of these well-known philosophical problems specifically with respect to sustainability. He emphasizes conceptual puzzles that arise when we formulate our obligations to posterity in the language of rights. How can people who do not exist have rights, for example? He concludes that although such rights may be rather limited in comparison to the rights of people who actually exist, there are four categories in which we clearly have obligations to the future: We must ensure the capacity to feed the world's population in the future. We must ensure their capacity to undertake scientific investigations. We must provide a robust set of institutions for democratic governance. And finally, we must bequeath them a tradition of moral trust and respect. Burkhardt's analysis is similar to that of Avner de Shalit, who addresses the Parfit paradoxes by rejecting the view that we should understand the moral significance of future generations as a population of individual lives. Instead, he argues that we should think of our duties to future generations as part and parcel of our duties to the larger human community, rather than as duties owed to specific rights-holding individuals. Since posterity will have needs that we can anticipate, the bonds of trust that bind the human community preclude practices that make those needs impossible to satisfy.

The Parfit paradoxes and responsibilities to future generations are among the most thoroughly studied topics in environmental philosophy. Further discussion of the debates in this area would take the present inquiry too far off course. The key point here is simply that conceptualizing sustainability in terms of resource sufficiency leads one fairly naturally to the philosophical problem of obligations to future generations. One can broaden this discussion by noting that people care about animals and wild environments, and we can assume that future generations will care about nature as well. Thus it is possible to generate fairly wide-ranging concern for the future of endangered species and threatened habitats within a philosophical framework that emphasizes obligations to future generations. Bryan Norton and Eugene Hargrove are two environmental philosophers who have explored this approach to conceptualizing the moral significance of preserving biodiversity, an approach they call "weak anthropocentrism." Again, this is familiar turf for environmental philosophy, but a detailed discussion of these themes is not germane to the issues at hand. Resource sufficiency provides a frame for sustainability that is compatible with a wide range of existing ideas in environmental economics and environmental philosophy. Debates over these ideas can be imported into an attempt to specify resource sufficiency in a fairly straightforward way. But is there an alternative?

Sustainability as Functional Integrity

Unlike sustainability as resource sufficiency, the notion of functional integrity has its roots in ecology and in ecological models developed well before *Our Common Future* was published in 1987. Old-style ecology had presumed that ecosystems would evolve toward an ever richer and more complexly balanced composition of plant and animal species. Plant and microbial life would, in most cases, draw on the solar and chemical energy present within the environment, and the configuration of ecosystem flora would thus reflect soil, water, and climatic constraints. Some animals would be predators of plant life, while others would be predators of lower animals. This evolution in the composition of life-forms present in the ecosystem would eventually "max out" in a climax state, where the composition of species would remain in balance. To say that such a system has integrity is simply to say that the elements of the system—soil, water, flora, and fauna—are reproducing within ranges that allow them to neither increase without limit nor decline into extinction.

Climax ecology envisioned an ideal of "natural order" within ecosystems that was already passé by the late 1970s. Yet ecologists continued to focus on the systematic interaction of both the physical elements of a given environment (soil and climate) and the flora and fauna. They began to recognize a great deal of arbitrariness and contingency in the way these relationships play out, to the extent that any talk of natural order gradually disappeared. Yet relatively stable patterns of interaction in populations of predators and prey organisms, for example, could still be recognized in the data ecologists were analyzing. And they began to identify and classify perturbations in these patterns of interaction, distinguishing those that only temporarily interrupt a pattern of interaction from those that so thoroughly disrupt interactions that the pattern is never reestablished. In the latter cases, contingency is sufficient to allow wholly new groups of individuals to establish new patterns within the spatial environment where the disrupted pattern had been stably reproduced before the perturbation. Such disruptive perturbations can be said to violate the integrity of the (previously existing) system of interaction.

If certain ecosystems can be described as the high points in evolutionary development, it is plausible to understand them as having a kind of value that degraded ecosystems lack. This is undoubtedly one source of the idea that natural ecosystems have intrinsic value, wholly apart from any use that human beings will ever make of them. As ecologists' understanding of ecosystem stability developed, the idea of maximally rich climax ecology gave way to the recognition that one system of interacting organisms is simply succeeded by another. The implicit basis for a "best" state of the system lost any underpinning of scientific support. Nevertheless, it is still possible, as a matter of ethics, to see human-caused perturbations as morally significant in a way that natural perturbations are not. In this manner, the ethics of functional integrity points toward environmental philosophies that value nature and natural systems in themselves, without regard to their utility or usefulness to the human species. Human practices should not disrupt the integrity of natural ecosystem interactions.

How would such a norm be operationalized? First, humans can do things that push stable systems into a disequilibrium from which they do not recover. Overfishing is a good example. Like all vertebrate animals, fish engage in reproductive behavior such that if all the progeny were to survive, populations would grow to the point that they outstripped their food supply. Then the fish would starve and the population would crash. In a stable aquatic environment, the fish population is held in check by predators, humans among them. The natural reproductive rate of the fish allows the total population to rebound after a certain percentage of the population is caught in each generation. This is the "sustainable yield" of the fishery. If humans dramatically increase their predation (say, by dramatically increasing their catch to exploit an economic opportunity), the population will be driven so low that it cannot rebound. This gives other organisms an opportunity to exploit the ecological niche the fish have been occupying, a circumstance that can lead to a permanent decline in the fishery.

This way of looking at ecosystem perturbation is actually quite compatible with a resource sufficiency model of sustainability. Indeed, sustainable yield can be calculated with the same stock and flow mathematics described earlier. Concern for posterity might also provide an adequate basis for describing the sustainable yield of a fishery as a moral norm. People in the future will need to eat fish, so to respect our obligation to futurity, we should not push the fishery beyond its capacity to regenerate the fish population. But an alternative way to understand overfishing is to see human practices as part of the system in question, rather than as actions that impinge on it from without. Here, one might see the rate of fishing as something that is itself regulated within a sustainable system, either by tradition and community norms or by a formal authority established to monitor fishing activity. In this case, overfishing is seen as a breakdown within the system, as a failure in those functional elements that regulate how many fish human beings take from the fishery. It is a problem of functional integrity, albeit beyond the strictly biological elements of a conventional ecosystem. The system in question is now a complex web of social, political, and psychological institutions that reproduce and constrain patterns of human behavior.

As we shift to this more radical point of view, the relevant system includes not only geology, climate, flora, and fauna. It also includes human institutions: habits, traditions, standing practices, and organized forms of collective behavior such as governments, corporations, trade associations, and political pressure groups. Clearly, when we evaluate the current status quo, we are not likely to conclude that these social institutions form a system of interacting elements that is working especially well in all its particulars. Much of our public life is dedicated to reforming, revising, or modifying the activities of other human beings, especially with regard to organized social entities such as governments and corporations. Yet to the extent we see maintaining the integrity of biological subsystems as a social goal, we should also take an interest in maintaining the elements of our social subsystems that are functioning to regulate human behavior in a satisfactory manner.

Of particular importance are those elements in our traditions, our folklore, and our material practice that are most responsible for reproducing moral norms. We want people of good moral character, and in the context of discussing the integrity of biological interactions, we want people who possess the virtues of stewardship and restraint. It is at this point that we circle back to the discussion of agrarian virtues that occupied the first six chapters of this book. The agrarian virtues are precisely those that have been regarded throughout history as critical to the maintenance of communities well integrated into their biological environment. As a people's daily practice reinforces habits of industriousness, community solidarity, citizenship, husbandry, and solicitude, the virtues needed to ensure the integrity of both natural and social patterns of interaction are produced and reproduced from one generation to the next. Formal organizations such as schools and churches may teach these virtues explicitly, but there is no substitute for patterns of work activity and sociability whereby virtue is rewarded with success.

When the system of reference becomes inclusive enough to encompass those practices that give us our sense of morality, of virtue, and of what is right, we have begun to think at a level where purely instrumental conceptualizations of sustainability no longer suffice. We do not value the system that gives us our identity as individuals and communities because it makes us feel happy or satisfied. This system *determines* our ideas of happiness and satisfaction. What is more, the system of institutions that reproduces human culture tends to include elements that actually cultivate dissatisfaction and critical awareness. One of the things we *want* to reproduce in our cultural norms is the capability to change our norms. We cannot help but stand within our cultural institutions when we do this. There is no way to stand outside these institutions and ask how well they serve our ends. We cannot help but value them (participate in them?) as a whole, yet we are able to deploy one institution against another to revise, reformulate, and adjust our cultural bequest. Indeed, the functional integrity of our system of morality depends entirely on our ability to do this. When we have started to think systemically in this way, we arrive at a sui generis understanding of sustainability as a norm.

Parsing Sustainability Redux

Relatively few authors on sustainability have chosen to approach the topic in terms of resource sufficiency and functional integrity, yet there are many points of connection and overlap between these notions and the existing literature. As the previous chapter notes, the 1990s debate over sustainability was framed as a debate between advocates of weak and strong approaches. Following the work of economist Robert Solow, advocates of weak sustainability hold that reproduced capital (that is, the investment of accumulated wealth into new technology and infrastructure) can substitute for the depletion of natural resources. Weak sustainability thus means that one makes a commitment to sustain a general level of welfare for future generations, just as the Brundtland Report said, but it makes no specific commitments about the kind of life future generations will be able to lead. Strong sustainability means a commitment to maintaining "stock" or "natural capital." The strong sustainability view entails, at a minimum, the preservation of those natural resources that have been critical to producing the flows of goods necessary for human welfare.

What is the difference here? It is possible that there is very little difference at all, but some of the debate reprises the themes discussed above. Perhaps a speculative example can help flesh out what is at stake. Today we grow food in farmers' fields and truck it to restaurants or people's homes. Sustaining that system means sustaining soils and having fuel to move the food around. But perhaps tomorrow we could produce massive quantities of algae in slime pits, pipe it directly to your grandchildren's house the way we do water or natural gas, and then have a device filled with nanotechnology and genetically engineered organisms transform the sludge into anything you want. According to weak sustainability, this is perfectly fine. People of tomorrow are still eating, and they do not need soil or gasoline, anyway. According to strong sustainability, we foreclose our grandchildren's future possibilities when we bet heavily on this scenario. We need to save soils, ecosystems, and maybe some petroleum, too.

Bryan Norton summarized the disagreement by writing that weak sustainability is simply a commitment to maintaining economic growth, while strong sustainability is a commitment to maintaining "stuff."[2] One component of the debate centers on whether science and technology can provide substitutes for natural resources, a theme discussed earlier in connection with the resource sufficiency approach. A robust model of agricultural production as we currently know it would reflect the need to maintain soil fertility and genetic diversity in order to maintain productivity. Perhaps new biotechnologies can compensate for the need to do this in ways that are less fantastic than my slime pit model. Improved crops might grow in degraded soils or allow farmers to use more marginal land. Whether one thinks this is a reasonable assumption depends a great deal on one's faith in the innovation process, as well as one's views about the pliability of natural systems. Another component of the debate concerns the nature of our responsibilities toward future generations. Do they have the right to enjoy the same natural amenities that we ourselves have enjoyed? Or does the Brundtland commitment to "needs of the future" simply mean that they should be able to enjoy a secure income, health care, and the other elements listed in Pearce, Barbier, and Markandya's development vector?

It is also plausible to interpret the difference between weak and strong sustainability as the difference between an anthropocentric and an ecocentric environmental philosophy. Alan Holland has followed this line of argument. The former sees all environmental values as being grounded in human attitudes, in uses that humans make of nature (even if *use* just means feeling secure in knowing that nature is "out there"). The latter says that nature has intrinsic value and that it would be wrong to cause the destruction of species or natural places even if there were no more human beings around to enjoy them. On this reading, someone who thinks that only humans matter would endorse weak sustainability, and those who think that natural habitats should be preserved for wild flora and fauna, or just because they are there, would advocate strong sustainability. This, too, suggests a rough equivalence between weak sustainability and resource sufficiency, on the one hand, and between strong sustainability and the integrity of biological systems (but not social institutions), on the other.

Indeed, economists have tended to approach sustainability using accounting-based thinking, while ecologists have long been interested in ecological integrity—a subclass of the approaches I call functional integrity. Solow sustainability was developed specifically in response to post-Brundtland discussions on sustainable development. *Development,* as the term is understood in economics, is explicitly committed to the expansion of human welfare, and Solow's interest lay in whether this expansion of welfare could be made sustainable. Accounting-style methods have long been applied to measure development, so Solow sustainability naturally falls into the mold of resource sufficiency. In contrast, Holling sustainability is grounded in work on the resilience and stability of ecosystems dating back to the 1970s. This work had little to do with development as such and was originally conceived in connection with ecosystems in which humans were involved as little as possible. As Holling expanded his ideas to include the possibility of "panarchy"—resilient, self-organized systems within and between the domain of both nature and human society—his ideas on sustainability got closer and closer to a general notion of functional integrity.

There is thus something of a matchup between Solow sustainability and resource sufficiency, on the one hand, and between Holling sustainability and functional integrity, on the other. Solow sustainability is understood as weak sustainability, and Holling sustainability as strong sustainability, so this lends further support to the idea that resource sufficiency versus functional integrity is just the weak versus strong debate all over again. The technical side of the debate has investigated whether the equations used by someone like Solow differ from the equations used by someone like Holling. Just as the earlier discussion used a stock and flow analysis to explain sustainable yield in fishery ecology, the underlying mathematics of the two notions may turn out to be equivalent. But I argue in the next chapter that the contrasts between weak and strong sustainability do not adequately articulate the most important differences between resource sufficiency and functional integrity and that, in fact, it doesn't really matter if the math is the same.

By the same token, what I have in mind might not be reflected in the technical specifications of an economic or ecological model at all. Resource sufficiency and functional integrity are leading ideas for thinking through the concept of sustainability. Somewhat like a scientific paradigm, a leading idea shapes the way one pursues an inquiry. It helps one formulate which questions it is important to ask. It is at least logically possible that some analysts working with different leading ideas might follow them to mathematically equivalent representations of system dynamics. But even so, resource sufficiency and functional integrity do not amount to the same thing in terms of how we decide what it is important to know or how we conceptualize the links between empirical and normative issues. That is, although either may provide a way to answer the yes-or-no question "Is this system sustainable?" each suggests a different logic for how that question gets connected to moral and political norms.

Given the development of sustainability as a norm in this chapter, it is, in fact, difficult to imagine how someone thinking in terms of resource sufficiency would ever come around to the thought that agrarian ideals are of any importance at all. Yet as we ponder functional integrity from a systemic perspective, we realize that not only we ourselves but also our culture and philosophic traditions are components of a system that includes plants, animals, and habitat as well. Neither social institutions and cultural traditions nor ecosystem elements are fully controlling of the other. Our ideas are shaped by our environment, and our environment is assuredly reshaped by our ideas. Just as we wish to preserve those aspects of the natural world that seem to be functioning well enough (in the sense that resilient patterns of interaction among populations of organisms and key biophysical processes are evident), we should wish to preserve those elements of our social institutions and culture that are functioning well enough. In the case of agrarian ideals, we may need to revitalize (or replace) a set of traditions, practices, and norms that functioned very well in the past to regulate the human use of nature and reproduce sociality and community.

CHAPTER 11

Sustainability

What It Is and What It Is Not

The somewhat presumptuous title of this chapter is not intended to suggest that I will now define *sustainability* once and for all. On the contrary, the continuing debate over the meaning of sustainable practice will increasingly prove useful and important for future generations. In fact, I have three main purposes. First, I review and consolidate themes related to the idea of sustainability that have been introduced throughout the book. In that modest sense, I say what sustainability *is*. Second, I discuss a trend only hinted at previously: that sustainability is best understood as a social movement. Although there are helpful and useful elements in this trend, in the next chapter I argue that we rest content with the idea that sustainability is just a social movement at our peril. In that modest sense, I say what sustainability *is not*. Finally, I try to sort out the puzzle that concluded the last chapter: how my leading ideas— resource sufficiency and functional integrity—match up with the more widely discussed notions of weak and strong sustainability.

Accounting-based approaches typical of resource sufficiency have been the main focus in technical literature emanating from the discipline of economics, but these approaches are not always associated with what is called weak sustainability. Similarly, ecologists have tended to do the kind of system modeling suggested by the idea of functional integrity, but again, this kind of modeling is not necessarily associated with strong sustainability. It is thus a mistake to read the terms of the weak versus strong debate into the difference between resource sufficiency and functional integrity. I argue that when taken as leading ideas, the philosophically important difference between resource sufficiency and functional integrity is that different types of value judgment inform each approach. This suggests that resource sufficiency and functional integrity represent a fundamental moral ambiguity in the way sustainability functions as an ideal. The value judgments implicit in any conceptualization of resource sufficiency are fairly clear: enough for whom, and to do what? For functional integrity, however, values specify the borders of the system in question and implicitly rely on a community ideal. Consonant with themes argued in previous chapters, I believe this makes functional integrity a more promising framework for a public discourse about what we want to achieve in pursuing sustainability.

The "paradox of sustainability" arises because substantive, research-based approaches to sustainability may be too complex to effectively motivate appropriate social responses, especially in a culture where science is presumed to be "value free." We want to pursue sustainability, but we don't really want to be very clear or honest about what that means. Nevertheless, I conclude that debate over the meaning of sustainability can stimulate a fuller appreciation of the complex empirical processes and potentially contestable values implicated in any attempt to accomplish sustainability. In some quarters, it will be possible to pursue this debate in much more complicated mathematical, theoretical, and empirical terminology than I use here. In broader interdisciplinary and public contexts, it will be more effective to use language that is much simpler and more emotionally evocative than mine. In such contexts, it will prove useful to discuss functional integrity in terms of agrarian ideals.

Sustainability and Philosophy

Philosophers spend a large part of their time scrutinizing words and concepts, attempting to clarify what they mean and the implications of their meaning for human endeavors. Philosophical analysis of words and concepts yields a more explicit statement of assumptions that are generally taken for granted when people speak in a certain way. Analysis can reveal ambiguity that leads to confusion and miscommunication, and it can provide insight into how interpreting a concept in one way or another can lead to large and systematic differences in the way two people using a single vocabulary approach a given topic. Again, agriculture is a case in point. Programs in sustainable agriculture apply human, biological, and financial resources to the development of technology and social institutions. They generally draw on agronomy and other agricultural sciences to research and disseminate tools and techniques that farmers can use, or they draw on the applied social sciences to support decision making and social organization to address the local problems of rural communities. Philosophy is a very abstract activity, and sustainable agriculture is a very concrete activity. What do they have to do with each other?

There are at least two points of contact. Sustainable agriculture programs are constantly subjected to criticism and debate about what, precisely, they should be doing. Some believe that resources should be allocated to agronomic techniques characterized by reduced chemical use or low inputs. Some believe that resources should be allocated to programs that make farms of a certain scale or pattern of land use more profitable. Still others believe that conventional agriculture is just fine as it is, and there is no need or basis for special programs on sustainable agriculture. Each of these viewpoints involves a different perspective on what it means for a farm, a production system, or a more comprehensive food system to be sustainable. The variety of views on what it means to be sustainable has multiplied since the early 1980s, when critics of conventional agriculture began to claim that it was unsustainable. The debate is no longer confined to agriculture. Others now want to talk about sustainable development, sustainable land use, and even sustainable architecture. Yet few participants in these debates have the time, inclination, or skills to step back and analyze whether they are separated by a difference in values and perspectives or engaged in a simple verbal dispute.

Philosophy can at least help clarify what is being disputed, even if it cannot resolve the dispute. It is possible that the philosopher's task will end when the terms of debate have been clarified. Yet I have already suggested that sustainability will turn out to be a contested ideal of more enduring and fundamental interest. In some cases, our thinking and communication can be clarified simply by attending closely to a specific definition. Other times, we find that a particular concept is so important to the way we understand ourselves and our world that we cannot gain mastery over it simply by specifying a definition for a given context. Concepts such as truth, objectivity, causality, and justice have been contested throughout human history. Such concepts have resisted our attempts to specify them in any final sense, yet it seems that we must use these concepts to think at all. I believe that as we come to think more deeply and carefully about the impact of human activity on the broader environment and on the opportunities of future generations, we will find that our conceptions of sustainability have a tremendous impact on the way we frame these problems.

Bryan Norton's book on sustainability introduces the themes I am discussing here by using the idea of a "wicked problem." Horst Rittel and Melvin Webber coined the term *wicked problem* in the 1970s to describe a class of planning problems that resisted straightforward, science-based problem solving. Wicked problems lack clear definitions. They do not have clear right and wrong answers. They are saturated with moral concepts and idealizations, and many of these moral ideals are contentious. Attempting to treat them as optimization problems thus neglects much of what makes a wicked problem problematic. Sandra Batie has argued that addressing wicked problems in connection with the analysis of sustainable agriculture cannot succeed through the application of economic models associated with resource sufficiency. Instead, analysts must become comfortable with ambiguity and contested definitions of the problem formulation. So philosophy encounters sustainability in these practical domains first by offering tools to better understand disputed visions of what a sustainable practice might involve, and second because the debates over sustainable agriculture, sustainable development, and even sustainable architecture may well be the opening to an important new area for environmental ethics.

Philosophers generally began to take an interest in the concept of sustainability in the late 1980s, and I have been working on it myself for twenty years. My thinking on sustainability has had three main phases. From about 1988 until about 1994, I was fairly skeptical and even cynical about the idea of sustainability. This is not to say that I was ever opposed to sustainable agriculture, for I was not. However, for about six years I believed that the debates over sustainable agriculture and sustainable development were driven by different conceptions of social justice, at best, and by underlying economic interests, at worst. To big fertilizer, seed, and equipment firms, sustainability meant continued profitability for those firms; to small farmers in Nebraska, sustainability meant being able to continue farming at a small scale in Nebraska; to advocates for Latin American peasants, sustainability meant social justice for Latin American peasants; and so on. My writing from this period argued that there was little ethical significance to any claim announcing that one type of agriculture was sustainable or that another was not. It was, I believed, much better to articulate the ethical claims that might be made on behalf of the environment, farmers, peasants, or the capitalist system in more direct and conventional language. However, I also believed that there were important empirical questions to answer about whether a given practice or ensemble of technologies was or was not sustainable. In other words, I believed it was meaningful to question how long one would be able to continue doing what one was doing before a scarcity of resources or some internal contradiction in one's practice would lead to its undoing.

Two other dimensions of my early thinking were covered in previous chapters. First, I believed then and still believe that it is impossible to answer the empirical question about sustainability without taking a systems view of agriculture, development, or whatever practice is in question. By this I mean that no particular production technology, form of land tenure, or other human practice is either sustainable or unsustainable in isolation. One examines a practice within a system context and then asks whether the total system is sustainable, presuming that conditions outside the system borders remain stable. Taking a systems view, however, involves value judgments, and these value judgments open the door for philosophical inquiry and debate. It is, for example, possible to assess sustainability at the level of a farmer's field, and such an assessment might focus on nutrient exchange, the population of soil microorganisms, or physical changes in the field due to erosion or soil compaction. Assessing sustainability in such terms presumes that the farmer is outside the system—not outside in the sense that the farmer's actions have no impact on the system, but in the sense that this way of understanding sustainability presumes that there will always be a farmer present to manage inputs. What if the continued presence of the farmer is itself in doubt? One can then reframe the question of sustainability by asking what system has to be in place to ensure that a farmer (either a particular farmer or any given farmer) will always be there to farm. Understanding this new system may involve credit markets and farm subsidies, so as systems expand, problems become more wicked.

The broader point here is to illustrate how the definition of system borders involves a value judgment that frames the empirical assessment of sustainability. If one takes the farmer for granted, one gets a set of borders and a corresponding system that may consist largely of soil, water, and microorganisms; if one asks how the farmer's continued involvement can be assured, one is dealing with a very different system that may involve banks, loans, and government payments. Which of these perspectives, which way of defining system borders, is appropriate? My answer to this question is that it depends on what kind of practical problem one is trying to solve. Some people who write about sustainability seem to think that advanced systems modeling is a wholly value-free process that will, through pure science, generate the information we need to save the planet. But the view supported by Norton and Batie (and the view I argued for in *The Spirit of the Soil*) is that the way we conceptualize a system is deeply value laden and reflects judgments about what is thought to be problematic, as well as likely guesses about where the solutions might lie.

Second, because of this systems approach, I argue in chapter 8 (which is to say, back in 1986) that it is possible for a person who is morally committed to sustainability to be overwhelmed by a more comprehensive and unsustainable system. By this I mean that someone who tries to farm or eat sustainably can be part of a society that is, in the aggregate, doing itself in, and there may be very little that any individual's commitment to sustainable farming can do about it. It is also possible for someone who neither thinks nor cares about sustainability to farm or engage in other practices that nevertheless contribute to the sustainability of the overall system. We can presume that many people in the past did so, for thinking and caring about sustainability are of comparatively recent origin. As such, it matters less that we promote sustainability as a personal ideal than that we pursue sustainability at a system level. This may mean that we are careful to maintain norms and beliefs that contribute to sustainability, even if they are not articulated as injunctions to pursue sustainability as such. This aspect of my earlier views has drawn the most comment, as well as some caustic and critical responses (discussed later).

In 1994 several colleagues and I undertook a fairly extensive review of the way people were defining and using the concept of sustainability in a variety of problem-solving and policy contexts. Many of the authors we read were trying to find ways to answer the empirical questions I had already identified as meaningful. This research did not lead me to recant my earlier views, but it did lead me to recast them. I recognized that attempts to answer the empirical questions would not be straightforward and would involve a number of subtle value judgments. Furthermore, I concluded that although there are dozens, perhaps hundreds, of distinct methodologies for measuring and pursuing sustainability through technical research, there are two leading ideas for conceptualizing sustainability. These two leading ideas do not contradict each other so much as they represent alternative approaches, each of which tends to subsume

the other. They differ in which questions they take to be most fundamental, and this difference has implications for how one organizes and
conducts research on sustainability, how one understands our ethical responsibility to make our practices more sustainable. The tension between
these competing ideas also led me to think that there may be something
of enduring philosophical interest here, after all. As a result, beginning
with the 1997 paper "Sustainability as a Norm" (see chapter 10) and continuing through this book, my writing has had a more hopeful tone, and
it takes sustainability more seriously.

As noted in the previous chapter, many of the technical approaches
my colleagues and I reviewed conceptualize sustainability as a problem of resource sufficiency. People working within this paradigm arrive at working definitions of sustainability through their approach to
two measurement problems. First, one must measure the rate at which a
given production or consumption practice depletes or utilizes resources.
Second, one must estimate the stock or store of resources available. The
relative sustainability of a practice is then determined by predicting how
long the practice can be continued, given the existing stock of resources.
The other approach conceptualizes sustainability in terms of the functional integrity of a self-regenerating system. In this view, a practice that
threatens the system's capacity for reproducing itself over time is said
to be unsustainable. This approach requires an account of the system
in question that specifies its reproductive mechanisms, as well as an
account of how specific practices, conceived as system activities, place
those mechanisms at risk.

On reflection, however, I recognize that when I carve up the discourse on sustainability, there are actually three groups rather than two.
In addition to these two paradigms, there are still a number of people
writing and talking about sustainability who seem to be making a *nonsubstantive* use of the word. There is a sense in which calling a practice or
a pattern of conduct unsustainable is just a way of saying, "You may get
away with it this time, but eventually you'll be sorry!" This might point
toward a deeper sense in which the practice or conduct will lead to its
own undoing, but more frequently it is just a general form of moral or
prudential rebuke. In this sense, calling something unsustainable is just
a mild way of calling it bad. I was harshly critical of such talk in earlier
publications, arguing that it created confusion and muddled thinking.
However, I must admit that mildness can be important, especially in

the Midwest, where the only thing worse than accusing someone of bad farming is to praise oneself as being a good farmer (or as knowing more about farming than someone else). In such contexts, "sustainable agriculture" is just a polite way of saying "good agriculture."

One goal of this chapter is to push our thinking on sustainability a little further into a third phase by exploring some of the implications of resource sufficiency and functional integrity within environmental ethics. Eventually, I will examine how these competing conceptions play out in the debate over weak and strong conceptions of sustainability: our broad obligations to nature and to future generations. This discussion should be relevant beyond agriculture. However, it may be useful to begin by returning briefly to some of the nonsubstantive uses of sustainability and to consider how this way of talking about sustainability enables and promotes some healthy activities within local and global debates. Here, sustainable agriculture proves to be a useful focus.

Nonsubstantive Sustainability

Dale Jamieson traces the concept of sustainable development from a 1980 report by the International Union for the Conservation of Nature and Natural Resources, through the 1987 Brundtland Report, to its current plethora of uses and applications. Jamieson concludes that the word *sustainability* is useful in structuring popular discussions and debate but has little philosophical content or motivational power. The philosophical indictment amounts to the claim that conceptualizing human activities in terms of sustainability does nothing to enhance our understanding of moral and prudential obligations associated with those activities. The claim that sustainability has no motivational power amounts to the assertion that characterizing one course of action as more sustainable than another has little effect on human behavior. These are important criticisms for anyone who wants to take sustainability seriously, and I consider each in turn.

First, Jamieson is right to point out that *sustainability* is a good conversation starter and a way to bring different interests to the table. What I have called nonsubstantive uses of the word *sustainable* can be important in bringing people with different interests and values together. When this use generates definitions of sustainability, they tend to be extremely general. Two economists offered this definition: "We define sustainable agricultural development in this paper as an agricultural system which over the long run, enhances environmental quality and the resource base on which agriculture depends, provides for basic human food and fiber needs, is economically viable, and enhances the quality of life of farmers and society as a whole."[2] This definition acknowledges that agriculture feeds the human population, provides income for farmers and rural communities, and affects the environment, and in doing so, it at least acknowledges multiple interests and multiple objectives. Yet, has there ever been an agricultural technology or development project that was not intended to be sustainable, given this definition? Not every project succeeds in meeting these goals, but that just brings us back to equating *sustainable* with *good*.

Nonsubstantive uses of the term *sustainable* are often intended to link environmental impact with social justice. Gordon Douglass notes this in his 1984 essay on different approaches to sustainability. In most instances, authors simply assert that socially unjust practices are unsustainable.[3] Patricia Allen and Carolyn Sachs defended this use of the term *sustainable* in 1992 when they described sustainable agriculture as a "banner" under which a number of groups interested in the environment and social justice have assembled. A year later, Allen and Sachs argued that an adequate conception of sustainability must include the interests of labor, of the poor, and of marginalized groups, but this claim derives its warrant solely from the judgment that the interests of these politically weak groups should be adequately considered in any politically defensible discussion of agricultural practices. Allen and Sachs do not provide any argument that explains why the inclusion of these interests is related to sustainability as such.

This suggests that we can lump people who make nonsubstantive uses of sustainability into the "mildness" camp and the "banner" camp. Neither is particularly interested in what the word *sustainability* might mean. The mild camp wishes to use the term as a way of conveying approval and disapproval in an inoffensive manner. Banner-waving organizers want to use sustainability to unify political and social causes. As Allen and Sachs are aware, one problem with the banner approach is that people with different conceptions of social justice are likely to propose different definitions of sustainability. Indeed, some authors writing on sustainable agriculture have equated sustainability with ordinary profitability, both for agricultural producers and for agribusiness firms.[4]

Neither mildness nor banners get us very far in understanding what criteria should be used when judging a practice to be sustainable, however. No one (well, hardly anyone) sets out to practice bad or unjust agriculture as his or her primary goal. Telling people that they should not be bad or unjust is virtually meaningless in the context of agriculture, unless one also lays out some agriculture-specific criteria as to what bad or unjust means. The substantive debate concerns the standard by which sustainability is to be judged, going beyond anything that mildness and banners can hope to accomplish. The debate over standards becomes acrimonious when either money or social approval is attached to sustainability. Everyone wants to make sure that sustainability is measured in a manner that leaves them qualified for the rewards. People scramble to define sustainability in ways that resemble the annual society page listing of who is "in" and who is "out," and what may have started out as politeness evolves into factional politics. Replaying the debate over social justice within a rhetoric of sustainability has not altered the familiar pattern of political alliances and ideological positions.

Nonsubstantive conceptions of sustainability are certainly useful conversation starters, but Jamieson's point is that the conversation does not go very far unless it eventually turns toward a serious attempt to understand what sustainability could mean in a substantive sense. Other critics of sustainability have been even less charitable. Adrian Parr argues that sustainability has become the "new black," meaning that it is little more than a fashion term. Corporations and politicians engage in greenwashing—concealing environmentally destructive practices behind a rhetoric of environmental stewardship—when they describe products and company policies in the language of sustainability. Julianne Lutz-Newton and Eric Freyfogle offered a dissent against sustainability in the pages of *Conservation Biology* that generated a flurry of debate. Lutz-Newton and Freyfogle argue that a focus on sustainability has contributed little new to conservation efforts and has actually diverted attention from issues of ecological integrity. All these critics emphasize the need to take substantive notions of sustainability seriously if the concept is to have any value in steering environmental policies or human practices, and all have become cynical about whether the word *sustainability* has the rhetorical force to do this.

Why Sustainability Is Important

One problem with nonsubstantive claims is that when we call something sustainable or unsustainable, we are generally making a statement that could be shown to be true or false. We thus need some conception of sustainability that does more than indicate mild approval or that reiterates the work being done by contested concepts such as social justice. One solution to this problem is to allow the values and interests of individuals working within a specific decision-making context to determine the parameters of sustainability.[5] This has been the de facto approach of most applied researchers for the last decade. The result is that the literature contains many technical definitions of sustainability that are inapplicable beyond the specific agronomic, economic, or ecological problems for which they were tailored. Although such problem-solving research may be useful to farmers or natural resource managers, it does little to inform public debate. Can any of these problem-specific approaches to sustainability be generalized?

In the first phase of my work I approached the question of sustainability by asking whether it represented some sort of intrinsic good or some comprehensive synthesis of goods. If this were the case, information about sustainability would be important because we would have an ethical obligation to pursue sustainability as such. I concluded that this is not the best way to characterize the ethics of sustainability. The argument can be summarized by considering an extreme question. We can ask whether murder is sustainable in terms of resource sufficiency by measuring the rate at which murder consumes victims and the number of victims available. We can ask whether murder is sustainable in terms of functional integrity by asking how murder threatens the human population's ability to reproduce itself. As an empirical matter, it seems likely that murder would turn out to be relatively sustainable, so long as more people are born than are killed. We are not inclined to view this fact about murder as indicating our being in favor of the practice. We are not in the least inclined to say, "Well, at least it's a *sustainable* practice." From this kind of argument, I have concluded that we should view sustainability as an "add-on" value rather than as an end in itself. Once we have deemed a practice worthwhile on other grounds, it becomes meaningful to ask whether it is sustainable and to seek relatively more sustainable ways of securing the values or achieving the goals that make a practice worthwhile in the first place.

Although sustainability is not intrinsically valuable, there is still the fact that there may be several ways to further other values that *are* fundamental, and it is important to know which of these several ways is most sustainable. Yet even this judgment may need to be qualified. For example, consider a hypothetical problem for the resource sufficiency approach. Assume that we have determined that one food production strategy will produce a great deal of satisfaction for society at large over a few generations. Assume further that an alternative is more sustainable, in that it will endure for a few more generations, but at such drastically reduced levels of satisfaction that there will be less total well-being produced, even over the long run. It is not at all clear that we should choose sustainability in this case. We would likely choose the alternative that leads to more satisfaction overall.

This suggests that sustainability over time is just a dimension of the general utilitarian maxim proposed by Jeremy Bentham more than 200 years ago. The maxim states that we should choose practices that maximize total well-being or utility, and Bentham describes several ways to measure utility. One of these is to increase the duration of pleasurable or satisfying experiences, but an increase in duration can be swamped by an increase in intensity or extent (that is, in the number of parties experiencing satisfaction).[6] The underlying principle is optimization, not sustainability. Nevertheless, it must be admitted that even if sustainability simply points us toward the duration of well-being over time, it is worth including in a comparison of alternative social policies. Information about sustainability in the sense of resource sufficiency is important for planning, but not in a way that adds anything to the traditional statement of utilitarian philosophy.

So far, my argument does not provide any basis to contradict the collective judgment of Jamieson, Parr, and Lutz-Newton and Freyfogle that there is nothing novel or philosophically interesting about sustainability, but perhaps this is simply a result of the resource sufficiency approach. To examine this possibility, consider again the practice of murder. Taking first the sustainability-as-duration idea suggested by the resource sufficiency approach, we could argue that society's capacity to sustain a murder rate over time is of little value because the costs or harms associated with almost any given murder outweigh any benefits. Lengthening the duration of a murder rate for society might be a good thing in comparison to an alternative whereby the murder rate increases, but not because of sustainability. The moral judgment is simply a matter of the total welfare produced by each alternative. Duration, again, is only one dimension of the increase or decrease in total utility, total benefit, and harm.

Switching to a functional integrity approach, we ask how murder threatens a society's ability to reproduce itself. We might first assess the question in terms of biological births and deaths, but the sustainability of murder is, on the face of it, a much more complicated question than whether there are enough victims to keep up the killing. We are led immediately to consider whether a given murder rate, or perhaps murders of a particular kind or within a particular sector of society, might threaten democratic or family institutions. Answering these questions might, in turn, lead us conclude that even if the birth rate is adequate to supply a continuous stream of victims, murder *does* threaten a society's ability to regenerate its fundamental institutions. This conclusion adds something to the urgency with which murder is understood as a social problem. The harm done by murder is itself sufficient reason to expend resources on police and courts, but the stakes are even higher when we become convinced that it threatens fundamental institutions.

I believe that a similar comparison can be made for ecological, environmental, and agricultural applications of these two approaches, although the issues are more complex. If we take a resource sufficiency approach to food production, the problem is still one of balancing costs and benefits. The accounting becomes very complicated and contentious, in part because there is little consensus about the environmental costs of food production and far less agreement than about the costs and benefits of murder. Yet if we did reach a consensus on the costs and benefits of food production, the value of sustainability would be entirely subsumed in this larger optimization problem. We would compare the relative costs and benefits of different ways of producing food. The comparison would be difficult because of the disparity between different kinds of costs or benefits (gustatory versus nutritional value, producer versus consumer benefit, human versus ecosystem health), but sustainability-as-duration would certainly be one of the least difficult aspects of the comparison to accomplish.

Consider, then, how food production affects our society's ability to reproduce itself. This, too, is a problem of almost overwhelming complexity, for society must be understood as a system comprising many subsystems that are threatened in different ways by different approaches to producing food. One aspect of social reproduction is the regeneration of our bodies, a reproductive process that requires food consumption. The human population's need for food sets one system parameter, but in meeting this parameter, it is possible to deplete soil, water, and genetic resources used in food production. Since each of these is a regenerative subsystem, threats to these subsystems represent threats to total system sustainability. Similarly, farms and rural communities represent subsystems. If farming is unprofitable, or if the local institutions that support farming are not regenerated, the sustainability of the larger system is threatened. Our desire to maintain the functional integrity of all these subsystems might make us conservative in the sense advocated by noted eighteenth-century commentator Edmund Burke. That is, we might be very cautious about "improving" a subsystem that seems to be functioning well enough, for fear that we might upset the complex interconnection of the whole.

Far from understanding sustainability as one dimension of optimization, we would understand it as a relative equilibrium among social and natural subsystems, an equilibrium that we challenge at our peril. We might say that we value these natural and social subsystems because they provide the context or the constitutive basis for personal and group identity and for the formation of preferences that would give rise to a given conception of well-being. This is quite consistent with Norton's and Batie's suggestion that we must understand sustainability as a wicked problem. There is nothing to optimize here because optimization presupposes stable identities that, in turn, generate stable preference functions. Our interest in sustainability, in contrast, calls into question the entire system of influences, legacies, and understandings that contribute to identity. Nevertheless, I believe this view stops short of making sustainability into an intrinsic value, for we would feel considerably less compunction about interfering in a system that did not seem to be functioning well. It might be worth some risk, in other words, to change a social system that produces wretchedness and social injustice in large measure. I also hasten to add that this conception of sustainability would not entail conservatism in every case. If our knowledge about threats to system integrity indicated that our food production system was headed for collapse, sustainability–as–functional integrity would provide a basis for even extreme restorative measures.

We can summarize and tie this discussion to a broader literature in ethics and political philosophy. Resource sufficiency points toward an interpretation of sustainability as a measure of the duration associated with practices that produce (or detract from) well-being. It leaves open certain questions about whose well-being and the relative measure of different forms of satisfaction. It is consistent with the general form of the utilitarian maxim and, indeed, seems to specify nothing more than the temporal dimension of it. It is therefore an important component of the information we need to carry out moral and political duties conceptualized in utilitarian terms, but it is not particularly interesting from a philosophical perspective. The resource sufficiency approach might also be made compatible with rights- or autonomy-based ethics if we understand access to a certain minimal amount of resources as a component of the basic endowment individuals need to experience a meaningful sense of freedom or control over their lives. John Rawls's idea of primary goods and Amartya Sen's idea of capabilities are recent philosophical innovations that articulate how this might be done. What is more, if one relaxes the requirements for being a subject whose welfare matters in this calculation, it is possible to include nonhuman animals (as recommended by Peter Singer and Tom Regan) or even to see nature or natural ecosystems themselves as moral subjects whose welfare must be taken into account. It is difficult to imagine how the economic accounting for some of these philosophically radical approaches might go, but they are all quite compatible with an idealization of sustainability specified in terms of resource sufficiency.

Functional integrity, however, describes the mechanisms that allow whole systems (such as human societies or human-dominated ecosystems) to regenerate themselves over time. System-level stability manifests itself in social institutions; renewal of soil, water, and genetic resources (including wildlife); and cultural identity. The basis of our obligation to maintain this stability is sometimes obscure, but it can be expressed as prudential advice to be cautious about very uncertain risks. It can also be expressed in more communitarian terms as a duty to maintain the integrity of institutions and natural processes that are the basis for our collective sense of identity and purpose. Part of the difficulty in articulating obligations to maintain functional integrity is that as we are pressed to expand the scope of the system whose functional integrity we are interested in preserving, we eventually find that the institutions (including education and language) we rely on to formulate and defend moral norms are actually part and parcel of the system itself. At this point, we must be content with ideals that are inherently vague and often ambiguous, for we are, in effect, trying to formulate how we ourselves would like to be, how we could be better people if only we existed in a socio-natural system with inducements, deterrents, and common practices that reinforced better mentalities and habits than those that allowed us to raise questions about sustainability in the first place. Or, in a more conservative mood, we may be fending off a decline in natural or social subsystems that would make us (or our children) less able to realize personal virtue and community solidarity than we currently are. Less virtuous people might have totally different conceptions of personal welfare and freedom, so ethical philosophies that eschew ideals and attempt to fully operationalize norms in terms of rights or preference satisfaction can never hope to address the moral significance of systems that produce and reproduce our very capacity for ethical judgment.

Resource Sufficiency versus Functional Integrity

The concepts sketched out above are problematic in more ways than can be covered even in the pages of a book. In fact, it is the problematic character of these general approaches to sustainability that makes sustainability a wicked problem and thus accounts for their philosophical significance. If sustainability were just the temporal dimension of a maximization rule, it would merit some analysis and debate among philosophers, economists, and policy wonks. But sustainability is a contested ideal, with functional integrity advocates claiming that it describes part-whole relationships in a way that is central to the socio-natural organization of human activity. It is therefore worth taking some pains to clarify and understand what is being contested and how functional integrity is different from resource sufficiency. In fact, I must admit that resource sufficiency and functional integrity are not so easily distinguished once empirical analysis begins. When it comes to applied science, there is less difference in the way these two approaches characterize the facts than might appear. However, the empirical interconnections only serve to underscore that advocates of each approach are interpreting facts in normatively different ways.

Any attempt to carry out the empirical measurement and system modeling implied by resource sufficiency and functional integrity tends to bring these two approaches to sustainability together. Consider what an analyst attempting to evaluate the sustainability of a given strategy for food production would do. Measuring the resources needed to produce food leads one immediately to renewable soil, water, and genetic resources. Accounting for the availability of these resources over time requires knowledge of the rates at which they are replenished. The resource sufficiency analyst is thus led to many of the same questions as the functional integrity analyst. Production strategies that maintain the functional integrity of regenerative subsystems for renewable resources are likely to come out as more sustainable, regardless of the approach.

Given this similarity, why is there a debate at all? Jamieson reviews the debate between advocates of strong sustainability, who insist that natural capital must not decline over time, and advocates of weak sustainability, who insist that human well-being must not decline over time. Both groups operationalize their respective conceptions of sustainability with accounting arguments of a resource sufficiency kind. The primary difference is that weak sustainability presumes that one means for maintaining human well-being is as good as any other. Crucially, advocates of weak sustainability believe that it is possible to maintain well-being by substituting human for natural capital. Advocates of strong sustainability believe that future generations have a right to the same amount of natural capital enjoyed by present generations, and they believe that protecting this right places a prior constraint on preference maximization by present generations. Norton also stresses the difference between strong and weak sustainability as approaches in ecosystem management. Here again, my illustrative case emphasizes agriculture.

Strong and weak sustainability represent significantly different perspectives for evaluating agriculture. Specifically, advocates of weak sustainability may see agricultural science as a way to compensate for declining soil fertility, water quality, or genetic variability. To say that human capital is substituted for natural capital is economists' way of saying that science will continue to increase yields, even as the renewable resource base declines. Norton and other advocates of strong sustainability reject this strategy, claiming that it violates the rights of future generations. This approach is consistent with resource sufficiency approaches to the measurement of sustainability. It is consistent with the welfarism of utilitarianism (the view that the well-being of individuals is ethically important) and differs from classical utilitarianism primarily by "taking rights seriously"— in this case, the rights of unborn future generations. Thus, the basic philosophical machinery in this approach to strong sustainability is consistent with recent work in ethics and political theory that is largely unconcerned with and uninformed by ecology or principles of functional integrity. Key work in reconciling rights and autonomy approaches with consequentialism (that is, understanding ethics as being intrinsically engaged in comparing the expected consequences of alternative courses of action) was accomplished by Ronald Dworkin and Amartya Sen. This approach does not demand a systems analysis or orientation, and it presupposes only that one has some reasonably reliable means of predicting the outcome of one's action, generally as a sequence of causal relationships.

Yet one wonders whether there is not a functional integrity argument lurking in the background of strong sustainability. One way that systems can creep into the strong sustainability view is when the consequences of human action are predicted using models that are, effectively, systems based. However, this makes it seem as if the predicting is purely a scientific activity. One of Norton's key points is that it is important to avoid a "value-free" notion of science, precisely because doing so conceals key value judgments that may have been made in conceptualizing system borders. The chance of such concealment is significant when the systems orientation is buried in the model being used to predict outcomes. Thus, one philosophical advantage of functional integrity is that the language in which sustainability is articulated invests the system of interest with significance in an obvious way. Clearly, the only way that natural capital can be preserved consistent with the rights of present generations (let alone future ones) is to utilize renewable natural resources within their capacity for regeneration and renewal. In saying that sustainability is about the integrity of the renewable resource subsystem, as opposed to welfare or rights, one brings into view the values implicit in understanding natural resources as a system capable of regeneration.

Another argument for resisting the dependence on science that is implicit in a resource sufficiency approach also points us toward functional integrity by stressing that key vulnerabilities reside in social (rather than soil and water) subsystems. First, if science is generating the technology crucial to meeting food needs, we must be sure that the subsystem that supports agricultural science is itself secure and that there are good reasons to think that continuous increases in yield are in store. Yet funding for agricultural science has declined steadily over the last two decades, and as the number of farmers who lobby for research declines, it is not at all clear that the social apparatus needed to support the research system (and hence the biological productivity of agricultural systems) is stable. Second, increases in yield have been accompanied by patterns of industrialization in agriculture that deplete rural populations and shift farmers' economic livelihood away from dependence on soil, water, and genetic resources and toward dependence on finance. This shift strikes at the heart of the sustainable agriculture movement, for people fear that the social and biological systems that support agriculture have been weakened and that farming has shifted toward greater dependence on an inherently risky system for regenerating financial capital. Each of these subsystems is seen as becoming more brittle as we drift toward industrial agriculture.

I am not asserting that risks to the science subsystem or the rural community subsystem have been proved. My intent is simply to sketch the implicit links between Norton's view of strong sustainability and a functional integrity point of view. However, this sketch suggests that a more explicit statement of the functional basis for imputing rights to future generations would result in a more plausible and potent philosophical statement of the case for strong sustainability. Although many advocates of strong sustainability use the accounting language of resource sufficiency, it seems likely that their conservatism about "stuff" derives from a deeper consideration of the way food production (not to mention the rest of our lives) depends on the continued performance of many interlinked subsystems. They believe that unbridled industrial agriculture poses significant risks to the stability of social, scientific, financial, and renewable resource subsystems. They therefore challenge the weak sustainability estimate of resource availability. Ultimately, a defense of this viewpoint depends more heavily on a plausible account of risks to system integrity than on the imputation of rights to future generations.

The Paradox of Sustainability

Jamieson's negative assessment of the philosophical richness in various conceptions of sustainability is unwarranted, as is the pessimism of Parr, on the one hand, or Lutz-Newton and Freyfogle, on the other. Even if one is inclined to favor a simple norm of optimization, one must admit that resource sufficiency and functional integrity present philosophically complex alternatives for conceptualizing the nature of human responsibility to act sustainably. However, until quite recently I was only slightly less pessimistic than Jamieson about the motivational effectiveness of sustainability. On the one hand, I hope this book will show why sustainability as functional integrity is important and why getting a clearer understanding of sustainability is crucial to policy planning and project management. On the other hand, the sheer complexity of functional integrity (which is part of my argument for treating it as a philosophical problem) weighs against its use as an idea that can mobilize mass political movements. It is questionable whether it can be useful in motivating individual behavior.

This leaves us with the paradox of sustainability: the human polity ought to act sustainably, but the human polity cannot mobilize around the goal of sustainability. Looked at in one way, there is no contradiction here. It is just a way of saying that it is better to be lucky than smart. If we have simple norms that provide little insight into the regenerative systems of ecology and society but that guide our behavior in ways that allow those systems to function, we should retain those simple norms. We ought not replace them with complicated conceptual or mathematical models that are "smart" in terms of providing predictive knowledge of system failure but are too complex for people to follow on a day-to-day basis.

This is not strictly paradoxical, but the upshot is at least ironic. Although we ought to improve our understanding of sustainability in a deep sense, and despite the fact that nonsubstantive discussions of sustainability make this more difficult, nonsubstantive talk about sustainability may be more sustainable (in the sense of promoting a genuinely sustainable society) than reforming the public discourse with an ecologically and philosophically richer idea. Mora Campbell has taken me to task for advocating this position. She claims that since my conceptualization of sustainability establishes a system perspective that is unavailable to people making decisions on a day-to-day basis, I have established a normative framework that is inherently elitist and exclusionary. According to Campbell, a conceptual apparatus that demands an ideal observer's perspective for establishing its normative claims is normatively unacceptable because any acceptable normative perspective must, in principle, be accessible to all. Campbell does not mean that every person must be able to "occupy" or to have deep affective sympathy with a perspective for it to have moral validity. That would be contrary to the general principles of the feminist critique her paper undertakes. Feminist thought in environmental ethics has promoted an interpretation of rightness (or the normatively correct) that is capable of accommodating deep incompatibilities in perspective.[7] This is not the place to launch into a detailed discussion of feminist thought, but Campbell's critique shows, contra Jamieson, that even if my approach to sustainability is motivationally weak, it is motivationally weak in a philosophically interesting way.

In reply I offer two concluding disclaimers and qualifications that will hopefully deflate the elitist and exclusionary pretensions Campbell associates with my position. First, although I have argued that the systems-modeling approach to sustainability yields a conceptualization more adequate to the task of reforming conduct and policy, I have *not* argued that adopting this approach is either a necessary or a sufficient condition for adequate moral decision making. Normative inquiry is complex, and I agree with the main thrust of the feminist critique: it is important to both figuratively imagine and actually conduct inquiries into the norms and goals that guide our lives in an open and welcoming manner. We should not dismiss different views as irrational, nor should we try to police our normative discourse in light of philosophical conceits. We should instead try to hear and accommodate each other's voices.

Second, I have *not* argued that we should allow the numbers generated by hard systems models to override other considerations when reviewing how to adjust our conduct or policy. Indeed, I do not think specific predictions and measurements of either resource sufficiency or functional integrity should be given much weight at all. In fact, I think it is very likely that current models omit crucial factors, and relying on them too heavily in policy making would be to fall victim to the fallacy of "state simplifications" articulated so forcefully by James C. Scott's book *Seeing Like a State*. My argument is that the systems-modeling approach yields an informative and normatively more adequate *conceptualization* of sustainability, one that gives us a better sense of what we are shooting for, one that helps us better understand what our adjustments, approximations, and ameliorative strategies should be striving toward. Models can also reveal patterns of association and interaction that tend to be maintained among various system elements, including human activity. Such revelations are normatively useful, even when the predictions are imprecise.

In fact, Campbell's concerns speak directly to the reason why this book is about both sustainability and agrarian ideals. Agrarian ideals speak to us in accessible and actionable ways. They can be translated into daily activities such as growing one's own food, shopping at farmers' markets, eating seasonal produce, participating in community-supported agriculture, buying fair-trade coffee, or reading up on Wendell Berry or biodynamic farming. Yet a too simple commitment to agrarian ideals lacks the critical consciousness we need to convert a set of quotidian habits or traditional practices into a moral philosophy. One problem with the social movement view of sustainability is that it threatens to become a group-think bandwagon, while demonizing people who do not fit comfortably with the in-group's ideas (industrial agriculture?). As such, it is crucial to return to the agrarian versus industrial theme introduced in early chapters now that we have developed a richer statement of how agrarian ideals relate to sustainable agriculture.

In my view, sustainability is not equivalent to the agrarian ideals we have long associated with democracy and social justice, nor should it be presumed that achieving these ideals will necessarily result in a sustainable society. Yet people seeking to make their societies both more sustainable and more democratic or more just would be well advised to develop an understanding of sustainability that has been informed by the lessons of ecology and systems modeling. They should also regard the definition and conceptualization of sustainability as a philosophically open-ended and always evolving task. It may be most productive to revitalize a moral tradition that understands individual personality and cultural identity to be strongly dependent on environmental influences. Such a tradition, a tradition of agrarian ideals, allows us to argue for nature education, outdoor experiences, and a culture of the table on the grounds that these activities make us better people. But we must also recognize that formulating moral significance in terms of moral ideals means that we will never have a complete understanding of sustainability. We must always be willing and eager to think it through again.

CHAPTER 12

Sustainability, Social Movements, and Hope

Highly technical approaches to sustainability proliferated in the decade between the publication of the Brundtland Report and the end of the millennium. By 2001, Australian philosopher Aiden Davison was calling for an end to the contentious debates over sustainable development on the ground that these technical definitions simply promoted the idea that environmental problems were a domain for expert decision making and technological innovation. The idea that there might be something about modern life that needed deep reform in which many (if not all) people should participate had been driven from the field. Davison's hope was that by turning the discussion away from sustainable development and toward sustainability as such, we would open a space in which more probing but ultimately more hopeful discussions of the question "How should we live?" might emerge. Like me, Davison draws heavily on the thought of Albert Borgmann in describing the way he hopes a conversation on sustainability might develop.

Less than a decade later, sustainability seems to be on everybody's lips. Has the conversation Davison hoped for now begun in earnest? One reason to be hopeful is that the influence of the Brundtland Report seems to have waned. Discussion now seems to focus on sustainability as such, rather than relying exclusively on the idea of economic development. One reason to be skeptical is the nonsubstantive manner in which the word *sustainability* often seems to be used. For many in business and politics, sustainability encompasses all that is good. Saluting sustainability is a way of saying "We want to be good" while avoiding any serious discussion of what that goodness might actually involve.

This usage has also developed a theoretical underpinning in the form of social movement theory. More than fifteen years ago, Patricia

Allen and Carolyn Sachs were calling for us to think of sustainability as a "banner" under which a variety of causes can unite. Today, many people have given up attempting to sort out the various ways we might understand sustainability, notwithstanding my attempt in the previous two chapters. Indeed, they have come to think of sustainability as a banner that describes a broad and important social movement, one of the first to have nearly global status and also one of the first to take shape in the twenty-first century.

Social Movements

One version of the idea is that, like major social movements of the twentieth century, sustainability is a cause that has gripped a significant portion of society. In the first half of the twentieth century, an international labor movement resulted in the formation of trade unions and created a political shift in many industrial countries that substantially increased the influence of the working class. It was formed by men and women with diverse ideologies: communists, socialists, anarchists, and social democrats who (unlike the others) hoped all along for relatively modest reforms. In addition to the revolutionaries, some saw the need for better treatment of workers in religious terms, while others saw it as an evolution in our understanding of democracy. Still others had more narrowly and practically defined objectives in the form of improved wages or working conditions. The labor movement became effective because it was able to transcend the divisions implied by these diverse goals and ideologies, and its ultimate accomplishments may not have been envisioned by any of the individuals who participated in it.

The civil rights movement in the United States during the 1950s and 1960s was similar, in that it represented the coalescence of many goals and ambitions shared initially by American blacks and increasingly embraced by white society. On the one hand, it was aimed at fairly specific political reforms, such as voting rights and the repeal of state-sanctioned segregation. The philosophical basis for these reforms could have been drawn from the founding documents of the American republic, a thought expressed by Martin Luther King Jr. (1929–1968) in the inspiring words of his August 28, 1963, speech in Washington: "I have a dream that one day this nation will rise up and live out the true meaning of its creed: 'We hold these truths to be self-evident, that all men are created equal.'" On the other hand, the civil rights movement unleashed a number of conflicting trends in the way black Americans thought of themselves and in the way blacks and whites interacted with each other. These included ideals of school, neighborhood, and social integration, as well as the idea of a distinct black culture that could thrive in a socially protected space. In this sense, the civil rights movement penetrated patterns of speech, as racial epithets and the words *Negro* and *black* took on new meanings and nuances that were often dependent on where and by whom they were spoken. No logically consistent or philosophically coherent conceptualization of civil rights would easily encompass or express the diverse goals, ideologies, and values we now associate with the civil rights movement.

The international women's movement of the 1970s and 1980s was similar in encompassing an extremely diverse collection of social, political, and economic reforms, while also designating a number of powerful cultural changes. Women today have economic opportunities that were denied to their mothers and grandmothers, including access to consumer and commercial credit and opportunities to assume leadership positions in business, law, and politics. Internationally, rates of literacy among women are rising dramatically. Development schemes such as microcredit emphasize the empowerment of poor women. Although the idea of women's rights articulated the philosophical rationale for some of these changes, others had little to do with any legally effective notion of rights. In the United States, the equal rights amendment, which would have expanded the legal rights of women, failed, yet its failure did not prevent large-scale attitudinal changes that affected women's opportunities for the better. Like the civil rights movement, the accomplishments of the women's movement included deep changes in our very language. When I took logic courses in the 1960s, "All Greeks are men" was considered to be a true sentence. Today it is false.

The general point of these examples is that while social movements are dedicated to objectives and goals that can be articulated, advocated, and defended as moral or political norms, effective social movements go well beyond the specific prescription or recommendation of any particular norm. Indeed, one lesson cited by scholars of such social movements is that the labor movement, the civil rights movement, and the women's movement became effective *because* they were not understood strictly in terms of a narrow or clearly specified set of norms. This is a crucial lesson for anyone who hopes that important environmental changes will be taken up by broader society. It is especially important because, as the Brandt and Brundtland reports both made clear, efforts to promote environmental sustainability will not succeed if they come at the expense of peoples whose economies are only now entering the phase of growth and industrial development that occurred throughout the Northern Hemisphere during the nineteenth and twentieth centuries. And why would we want to endorse any vision of sustainability that perpetuates the extreme poverty in which millions of people now live? To assert that goals of sustainability override fundamental human rights is morally offensive. In the spirit of making our movement for reform and improvement broader, more appealing, and morally acceptable, it is far more attractive to say that sustainability *includes* human rights and social justice. From the perspective of a social movement for sustainability, we should want this movement to be as committed to improving the lot of downtrodden and oppressed people as it is to protecting the environment.

Is Sustainability a Social Movement?

If social movements are cultural transformations that enroll a diverse spectrum of people in broad social change, the answer to the question, "Is sustainability a social movement?" has to be, "Let us hope so." But for social theorists who study social movements, such hopefulness may seem misplaced. These specialists can draw more detailed and poignant lessons from the social movements discussed above. The first lesson is that most social movements fail. They never catch on, and the changes that participants hoped for do not occur. Thus, to say that sustainability is a social movement is simply to say that some people are working toward a vision of social change, and this in itself is no particular reason for hopefulness. What is more, as we saw in chapter 8, achieving sustainability does not necessarily depend on pursuing sustainability. It is possible to have a sustainable society without anyone in society setting out to achieve this social goal.

Another lesson is that even when social movements are effective in bringing about broad changes, those changes may not necessarily reflect the ideals that attracted people to the movement in the first place. Although the labor movement, the civil rights movement, and the women's movement are models of successful social movements, the changes associated with each were not always the changes that participants anticipated or sought. Many labor advocates, for example, envisioned a society

people leading movement are the ones defining sustainability in which the power and influence of corporations would be sharply curtailed. Although the labor movement succeeded in improving working conditions and quality of life for working-class people, corporations are at least as dominant and powerful today as during the heyday of labor activism. So with respect to sustainability as a social movement, I repeat, it is better to be lucky than smart. We may hope that sustainability catches on and becomes an effective social movement, but we must recognize that this is no guarantee that sustainability will actually be achieved.

The sociologists, geographers, and anthropologists who study social movements also have a number of theoretical issues they are arguing about among themselves. One of these is "new social movement theory," which is an attempt to understand and explain a new breed of social movement that sociologists have seen emerging in recent decades. Classic social movements (such as the labor movement) were pretty much full-time affairs to which participants devoted a major chunk of their lives. They often involved causes that penetrated class identity, thus creating a unifying force. And they were focused on basic economic rights: the right to work, to fair working conditions, and to equal pay. New social movements, in contrast, are often social causes that people participate in by sending donations to nongovernmental organizations (NGOs), which lobby for reforms. People may indicate their commitment to these causes by altering their purchasing behavior—by refusing to buy clothing produced in sweatshops, for example. But these movements can hardly be said to involve their advocates in the whole of their being, and they often extend to causes that have little to do with economic rights. At the same time, the theory of new social movements has been subjected to strenuous criticism, and scholars disagree as to whether consumer actions or donating to NGOs qualifies as a social movement of any kind.[1]

I have no wish to embroil myself or my readers in the details of this debate, but I am compelled to bring it up because this thinking has become influential in the public conversation about sustainability. It is not unusual for academic social scientists who support a given social cause to integrate their activism with their research. Publishing on how civil rights, women's issues, environmentalism, or even local food activism embodies the principles of social movement theory is a way to do this. What is more, someone conversant in social movement theory can apply principles of the theory in pursuing an activist cause. For example, one might recognize the theoretical grounds on which modifications or compromises in one's goal or message will expand or contract the movement by attracting or repelling people with compatible interests and goals. Pretty soon it is possible to start talking as if the word *sustainability* is nothing more than a banner under which diverse groups and causes unite. Sustainability then comes to mean whatever list of causes or norms is encompassed by the social movement.

This phenomenon is relevant to a key philosophical question: is social justice a component of sustainability? This question was central to the approach Allen and Sachs took toward sustainable agriculture in the early 1990s. If sustainability is only about the environmental impact of agricultural production, issues such as a living wage for farmworkers or fair trade for smallholders in the developing world seem to fall outside the parameters of sustainability. But perhaps environmental activists and social justice activists can both get a boost by forming an alliance against a common enemy, identified in this case as the firms and institutions that benefit from industrial agriculture. So seeing sustainability as a banner that can encompass a number of causes is a way to see it as social movement that gains strength and efficacy by uniting diverse interests against a common foe.

What happens is that social movement theorists provide a kind of scholarly expert support for certain ways of talking about sustainability. If one says, "An agriculture that exploits people is unsustainable," how are we to evaluate this claim? In the mildness view discussed in chapter 11, the statement is clearly true; however we ultimately cash out the word *exploits*, we know it is not a good thing. But how would a more theoretically rich and textured approach to sustainability evaluate the claim? Later I consider a related question in light of resource sufficiency and functional integrity, but social movement theory has now created a sociological competitor to these approaches grounded in economics and ecology, respectively. There are several ways that our fictional social movement theorist could go. One is to understand the issue as a straightforward inquiry into the current facts related to the sustainability social movement. A strictly fact-oriented sociologist might collect data on groups or individuals who identify themselves as pursuing sustainability. If these people say that social justice is a key component of their goals, then social justice is a component of sustainability. If the data do not support the claim that sustainability activists are pursuing causes of social justice, then social justice is not a component of sustainability.

But neither economists nor ecologists intend to be narrowly descriptive in their treatments of sustainability. Both hope to use their science to tell us what we ought to do. Why should we expect sociologists to be any different? A more normatively inclined sociologist can look at the causes currently clustered under the banner of sustainability and make a judgment about whether human rights advocacy fits. In particular, if stretching the banner to include opposition to exploitation would strengthen the likely effectiveness of the social movement, perhaps by adding new allies or by bringing in a cause that already has widespread social appeal, a normatively inclined sociologist will tell us that we are correct to include a consideration of human rights in our conception of sustainability. Or perhaps our normative sociologist is someone who is deeply committed to human rights already. If so, that person might see linking up with the environmental sustainability crowd as a way to promote his or her own ethically important goals. Either way, no agriculture that exploits people can possibly be sustainable.

I think there is a problem here. My concern at this point has nothing to do with how I feel about exploitation, which I am emphatically against. What is more, as an activist, I would like to know what my social movement theorist thinks about the prospects for mobilizing human rights advocates in the broader social movement for sustainability. But as an environmental philosopher, I just don't think this is how we should settle questions about whether a system or practice is sustainable. Allen and Sachs had similar considerations in mind when they advocated the concept of sustainability as a banner, and their thinking is becoming increasingly commonplace. It has become the basis for thinking that human rights, fair trade, and corporate responsibility are components of sustainability. Sustainability becomes a cluster concept that includes these elements as well as (or perhaps instead of) resource sufficiency and functional integrity. Animal welfare is also on that list. Now science is becoming enrolled. One of my (very distinguished) colleagues in sociology tells me that we can understand sustainability science not as science dedicated to understanding resource sufficiency or functional integrity but as a social movement among scientists. Sustainability is whatever the scientists in the social movement are supporting (and most are focused on forestalling climate change).

Sustainability Indicators

My concern can be made more concrete by examining some indicators that have been suggested for promoting sustainability in livestock production. Indicators are measurable quantities that fall short of an exhaustive characterization of the phenomenon under investigation but can be taken as a sign of relative progress toward it. Indicators have long been utilized in a variety of social policy contexts, including development studies in which *development* has been recognized as a complex and multifaceted phenomenon. Well before the 1987 Brundtland Report called for "sustainable development," development theorists had begun to integrate diverse indicators into an index that would streamline evaluation and simplify decision making for development projects and policy planning. It is therefore not surprising that the use of indicators would be proposed for sustainable development. Subsequent efforts such as the millennium ecosystem assessment developed a number of specific indicators to serve as benchmarks in the progress toward sustainability.

Bryan Norton has argued that we can avoid a lot of confusion and wheel spinning by focusing on indicators instead of on broad definitions or philosophies of sustainability. He points out that abstract debates (like the one between weak and strong sustainability) mean little to the average person, but once sustainability becomes specified in terms of indicators we can actually keep track of, almost everyone can make sense of the problem, and many people will have useful information and helpful ideas to contribute. What is more, implementing any broad approach to sustainability requires attention to many details that do not become evident until a specific problem and a specific locale have been identified. Norton believes that when the process of choosing indicators is carried out publicly in the community where the indicators are to be monitored, the very task of identifying and specifying indicators helps the community reach a consensus about the values and ideals that are most important for its continued well-being.[2]

But in moving from broad thinking about sustainability to specific indicators of sustainability, we introduce a new set of philosophical, practical issues. One can imagine situations in which the consensus advocated by Norton fails to emerge because people do not agree that a given indicator is actually relevant to sustainability. We can begin to appreciate this problem by examining the work done by a group of Dutch researchers hoping to specify indicators for the sustainability of livestock production. Their indicators include economic measures of farm viability such as productivity or net farmworker income, ecological measures such as eutrophication or acidification of surface water, and animal welfare measures such as mortality or air quality. It is important to note that these are, in fact, nested indicators. Farm viability, ecological impact, and animal welfare are the overall indicators of sustainability, but the research group has identified more detailed indicators or measures for each of these three elements. A livestock production system that does well with respect to these three components is deemed to be sustainable. Weakness in any element reduces sustainability, as these researchers have defined it.

These three groups of indicators for the sustainability of farm animal production systems provide a nice test case that illustrates three ethical issues. First, how does the practice of seeing sustainability as a social movement influence the process of selecting and justifying indicators? Second, how might thinking in terms of resource sufficiency or functional integrity influence the way we frame the ethical issues? Third, what are some of the specific problems that arise when we use indicators to fix our interpretation of either sustainability itself or one of the nested concepts such as animal welfare? The second question is taken up in the next section, and the third question is treated only briefly here, although versions of it are critical to any specific proposal for more sustainable practices. For now, I focus on the troubles we encounter when we shift from substantive understandings of sustainability to the idea that the meaning of sustainability flows from its understanding as a social movement. Although the problems can be generalized to almost any discussion of sustainability, I stick closely to the topic of the Dutch research team.

If the word *sustainability* is taken to refer to a social movement for change in agricultural production systems, then sustainability indicators should reflect the goals and values that participants in this social movement wish to promote. According to one view, this is largely an empirical question that can be answered through various kinds of social science research and political processes. The relevant questions are (1) whether the indicators chosen for farm viability, ecological impact, and animal welfare are in fact endorsed by individuals involved in the social movement; and (2) whether these indicators broadly represent the values that participants in the social movement see as relevant to animal production systems. The Dutch researchers asked these questions with respect to milk and egg production.

The Dutch project to achieve more sustainable animal production systems did, in fact, undertake social science research and organize public forums designed to ascertain the answers to these questions. The livestock sustainability project in question defined the social movement toward sustainability as something that has been broadly endorsed by the public at large. The Dutch researchers utilized social science and public engagement techniques that involved representative samples of public opinion and open forums for the discussion of indicators.[3] This may be a reasonable approach in the Netherlands, where recent events may be said to have created a national consensus on sustainability.[4] But in the United States, at least, sustainability continues to be a highly contested concept. If there is a social movement for sustainability in the United States—and I believe that there is—it would need to be conceptualized as one that enrolls much less than a majority of the American public. For agriculture, any movement for sustainability has been, until recently, opposed by many mainstream farm producers and producer organizations. As such, measures of opinion that reflect the U.S. population as a whole might not adequately reflect the values and goals that hold the social movement for sustainable agriculture together in a U.S. context.

In short, if one sees sustainability as a social movement, the question of what indicators represent movement values depends heavily on the local context. However, to the extent that specific indicators arise from or are endorsed by research or by a participatory process, they are taken to be indicators of sustainability. Researchers may then develop indices or scenarios that reflect trade-offs among these indicators, which in turn may be turned over to decision makers or fed back into an iterative process of public engagement.[5] In the former case, bureaucrats or regulators make decisions based on scientifically derived measures to flesh out and specify the broad indicators identified through surveys or focus groups. In the latter case, members of the public have an opportunity to validate, criticize, or otherwise respond to the work of the scientists. Decision making might even be carried out directly by citizen groups (although this is rare in the United States). In either case, these indices or scenarios can reasonably be said to inform public decision making.

Ethics has no clear role in this process, except insofar as ethics has something to say about any process that involves members of the public or a specific group in decision making. In other words, this general way of approaching environmental decision making is a reasonable attempt to make decision making more democratic, and in that sense, it responds to an ethical concern. But there is no ethical content specifically associated with sustainability, nor does there appear to be any ethical work involved in ascertaining the indicators for sustainability or animal welfare. These indicators simply reflect whatever values people happen to have. Researchers must be ethical in reporting data and recruiting participation; members of the public can be expected to reflect their own ethical values in participating in the exercise. Followed faithfully, such an exercise can be expected to reflect the prevailing opinion of those deemed to be included in the social movement for sustainability to a significant degree.[6]

Sustainability as a Norm

If we think that sustainability should be understood as a norm focused on maintaining the functional integrity of an animal production system or, alternatively, resource availability in the future, there are two points of entry for ethics. First, there is the specification of relevant system parameters to generate measures on indicators. Second, there is the evaluation of trade-offs among the respective indicators (as well as additional values that might be relevant to decision making). It may be helpful to begin with the second point of entry, since it involves the most obvious ethical dimension. Clearly, the development of an index that represents the performance of alternative animal production systems with respect to economic, ecological, and welfare indicators has the potential to facilitate deliberative decision making by providing a scientific basis for evaluating trade-offs among economic performance, environmental impact, and animal welfare. This is a useful tool for ethical deliberation, subject to some qualifications discussed later. The question is, is it appropriate to frame indicators that relate to economic performance, environmental impact, and animal welfare as *sustainability* indicators? The answer to this question depends on the way sustainability is conceptualized in normative terms.

As I argued in chapter 10, to understand sustainability as a norm might be to understand the functional integrity of a system as one of several goals or norms to be considered in decision making, where functional integrity is, in turn, the system's capability of reproducing itself through a series of cycles. Alternatively, we could understand sustainability as a norm concerned with whether the resources needed to carry out the activity are foreseeably available. Let us first consider how economic performance, environmental impact, and animal welfare can be understood in terms of resource sufficiency. Recall that the idea behind resource sufficiency is that one estimates the rates of resource consumption and renewal, then calculates whether (or how long) the practice—in this case, an animal production practice—can continue. In this view, we can peg environmental indicators to tell us things such as whether manure leaching into the water supply is causing eutrophication, a buildup of nitrogen or phosphorus that will eventually make the water unusable for human consumption. Economic indicators might focus on whether the farm operator's returns are sufficient to support his or her family, but they might also include the price points for animal products: are they affordable for people on low incomes?

Both kinds of indicators involve ethical questions that fall roughly under the category of "Enough for whom?" The meaning of "enough" and "whom" is very clear on the economic side. For example, a system of egg production that puts the price of eggs out of reach for those Americans who depend on the roughly $1 per person per day that is currently allocated under food stamps would be sustainable only for those whose incomes could be stretched to afford significantly more expensive eggs. Environmental indicators broach the question "Enough for whom?" in terms of both impacts on future generations and impacts on poor people who may not be able to shield themselves from environmental pollutants. One might also wonder whether a system that addresses eutrophication with a technical fix to the human water supply is adequate for the nonhuman residents of the ecosystem. So it is possible to interpret the environmental "Enough for whom?" question quite broadly.

One might think that animal welfare indicators would involve similar applications of the "Enough for whom?" question. That is, we would ask whether the interests of the animals being kept under these production systems had been adequately taken into consideration. The Dutch study cited above, however, took Dutch citizens' feelings about animal welfare as a proxy for actual impacts on the animals. This may seem justified if sustainability is just a social movement, but if we are really interested in how the animals fare in a production system, hard scientific and philosophical questions need to be addressed in configuring an animal welfare indicator. As discussed briefly below, this raises the question of whether the chosen indicators really tell us very much about animal welfare.

Given the functional integrity orientation, we need to understand economic performance, environmental impact, and animal welfare in terms of system cycles. This is reasonably straightforward with respect to environmental impact indicators, because eutrophication and acidification can be related to nutrient cycling ecological models that suggest tipping points at which the pollutants released from the production system exceed the ecological capacity for absorption and utilization of phosphorus or nitrogen, making the system functionally unsustainable. Economic performance is a little trickier. Producers must certainly derive sufficient income from farming operations to cover their costs, including costs associated with a reasonable standard of living. Yet we cannot assume that there is a direct correlation between profitability and sustainability, because there is certainly a point at which profits exceed the amount needed to maintain economic viability. That is, although profits can go up and up and up, there is a certain point at which one would say "enough" with respect to sustainability.

Nevertheless, productivity measures together with models for credit and commodity markets provide a way to conceptualize economic performance in terms of system sustainability. However, a system that demands an annual government subsidy to remain economically viable is sustainable only if the political system that produces the subsidy is sustainable. In U.S. animal production systems, the nature and source of these subsidies are exceedingly complex and difficult to identify clearly. For example, subsidies critical to the economic viability of animal production may be paid to those who produce feedstuffs rather than to animal producers themselves.[7] Subsidies to grain growers allow animal producers to keep feed costs low. The problem of subsidies points to a key value judgment that must be made when developing system models in the economic sphere.

Some economic models for animal production systems are capable of predicting the amount of subsidy needed to maintain economic viability, given data or assumptions about the price points that must be met for the meat, milk, and eggs that livestock farmers produce. But these models do not incorporate the political system itself. Thus, a subsidy is an exogenous input that must be presumed to be secure in order for the system to be deemed economically sustainable. Are we justified in assuming that the economic system is entirely cut off from political influences and policy mechanisms that regenerate political decisions to provide farm subsidies? Or should we see economic exchange as embedded within a larger and more complex system of social relations that also produces and reproduces political action? The parameters (or borders) of the economic system that is to be sustained can only be established in reference to assumptions that reflect either broad philosophical values or methodological values that facilitate the pursuit of research programs in disciplinary areas.

We can, for example, make the value judgment that a subsidy for farmers is always a legitimate political goal. Perhaps we, like Jefferson, think that farmers make the best citizens, and we want to keep as many of them around as possible. Or we can make the very difficult value judgment that a subsidy distorts the playing field for economic actors. Value judgments of this kind are often hidden in the analyses done by competing policy think tanks. We can also ask our economic modeler to include the various forces that create or deplete the political will to enact subsidies. This makes the question of political sustainability look more like an empirical question that better research could answer, but this is a difficult request for any present-day modeler to comply with. Because of the sheer complexity and high levels of uncertainty that accompany any model of political will, analysts of economic sustainability would likely duck this question for methodological reasons. What matters most in the present context is that these "system border" value judgments are exactly the kind of questions that arise when we think of sustainability in terms of functional integrity, but that might remain in the background when we think in terms of resource sufficiency. Although I have used the parameters of the economic system to illustrate the sensitivity of the modeling process to value judgments, biological models involve similar value judgments.

In contrast to economic performance and environmental impact, animal welfare is not easily modeled as a dimension of system cycles. In livestock farming, reproduction of the animal population is accomplished by having a side enterprise such as a hatchery or a calf farm that supplies animals to the farms where eggs or meat are produced for market. There will always be plenty of new animals, no matter how badly they are treated, so from the standpoint of whether animal welfare is required to get a new herd or flock of animals, there is little question that it is not. Like human welfare indicators, animal welfare indicators are typically framed to provide some measure of the creatures' well-being, which is understood to encompass mortality, morbidity, and measures of experiential quality of life. Indicators for human and animal welfare are typically developed to specify levels of well-being that far exceed the capacity of a population to reproduce itself. In the Dutch study, mortality and air quality were selected. As such, although animal welfare is one of the important ethical parameters for evaluating a production system, it is not easy to see how it can be formulated as an indicator of the system's functional integrity.

In fact, when we think of sustainability as a norm in light of the system's functional integrity, we might be more inclined to see the ethical issues of animal welfare as framing a trade-off between sustainability and other, more fundamental ethical goals. This thinking draws on the point made earlier when I suggested that sustainability might be thought of as an "add-on" goal. We can think of our first ethical priorities in terms of basic human rights and human well-being, and then ask what it would take to make a society that satisfies these priorities more sustainable in the functional integrity sense. I agree with those who suggest that animal rights and animal welfare should be added to our list of fundamental priorities. Just as we might be willing to accept some weakness in the integrity of a system to achieve goals of social justice and welfare for humans, we might get a clearer picture of animal welfare if we think of it as something that is ethically more fundamental than functional integrity.

At this point, we are much too far into a long and complicated argument to do real justice to the issues of animal welfare and animal rights, but I want to close this discussion by briefly considering the third question asked earlier. Which indicators really tell us something about animal welfare? Identifying animal welfare indicators is difficult because, like human welfare, it has multiple dimensions. Some animal welfare scientists have argued that the most reliable indicator of animal welfare in livestock production is the most obvious one: how many animals die because of their living conditions? Animal advocates might react by saying that this is an extremely conservative and underambitious indicator. Animals might endure suffering that should be regarded as intolerable well before they actually die from it. But in other respects, mortality seems a far too stringent test of welfare. Mortality rates are generally higher on farms where animals are kept outdoors under conditions that a casual observer might regard as idyllic. On old-fashioned farms, animals were vulnerable to predators and pathogens. They died much more frequently than do animals on industrial farms, but was their welfare worse? How would we decide?

In 2008 California voters passed a ballot initiative that bans any livestock production system that does not allow animals to perform the full range of movement typical of the species. When implemented, the referendum will put an end to the industrial-style egg production facilities typical of the U.S. egg industry at this writing, but it will permit systems that are known to exhibit much higher levels of disease and mortality among birds. It is at least arguable that the birds are better off in these alternative systems, even if more of them die. Few human beings would choose a lifestyle that minimizes their own mortality risk. My larger point here is that truly integrating animal welfare into a conceptualization of either resource sufficiency or functional integrity would require us to work through this puzzle and many others. Not the least of them is the still unsettled matter of when it is appropriate to utilize animals for human ends. It is an important task for agricultural ethics, but not one to be pursued in the present context. More pointedly, it is not a task that is illuminated or better understood by conceptualizing animal welfare as an indicator for sustainability.

Norm versus Social Movement

Whether we are thinking of resource sufficiency and functional integrity, on the one hand, or thinking of sustainability as a social movement, on the other, we can use indicators to create indices or scenarios that simplify and communicate trade-offs in a decision-making process. In both approaches, the evaluation of these trade-offs can be conceptualized as a deliberative, reflective, or democratic process in which the role of indicators is to facilitate clear and informed decision making. In both approaches, this process is informed by ethics, but it is not reducible to any ethically rationalized algorithm or decision rule. Thus, for both these approaches, ethics comes in at the stage of decision making, and it can be understood as providing a statement of values or a philosophy that is intended to guide decision making in light of trade-offs. This decision making involves ethical deliberations about how much weight to give each dimension for which an indicator has been selected, and clearly, an

in order for sost. to be a social moreant, laymen need to understand and be inspired by it index of indicators is helpful in conducting these ethical deliberations. One might reasonably ask, given these similarities, what is the debate between sustainability as a norm and sustainability as a social movement all about?

There are two points to make in this connection. The first has to do with ordinary language and effective communication. Twentieth-century philosophers devoted a great deal of effort to examining how decision trade-offs might be framed and evaluated. This included using economic and quasi-economic valuation methods to assign common scales to multiple indicators, weighting indicators associated with morally significant features such as harm or compromise to rights, and identifying rationales for regarding outcomes associated with a specific class of indicators (such as rights) as unacceptable, regardless of trade-offs for other dimensions. Some multivariable decision-making theories attempted to reflect these philosophical considerations, although I think it is fair to say that the current consensus favors the conversion of an index into more intuitive scenarios so that citizens who lack expertise in quantitative decision making can still provide input into the decision-making process. To the extent that this is so, it is important to ask whether thinking of an indicator such as animal welfare as a *component* of sustainability aids or detracts from the understanding of the normative issues at hand. My suspicion is that simply allowing everything to be seen as a dimension of sustainability obscures the importance of functional integrity and resource availability in decision making. This is a hypothesis that is amenable to empirical research, so we will simply have to wait and see.

If you began to lose the train of thought in the previous paragraph somewhere around the point where I brought up quasi-economic valuation methods (or even if you hung in there until we got to multivariable decision-making theories), you may be one of the people who hopes that key value decisions made in connection with sustainability can be expressed in plain English. This is one of the key recommendations Bryan Norton makes in his monumental study of sustainability, and it is critical not only to ensure that the broadest possible range of the public can participate in conversations about sustainability but also because even technical specialists tend to talk past one another when they are allowed to continue indefinitely in the jargon of their disciplinary specializations.

The second point acknowledges what the social movement view gets right. Although it is better to be lucky than smart, it would be highly irresponsible to count on luck. Motivating people to take personal and political action simply must be a part of sustainability. Thus, although an overly broad view of sustainability may obscure the important "system maintenance" aspects that are brought to the foreground in both functional integrity and resource sufficiency conceptualizations, these approaches rely on technically complex, deeply theory-laden ideas from environmental science. And this technical complexity threatens to undercut their motivational potential altogether. Social movement theorists move directly to conversations with real people, to procedures for bringing more voices into the mix. They fail only insofar as they allow us to forget that our ability to keep our society, our way of life, going hangs in the balance. But keeping things going is what sustainability was originally all about, before the social movement theorists got their mitts on it.

Here it is worth reiterating the central theme of this book. The appeal to agrarian ideals can bridge the gap between abstruse theory and common sense. Agrarianism has taken numerous forms throughout human history, but agrarian views have always communicated that a human practice achieves its potential only when it is adaptively responsive to the broader environment in which it is embedded. As such, it is more than plausible to suggest that agrarian ideals have the potential to provide a broad segment of the public with access to the important themes articulated in functional integrity and resource sufficiency conceptualizations of sustainability. And they may well accomplish this more effectively than do the terms *functional integrity* and *resource sufficiency*.

Social Sustainability and Social Hope

Perhaps the problem is all too obvious. Livestock production systems that confine animals indoors in small spaces will inevitably generate political opposition because people do not like to think of animals confined in that way. Such systems are not sustainable because social movements will rise up and call for reform, just as the labor movement, the civil rights movement, and the women's movement achieved significant social change through alternating activities of confrontation and compromise. This rather straightforward and commonsense way of thinking suggests that social movements *do* have something to do with sustainability in a much more direct way than my analyses of resource sufficiency and functional integrity have thus far acknowledged. Does this implicit linkage between social movements and progressive change provide a third way to conceptualize sustainability, or does it devolve back into norms and ideals that are better articulated in terms of social justice?

Arguments for the latter alternative have been suggested several times already. No one is against progress understood in terms of greater justice, fairness, or goodness, so linking sustainability and progressive social movements looks very much like a nonsubstantive use of the word. Either we are politely hinting that animals are being treated badly (the mildness approach) or we are rallying the troops for a serious political campaign (the banner approach). But in neither case are we saying more in ethical terms than that animal welfare is an ethical imperative. Or perhaps this kind of social sustainability is just good strategic advice for the corporate sector—in this case, livestock producers: don't anger your customers; hire a sociologist to figure out what they will and won't accept. Here social sustainability seems to be emptied of all normative content whatsoever. But with these qualifiers firmly in mind, it may still be possible to articulate a sense in which progressive social change brought about through social movements can indeed be understood to involve a kind of sustainability.

Walter Kaufmann (1921–1980) described G. W. F. Hegel's *Phenomenology of Spirit* as a "pageant of human consciousness" in which a sequence of mentalities or self-understandings unfolds as a result of confrontations between one self and another. The central motor of this unfolding is the master-slave dialectic, in which one self, one consciousness, seeks to realize itself most fully by subjecting another consciousness (another person) wholly to its own desires and will. Ironically, in doing so, the master becomes wholly dependent on the slave, for it is the slave who actually acts by working to do the master's bidding. As master and slave alike become conscious of this ironic dependence relationship, a new stage of consciousness emerges in which each recognizes his self in the consciousness of the other. As readers of this notoriously difficult book know, the sequence of oppositions moves through ever more complex and subtle forms of revelation and self-recognition. Consciousness eventually recognizes its inherently social being through its dependence on culture, history, and social embodiment in the ideal of the church, the state, and the abstract moral community of all people.

Hegel's thought assumed profound influence among nineteenth-century intellectuals because they were able to believe that history was actually fulfilling something like this sequence. Societies in which literal forms of subjection and slavery had persisted were giving way to social democracies that recognized the worth and value of all people. A consummation of human community seemed just on the horizon, although it was imagined somewhat differently, it is worth noting, by those who invested their hopes in the church and those who stressed reforms in the organization of labor and material production. Progress itself seemed to be driven along by the dialectic of confrontation sketched in the master-slave dialectic. Karl Marx and Friedrich Engels (1820–1895) developed a version of Hegel's dialectic in which social consciousness progressed through material confrontations between dominant and subservient social classes. In the heady atmosphere of the nineteenth century, it was possible to hope that social conflict would lead to a widespread mutual consciousness of human potential, human interdependence, and solidarity.

The wars, genocides, and environmental decay of the twentieth century did much to dash such hopes for progress. Back in 1992 I was referencing Hegel and writing, "Where we once hoped that history would convert individual misery and folly into a comprehensive progress for all humanity, we now hope for sustainability."[8] My thought was completed by Tarla Rae Peterson, who argues that giving up on ideals of progress is a feature of the postmodern era, and we have settled on sustainability as a substitute. But if this is so, perhaps the social movement theorists are right in seeing social conflict as the cauldron in which a new environmental consciousness will emerge. This is not the same thing as saying that justice or animal welfare is part and parcel of sustainability, but it does suggest that social movements aimed at promoting justice or animal welfare will play an indispensable role in shaping how sustainability comes to be conceived.

Deep social conflicts are not sustainable because the sense of hope implicit in any conceptualization of sustainability as a moral ideal implies a realization of community consciousness. The recognition and discovery that occur in conjunction with the resolution or sublimation of social conflict feed a process of personal learning on the part of individual participants in social struggles and, in the best cases, promote social learning that realizes an expanded sense of community and shared fate. This is the case even though there have been episodes of human history in which forms of oppression and subjugation have been sustained for protracted periods, even millennia. To suggest that Egyptian slave agricultures must have been sustainable because they endured for thousands of years is to presuppose an overly literal sense of temporality. The focus on social conflict suggests a historical notion of time that implies that subjection and social conflict are symptoms of unrealized hope. Unrealized hope points us toward a future that, even when forever unrealized, animates our consciousness of collective practice in light of moral ideals. Even failed social movements (whether focused on sustainability or on something else) reflect the motivating power of ideals in human affairs.

Agrarian ideals are relevant for social movements focused on sustainability because they model and make transparent the manner in which an existing way of life, conditioned and structured by its history as well as its environment, succeeds or fails to renew itself through cycles of time that can be measured week to week, year to year, or generation to generation. They illustrate how our personal and group identities are part and parcel of an ecology that begins in the natural order, and they make our collective vulnerabilities visible to us far better than do Enlightenment ideals of equality, welfare, or human rights. Group conflict is one of those vulnerabilities, as agrarian ideals from ancient Greece emphasized by linking the farm household to virtues of courageous common defense. Resuscitated and revitalized ideals for the twenty-first century will strike different notes, but those who try to refashion ideals for today's social movements would do well to study Jefferson's praise of farming very carefully.

Conclusion

Jefferson's Bequest

When it comes to sustainability, it is better to be lucky than smart. This does not mean that we should abandon intelligence completely. Thomas Jefferson's approach to the political sustainability of the new American republic illustrates how intelligence can be applied to the problem of sustainability with cunning and guile. When Jefferson became president of the United States in 1801, the immediate threats to the sustainability of America lay in factionalism and in the potential for foreign invasion. Jefferson might have approached this problem by appealing to Americans' patriotic zeal, buttressed, perhaps, with a bit of fear. Instead, he followed a course outlined in his writings from the 1780s, pursuing policies to encourage the growth of farming at the expense of manufacturing and urban growth.

Jefferson's legacy resides in the indirectness of this approach. Jefferson's goal was to avoid both dissolution and subjection from foreign powers, but he was also wary of consolidating too much power in the executive office. As such, the path he followed was to populate the American republic with citizens whose abiding interest was coincident with the medium-term stability of the government. As Americans have seen in recent times, traders and manufacturers are not "tied to their country & wedded to its liberty & interests by the most lasting bonds." Indeed, traders and manufacturers operate wherever in the world they find the most advantageous terms. Economic risks from insolvent or unstable governments are part of their calculations, to be sure, but these risks might be overshadowed by cheap labor or materials. And the economic risk of operating in an unstable political climate can be mitigated by an ironfisted application of power. Repressive regimes have proved to be quite capable of generating conditions favorable to manufacturing and trade.

Farmers, in contrast, are invested in the improvement and development of their land. They are "tied to their country" (Jefferson's words) in a literal sense. The word *country* in this phrase is felicitously ambiguous. It can mean "rural districts, including farmland, parkland, and other sparsely populated areas," or, more simply, just "a tract of land," but it also means "a state or nation" and "the land of one's birth or citizenship."[1] It is the tie to the tract of land on which they farm that bonds farmers to the land of their citizenship so firmly. In choosing the Louisiana Purchase over Alexander Hamilton's plan for industrial development, Jefferson thus exhibited a cunning in his approach to the sustainability issues of America circa 1800 that serves as a model for us today. It is worth exploring how this mode of thinking differs from a more direct approach.

We might think of straight-line rationality as fixing one's goals, then choosing the shortest, most direct route toward them. This is the classic model of rational action favored by economists and utilitarian philosophers. This mode of thinking might lead us to think of sustainability in terms of resource sufficiency and then to calculate which public policies would achieve that goal. Had Jefferson thought in this mode, he might have favored Hamilton's plan. It would all depend on how the comparative economic evaluation of the Louisiana Purchase versus investment in industrial development played out. Indeed, from this point of view, the Louisiana Purchase *was* industrial development: we could spend the money on factories or on land. In resource sufficiency terms, we evaluate this choice by computing the long-run returns on either option and then choosing the one with the most favorable returns, once externalities have been included. Consistent with an industrial philosophy of agriculture, farming is just one sector of an industrial economy. Using straight-line rationality to think about sustainability, we must evaluate investments in different sectors of the economy in common terms if we are to make a valid comparison of how each contributes to resource sufficiency. That is what it means to be smart.

Jefferson, however, was thinking more along the lines of functional integrity, although his notion of functional integrity was especially attentive to the economic and political conflicts that can rip a society apart. An industrial society might have sufficient resources to sustain itself, but the "mobs of great cities" may well incite political tensions that cannot be overcome without violence or repressive applications of state power. Recall that Jefferson had been ambassador to France not long before the

Reign of Terror that lasted for nine months beginning in September 1793. The sustainability that Jefferson was seeking required "the manners and spirit of a people which preserve a republic in vigour," and these were to be achieved by facilitating vocations that would encourage Americans to see themselves as irrevocably wedded to a common fate. Citizens in this mold would be less tempted by factions that sought dissolution into smaller and weaker political units. They would turn up for military service and would not abandon their country in search of more attractive terms for trade. They would be equally leery of too much consolidation at the federal level. Because they could not preserve both their wealth and their freedom by immigrating to new lands, they would guard their liberty through "eternal vigilance." Jefferson's praise of farming must be seen in this historical context if we are to appreciate his legacy for approaching sustainability today.

Jefferson, of course, did not speak in terms of sustainability, much less functional integrity. Jeffersonian democracy was articulated by an appeal to agrarian ideals. It was a language quite unlike that of the complex economic and ecological models used to flesh out resource sufficiency or even ecological integrity today. There is no calculating "the greatest good for the greatest number" with Jefferson and no appeal to the general welfare at all. This omission is not because Jefferson suffered from math anxiety. The man loved numbers, but he did not appeal to them in his moral and political writings. Contemporary historian Garry Wills is fond of quoting a passage from a letter Jefferson wrote to his ward Peter Carr in 1787: "State a moral case to a ploughman & a professor. The farmer will decide it as well, & often better than the latter, because he has not been led astray by artificial rules."[2] One point we should take from this is that the language of virtue and moral character may possess more cunning than putatively smart approaches that address sustainability solely through the lens of complicated mathematical models.

It is also quite striking that Jefferson's approach to the problem of sustainability eschews any talk of rights and justice. The reason is simple. The problems that Jefferson was addressing in his celebrated passages on farming and democracy were not *about* rights and justice. They were about the sustainability of a democratic polity. This is an especially poignant observation in light of Jefferson's status as an advocate of human rights through his authorship of the Declaration of Independence and the Virginia Statute for Religious Freedom (1779), as well as his insistence on the inclusion of a Bill of Rights in the U.S. Constitution. As historian Edmund Morgan writes, "Jefferson himself, whatever his shortcomings, was the greatest champion of liberty this country has ever had."[3] If there is one thing we can be sure of, it is that Jefferson was fully conversant in the philosophical language of rights as well as its applicability to problems of justice and liberty. Yet unlike contemporary political theorists who presume that all public goals (including sustainability) must be rationalized in terms of welfare and utility, on the one hand, or rights and justice, on the other, Jefferson did not hesitate to express one of the most fundamental tenets of Jeffersonian democracy in terms of moral character, "the spirit of a people," and agrarian ideals.

We dishonor Jefferson's bequest if we insist on reading the agrarian passages too literally. These are not simpleminded exhortations to engage in farming! Even in his own time, Jefferson realized that encouragement of manufacturing was essential to the future of American independence. What we should take from Jefferson's agrarian writings is his general approach to the problem of sustainability. It is notable for being indirect rather than "smart," for its reliance on the moral and philosophical language of virtue and character, and for the way it grounds that language in the daily, material habits of citizens. These material habits do indeed affect our thinking, but not by encouraging us to "make better choices," as an advocate of straight-line rationality might suggest. The habits of the farmer make certain needs, problems, and interdependencies transparently obvious. And it is through cultivating such habits that we get lucky instead of smart.

But it is patently obvious that the problems of sustainability we face are quite different from those faced by Jefferson. As such, our use of agrarian ideals requires adaptation and even revision if they are to serve us well. Perhaps at this point it is worthwhile to return to Thomas Inge's five themes:

1. *Religion.* Farming reminds humanity of its finitude and dependence on God.
2. *Romance.* Technology corrupts; nature redeems.
3. *Moral Ontology.* Farming produces a sense of harmony and integration, while modern society is alienating and fragmenting.
4. *Politics.* Rural autochthony provides the backbone for democracy.

5. *Society.* Rural interdependencies and reciprocities provide a model for healthy community.

A reformulation of Inge is clearly in order if we are to move toward an adequate conceptualization of sustainability. Although earlier chapters provided the basis for rethinking some of Inge's themes, others have only been touched on.

Religion

The dependence on God mentioned by Inge should stress ecological integrity, or it should involve an explicit theology that links God and nature (as contemporary ecology understands it). My discussion of agrarian ideals in chapter 1 draws on the ancient Greek poet Hesiod, who understood all of nature to be imbued with the divine presence. The connection with the religion of Hesiod thus links God, as Inge understands the deity when he talks of finitude and dependence on God, directly with nature or ecological integrity as I understand it throughout this book. The theology gets more complicated as we move into the Christian era. Historian Lynn White wrote a very influential article in 1967 arguing that some Christian beliefs might be the source of our present-day ecological crisis. White's thesis is debated, but it is clear that early Christians took great pains to distinguish the Christian conception of God from the pantheistic ideas of Hesiod. Thus, some bridge building is required between my development of nature as ecological integrity and a religious understanding of God that would be familiar to contemporary Americans. There are many contemporary theologians who have undertaken this kind of bridge building. The best known may be John Cobb, whose book *For the Common Good,* written with economist Herman Daly, is already a classic in the literature of sustainability.

Norman Wirzba has developed a theological approach that is directly mindful of agrarian ideals. Wirzba argues that one key task for a reformulation of the religion tenet is to disentangle it from the metaphysical assumptions of the Cartesian age, which saw "mind" and "matter" as wholly discrete realms of being. The soul comes to be identified with Descartes' idea of the "subject"—a disembodied onlooker to the events of a person's life. It is a conceit seductively conducive to religious traditions that stress the immortality of the soul. It encourages religious believers to dissociate themselves from their embodied experience. It is easy to see how this picture becomes attractive to anyone approaching death. My own mother (hardly a conventional Christian) spoke of her own death in terms of leaving behind a body racked with multiple debilities and dancing on the clouds. But however consoling this picture might be, a religious faith constructed around mind-body dualism becomes bogged down in numerous difficulties when it is used as a guide for life. It can be taken to imply that we need not take care of our bodies or, in extreme cases, that we can denigrate and even torture our bodies (and others') in pursuing purity of soul. Most especially, it suggests that the earth is not really our home and that faith is primarily about something that happens elsewhere. Religious faith ceases to address living in this world and becomes obsessed with how to get out of it. Wirzba's subtle and rewarding treatment of these themes draws on Wendell Berry's work, and especially on the long chapter "The Body and the Earth" from *The Unsettling of America*. That same text was the primary focus of my discussion of Berry in *The Spirit of the Soil*, and I refer readers to Wirzba or to my book for a more developed discussion of how we might take a more fully embodied and alive approach to Inge's religion tenet.

There are also more straightforward connections between religion and food. British philosopher Roger Scruton interprets the contemporary environmental movement as an attempt to recover some sense of piety "in a world where the results of human presumption are so apparent." He sees vegetarianism, for example, as an instinctive response to "the impious nature of much that we do by way of supplying, fulfilling, and displaying our appetite for the flesh of other species." In a passage reminiscent of Albert Borgmann's remarks on the culture of the table, Scruton writes: "Rational beings are nourished on conversation, taste, manners, and hospitality and to divorce food from these practices is to deprive it of its true significance." The traditional religious practices of saying grace and of fasting or feasting situate food consumption within a nexus of meaning that gives rise to fundamental understandings of personal and community identity. Like Borgmann, Scruton decries fast food because it has deprived us of the full sense of being at home. Eating, in other words, is a proper domain for piety, which Scruton defines as "the underlying recognition of our fragility and dependence, and the attitude of respect toward the world and the creatures that live in it, upon which religions draw for much of their inspiration."[4]

Clearly, nothing that can be said in a brief conclusion will satisfy the need for a full-scale revision and reconstruction of any of Inge's tenets. This may be especially true of the religion tenet. The important point about the farmer's sense of humility before God is that it comes readily to an agrarian people by virtue of their closeness to and dependence on divine providence as expressed through changes in the weather; raiding by insects, birds, or other "pests"; and the loss of fertility through erosion, nutrient depletion, and genetic drift. Can more mindful food practices help us recover a sense of natural piety? One would think that food practices need to recapture some of farming's vulnerability to the vicissitudes of nature to do so, but that is a question that only a more extended effort in environmental philosophy (abetted, one would hope, with some experimentation) can answer.

Romance

Antitechnology Romanticism is rampant in contemporary debates on food and agriculture. The photographic images in Andrew Kimbrell's *Fatal Harvest: The Tragedy of Industrial Agriculture* emphasize the tectonically built and technologically maintained appearance of modern farming. In contrast, the front cover of Tom Lyson's *Civic Agriculture* shows a barefooted young woman harvesting vegetables in a basket. Opposition to genetically engineered crops has been a signature for those enrolled in the sustainable agriculture movement, while boosters of industrial agriculture continue to insist that it will be needed to feed the world. There is thus a sense in which Inge's romance tenet—that technology corrupts while nature redeems—hardly needs any revising at all. Although few contemporary advocates of alternative agriculture would be comfortable spouting faith in the farmer's natural piety, many seem quite at home with the view that technology will inevitably lead us astray.

This attitude hardly seems generalizable to larger questions of sustainability. It seems obvious that achieving any semblance of sustainability with respect to energy use, pollution and toxins in the environment, or climate change will require us to embrace new and better technology. Modern bicycles, hybrid cars, wind turbines, geothermal heating cores, and solar energy technologies are in no sense a throwback to earlier technologies, much less a return to nature. Although many people seem to think that we can preserve a romance tenet when it comes to food and farming, almost no one thinks we can do so when it comes to other aspects of sustainability. So here, it appears, the articulation of agrarian ideals provides little insight into problems that are not directly related to farming.

I would caution against this reading of Inge's remarks on technology, however. A revised version of the romance tenet should be fully articulated in terms of the link between environment and technology expressed by Albert Borgmann and David Strong. This theme is discussed at some length in chapters 5 and 6. My point there is that the agrarian ideal of community is still critical for a meaningful and rewarding life and that technologies have been inimical to the habitual daily practices that create meaningful lives. Borgmann's view of technology is also a key topic for Aiden Davison in his book *Technology and the Contested Meanings of Sustainability.* Davison follows Borgmann in claiming that technology corrupts because the convenience provided by technical devices eventually drains our lives of meaningful encounters with people and things. The entanglements and complications of working out our material lives—eating, staying warm, getting dressed, cleaning up—may seem annoying, but one may find that being relieved of these entanglements and complications also leaves one disembedded, alienated, and adrift.

An important task for sustainable living is to find patterns and habits that connect one to nature and to other people. There is thus an important complementarity between meaningful work and the religious virtue of piety. Although one can hardly object to devices that relieve human beings of toilsome entanglements, the simple fact is that friendship, community, appreciation of beauty, enchantment, and personal satisfaction grow out of the trouble we take to accomplish the normal tasks of daily life. One by one, technologies relieve us from toil and entanglement, and we are satisfied that the benefit of such relief compensates for any decline in the satisfaction we take from our trouble. When all those tasks can be accomplished well enough without an engaging, open-ended encounter with things—without what Borgmann calls a focal practice—life becomes empty of meaning. Our interactions with others become defined by the paradigm of commodity exchange, and we find ourselves isolated, alone, and profoundly disappointed by technology's unfulfilled promise. Nature redeems in the sense that natural things are replete with possibility, but also in the sense that the classic agrarian lifestyle paints a picture of the way the farm household becomes thoroughly embedded in nature through normal practices of husbandry and household care. We need not all become farmers, but we may indeed recapture focal meaning in our lives by pursuing what Borgmann calls "the culture of the table."

Moral Ontology

Moral ontology is not a phrase that comes dripping off the tongue of the common person. But the theme of moral ontology has appeared throughout the chapters of this book, even if it surfaced as an explicit topic only briefly in chapter 6. The great French philosopher Michel Foucault (1926–1984) characterizes moral ontology as having a four-part structure: (1) the *substance éthique,* or the aspect or part of myself that is concerned with morality; (2) the *mode d'assujettissement,* or the way in which people are invited or incited to recognize moral obligations; (3) *tekhné,* or the means available for becoming ethical; and (4) *téléology,* or the kind of being to which we aspire when we behave in a moral way. Foucault's schema can help us unpack what Inge means by moral ontology.

Inge's statement of the moral ontology tenet overlaps substantially with the way I reformulated his romance tenet: farming produces a sense of harmony and integration, whereas modern society is alienating and fragmenting. It can also be read as expressing what Foucault calls a *téléology:* we aspire to harmony and integration when we behave in a moral way. Many moral philosophers would interpret "harmony and integration" as holding an internally consistent set of moral beliefs, but Inge's contrast with the alienation and fragmentation of modern society suggest a different *mode d'assujettissement.* We are invited into morality not through an adjustment of our beliefs but through an appreciation of how the life lived by farmers creates a whole that is greater than the sum of its parts. The *tekhné* at work here is practice, rather than rational reflection. All this suggests a *substance éthique* in agrarianism that can best be appreciated in contrast to the *substance éthique* that characterizes most of twentieth-century philosophical ethics, including the main approaches in environmental philosophy discussed in chapter 1.

In mainstream environmental philosophy (and in much of philosophical ethics in general), each element in Foucault's structure revolves around the Cartesian subject, understood implicitly as a disembodied decision maker. It is one's facility of choice, one's will, that is the focus of morality: the *substance éthique.* One is invited into a consideration of morality (*mode d'assujettissement*) in environmental ethics through a challenge to one's beliefs, by considering environmental impacts. The *tekhné* is argument, persuasion, and the application of standards for logical consistency. For utilitarians and other consequentialists, one aspires to be ethical by aligning one's preferences with those outcomes that produce the best result for everyone affected. Those who emphasize rights or intrinsic values in nature hope to align their conduct with the appropriate constraints on one's opportunity set that make us moral. The behavior that defines the *téléology* of both approaches is that of rational decision making in full cognizance of environmental impact: being smart. These approaches differ from one another in only the narrowest terms.

Contemporary environmental philosophy (and here I include environmental economics and other approaches to environmental policy) has been embroiled in an unsatisfying debate over the way this dogma of environmental impact should be understood. Is the value we attach to environmental impacts human centered or nature centered? Under the reign of the Cartesian subject as the only credible *substance éthique,* valuation is an exercise in reflecting and respecting subjectivities. The most politically persuasive approaches have been anthropocentric: it is consideration for other human subjects that we should find persuasive. Radical environmentalists have labored to persuade us that animals, ecosystems, Gaia, and other entities in nature are adequately subject-like. In this they broaden the *substance éthique* beyond the conventional notion of will, and they suggest a *téléology* inclusive of a capability for recognizing this broadened conception of value. Yet by maintaining a commitment to the *tekhné* of rational persuasion, they ultimately return to a very human notion of the *substance éthique.* It is ultimately the will, the decision-making facility, that is affected by argument.

In suggesting that harmony and integration are achieved through practice rather than rational persuasion, agrarian ideals point toward a different *substance éthique.* They express profound senses in which humans are both dependent on nature and more fully realized when they are at home within it. Humans risk all and forgo any chance of true fulfillment when human will becomes the touchstone for moral philosophy, but an ideal of pristine nature in which humans are absent is of little help at all. It is thus *not* the case that we must look for analogues to the Cartesian subject in the natural world. My frequent references to Aristotle and the ancient Greeks hint that a moral ontology focused on the rights and duties (or pains and pleasures) of conscious or sentient creatures is much less salient for sustainability than a moral ontology attentive to virtues, to the formation of moral character, and to the expression and realization of the community ideal.

This suggests that a more appropriate *substance éthique* might be embodied practice, especially in quotidian tasks in which one's sense of self as a subject recedes entirely into the background as one becomes fully absorbed in a task. It suggests further that the *téléology* of harmony and integration is pointed toward relatively unreflective habits, where one may not experience oneself as a decision maker at all. We aspire to be lucky rather than smart. The *mode d'assujettissement* is very indirect, as when Jefferson tried to promote sustainability not through exhortation but by the encouragement of farming. *Tekhné* emphasizes doing and practice over thinking. Of course, Jefferson and I both exhort others to consider their beliefs and to think in new ways. It is not as if intelligence is irrelevant to sustainability. The point, however, is that an environmental ethic is much less concerned with valuation and decision making and far more focused on trying to understand how our habits and material practices can be made more sustainable.

Politics

This book has dealt quite a bit with questions of political theory. Readers who want more should consult Kimberly Smith's book *Wendell Berry and the Agrarian Tradition* for a complementary approach to agrarian political theory. We have gradually moved through many of the keystone ideas showcased by one political theorist or another: utility, libertarianism, the social contract. In every case, I have tried to soften the way contemporary professors of politics have formulated these ideas in terms of what Jefferson would have called "abstract rules" and tried to articulate them in light of agrarian ideals. This means that my own approach to politics is rather unlike Inge's emphasis on rural autochthony, although one can articulate autochthony in various ways. Inge's approach to politics is actually rather close to the central agrarian tenet: farmers make the best citizens. Yet unless I am just dead wrong about Jefferson, he did not believe that rural autochthony is the backbone of democracy. What he believed was that farmers' interests and practices were more consonant with those of an emerging republic. In lieu of recapitulating the argument of the entire book under the heading of the politics tenet, it may be more useful to make a few additional comments on Jefferson's bequest.

Jeffersonian democracy is, as I understand it, committed to liberal political ideals that are familiar points of debate among utilitarians, libertarians, and egalitarians. It differs from contemporary political theory in two important ways. First, it takes agrarian ideals quite seriously. Part of what is important here is merely the word *ideals* as distinct from *utilities* or *rights*. *Efficiency*, too often overspecified in economists' definitions, is a perfectly respectable ideal and one that, as I argued at length in *The Spirit of the Soil*, is a great legacy of the agrarian tradition. As an experientially based and slightly vague notion that informs our thinking without dominating it, the ideal of efficiency gives useful direction to political debates. It may even counterpoise ideals of liberty and equality in some settings. But consonant with the main thrust of this book, there is more than just this theme of ideals. Jefferson's rhetoric of farming was actually his way of addressing problems of political and social sustainability—problems that might be articulated in terms of solidarity. By countenancing agrarian ideals, the Jeffersonian democrat adopts a political vocabulary in which the polity's ability to reproduce itself from one generation to the next is both a problem worthy of attention and deliberation and one that is addressable by attending to those practices that both reproduce material culture and situate human activity within the natural environment.

Second, the Jeffersonian democrat takes the notion of place very seriously and gives it a legitimacy that it lacks in mainstream liberal politics. This is one way in which we might interpret autochthony. Arguably, Steinbeck learned this lesson by following the harvest gypsies as he was researching *The Grapes of Wrath*. Steinbeck may have set out to document the emergence of a true working-class mentality, one forged in resistance to the dominating power of elites. He ended by tempering this theme with a voice that speaks of reciprocities and solidarities defined and articulated as being *of* the soil at a given place. But this is a qualified notion of indigenous identity, and it should not be confused with a celebration of autochthony that sees the farming family as a world unto itself, caring little for commerce and needing nothing from the manufacturing classes. As Donald Worster shows in his treatment of the American Dust Bowl, the reality of the Great Plains was very far from any such notion of autochthony in the 1930s. The idea of radical independence and self-sufficiency that is sometimes associated with autochthony has thus been thoroughly reworked in the notions of place and community that emerge from this book.

The politics tenet needs to be further reformed by becoming more complicated and less central than the central agrarian tenet. The solidarity and place politics celebrated in agrarian ideals must be understood as one thrust among many in the complex dialectic of democratic politics. Throughout, my hope has been to resuscitate agrarian ideals for the role they can play in environmental ethics and the political pursuit of sustainability. I see them as offering an important counterwisdom to political excesses that occur when utilitarian, libertarian, and egalitarian ideals—the philosophical ideals that underlie an industrial philosophy of agriculture—become dominant in the shared vocabulary of a people. But this does not mean that we abandon human rights, fairness, and promotion of the general welfare. That would hardly be a fitting tribute to Jefferson. A healthy conception of sustainability will arise when industrial and agrarian ideals are incorporated in the mix of goals, hopes, and story lines that shape our public life.

Society

Inge's society tenet already provides a dialectical counterpoint to an overly strong emphasis on autochthony. Rural life is valued for its independence and self-reliance, but those traits are attained through interdependence and reciprocity. Clearly, however, the society tenet needs to be continually updated with a thorough study of changes brought about by agricultural industrialization. Nor would we want to take its implied praise of rural life too seriously today. I have hinted at this throughout the book, but it is a task that has been executed more thoroughly in the sociology of agriculture. Starting with Walter Goldschmidt's landmark study, it has become clear that the realization of industrial values in the rural countryside has rather thoroughly upset interdependencies and reciprocities in today's heartland. Yet if we have truly agrarian ideals in mind, perhaps there is little need for a dramatic reformulation of Inge here. Rural interdependencies and reciprocities can provide a model for healthy community, especially when it is the rural America of Jefferson, Emerson, or even Teddy Roosevelt we have in mind.

A growing number of contemporary authors have taken up the call to update the society tenet in light of contemporary experience. Tom

Lyson stands at the forefront. Like Goldschmidt, Lyson conducted empirical studies on social institutions and community development activities throughout the United States, but especially in the South. He became increasingly impressed by his findings that relatively low-tech and small-scale enterprises such as vegetable farms, farmers' markets, craft activities, and voluntary efforts had more enduring effects in terms of the livability and economic vitality of American communities than seemingly larger and better capitalized efforts. His book *Civic Agriculture* continues this work by exploring how community gardens and community-supported agriculture experiments become the basis for social bonds that allow communities and the individuals that live in them to sustain themselves economically and spiritually. More thoroughly than anything I can provide in this limited space, Lyson's work (along with that of Fred Buttel and of Europeans such as Terry Marsden and Jan Douwe van der Ploeg) lays the foundations for a thorough revision and updating of Inge's society tenet.

My theme, however, is that the now almost forgotten interdependencies and reciprocities of agrarian life underwrote an implied experience of functional integrity within the agrarian world. The families that peopled this world felt that it had some semblance of stability at the same time that they recognized the precariousness of their situation. The tension between a stable future, somewhat like the past, and the vulnerability inherent in a way of life dependent on weather and other natural forces made them attentive to the role that reciprocity and mutual interdependence play in the reproduction of agrarian society. As such, I might revise Inge thus: rural interdependencies and the reciprocities of the agrarian farming style provide the model for sustainability. But sustainability is not the whole of what we want from society or even from farming. I concluded *The Spirit of the Soil* by writing that we might sacrifice a little sustainability to achieve some justice and equality. I don't think that's incompatible with agrarian ideals, although a hardscrabble agrarian might well balk at sacrificing much sustainability for improved welfare and personal comfort. But we in contemporary American society fail to devote much attention at all to sustainability, and we do so at great peril to justice and equality, not to mention the other living organisms on planet Earth.

The great virtue of agrarian ideals in this connection is the transparency with which the problems of sustainability come to be seen. Were contemporary Americans to fully appreciate Aldo Leopold's warning about the two spiritual dangers of not owning a farm (thinking that breakfast comes from the grocery store and that heat comes from the furnace), it might be far, far easier for us to undertake the challenges that lie before us in an era of climate change, declining oil reserves, and competition for resources. Furthermore, although too many environmental philosophers have neglected the way ecological reciprocities draw on the agrarian ideal of community, Leopold was one who did not. Leopold's land ethic stresses the importance of expanding our notion of community so that it is inclusive of the land, of place, of our environment. My attempt to frame the social goals of agriculture, to examine food and community, and then to explore the various meanings of sustainability has all been undertaken in service to Leopold's hoped-for expansion.

So Inge's summary provides a sketch of some key agrarian tenets and yields a program for philosophical renovation and reform that might well result in a new kind of ecological ethic. It is an ambitious program. Sustainability itself is an ongoing project. Agrarian ideals can provide a potent and largely neglected set of considerations for understanding and pursuing sustainability. Chapter 12 attempted some reconciliation with those who understand sustainability as social movement that is deeply committed to social justice, animal welfare, and human rights, but there is an important sense in which the philosophical rationale for these commitments is different from the way my agrarian interpretation of Inge's society tenet speaks to the problem of sustainability. Critical ideals associated with human rights and welfare are almost certainly more reliably sourced in the ethical and political philosophies that gave rise to our conception of industrial society. I am not suggesting that we can forget them for a moment: eternal vigilance is the price of liberty. I end, therefore, with a tentative and hesitant move toward what I hope will be sustainability. As I envision it, sustainability is something we must both do and discuss together. No one's book can possibly have the answer.

Notes

To minimize distracting breaks in the flow of the text, I have not included notes for source materials that can easily and unambiguously be found in the references based on identifying phrases in the text. Notes have been used when there are multiple supporting sources and when it is important to provide specific page references. In addition, a few notes amplify points in the text that would be of interest only to specialist readers. Except in these special cases, scholars and bibliophiles should consult the reference list at the end of the book for full bibliographic information.

Introduction

1. This quotation appeared on Wikipedia as an entry under "Agrarianism"; http://en.wikipedia.org/wiki/Agrarianism (accessed September 12, 2008). The passage is described as being "adapted from M. Thomas Inge." The perhaps overenthusiastic portrayal of farming is not atypical of the way agrarianism has been understood in popular culture.

1. Sustainability and Environmental Philosophy

1. Brown 1997, 31.

2. Leopold 1949, 6.

3. Many philosophers take the word *impact* to be strongly associated with consequentialist approaches in ethics that evaluate action in terms of impact on welfare or well-being. In contrast, deontological, "rights-based," or Kantian approaches evaluate action in light of its consistency with principles, rules, or reasons. In discussing a "dogma of environmental impact," I am using the term more broadly to indicate any approach that looks to features or attributes of events that are caused by human action or decision making. In this sense, both classical utilitarian ethics (which is the paradigmatic example of consequentialism) and ethical theories that are sometimes characterized as "a consequential-

ism of rights" focus on outcomes or impacts. In the latter case, the impact or outcome of an action might be a violation of rights instead of or in addition to an adverse effect on welfare. One still evaluates a prospective action in light of its expected outcomes, but one includes outcomes that are defined considerably more broadly than the classical utilitarian notions of pleasure and pain, or satisfaction and dissatisfaction. Such approaches are used widely in environmental economics and environmental law, and they have been the subject of debate among philosophers who are self-described consequentialists (see Armstrong 2006).

4. Sachs 2005, 137.

5. Ibid., 177.

6. This interpretation of Hesiod relies heavily on Nelson 1998.

7. See Griswold 1948. Gene Wunderlich (2000) provides an excellent interpretive analysis of Griswold's use of Thomas Jefferson and his impact on agricultural policy.

8. On Benjamin Franklin, see Campbell 2000.

2. The Philosophy of Farming in America

1. Cooper and Holmes (2000) describe the phenomenon of industrial versus alternative agriculture as a philosophical debate. Wright and Middendorf (2008) use the more colorful term *fight*, but they clearly have both contesting interest groups and philosophical principles in mind.

2. See Wojcik (1984) for a discussion of Crèvecoeur and his views.

3. Jefferson 1984, 291, 290, 818. I provide a more extensive philosophical discussion of these quotations and the relationship to Jefferson's agrarianism in Thompson 2000b.

4. See Meinig 1993.

5. Garry Wills (1997) provides an argument for this reading of Jefferson's intent.

6. Sidney Mintz (1986) discusses this phenomenon as it occurred in industrial England.

7. I owe this interpretation of American agricultural history to Robert Kirkendall (1984).

8. John Brewster (1966) offers a sweeping portrait of Jeffersonian agrarianism as a response to Griswold. Gene Wunderlich (2000) analyzes the history and policy impact of this debate.

9. The analysis in this section relies on Browne, Skees, Swanson, Thompson, and Unnevehr 1992.

10. See Stoll 1998.

11. The Thoreau passage is quoted by Stanley Cavell (1981, 9).

12. For a discussion of Emerson, see Corrington 1990. For Thoreau, see Anderson 2000. I have a slightly more in-depth treatment of Emerson, Thoreau, and transcendentalism in Thompson 1998a. This phase of American history is also discussed by Montmarquet 1989.

3. Political Values and the Future of U.S. Agriculture

1. The ideals I am emphasizing have been the subject of hundreds of years of debate and scholarship. Their philosophical history and the argumentative structure that supports them are of interest only to specialists. Although these details become more important in the context of specific policy proposals, they have been omitted from the present treatment in order to develop coherent and accessible statements of the overarching philosophy that underlies each vision of agriculture.

2. I rely heavily on the distinction between an understanding of private property and efficiency as expressing moral ideals, on the one hand, and the particular configuration of these ideals that emerges when they are specified more rigorously in economic theory, on the other. As my friends A. Allan Schmid and Daniel Bromley have argued tirelessly, attempts at rigorous specification have frequently embroiled economists in circular reasoning of the sort sketched briefly in my critical comments about the interdependence between notions of efficiency and the rules for exchange reflected in property rights. One of the most pernicious (and most influential) equivocations was Ronald Coase's argument against the notion of externality as I use it here. Coase argues (in effect) that since we are free to organize and lobby against putative external costs, the fact that we do not do so proves that we are in a kind of equilibrium state in which efficiencies are actually being achieved! When I originally read Coase's article "The Problem of Social Cost," I thought it a brilliant reductio ad absurdum against the idea of efficiency. Only later did I learn that Coase and his followers were actually serious about this.

Schmid's critique in *Property, Power and Public Choice* is devastating, but he too thinks that the very idea of externality is pernicious: one person's externality is another person's noninterference. Bromley agrees to the extent that one would be seriously deluded if one thought that identifying efficiencies and externalities was a purely objective accomplishment of economic science. But like me, he seems more willing to countenance the use of these ideas in a philosophical context. Clearly people do slide back and forth between engineering notions of efficiency, such as "miles per gallon," and moral notions, such as those I associate with Jeffrey Sachs's comments on the inefficiency of poor farmers. The vague and equivocal nature of such usage is totally consistent with the way I am characterizing moral ideals. Although we should be mindful of circularity in how these ideas are being specified to justify any given policy proposal, they do not strike me as wholly unpersuasive when one is trying to give some general shape to a philosophical proposal.

3. Roosevelt is quoted in McGovern 1967, 28.

4. The Moral Significance of Land

1. See Lisca 1972.

2. Steinbeck 1972, 206.

3. See Wilson 1940; Lisca 1972.

4. See Cochrane 1979. The passages from Marx's *Das Kapital* that can be linked to the treadmill concept are analyzed in Thompson 2007a, 197. Griswold 1948 links the treadmill to Roosevelt.

5. For the application of the prisoner's dilemma–tragedy of the commons analysis to the Dust Bowl, see Scherer 1983.

6. Steinbeck 1988 reprints these newspaper articles and includes an introductory essay by Charles Wollenberg.

7. Worster 1979, 179, 180.

8. These metaphors and their links to communitarian thought are explored in Lukes 1993.

5. Farming as a Focal Practice

1. Borgmann 1984, 219.

2. Logsdon 1994, 90–91.

3. Borgmann 1984, 209.

4. See Wolf and Buttel 1998.

5. Lisa Heldke (2003) has developed an especially thoughtful critique of the elitism that might be associated with trendy food habits. She does not discuss Borgmann or the culture of the table.

6. Even a brief summary of the philosophical critiques of dualism would be out of place in the present context. Dualism and the Cartesian idea of subjectivity both continue to reverberate through a number of theoretical constructs and a few widely shared cultural beliefs. But it is doubtful that the excruciatingly detailed and complex philosophical criticisms of these legacies from the sixteenth century that set the standard for academic philosophy would be helpful to many readers. My strategy is to make a few superficial comments on the obvious way that dualism does not square with common sense and to refer readers who may be seriously tempted by Cartesian abstractions to the work of philosophers such as Husserl, Heidegger, and Dewey.

7. For a representative sample, see Williams, Patterson, and Roggenbuck 1992; Eisenhauer, Krannich, and Blahna 2000; Jorgenson and Stedman 2001.

Stedman 2003 offers an interesting critique of the subjectivism assumed by most research on place.

8. For the contested character of the idea of nature, see McNaughten and Urry 1998. For a review of the literature on the rural idyll, see Bell 2006. Castree and Braun (2006) give a probing and lucid discussion of the role that "social construction" has played in the literature of rural studies.

9. Husserl's essay "The Origin of Geometry" was brought to widespread attention by Jacques Derrida (1978).

10. See Heidegger 1947. Ian Hacking (2006) discusses the phenomenon of counting sources to establish the credibility of a statement in his development of the modern notion of probability. In fact, Michel Foucault's widely read studies on the construction of subjectivity presume Husserl's critique of Cartesianism and Heidegger's rejection of the neo-Platonic view. Foucault notes that "subject" is understood in a dual sense. As Descartes' ontological substrate for the mental realm, the subject inherits a number of traits from the Greek notion of psyche and the Christian notion of soul. As a political notion, a subject is one who is beholden to the authority of a king or prince, one who is obligated to perform certain duties. This leads to the emergence of governmentality, on the one hand, but also to the medical and social science disciplines, on the other, where subjects are constituted so that they will discipline themselves rather than having to rely on the physical coercion of the lordly class. Thus in Foucault's work, the very notion of a subject becomes suspect, a construction of a historical discourse. It is ironic that the social science of rural space has adapted Foucault's thought into a set of philosophical commitments that seem to privilege this very concept.

11. See Casey 1993.

6. Food and Community

1. Sagoff (2006) engages in an extended debate with Norton (2006) on this very point in an exchange published in *Ethics, Place and Environment*. Much of my confidence in the report I give here of Sagoff's Kantianism is based on his reply to my own exchange with him (Thompson 2006), published in the same volume.

2. My own views on community owe more to Josiah Royce (1855–1916) than to Kant or Sellars. Royce clearly started out as a robust Hegelian, indebted to T. H. Green and F. H. Bradley. After studying the logical writings of C. S. Peirce, Royce migrated to a semantics-based view in which the relevant notion of community is reflected in the common practice of interpretation or hermeneutics. This practice is shared and made real by the historical reality of the Christian church (Royce 1913). He offers a shorter and less overtly religious ver-

sion of this interpretation-oriented understanding of community in one of his last works, *The Hope of the Great Community* (Royce 1916). Although I would have liked to develop the ideas in this chapter with reference to Royce, I was unable to solve practical problems (such as holding a reader's attention) while doing so.

3. Fischler's works are included in the references. For this point, see especially Rozin, Fischler, Imada, Sarubin, and Wrzenjiewski 1999.

4. I have devoted entirely too much of my life to analyzing the ethical issues associated with genetically engineered food. An article entitled "Why Food Biotechnology Needs an Opt Out" (Thompson 2002) is most relevant to the point at hand. Thompson 2007b provides a concise and lighthearted synopsis of my work; Thompson 2007a gives you the full course.

7. Why Philosophy Matters for Agricultural Policy

1. Jefferson 1984, 290, 818.

2. See Calhoun 2002 for a particularly lucid and informative discussion of this point.

8. Sustainability and the Social Goals of Agriculture

1. Locke 1789, 23–24.

2. Jefferson 1984, 290, 818.

3. Berry 1977, 143, 144.

4. Ibid., 21.

5. Cowan 1983, 25.

6. The quotation is from a speech Lincoln gave at a Wisconsin agricultural fair (see Lincoln 1859).

7. Emerson 1870, 153–54.

8. Roosevelt is quoted in McGovern 1967, 28.

9. Jefferson's "Farm Book" is a compendium of communications, records, and notes compiled in conjunction with his farming operation at Monticello. See Betts 1953.

10. Schumacher 1972, 109, 113.

11. Leopold 1949, 201, 203.

9. The Road to Sustainability

1. United Nations 1983.

2. Independent Commission on International Development 1980, 18.

3. World Commission on Environment and Development 1987, 46, 47, 48–49.

4. Pearce, Barbier, and Markandya 1990, 3.

5. See Murasinghe and Shearer 1995.

6. See Solow 1992, 1993. Weak or Solow sustainability is discussed and analyzed in Howarth 1997, among many other sources. Bryan Norton (1995) uses the "weak" versus "strong" language to characterize the difference between Solow's approach and that of Herman Daly.

7. See Hediger 1999; Harris 2000.

8. For a more detailed discussion of the links between war and agricultural technology, see Russell 2001. For a discussion of Liebig and the abandonment of a more biologically oriented approach, see Uekoetter 2006.

9. Tobie 1949.

10. Uekoetter 2006, 336.

10. Sustainability as a Norm

1. Burkhardt 1989, 114.

2. Norton 2005, 311.

11. Sustainability: What It Is and What It Is Not

1. This aspect of my work is derived from Thompson 1992, 1995, 1997, and 1998a, as well as Thompson, Matthews, and van Ravenswaay 1994.

2. Davis and Langham 1995, 21–22.

3. For examples, see George 1992; Thrupp 1993; Barkin 1998.

4. Lynam and Herdt (1989) discuss producers; Richgels, Barrick, and Foells (1990) express the viewpoint of agribusiness firms.

5. Walters, Mortensen, Francis, Elmore, and King (1990) argue for this perspective.

6. Bentham (1789, 30) discusses this point.

7. See, for example, Warren 2000; Plumwood 2002.

12. Sustainability, Social Movements, and Hope

1. See Habermas 1981 for the paradigmatic statement of new social movements, and Pichardo 1997 for a critical and skeptical review. My thanks to Aaron McCright, whose comments on the original draft of this section were extremely helpful.

2. See Norton 2005, especially 388–99.

3. Van Calker, Berentsen, Giesen, and Huirne (2005) provide a good discussion of how Dutch researchers have used participatory public input processes very much like those that Norton envisions to specify indicators for sustainability in dairy production. The article by Cornelissen, van den Berg, Koops, Grossman, and Udo (2001) is another example. This group is also developing a logic model that will allow multiple indicators to be weighted, each

reflecting a contribution to sustainability (see de Boer and Cornelissen 2002; Bosma, Kaymak, van den Berg, and Udo 2005). This raises yet another potential problem with indicators—namely, that when these technically complex modeling techniques are used to blend indicators, it is far from clear that Norton's goals of community transparency and consensus can also be served.

4. Norton (2005, 484–94) discusses "the evolving Dutch system of environmental management" in such broad terms, but he does not refer to social movement theory.

5. The Dutch research cited above is also very much concerned with the problem of integrating diverse values into an overall measure that can inform such efforts in a meaningful way. Just as social movement theory generates a research program based on determining what people who organize to promote sustainability think they are trying to promote, this approach has spawned a small industry of social science research projects that deploy complex methods for integrating and representing the measures that people say they care about.

6. I will note in passing that this kind of social science is highly susceptible to researcher bias. Participants in these public processes may be influenced by the way questions and scenarios are initially framed. As such, the difference between an empirical social movements approach and one in which the researcher takes an activist stance committed to certain values may be less than one might think. From the perspective of ethics, the problem is that there may be precious little opportunity for deliberative and thoughtful debate in which ethical values, ideals, and goals are explicitly framed.

7. In fact, U.S. farm policy does not provide direct subsidies for animal products, with the exception of milk. Subsidies to corn and soybean growers indirectly support livestock production because they have historically ensured that animal feed is available at reasonable prices. This additional bit of complexity is not reflected in the example described in the text.

8. Thompson 1992, 17.

Conclusion

1. These definitions were taken from Dictionary.com. http://dictionary .reference.com/browse/country (accessed August 3, 2009).

2. Jefferson 1984, 902.

3. Morgan 1975, 376.

4. Scruton 2004, 86, 82, 86. Scruton is an opponent of "animal rights" philosophies, although in the article from which these passages are quoted, he is quite critical of industrial livestock production practices.

References

Aiken, W. 1978. The Right to Be Saved from Starvation. In *World Hunger and Moral Obligation,* ed. W. Aiken and H. LaFollette, 85–102. Englewood Cliffs, NJ: Prentice-Hall.

———. 1984a. Ethical Issues in Agriculture. In *Earthbound,* ed. T. Regan, 247–86. New York: Random House.

———. 1984b. The Goals of Agriculture. In *Agriculture Change and Human Values,* ed. R. Haynes and R. Lanier, 29–54. Gainesville: University of Florida Humanities and Agriculture Program.

———. 1986. Evaluating Agricultural Research. In *New Directions for Agriculture and Agricultural Research,* ed. K. Dahlberg, 31–41. Totowa, NJ: Rowman and Allanheld.

Allen, P. 1993. *Food for the Future: Conditions and Contradictions of Sustainability.* New York: John Wiley and Sons.

Allen, P., and C. Sachs. 1992. The Poverty of Sustainability: An Analysis of Current Positions. *Agriculture and Human Values* 9(4): 29–35.

———. 1993. Sustainable Agriculture in the United States: Engagements, Silences, and Possibilities for Transformation. In *Food for the Future: Conditions and Contradictions of Sustainability,* ed. P. Allen, 139–67. New York: John Wiley and Sons.

Altieri, M. 1991. An Agroecological Analysis of the Environmental Degradation Resulting from the Structure of Agriculture. In *Beyond the Large Farm: Ethics and Research Goals for Agriculture,* ed. P. B. Thompson and B. A. Stout, 125–36. Boulder, CO: Westview Press.

Anderson, D. R. 2000. Wild Farming: Thoreau and Agrarian Life. In *The Agrarian Roots of Pragmatism,* ed. P. B. Thompson and T. C. Hilde, 153–63. Nashville, TN: Vanderbilt University Press.

Armstrong, W. S. 2006. Consequentialism. *Stanford Encyclopedia of Philosophy.* http://plato.stanford.edu/entries/consequentialism/#ConWhaRigRelR ul (accessed December 16, 2008).

Attfield, R. 1998. Environmental Ethics and Intergenerational Equity. *Inquiry* 41: 207–22.

——. 2003. *Environmental Ethics: An Overview for the Twenty-first Century.* Cambridge: Cambridge University Press.

Bailey, L. H. 1911. *Report of the Commission on Country Life, with an Introduction by Theodore Roosevelt.* New York: Sturgis and Walton.

Barkin, D. 1998. Sustainability: The Political Economy of Autonomous Development. *Organization and Environment* 11: 5–32.

Batie, S. 1984. *Soil Conservation Policy for the Future: The Farm and Food System in Transition No. 23.* East Lansing: Cooperative Extension Service, Michigan State University.

Batie, S., and R. G. Healy. 1980. *The Future of American Agriculture as a Strategic Resource.* Washington, DC: Conservation Foundation.

Batie, S. S. 2008. Wicked Problems and Applied Economics. *American Journal of Agricultural Economics* 90: 1176–91.

Bawden, R. J. 1991. Systems Thinking and Practice in Agriculture. *Journal of Dairy Science* 14: 2362–73.

Bawden, R. J., and R. G. Packham. 1993. Systemic Praxis in the Education of the Agricultural Systems Practitioner. *Systemic Practice and Action Research* 6: 7–19.

Bell, D. 2006. Variations on the Rural Idyll. In *The Handbook of Rural Studies*, ed. P. Cloke, T. Marsden, and P. H. Mooney, 149–60. London: Sage Publishing.

Bellah, R., R. Madsen, W. M. Sullivan, A. Swidler, and S. M. Tipton. 1986. *Habits of the Heart: Individualism and Commitment in American Life.* New York: Harper and Row.

Bennett, W. J. 1996. *The Book of Virtues.* New York: Simon and Schuster.

Bentham, J. 1789 [1948]. *The Principles of Morals and Legislation.* New York: Hafner Press.

Berry, W. 1970. *Farming: A Handbook.* New York: Harcourt, Brace, and Jovanovich.

——. 1977. *The Unsettling of America: Culture and Agriculture.* San Francisco: Sierra Club Books.

——. 1981. *The Gift of Good Land.* San Francisco: North Point Books.

——. 1985. *Collected Poems.* San Francisco: North Point Books.

——. 1987. *Home Economics.* San Francisco: North Point Books.

——. 1991. *What Are People For?* San Francisco: North Point Books.

Betts, E. M. 1953. *Thomas Jefferson's Farm Book, with Commentary and Excerpts from Other Writings.* Princeton, NJ: Princeton University Press.

Bonnen, J. 1983. Historical Sources of U.S. Agricultural Productivity: Implications for R&D Policy and Social Science Research. *American Journal of Agricultural Economics* 65(5): 958–66.

Borgmann, A. 1984. *Technology and the Character of Contemporary Life: A Philosophical Inquiry.* Chicago: University of Chicago Press.

——. 1992. *Crossing the Postmodern Divide.* Chicago: University of Chicago Press.

——. 2006. *Real American Ethics: Taking Responsibility for Our Country.* Chicago: University of Chicago Press.

Bosma, R., U. Kaymak, J. van den Berg, and H. M. J. Udo. 2005. Fuzzy Modelling of Farmer Motivations for Integrated Farming in the Vietnamese Mekong Delta. Presented at the Fourteenth IEEE International Conference, 827–32.

Brewster, J. M. 1966. The Relevance of the Jeffersonian Dream Today. In *Land Use Policy in the United States,* ed. H. W. Ottoson, 86–136. Lincoln: University of Nebraska Press.

Bromfield, L. 1948 [1999]. *Malabar Farm.* Wooster, OH: Wooster Book Co.

Bromley, D. W. 1998. Searching for Sustainability: The Poverty of Spontaneous Order. *Ecological Economics* 24: 231–40.

——. 2006. *Sufficient Reason: Volitional Pragmatism and the Meaning of Economic Institutions.* Princeton, NJ: Princeton University Press.

Brown, L. 1995. *Who Will Feed China? Wake-up Call for a Small Planet.* New York: W. W. Norton.

——. 1997. *The Agricultural Link: How Environmental Damage Could Disrupt Economic Progress.* Worldwatch Paper No. 136. Washington, DC: Worldwatch Institute.

Browne, W. P., J. R. Skees, L. Swanson, P. B. Thompson, and L. Unnevehr. 1992. *Sacred Cows and Hot Potatoes: Agrarian Myths and Policy Realities.* Boulder, CO: Westview Press.

Burkhardt, J. 1989. The Morality behind Sustainability. *Journal of Agricultural Ethics* 2: 113–28.

——. 2000. Coming Full Circle? Agrarian Ideals and Pragmatist Ethics in the Modern Land Grant University. In *The Agrarian Roots of Pragmatism,* ed. P. B. Thompson and T. C. Hilde, 279–303. Nashville, TN: Vanderbilt University Press.

Busch, L., and W. Lacy. 1984. *Food Security in the United States.* Boulder, CO: Westview Press.

Buttel, F. H. 1993. The Production of Agricultural Sustainability: Observations from the Sociology of Science and Technology. In *Food for the Future: Conditions and Contradictions of Sustainability,* ed. P. Allen, 19–46. New York: John Wiley and Sons.

——. 2005. Ever since Hightower: The Politics of Agricultural Research Activism in the Molecular Age. *Agriculture and Human Values* 22: 275–83.

Cafaro, P. 2004. *Thoreau's Living Ethics: Walden and the Pursuit of Virtue.* Athens: University of Georgia Press.

——. 2007. Split Decision. *Conservation Biology* 21: 888–90.

Cafaro, P., and R. Sandler. 2005. *Environmental Virtue Ethics.* New York: Rowman and Littlefield.

Calhoun, C. 2002. The Class Consciousness of Frequent Travelers: Toward a Critique of Actually Existing Cosmopolitanism. *South Atlantic Quarterly* 101(4): 869–97.

Callicott, J. B. 1988. Agroecology in Context. *Journal of Agricultural Ethics* 1: 3–9.

Campbell, J. 2000. Franklin Agrarius. In *The Agrarian Roots of Pragmatism,* ed. P. B. Thompson and T. C. Hilde, 101–17. Nashville, TN: Vanderbilt University Press.

Campbell, M. 1994. Beyond the Terms of the Contract: Mothers and Farmers. *Journal of Agricultural and Environmental Ethics* 7(2): 205–30.

——. 1998. Dirt in Our Mouths and Hunger in Our Bellies: Metaphor, Theory-making and Systems Approaches to Sustainable Agriculture. *Agriculture and Human Values* 15: 57–64.

Caplan, A. L. 1986. The Ethics of Uncertainty: The Regulation of Food Safety in the United States. *Agriculture and Human Values* 3(1–2): 180–90.

Carpenter, F. I. 1941. The Philosophical Joads. *College English* 2: 315–25.

Carson, R. 1962. *Silent Spring.* Boston: Houghton Mifflin.

Casey, E. 1993. *Getting Back into Place: Toward a Renewed Understanding of the Place-world.* Bloomington: Indiana University Press.

Castree, N., and B. Braun. 2006. Constructing Rural Natures. In *The Handbook of Rural Studies,* ed. P. Cloke, T. Marsden, and P. H. Mooney, 161–70. London: Sage Publications.

Cavell, S. 1981. *The Senses of Walden,* expanded ed. San Francisco: North Point Press.

Clancy, K. 1997. Reconnecting Farmers and Citizens in the Food System. In *Visions of American Agriculture,* ed. W. Lockeretz, 47–58. Ames: Iowa State University Press.

Cloke, P. 2006. Rurality and Racialized Others: Out of Place in the Countryside. In *The Handbook of Rural Studies,* ed. P. Cloke, T. Marsden, and P. H. Mooney, 379–87. London: Sage Publications.

Coase, R. H. 1960. The Problem of Social Cost. *Journal of Law and Economics* 3: 1–44.

Cochrane, W. 1979. *The Development of American Agriculture.* Minneapolis: University of Minnesota Press.

Cooper, A., and L. M. Holmes. 2000. *Bitter Harvest: A Chef's Perspective on the Hidden Dangers in the Foods We Eat and What We Can Do About It.* New York and London: Routledge.

Cornelissen, A. M., G. J. van den Berg, W. J. Koops, M. Grossman, and H. M. J. Udo. 2001. Assessment of the Contribution of Sustainability Indicators to

Sustainable Development: A Novel Approach Using Fuzzy Set Theory. *Agriculture, Ecosystems, and Environment* 86(2): 173–85.

Corrington, R. S. 1990. Emerson and the Agricultural Midworld. *Agriculture and Human Values* 7(1): 20–26.

Costanza, R., ed. 1991. *Ecological Economics: The Science and Management of Sustainability.* New York: Columbia University Press.

Cowan, R. S. 1983. *More Work for Mother.* New York: Basic Books.

———. 1997. *A Social History of American Technology.* New York: Oxford University Press.

Cronon, W. 1991. *Nature's Metropolis: Chicago and the Great West.* New York: W. W. Norton.

———. 1996. The Trouble with Wilderness: Or, Getting Back to the Wrong Nature. *Environmental History* 1: 7–28.

Crosby, A. W. 1986. *Ecological Imperialism: The Biological Expansion of Europe, 900–1900.* Cambridge: Cambridge University Press.

Daly, H., and J. Cobb Jr. 1989. *For the Common Good: Redirecting the Economy toward Community, the Environment, and a Sustainable Future.* Boston: Beacon Press.

Davis, C., and M. Langham. 1995. Agricultural Industrialization and Sustainable Development: A Global Perspective. *Journal of Agricultural and Applied Economics* 27: 21–34.

Davison, A. 2001. *Technology and the Contested Meanings of Sustainability.* Albany: State University of New York Press.

de Boer, I. J., and A. M. Cornelissen. 2002. A Method Using Sustainability Indicators to Compare Conventional and Animal-Friendly Egg Production Systems. *Poultry Science* 81: 173–81.

Derrida, J. 1978. *Edmund Husserl's Origin of Geometry: An Introduction,* trans. J. P. Leavey Jr., ed. D. B. Allison. Stony Brook, NY: N. Hays.

de Shalit, A. 1995. *Why Posterity Matters: Environmental Policies and Future Generations.* London: Routledge.

Diamond, J. 1997. *Guns, Germs, and Steel: The Fates of Human Societies.* New York: W. W. Norton.

Donahue, B. 2003. The Resettling of America. In *The Essential Agrarian Reader,* ed. Norman Wirzba, 34–51. Lexington: University Press of Kentucky.

Douglass, G. K. 1984. The Meanings of Agricultural Sustainability. In *Agricultural Sustainability in a Changing World Order,* ed. G. K. Douglass, 3–29. Boulder, CO: Westview Press.

Dworkin, R. 1977. *Taking Rights Seriously.* Cambridge, MA: Harvard University Press.

Ebenreck, S. 1983. A Partnership Farmland Ethic. *Environmental Ethics* 5(1): 33–45.

Ehrenfeld, D. 1978. *The Arrogance of Humanism*. New York: Oxford University Press.

Eisenhauer, B. W., R. S. Krannich, and D. J. Blahna. 2000. Attachments to Special Places on Public Lands: An Analysis of Activities, Reason for Attachments, and Community Connections. *Society and Natural Resources* 13: 421–41.

Eisinger, C. 1947. Jeffersonian Agrarianism in "The Grapes of Wrath." *University of Kansas Review* 14 (Winter): 149–54.

Ellen, R. F. 1982. *Environment, Subsistence and System: The Ecology of Small-scale Social Formations*. New York: Cambridge University Press.

Emerson, R. W. 1870 [1904]. Farming. In *The Complete Works of Ralph Waldo Emerson*. Vol. 7. Boston: Houghton, Mifflin.

Feenstra, G. 1993. Is BGH Sustainable? The Consumer Perspective. In *The Dairy Debate: Consequences of Bovine Growth Hormone and Rotational Grazing Technologies,* ed. W. C. Leibhardt, 1–63. Davis: University of California Sustainable Agriculture Research and Education Program.

Fink, D. 1998. *Cutting into the Meatpacking Line: Workers and Change in the Rural Midwest*. Chapel Hill: University of North Carolina Press.

Fischler, C. 1988. Food, Self and Identity. *Social Science Information* 27: 275–83.

———. 2004. *Food Selection and Risk Perception*. Paris: Centre d'Etudes Transdisciplinaires—Sociologie, Anthropologie, Histoire.

———, ed. 1994. *Manger Magique*. Paris: Autrement.

Fisher, W. R. 1984. Narration as a Human Communication Paradigm: The Case of Public Moral Argument. *Communication Monographs* 51: 1–22.

Fite, G. C. 1981. *American Farmers*. Bloomington: Indiana University Press.

Flora, C. 1986. Values and the Agricultural Crisis: Differential Problems, Solutions, and Value Constraints. *Agriculture and Human Values* 3(4): 16–23.

Foucault, M. 1994 [1997]. On the Genealogy of Ethics: An Overview of a Work in Progress. In *Ethics, Subjectivity and Truth,* ed. P. Rabinow, 253–80. New York: Free Press.

Freyfogle, E. T. 2007. *Agrarianism and the Good Society: Land, Culture, Conflict, and Hope*. Lexington: University Press of Kentucky.

Friedman, M., and R. D. Friedman. 1962. *Capitalism and Freedom*. Chicago: University of Chicago Press.

Gardner, G. 1996. *Shrinking Fields: Cropland Loss in a World of Eight Billion*. Worldwatch Paper No. 131. Washington, DC: Worldwatch Institute.

Garrett, A. 2003. Anthropology: The "Original" of Human Nature. In *Cambridge Companion to the Scottish Enlightenment,* ed. A. Broadie, 79–93. Cambridge: Cambridge University Press.

George, K. P. 1992. Sustainability and the Moral Community. *Agriculture and Human Values* 9(4): 48–57.

Goldschmidt, W. 1947 [1978]. *As You Sow: Three Studies in the Social Conse-quences of Agribusiness.* Montclair, NJ: Allanheld, Osmun.

Grant, W. E., and P. B. Thompson. 1997. Integrated Ecological Models: Simu-lation of Socio-cultural Constraints on Ecological Dynamics. *Ecological Modeling* 100: 43–59.

Greene, J. 1993. The Intellectual Reconstruction of Virginia in the Age of Jef-ferson. In *Jeffersonian Legacies,* ed. P. S. Onuf, 225–53. Charlottesville: Uni-versity of Virginia Press.

Griswold, A. W. 1948. *Farming and Democracy.* New York: Harcourt Brace.

Grundy, S. M., D. Bilheimer, H. Blackburn, W. V. Brown, P. O. Kwiterovich Jr., F. Mattson, G. Schonfeld, and W. H. Weidman. 1982. Rationale of the Diet Heart Statement of the American Heart Association. Report of the Nutri-tion Committee. *Circulation* 65: 839A–54A.

Gussow, J. D. 1991. *Chicken Little, Tomato Sauce and Agriculture: Who Will Produce Tomorrow's Food?* New York: Bootstrap Press.

Gussow, J. D., and K. L. Clancy. 1986. Dietary Guidelines for Sustainability. *Journal of Nutrition Education* 18: 1–5.

Guthman, J. 2004. *Agrarian Dreams: The Paradox of Organic Farming in Cali-fornia.* Berkeley: University of California Press.

Habermas J. 1981. New Social Movements. *Telos* 49: 33–37.

———. 1990. *Moral Consciousness and Communicative Action.* Cambridge, MA: MIT Press.

Hacking, I. 2006. *The Emergence of Probability.* Cambridge: Cambridge Uni-versity Press.

Hanson, V. D. 1995. *The Other Greeks: The Family Farm and the Agrarian Roots of Western Civilization.* New York: Free Press.

———. 2000. *The Land Was Everything: Letters from an American Farmer.* New York: Free Press.

Hardin, G. 1968. The Tragedy of the Commons. *Science* 162: 1243–48.

Hargrove, E. C. 1989. *Foundations of Environmental Ethics.* Englewood Cliffs, NJ: Prentice-Hall.

Harris, J. M. 1996. World Agricultural Futures: Regional Sustainability and Ecological Limits. *Ecological Economics* 17: 95–116.

———. 2000. *Basic Principles of Sustainable Development.* Global Development and Environment Institute Working Paper 00–04. Medford, MA: Tufts University.

Harris, J. M., T. A. Wise, K. Gallagher, and N. R. Goodwin, eds. 2001. *A Survey of Sustainable Development: Social and Economic Approaches.* Washing-ton, DC: Island Press.

Harris, M. 1977. *Cannibals and Kings: The Origins of Culture.* New York: Ran-dom House.

Hays, S. P. 1959. *Conservation and the Gospel of Efficiency: The Progressive Conservation Movement 1890-1920*. Cambridge, MA: Harvard University Press.

Hediger, W. 1999. Reconciling "Weak" and "Strong" Sustainability. *International Journal of Social Economics* 26: 1120-43.

Heidegger, M. 1947 [1962]. Plato's Doctrine of Truth, trans. J. Barlow. In *Philosophy in the Twentieth Century*, vol. 3, ed. W. Barrett and H. D. Aiken, 173-92. New York: Harper and Row.

———. 1968. *What Is a Thing?* Chicago: H. Regnery.

Heldke, L. 2003. *Exotic Appetites: Ruminations of a Food Adventurer*. New York: Routledge.

Hightower, J. 1973. *Hard Tomatoes, Hard Times*. Washington, DC: Agribusiness Accountability Project.

———. 1975. *Eat Your Heart Out: Food Profiteering in America*. New York: Crown Books.

Hilde, T. C., and P. B. Thompson. 2000. Agrarianism and Pragmatism. In *The Agrarian Roots of Pragmatism*, ed. P. B. Thompson and T. C. Hilde, 1-21. Nashville, TN: Vanderbilt University Press.

Hobbes, T. 1651 [1981]. *Leviathan*. Ed. C. B. Macpherson. New York: Penguin Books.

Holland, A. 2001. Sustainability. In *A Companion to Environmental Philosophy*, ed. D. Jamieson, 390-401. Oxford: Blackwell.

Holling, C. S. 2001. Understanding the Complexity of Economic, Ecological and Social Systems. *Ecosystems* 4: 390-405.

Holthaus, G. 2006. *From the Farm to the Table: What All Americans Need to Know about Agriculture*. Lexington: University Press of Kentucky.

Hospers, J. 1971. *Libertarianism: A Political Philosophy for Tomorrow*. Los Angeles: Nash Publishing.

Howard, A. 1947 [2006]. *The Soil and Health: A Study of Organic Agriculture*. Lexington: University Press of Kentucky.

Howarth, R. B. 1995. Sustainability under Uncertainty: A Deontogical Approach. *Land Economics* 71(4): 417-27.

———. 1997. Sustainability as Opportunity. *Land Economics* 73(4): 569-79.

Hurt, C. 1996. Industrialization in the Pork Industry. In *The Best of CHOICES, 1986-1996*, ed. H. Ayers, 73-76. Ames, IA: American Agricultural Economics Association.

Independent Commission on International Development. 1980. *North-South: A Programme for Survival*. Cambridge, MA: MIT Press.

Inge, M. T. 1969. *Agrarianism in American Literature*. New York: Odyssey Press.

Jackson, W. 1985. *New Roots for Agriculture*. Lincoln: University of Nebraska Press.

Jaeger, W. K. 1995. Is Sustainability Optimal? Examining the Differences between Economists and Environmentalists. *Ecological Economics* 15: 43–57.

Jamieson, D. 1998. Sustainability and Beyond. *Ecological Economics* 24: 183–92.

Jefferson, T. 1984. *Writings.* Ed. M. D. Peterson. New York: Library of America.

Jonas, H. 1984. *The Imperative of Responsibility: In Search of an Ethics for the Technological Age.* Chicago: University of Chicago Press.

Jorgenson, B. S., and R. C. Stedman. 2001. Sense of Place as an Attitude: Lakeshore Owners' Attitudes toward Their Properties. *Journal of Environmental Psychology* 21: 233–48.

Kaufmann, W. A. 1965. *Hegel: Reinterpretation, Texts and Commentary.* Garden City, NY: Doubleday.

Kimbrell, A. 2002. *Fatal Harvest: The Tragedy of Industrial Agriculture.* Washington, DC: Island Press.

King, M. L., Jr. 1963. I Have a Dream. Speech delivered at the Washington Monument, August 28. http://www.americanrhetoric.com/speeches/mlki haveadream.htm (accessed September 3, 2008).

Kirkendall, R. 1984. The Central Theme of American Agricultural History. *Agriculture and Human Values* 1(2): 6–8.

Kloppenburg, J. J., J. Henrickson, and G. W. Stevenson. 1996. Coming into the Foodshed. *Agriculture and Human Values* 13(3): 33–42.

Kurzweil, R. 2001. Promise and Peril—The Intertwined Poles of 21st Century Technology. *Communications of the ACM* 44(3): 88–91.

LaFollette, H. 2000. Pragmatic Ethics. In *The Blackwell Guide to Ethical Theory,* ed. H. LaFollette, 400–419. Oxford: Blackwell.

Lakoff, G. 2004. *Don't Think of an Elephant: Know Your Values and Frame the Debate: The Essential Guide for Progressives.* White River Junction, VT: Chelsea Green.

Lakoff, G., and M. Johnson. 1980. *Metaphors We Live By.* Chicago: University of Chicago Press.

———. 1999. *Philosophy in the Flesh: The Embodied Mind and Its Challenge to Western Thought.* New York: Basic Books.

Leopold, A. 1949. *A Sand County Almanac: And Sketches Here and There.* Oxford: Oxford University Press.

Levine, J. 1986. Hearts and Minds: The Politics of Diet and Heart Disease. In *Consuming Fears,* ed. H. M. Sapolsky, 40–79. New York: Basic Books.

Light, A. 2001. Contemporary Environmental Ethics from Metaethics to Public Philosophy. *Metaphilosophy* 33: 426–49.

Light, A., and E. Katz. 1998. *Environmental Pragmatism.* New York: Routledge.

Lincoln, A. 1859. Address before the Wisconsin State Agricultural Society, Milwaukee, September 30. U.S. National Agricultural Library. http://www.nal.

usda.gov/speccoll/exhibits/lincoln/lincoln_wisconsin.html (accessed January 2, 2009).

Lisca, P. 1972. Editor's Introduction: The Pattern of Criticism. In The Grapes of Wrath: *Text and Criticism*, ed. P. Lisca, 695–719. New York: Viking Penguin.

Locke, J. 1789 [1980]. *The Second Treatise of Government.* Ed. C. B. Macpherson. Indianapolis: Hackett.

Logsdon, G. 1994. *At Nature's Pace: Farming and the American Dream.* New York: Pantheon Books.

Lowrance, W. W. 1986. *Modern Science and Human Values.* Oxford: Oxford University Press.

Ludwig, D. 1993. Environmental Sustainability: Magic, Science and Religion in Natural Resource Management. *Ecological Applications* 3: 555–58.

Ludwig, D., B. Walker, and C. S. Holling. 1997. Sustainability, Stability, and Resilience. *Conservation Ecology* 1(1): 7. http://www.consecol.org/vol1/iss1/art7/.

Lukes, S. 1993. Five Fables about Human Rights. In *On Human Rights: The Oxford Amnesty Lectures of 1993,* ed. S. Shute and S. Hurley, 19–40. New York: Basic Books.

Lutz-Newton, J., and E. T. Freyfogle. 2005. Sustainability: A Dissent. *Conservation Biology* 19: 23–32.

Lynam, J. K., and R. W. Herdt. 1989. Sense and Sustainability: Sustainability as an Objective in International Research. *Agricultural Economics* 3: 381–98.

Lyson, T. A. 2004. *Civic Agriculture: Reconnecting Farm, Food and Community.* Medford, MA: Tufts University Press.

MacIntyre, A. 1984. *After Virtue: A Study in Moral Theory.* South Bend, IN: University of Notre Dame Press.

Madden, P., and P. B. Thompson. 1987. Ethical Perspectives on Changing Agricultural Technology in the United States. *Notre Dame Journal of Law, Ethics, and Public Policy* 3(1): 85–116.

Malthus, T. 1798 [1983]. *An Essay of the Principle of Population.* New York: Penguin Books.

Mauss, M. 1966 [1925]. *The Gift: Forms and Functions of Exchange in Archaic Societies,* trans. I. Cunnison. London: Cohen and West.

Mazoyer, M., and L. Roudart. 2006. *A History of World Agriculture from the Neolithic Age to the Current Crisis,* trans. J. H. Membrez. London: Earthscan.

McClennen, E. F. 1983. Rational Choice and Public Policy: A Critical Survey. *Social Theory and Practice* 9(2–3): 335–79.

McGinn, R. E. 1994. Technology, Demography and the Anachronism of Traditional Rights. *Journal of Applied Philosophy* 11: 57–70.

McGovern, G. 1967. *Agricultural Thought in the Twentieth Century.* Indianapolis: Bobbs-Merrill.

McKibben, B. 2007. *Deep Economy: The Wealth of Communities and the Durable Future.* New York: Times Books.

McNaughten, P., and B. Urry. 1998. *Contested Natures.* London: Sage Publishing.

McWilliams, C. 1939. *Factories in the Fields: The Story of Migratory Farm Labor in California.* Boston: Little, Brown.

———. 1942. California Pastoral. *Antioch Review* 2 (March): 103–21.

———. 1948. *Ill Fares the Land: Migrants and Migratory Labor in the United States.* Boston: Little, Brown.

Meinig, D. W. 1986. *The Shaping of America: A Geological Perspective on 500 Years of History.* Vol. 1, *Atlantic America.* New Haven, CT: Yale University Press.

———. 1993. *The Shaping of America: A Geological Perspective on 500 Years of History.* Vol. 2, *Continental America.* New Haven, CT: Yale University Press.

Menand, L. 2001. *The Metaphysical Club: A Story of Ideas in America.* New York: Farrar, Straus and Giroux.

Miller, C. 2001. *Gifford Pinchot and the Making of Modern Environmentalism.* Washington, DC: Island Press.

Minteer, B. A., and J. P. Collins. 2005. Ecological Ethics: Building a New Tool Kit for Ecologists and Biodiversity Managers. *Conservation Biology* 19: 1803–12.

Mintz, S. W. 1986. *Sweetness and Power: The Place of Sugar in Modern History.* New York: Penguin Books.

Montesquieu, C. d. S., Baron de. 1748 [1823]. *The Spirit of the Laws.* London: J. Collingwood.

Montmarquet, J. A. 1989. *The Idea of Agrarianism: From Hunter-Gatherer to Agrarian Radical in Western Culture.* Moscow: University of Idaho Press.

Morgan, E. S. 1975. *American Slavery, American Freedom: The Ordeal of Colonial Virginia.* New York: W. W. Norton.

Morgan, P. A., and S. J. Peters. 2006. The Foundations of Planetary Agrarianism: Thomas Berry and Liberty Hyde Bailey. *Journal of Agricultural and Environmental Ethics* 19: 443–68.

Murasinghe, M., and W. Shearer. 1995. *Defining and Measuring Sustainability: The Biogeophysical Foundations.* Washington, DC: World Bank and United Nations University.

Nagel, T. 1977. Poverty and Food: Why Charity Is Not Enough. In *Food Policy,* ed. P. Brown and H. Shue, 54–62. New York: Free Press.

Narveson, J. 1988. *The Libertarian Idea.* Philadelphia: Temple University Press.

Nelson, Stephanie. 1998. *God and the Land: The Metaphysics of Farming in Hesiod and Vergil.* Oxford: Oxford University Press.

Norton, B. G. 1984. Environmental Ethics and Weak Anthropocentrism. *Environmental Ethics* 6: 131–48.

———. 1988. The Constancy of Leopold's Land Ethic. *Conservation Biology* 2: 93–102.

———. 1991. *Toward Unity among Environmentalists.* New York: Oxford University Press.

———. 1992. Sustainability, Human Welfare, and Ecosystem Health. *Environmental Values* 1: 97–111.

———. 1995. Evaluating Ecosystem States: Two Competing Paradigms. *Ecological Economics* 14: 113–27.

———. 2003. *Searching for Sustainability.* Cambridge: Cambridge University Press.

———. 2005. *Sustainability: A Philosophy of Adaptive Ecosystem Management.* Chicago: University of Chicago Press.

———. 2006. Mark Sagoff's *Price, Principle, and the Environment:* Two Comments. *Ethics, Place and Environment* 9: 337–43.

Nozick, R. 1974. *Anarchy, State and Utopia.* New York: Basic Books.

O'Neill, O. 1986. *Faces of Hunger.* London: Allen and Unwin.

Parfit, D. 1984. *Reasons and Persons.* Oxford: Clarendon Press.

Parr, A. 2009. *Hijacking Sustainability.* Cambridge, MA: MIT Press.

Passmore, J. 1974. *Man's Responsibility for Nature: Ecological Problems and Western Traditions.* New York: Charles Scribner's Sons.

Pearce, D. 1993. *Economic Value and the Natural World.* London: Earthscan.

Pearce, D. W., E. Barbier, and A. Markandya. 1990. *Sustainable Development: Economics and Environment in the Third World.* London: Earthscan.

Perelman, M. 1977. *Farming for Profit in a Hungry World.* Totowa, NJ: Allanheld, Osmun.

Peterson, T. R. 1997. *Sharing the Earth: The Rhetoric of Sustainable Development.* Columbia: University of South Carolina Press.

Petrini, C. 2003. *Slow Food: The Case for Taste.* New York: Columbia University Press.

Pichardo, N. A. 1997. New Social Movements: A Critical Review. *Annual Review of Sociology* 23: 411–30.

Pimentel, D., T. W. Culliney, I. W. Buttler, D. J. Reinemann, and K. B. Beckman. 1989. Low-Input Sustainable Agriculture Using Ecological Management Practices. *Agriculture, Ecosystems, and Environment* 27: 3–24.

Plato. 1961. *The Collected Dialogues of Plato.* Ed. E. Hamilton and H. Cairns. Princeton, NJ: Princeton University Press.

Plumwood, V. 2002. *Environmental Culture: The Ecological Crisis of Reason.* London and New York: Routledge.

Pollan, M. 1991. *Second Nature: A Gardener's Education.* New York: Dell Publishing.

———. 2007. *The Omnivore's Dilemma: A Natural History of Four Meals.* New York: Penguin Books.

———. 2008. Farmer in Chief. *New York Times Magazine,* October 12. http://www.michaelpollan.com/article.php?id=97 (accessed December 23, 2008).

Pray, C. 1993. Trends in Food and Agricultural R&D: Signs of Declining Competitiveness? In *U.S. Agricultural Research: Strategic Challenges and Options,* ed. R. D. Weaver, 51–67. Bethesda, MD: Agricultural Research Institute.

Putnam, R. D. 2000. *Bowling Alone: The Collapse and Revival of American Community.* New York: Simon and Schuster.

Rappaport, R. A. 1967. *Pigs for the Ancestors: Ritual in the Ecology of a New Guinea People.* New Haven, CT: Yale University Press.

Rawls, J. 1972. *A Theory of Justice.* Cambridge, MA: Belknap Press.

Regan, T. 1983. *The Case for Animal Rights.* Berkeley: University of California Press.

———. 1993. Vegetarianism and Sustainable Agriculture: The Contributions of Moral Philosophy. In *Food for the Future: Conditions and Contradictions of Sustainability,* ed. P. Allen, 103–21. New York: John Wiley and Sons.

———. 2001. *Defending Animal Rights.* Urbana: University of Illinois Press.

Richgels, C. E., S. J. Barrick, and R. H. Foells. 1990. Sustainable Agriculture, Perspectives from Industry. *Journal of Soil and Water Conservation* 45: 31–33.

Rittel, H. W. J., and M. M. Webber. 1973. Dilemmas in a General Theory of Planning. *Policy Sciences* 4: 155–69.

Roe, E. 1994. *Narrative Policy Analysis: Theory and Practice.* Durham, NC: Duke University Press.

Rolston, H., III. 1975. Is There an Ecological Ethic? *Ethics* 85: 93–109.

———. 1988. *Environmental Ethics: Duties to and Values in the Natural World.* Philadelphia: Temple University Press.

———. 1991. Environmental Ethics: Values in and Duties to the Natural World. In *Ecology, Economics, Ethics: The Broken Circle,* ed. F. H. Bormann and S. R. Kellert, 73–97. New Haven, CT: Yale University Press.

———. 1999. *Genes, Genesis and God: Values and Their Origins in Natural and Human History.* Cambridge: Cambridge University Press.

———. 2001. Natural and Unnatural; Wild and Cultural. *Western North American Naturalist* 61: 267–76.

Rousseau, J-J. 1754 [1761]. *A Discourse upon the Origin and Foundation of the Inequality among Mankind.* London: R. and J. Dodsley.

———. 1761 [1993]. *Emile.* Rutland, VT: J. M. Dent.

Royce, J. 1913. *The Problem of Christianity.* New York: Macmillan.

———. 1916. *The Hope of the Great Community.* New York: Macmillan.

Rozin, P., C. Fischler, S. Imada, A. Sarubin, and A. Wrzenjiewski. 1999. Attitudes to Food and the Role of Food in Life in the U.S.A., Japan, Flemish Belgium and France: Possible Implications for the Diet-Health Debate. *Appetite* 33: 163–80.

Russell, E. 2001. *War and Nature: Fighting Humans and Insects with Chemicals from World War I to Silent Spring.* New York: Cambridge University Press.

Ryle, G. 1984 [1949]. *The Concept of Mind.* Chicago: University of Chicago Press.

Sachs, J. 2005. *The End of Poverty: Economic Possibilities for Our Time.* New York: Penguin Books.

Sagoff, M. 1981. At the Shrine of Our Lady of Fatima, or Why Political Questions Are Not All Economic. *Arizona Law Review* 23: 1283–98.

———. 2006. Reply to My Critics. *Ethics, Place and Environment* 9: 365–72.

Sandel, M. 1982. *Liberalism and the Limits of Justice.* New York: Cambridge University Press.

Schelling, T. 1978. *Micromotives and Macrobehavior.* New York: W. W. Norton.

Scherer, D. 1983. The Game of Games. In *Ethics and Environment,* ed. D. Scherer and T. Attig, 204–13. Englewood Cliffs, NJ: Prentice-Hall.

Schmid, A. A. 1987. *Property, Power and Public Choice: An Inquiry into Law and Economics,* 2nd ed. New York: Praeger Press.

Schumacher, E. F. 1972. *Small Is Beautiful.* New York: Harper and Row.

Schweikhardt, D. B., and J. F. Whims. 1993. Trends and Issues in Agricultural Research Funding at the State Agricultural Experiment Stations. In *U.S. Agricultural Research: Strategic Challenges and Options,* ed. R. D. Weaver, 89–112. Bethesda, MD: Agricultural Research Institute.

Scott, J. C. 1998. *Seeing Like a State.* New Haven, CT: Yale University Press.

Scruton, R. 2004. The Conscientious Carnivore. In *Food for Thought: The Debate over Eating Meat,* ed. S. F. Sapontzis, 81–107. Amherst, NY: Prometheus Books.

Sen, A. 1981. *Poverty and Famines: An Essay on Entitlement and Deprivation.* Oxford: Clarendon Press.

———. 1987. *On Ethics and Economics.* Oxford: Basil Blackwell.

Sheehan, G. 1978. *Running and Being: The Total Experience.* New York: Simon and Schuster.

Shiva, V. 1991. *The Violence of the Green Revolution.* London: Zed Books.

Shue, H. 1981. *Basic Rights.* Princeton, NJ: Princeton University Press.

Simon, J. 1980. Resources, Population, Environment: An Oversupply of False Bad News. *Science* 208: 431–37.

Singer, P. 1975. *Animal Liberation.* New York: Avon Books.

———. 1993. *Practical Ethics,* 2nd ed. Cambridge: Cambridge University Press.

———. 2002. *One World: The Ethics of Globalization.* New Haven, CT: Yale University Press.

Smith, K. K. 2003. *Wendell Berry and the Agrarian Tradition: A Common Grace.* Lawrence: University Press of Kansas.

Solow, R. 1992. *An Almost Practical Step toward Sustainability.* Washington, DC: Resources for the Future.

———. 1993. Sustainability: An Economist's Perspective. In *Economics of the Environment: Selected Readings,* ed. R. Dorfman and N. Dorfman, 179–87. New York: W. W. Norton.

Stedman, R. C. 2003. Is It Really Just a Social Construction? The Contribution of the Physical Environment to Sense of Place. *Society and Natural Resources* 16: 671–85.

Steinbeck, J. 1963 [1936]. *In Dubious Battle.* New York: Viking Press.

———. 1972 [1939]. The Grapes of Wrath: *Text and Criticism.* Ed. P. Lisca. New York: Penguin Books.

———. 1988. *The Harvest Gypsies: On the Road to* The Grapes of Wrath. Ed. C. Wollenberg. Berkeley, CA: Heyday Books.

Steiner, R. 1958. *Agriculture,* trans. G. Adams. London: Bio-Dynamic Agricultural Association.

Stewart, B. A., R. Lal, and S. A. El-Swaify. 1991. Sustaining the Resource Base of an Expanding World Agriculture. In *Soil Management for Sustainability,* ed. R. Lal and F. Pierce, 125–44. Ankeny, IA: Soil and Water Conservation Society.

Stoll, S. 1998. *The Fruits of Natural Advantage: Making the Industrial Countryside in California.* Berkeley and Los Angeles: University of California Press.

Strange, M. 1988. *Family Farming: A New Economic Vision.* Lincoln: University of Nebraska Press.

Strong, D. 1995. *Crazy Mountains: Learning from Wilderness to Weigh Technology.* Albany: State University of New York Press.

Sylvan, R. 1973. Is There a Need for a New, an Environmental Ethic? In *Proceedings of the World Congress of Philosophy,* vol. 1, 205–10. Sophia, Bulgaria: Sophia Press.

Taylor, C. 1989. *Sources of the Self: The Making of the Modern Identity.* Cambridge, MA: Harvard University Press.

Taylor, P. W. 1986. *Respect for Nature: A Theory of Environmental Ethics.* Princeton, NJ: Princeton University Press.

Thompson, E. P. 1971. The Moral Economy of the English Crowd in the Eighteenth Century. *Past & Present* 50: 76–136.

Thompson, P. B. 1992. The Varieties of Sustainability. *Agriculture and Human Values* 9(3): 11–19.

———. 1995. *The Spirit of the Soil: Agriculture and Environmental Ethics.* London and New York: Routledge.

———. 1996. Markets, Moral Economy and the Ethics of Sustainable Agriculture. In *Rural Reconstruction in a Market Economy,* ed. W. Heijman, H.

Hetsen, and J. Frouws, 39–54. Wageningen, the Netherlands: Wageningen Agricultural University.

———. 1997. The Varieties of Sustainability in Livestock Farming. In *Livestock Farming Systems: More than Food Production*, ed. J. T. Sørensen, 5–15. Wageningen, the Netherlands: Wageningen Pers.

———. 1998a. *Agricultural Ethics: Research Teaching and Public Policy*. Ames: Iowa State University Press.

———. 1998b. Environmentalism, Feminism, and Agrarianism: Three Isms in Search of Sustainable Agriculture. *Agriculture and Human Values* 12: 170–76.

———. 2000a. Agrarianism as Philosophy. In *The Agrarian Roots of Pragmatism*, ed. P. B. Thompson and T. C. Hilde, 25–50. Nashville, TN: Vanderbilt University Press.

———. 2000b. Thomas Jefferson and Agrarian Philosophy. In *The Agrarian Roots of Pragmatism*, ed. P. B. Thompson and T. C. Hilde, 118–39. Nashville, TN: Vanderbilt University Press.

———. 2002. Why Food Biotechnology Needs an Opt Out. In *Engineering the Farm: Ethical and Social Aspects of Agricultural Biotechnology*, ed. B. Bailey and M. Lappé, 27–44. Washington, DC: Island Press.

———. 2003. Expanding the Conservation Tradition: The Agrarian Vision. In *Reconstructing Conservation: Finding Common Ground*, ed. B. A. Minteer and R. E. Manning, 77–92. Washington, DC: Island Press.

———. 2006. Mark Sagoff's Kantian Environmental Philosophy. *Ethics, Place and Environment* 9(3): 344–50.

———. 2007a. *Food Biotechnology in Ethical Perspective*, 2nd ed. Dordrecht, the Netherlands: Springer.

———. 2007b. Shall We Dine? The Strange and Horrifying Story of GMOs in Our Food. In *Food & Philosophy: Eat, Drink, and Be Merry*, ed. F. Allhoff and D. Monroe, 208–20. Oxford: Blackwell.

Thompson, P. B., R. J. Matthews, and E. van Ravenswaay. 1994. *Ethics, Public Policy, and Agriculture*. New York: Macmillan.

Thompson, P. B., and A. Nardone. 1999. Sustainable Livestock Production: Methodological and Ethical Challenges. *Livestock Production Science* 61: 111–19.

Thrupp, L. A. 1993. Political Ecology of Sustainable Rural Development: Dynamics of Social and Natural Resource Degradation. In *Food for the Future: Conditions and Contradictions of Sustainability*, ed. P. Allen, 47–73. New York: John Wiley and Sons.

Tobie, W. C. 1949. The Nature of Disease Institute First Annual Report by J. E. R. McDonagh, Mark Clement. *Quarterly Review of Biology* 24(3): 261.

Tweeten, L. 1983. *Food for People and Profit: Ethics and Capitalism*. The Farm and Food System in Transition—Emerging Policy Issues No. FS5. East Lansing: Cooperative Extension Service, Michigan State University.

Uekoetter, F. 2006. Know Your Soil: Transitions in Farmers' and Scientists' Knowledge in Germany. In *Soils and Societies: Perspectives from Environmental History,* ed. J. R. McNeill and V. Winiwarter, 322–40. Isle of Harris, UK: White Horse Press.

United Nations. 1983. *Process of Preparation of the Environmental Perspective to the Year 2000 and Beyond.* General Assembly Resolution 38/161, December 19.

Van Calker, K. J., P. B. M. Berentsen, G. W. J. Giesen, and R. B. M. Huirne. 2005. Identifying and Ranking Attributes that Determine Sustainability in Dutch Dairy Farming. *Agriculture and Human Values* 22: 53–63.

Walters, D. T., D. A. Mortensen, C. A. Francis, R. W. Elmore, and J. W. King. 1990. Specificity: The Context of Research for Sustainability. *Journal of Soil and Water Conservation* 45: 55–57.

Wargo, J. P. 1996. *Our Children's Toxic Legacy: How Science and Law Fail to Protect Us from Pesticides.* New Haven, CT: Yale University Press.

Warren, K. J. 2000. *Ecofeminist Philosophy: A Western Perspective on What It Is and Why It Matters.* Lanham, MD: Rowman and Littlefield.

White, L. 1967. The Historical Roots of Our Ecological Crisis. *Science* 155: 1203–7.

Williams, D. R., M. E. Patterson, and J. W. Roggenbuck. 1992. Beyond the Commodity Metaphor: Examining Emotional and Symbolic Attachment to Place. *Leisure Sciences* 14: 29–46.

Wills, G. 1997. American Adam. *New York Review of Books,* March 6, 30–33.

Wilson, E. 1940. The Californians: Storm and Steinbeck. *New Republic* 103 (December 9): 784–87.

Wirzba, N. 2003. *The Paradise of God: Renewing Religion in an Ecological Age.* New York: Oxford University Press.

Wojcik, J. 1984. The American Wisdom Literature of Farming. *Agriculture and Human Values* 1(4): 26–37.

Wolf, S. A., and F. H. Buttel. 1998. The Political Economy of Precision Farming. In *Privatization of Information and Agricultural Industrialization,* ed. S. A. Wolf, 107–16. Boca Raton, FL: CRC Press.

Wollenberg, C. 1988. Introduction to *The Harvest Gypsies: On the Road to* The Grapes of Wrath. Berkeley, CA: Heyday Books.

World Commission on Environment and Development. 1987. *Our Common Future.* Oxford: Oxford University Press.

Worster, D. 1979. *Dust Bowl: The Southern Plains in the 1930s.* Oxford: Oxford University Press.

Wright, W., and G. Middendorf. 2008. Fighting over Food: Changing the American Food System. In *The Fight over Food: Producers, Consumers and Activists Challenge the Global Food System,* 1–26. University Park: Pennsylvania State University Press.

Wunderlich, G. 2000. Two on Jefferson's Agrarianism. In *The Agrarian Roots of Pragmatism,* ed. P. B. Thompson and T. C. Hilde, 254–68. Nashville, TN: Vanderbilt University Press.

Index